- <u>topic</u>: practical justification

<u>Kant's approach</u>: to justify uncond. normative claims w/out recourse to assumptions/views/doctrines that are not justifiable

<u>reason for collection</u>: no systematic sustained study of this topic

<u>starting point</u>: successful account of justification of normative claims has to be <u>non</u> metaphysical

essays engage with this view + pursue implications

for   ethics
      legal
      political
      Religions

Kant on Practical Justification

Kant on Practical Justification

INTERPRETIVE ESSAYS

Edited by Mark Timmons
and
Sorin Baiasu

OXFORD
UNIVERSITY PRESS

OXFORD
UNIVERSITY PRESS

Oxford University Press is a department of the University of Oxford.
It furthers the University's objective of excellence in research, scholarship,
and education by publishing worldwide.

Oxford   New York
Auckland   Cape Town   Dar es Salaam   Hong Kong   Karachi
Kuala Lumpur   Madrid   Melbourne   Mexico City   Nairobi
New Delhi   Shanghai   Taipei   Toronto

With offices in
Argentina   Austria   Brazil   Chile   Czech   Republic   France   Greece
Guatemala   Hungary   Italy   Japan   Poland   Portugal   Singapore
South Korea   Switzerland   Thailand   Turkey   Ukraine   Vietnam

Oxford is a registered trademark of Oxford University Press in the UK and
certain other countries.

Published in the United States of America by
Oxford University Press
198 Madison Avenue, New York, NY 10016

Library of Congress Cataloging-in-Publication Data
Kant on practical justification : interpretative essays / edited by
Mark Timmons & Sorin Baiasu.
p. cm.
Includes bibliographical references and index.
ISBN 978–0–19–539568–6 (hardback : alk. paper)—ISBN 978–0–19–987536–8 (e-book)
1. Kant, Immanuel, 1724–1804.   2. Justification (Theory of knowledge)
I. Timmons, Mark, 1951–   II. Baiasu, Sorin.
B2799.K7K3625 2013
193—dc23
2012025461

978–0–19–539568–6
978–0–19–987536–8

1 3 5 7 9 8 6 4 2
Printed in the United States of America
on acid-free paper

{ CONTENTS }

{ ABBREVIATIONS }

In citing Kant's works the abbreviations listed below are used throughout this book. Pagination references in the text and footnotes are to the volume, page number, and (in some cases) line in the German edition of Kant's works, *Kants gesammelte Schriften*, edited by the Königlich Preußischen Akademie der Wissenschaften, subsequently Deutsche, now Berlin-Brandenburg Akademie der Wissenschaften (originally under the editorship of Wilhelm Dilthey) (Berlin: Georg Reimer, subsequently Walter de Gruyter, 1900–). References to the *Critique of Pure Reason* (*KrV*) follow the A (first edition), B (second edition) convention. Where applicable, translations used by each contributor are listed in the bibliography of the respective volume chapter.

AA	Kants gesammelte Schriften
Anth	Anthropologie in pragmatischer Hinsicht (*AA* 07)
FM	Welches sind die wirklichen Fortschritte, die die Metaphysik seit Leibnitzens und Wolff's Zeiten in Deutschland gemacht hat? (*AA* 20)
GMS	Grundlegung zur Metaphysik der Sitten (*AA* 04)
KpV	Kritik der praktischen Vernunft (*AA* 05)
KU	Kritik der Urteilskraft (*AA* 05)
Log	Logik (*AA* 09)
MAM	Mutmaßlicher Anfang der Menschheitsgeschichte (*AA* 08)
MS	Die Metaphysik der Sitten (*AA* 06)
RL	Metaphysische Anfangsgründe der Rechtslehre (*AA* 06)
Päd	Pädagogik (*AA* 09)
Prol	Prolegomena zu einer jeden künftigen Metaphysik (*AA* 04)
Refl	Reflexion (*AA* 14–19)
RS	Recension von Schulz's Versuch einer Anleitung zur Sittenlehre für alle Menschen (*AA* 08)
RGV	Die Religion innerhalb der Grenzen der bloßen Vernunft (*AA* 06)
SF	Der Streit der Fakultäten (*AA* 07)
TL	Metaphysische Anfangsgründe der Tugendlehre (*AA* 06)
TP	Über den Gemeinspruch: Das mag in der Theorie richtig sein, taugt aber nicht für die Praxis (*AA* 08)
V-Lo/Blomberg	Logik Blomberg (*AA* 24)
V-Mo/Collins	Moralphilosophie Collins (*AA* 27)

V-Mo/Mron	Moral Mrongovius (*AA* 27)
V-Mo/Mron II	Moral Mrongovius II (*AA* 29)
V-MS/Vigil	Die Metaphysik der Sitten Vigilantius (*AA* 27)
V-Phil-Th/Pölitz	Philosophische Religionslehre nach Pölitz (*AA* 28)
V-Th/Volckmann	Natürliche Theologie Volckmann nach Baumbach (*AA* 28)
WA	Beantwortung der Frage: Was ist Aufklärung? (*AA* 08)
WDO	Was heißt sich im Denken orientiren? (*AA* 08)
ZeF	Zum ewigen Frieden (*AA* 08)

{ NOTES ON CONTRIBUTORS }

Henry E. Allison is Professor Emeritus at the University of California, San Diego and Boston University. His books include *Lessing and the Enlightenment* (1966), *The Kant–Eberhard Controversy* (1973), *Kant's Transcendental Idealism: An Interpretation and Defence* (1983; rev. ed. 2004), *Benedict de Spinoza: An Introduction* (1987), *Kant's Theory of Freedom* (1990), *Idealism and Freedom* (1996), *Kant's Theory of Taste: A Reading of the "Critique of Judgement"* (2001), *Custom and Reason in Hume: A Kantian Reading of the First Book of the Treatise* (2008), *Kant's Groundwork for the Metaphysics of Morals: A Commentary* (OUP 2011), and *Essays on Kant* (OUP 2012). He has written numerous articles on Kant and also edited (with Peter Heath) *Kant's Theoretical Philosophy after 1781* (2002).

Karl Ameriks is McMahon-Hank Professor of Philosophy at the University of Notre Dame. His publications include *Kant's Theory of Mind* (1982, 2nd ed. 2000), *Kant and the Fate of Autonomy* (2000), *Interpreting Kant's Critiques* (2003) and *Kant and the Historical Turn* (2006). He cotranslated and coedited Kant's *Lectures on Metaphysics* (1997), coedited *Kants Ethik* (2004) and *Kant's Moral and Legal Philosophy* (2009), and edited the *Cambridge Companion to German Idealism* (2000).

Sorin Baiasu is Reader in Philosophy at Keele University. He published a monograph on *Kant and Sartre: Re-discovering Critical Ethics* and a collection (with Howard Williams and Sami Pihlström) on *Politics and Metaphysics in Kant*, both in 2011. He edited a special issue of the journal *International Political Theory* on "Kantian Justifications of Practical Norms" (2007), and (with Michelle Grier) a special issue of *Kantian Review* (2011) with papers presented to the APA Author Meets Critics Session on Graham Bird's *The Revolutionary Kant*. He is guest editor of forthcoming special issues of *Philosophia* (on toleration and pragmatism in the work of John Horton) and *Collingwood and British Idealism Studies* (on Kant and the British Idealists). He is the author of many other articles and volume chapters.

Paul Guyer is Jonathan Nelson Professor of Humanities and Philosophy at Brown University. His books include *Kant and the Claims of Taste* (1979, 2nd ed. 1997), *Kant and the Claims of Knowledge* (1987), *Kant and the Experience of Freedom* (1993), *Kant on Freedom, Law and Happiness* (2000), *Kant's System of Nature and Freedom* (2005), *Values of Beauty: Historical Essays in Aesthetics* (2005), *Kant* (2006), *Kant's 'Groundwork for the Metaphysics of Morals': A Reader's Guide* (2007) and *Reason, Knowledge and Taste: Kant's Response to*

Hume (2008). *A History of Modern Aesthetics* in three volumes is forthcoming from Cambridge University Press. He has translated several of Kant's writings and edited volumes of critical essays on Kant.

John Hare is Noah Porter Professor of Philosophical Theology at Yale University. He has written *The Moral Gap: Kantian Ethics, Human Limits and God's Assistance* (1997), *Why Bother Being Good: the Place of God in the Moral Life* (2002), and *God and Morality: A Philosophical History* (2006). He has authored many articles on Kant in journals and edited collections.

Otfried Höffe is Professor Emeritus of Philosophy and Director of the Research Centre for Political Philosophy at Tübingen University. His books include: *Ethik und Politik. Grundmodelle und -probleme der praktischen Philosophie* (4th ed. 2000), *Immanuel Kant* (7th ed. 2007; English tr. 1994), *Politische Gerechtigkeit. Grundlegung einer kritischen Philosophie von Recht und Staat* (3rd ed. 2002), *Kants Kritik der reinen Vernunft. Die Grundlegung der modernen Philosophie* (2003; 4th ed. 2004), *Lebenskunst und Moral. Oder Macht Tugend glücklich?* (2007). His work has been translated into more than twenty languages.

Larry Krasnoff is Professor of Philosophy at the College of Charleston. He has edited *New Essays on the History of Autonomy* (2004) and authored *Hegel's Phenomenology of Spirit: An Introduction* (2008). His essays have appeared in *European Journal of Philosophy, Journal of Philosophy, Kant-Studien*, and Philosophical Quarterly.

A. W. Moore is Professor of Philosophy at Oxford University. His publications include *The Infinite* (1990, 2nd edn 2001), *Points of View* (1997), *Noble in Reason, Infinite in Faculty: Themes and Variations in Kant's Moral and Religious Philosophy* (2003), and *The Evolution of Modern Metaphysics: Making Sense of Things* (2012). He has published articles on Kant in *Mind, Philosophical Quarterly, Ratio*, and *Philosophy*.

Andrews Reath is Professor of Philosophy at the University of California, Riverside. He has written *Agency and Autonomy in Kant's Moral Theory* (2006) and edited (with B. Herman and C. M. Korsgaard) *Re-claiming the History of Ethics: Essays for John Rawls* (1997). He has published many articles on Kant in, among others, *Journal of the History of Philosophy, Kant-Studien, Inquiry, Jahrbuch für Recht und Ethik*, and *Noûs*.

Sebastian Rödl is Professor of Philosophy at the Universität Leipzig. He is the author of *Selbsbezug und Normativität* (1998), *Kategorien des Zeitlichen: Eine Untersuchung der Formen des endlichen Verstandes* (2005; published in English as *Categories of the Temporal*), and *Self-consciousness* (2007). He has published articles on Kant and German idealism in journals and edited collections.

Houston Smit is Associate Professor of Philosophy at the University of Arizona. He specializes in the history of medieval and early modern philosophy and is currently writing a book with the working title *Kant's Theory of Cognition*. Smit and Timmons are coauthors of "The Moral Significance of Gratitude in Kant's Ethics," *Southern Journal of Philosophy* 49 (2011): 295–320.

Robert Stern is Professor of Philosophy at Sheffield University. He is the author of *Hegel, Kant and the Structure of the Object* (1990), *Transcendental Arguments and Scepticism* (2000), and *Understanding Moral Obligation: Kant, Hegel, Kierkegaard* (2012). He also edited *Transcendental Arguments: Problems and Prospects* (1999), and a collection of his papers has appeared under the title *Hegelian Metaphysics* (2009).

Mark Timmons is Professor of Philosophy at the University of Arizona. He has published widely on topics in metaethics, normative ethics, and Kant's ethics. He is editor of *Oxford Studies in Normative Ethics* and is currently working on a book with Terry Horgan tentatively entitled *Illuminating Reasons: An Essay in Moral Phenomenology.* Smit and Timmons are co-authors of "The Moral Significance of Gratitude in Kant's Ethics," *Southern Journal of Philosophy* 49 (2011): 295–320.

Howard Williams is Professor of International Politics at Aberystwyth University. His publications include *Kant's Political Philosophy* (1983) and *Kant's Critique of Hobbes* (2003). He has edited *Essays on Kant's Political Philosophy* (1992) and has published articles on Kant in *Kant-Studien, Kantian Review, Philosophical Quarterly*, and *Review of Politics*, as well as in several edited collections. He is editor (together with Graham Bird) of the journal *Kantian Review*.

Allen Wood is Ruth Norman Halls Professor of Philosophy at Indiana University. His interests are in the history of modern philosophy, especially Kant and German idealism, and in ethics and social philosophy. He has held professorships at Cornell and Yale, and at Stanford, where he is Ward W. and Priscilla B. Woods Professor emeritus. He has also held visiting appointments at the University of Michigan, University of California at San Diego, and Oxford University, where he was Isaiah Berlin Visiting Professor in 2005. He has been affiliated with the Freie Universität Berlin in 1983–4 and the Rheinische-Friedrich-Wilhelms-Universität Bonn in 1991–2. His publications include: *Kant's Moral Religion* (1970, reissued 2009*), Kant's Rational Theology* (1978, reissued 2009), *Karl Marx* (1981, second expanded edition 2004), *Hegel's Ethical Thought* (1990), *Kant's Ethical Thought* (1999), *Unsettling Obligations* (2002), *Kant* (2004), and *Kantian Ethics* (2008). He is general editor (with Paul Guyer) of the Cambridge Edition of the Works of Immanuel Kant, in English translation, for which he has edited, translated, or otherwise contributed to six volumes. Among the other books he has edited are *Self and Nature in Kant's Philosophy* (1984), *Hegel: Elements of the Philosophy of Right* (1991), *Kant: Groundwork for the Metaphysics of Morals* (2002), *Fichte: Attempt at a Critique of All Revelation* (2010), and (with Songsuk Susan Hahn), the *Cambridge History of Philosophy in the Nineteenth Century* (2012).

Introduction

PRACTICAL JUSTIFICATION IN KANT[1]

Sorin Baiasu

I. Outline

The literature on Kantian accounts of practical justification has been growing of late. This is not surprising given that Kant's approach seems so promising. Kant claims to be able to justify unconditional normative claims without recourse to assumptions, views, or doctrines, which are not in their turn justifiable. Within the context of modern pluralism, this is exactly what we seem to need: an approach which can demonstrate why certain normative claims are valid, and why the grounds of these claims are valid in their turn, and why the grounds of these grounds could also be justified, and why the freedom to question should not be stifled by assuming some matter-of-fact irreconcilable pluralism.

Although this has been a growth area in philosophy, no systematic and sustained study of the topic of practical justification in Kantian philosophy has

[1] Some of the chapters in this collection were originally papers presented to the 2006 Annual Conference of the UK Kant Society, organized at the University of Manchester. Thanks are due to the British Academy, the Analysis Trust, the Aristotelian Society, the Political Thought Specialist Group of the UK Political Studies Association, and the British Society for the History of Philosophy for sponsoring the event. I would also like to thank an academic, who prefers to remain unnamed, who supported the project of the conference and helped me with its organisation. I am also grateful to Adrian W. Moore for his encouragement and advice at the initial stages of this book project. I am grateful to all friends and family, who have helped me to free time for the editorial work. In addition, with their flexibility with marking and other administrative deadlines, administrative staff and colleagues in the School of Politics, International Relations and Philosophy at Keele University, allowed me to make progress with my work on this edited collection when it seemed impossible—I am very thankful to them for this. I would also like to thank my coeditor, Mark Timmons, for his support and help; the editor from Oxford University Press, Peter Ohlin, for his advice and patience; and the anonymous referee who provided very constructive and useful comments on the book manuscript. Finally, thanks are due to Sreejith Viswanathan, the project manager from Newgen Knowledge Works, for careful attention and patience at the copyediting and proof stages of the production process.

been undertaken so far. The aim of this volume is to provide a comprehensive and structured examination of this topic, as a starting point for a focused investigation on the Kantian approach to justification in practical disciplines (ethics, legal and political philosophy, or philosophy of religion). I would like to begin, in this introduction, by mapping some of the main areas of philosophical inquiry where practical justification is playing a role in Kant's writings and in the works of contemporary Kantians. Since practical justification is of claims or assertions, I will organize this introduction around the various types of claim that are defended by Kant or contemporary Kantians. This will also clarify the structure of this collection and will make clearer the main directions and areas of research on this topic. I present schematically these various areas and their various places in relation to practical justification in Diagram 1 below.

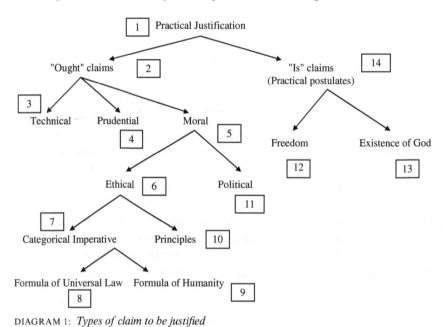

DIAGRAM 1: *Types of claim to be justified*

II. Distinctions

Some aspects of the mapping I plan to offer here will unsurprisingly be included as a result of making a choice between various ways in which distinctions can be drawn in Kant. For instance, concerning claims involving an "ought," we can divide the same universe of discourse into two or three areas, depending on the distinguishing criterion. We can, for instance, rely on Kant's distinction between hypothetical and categorical imperatives or, alternatively, on that between imperatives of skill, of prudence and of morality. Here, the choice between such alternative distinctions will ultimately depend on how useful each of them turns out to be for the purpose of providing orientation in a complex and growing research area.

Let me start with the most general relevant topic here, in order to identify the first area of research: Kant's view of practical justification in general, and, more exactly, his notion of justification [*Rechtfertigung*], the difference between this notion in the case of "ought" claims and in the case of "is" claims, as well as other general issues which bear on the notion as a whole. This part can be illustrated by reference to chapter 1 of this volume. There, in the first section, I discuss the etymology of Kant's notion of justification, and how Kant employs this notion in his writings. In the second section, in the context of the few texts of secondary literature available on the topic,[2] I contrast justification of theoretical and practical claims, and I argue for the epistemic character of both.[3]

Consider now what is perhaps the most general distinction we can draw in relation to practical justification: practical justification of theoretical and of practical assertions. The divide follows Kant's well-known distinction between theoretical and practical cognition:

> I shall here settle for explicating theoretical cognition as one whereby I cognise *what is,* and practical cognition as one whereby I conceive *what ought to be.* (A633/B661)

Accordingly, we have "ought" claims, which belong to practical philosophy. These claims are practical or related to the praxis, because they formulate certain prescriptions on *actions.* They do not simply describe how we act or how things happen in the world, but prescribe how we ought to act and how things ought to happen in the world. Let me identify this is as the second area where practical justification can be discussed.[4] Here examination of practical justification would refer to features of "ought" claims in general.

But the assertions based on practical cognition (the "ought" claims, which Kant also calls "imperatives"[5]) can also be of different types. In the *Groundwork*, Kant identifies three types:

> All sciences have some practical part, consisting of problems [which suppose] that some end is possible for us and of imperatives as to how it can be attained. These can therefore called, in general, imperatives of *skill.* Whether the end is rational and good is not at all the question here, but only what one must do in order to attain it.... There is, however, *one*

---

[2] I focus particularly on Chignell (2007); also pioneering in this area are Stevenson (2003) and (2011).

[3] This is the first area considered in the volume and I label it 1 in Diagram 1.

[4] I will label this area correspondingly with 2; see Diagram 1.

[5] More exactly, Kant says: "The representation of an objective principle, insofar as it is necessitating for a will, is called a command (of reason), and the formula of the command is called an *imperative*" (*GMS* 4: 413; original emphasis).

end that can be presupposed as actual in the case of all rational beings
(insofar as imperatives apply to them, namely as dependent beings) and
therefore one purpose that they not merely *could* have but that we can
safely presuppose they all actually *do have* by a natural necessity, and
that purpose is *happiness*....Now, skill in choice of means to one's own
greatest well-being can be called *prudence* in the narrowest sense....Finally
there is one imperative that, without being based upon and having as its
condition any other purpose to be attained by certain conduct, commands
this conduct immediately....This imperative may be called the imperative
of morality. (GMS 4: 415–16; original emphasis)

We can identify in this way three other areas where practical justification is 3, 4, 5
applied in order to ground claims of practical reason.[6] If such claims are imperatives concerning the best means to reaching an arbitrary end, then we deal
with justification of imperatives of skills. If the end is happiness and, hence, has
natural necessity for us, as limited rational beings, then the imperatives, which
prescribe the best means to happiness, are imperatives of prudence. Finally,
Kant identifies an imperative that does not simply formulate the best means to
some end, but directly determines the will and calls it the imperative of morality. This is the famous Categorical Imperative.

Obviously, research in these areas will rarely focus exclusively on only
one type of imperative. There will be discussions, which may put particular
emphasis on the normative aspects of one type of imperative, but examination may also span the divides, especially since how one should draw the
distinction between imperatives of skill, of prudence, and of morality is a
controversial topic. Let me now move on and focus on the fifth area identi-   5
fied so far, the area of moral theory, where practical justification refers to the
moral imperative.

In the *Metaphysics of Morals*, in "On the Division of a Metaphysics of
Morals," Kant distinguishes between two areas of morality:

All lawgiving can therefore be distinguished with respect to the
incentive...That lawgiving which makes an action a duty and also makes
this duty the incentive is *ethical*. But that lawgiving which does not include
the incentive of duty in the law and so admits an incentive other than the
idea of duty itself is *juridical*. (MS 6: 218–19)

By "lawgiving" (*Gesetzgebung*), Kant refers to both a law, which presents an
action as a duty, and an incentive, which connects a ground for this action
subjectively with the representation of the law. The domain of the ethical
is the domain where action in accordance with duty must be done out of

---

[6] Discussions of justification of these claims are labeled 3, 4, and, 5, respectively; 6 refers to
justification of ethical claims—see note 7 and Diagram 1 above.

duty, whereas the domain of the legal or political is the domain where the
incentive need not be given by duty. I identify accordingly two additional
areas of practical justification, depending on whether justification refers to
ethical or legal lawgiving.[7]

As we will see in chapter 1, Kant's *Rechtfertigung* applies to various
entities—judgments, processes, even persons (the relevant aspects of
which can of course be expressed by claims or assertions)—so it will also
be applicable to claims about incentives. Again, exactly how the distinction between ethical and legal philosophy is to be drawn is a matter of
controversy, but that there is such a distinction is not usually contested,
and this suffices for my purposes here.

Before I turn to the initial distinction I presented in this section and, in
particular, to the practical justification of theoretical cognition, I would
like to introduce two further distinctions. These will help me identify four
additional areas relevant for practical justification, where commentators
have done considerable work. The first distinction is quite standard in Kant
and Kantian studies, and one can find it formulated in, say, the second
Critique.

Thus, in "The Analytic of Pure Practical Reason," Kant formulates the fundamental law of pure practical reason as follows: "So act that the maxim of
your will could always hold at the same time as a principle in a giving of universal law" (*KpV* 5: 30). There is, therefore, an implicit distinction between this
fundamental law of practical reason, which, when applied to limited rational
beings like us, is a categorical imperative, on the one hand, and, on the other,
maxims of will, the validity of which is tested by the imperative. The first section of the Analytic includes a definition of maxims:

> Practical *principles* are propositions that contain a general determination
> of the will, having under it several practical rules. They are subjective, or
> *maxims*, when the condition is regarded by the subject as holding only
> for his will; but they are objective, or practical *laws*, when the condition
> is cognised as objective, that is, as holding for the will of every rational
> being. (*KpV* 5: 19)

Maxims are, therefore, subjective propositions that contain a general determination of the will. They are the principles, which actually determine the
will of the agents in action. Such principles may, but need not, be objective, that is, ethically valid. Hence, one distinct area of practical justification

---

[7] See Diagram 1 above. As I have already mentioned (note 6 above), I label the area of the justification of ethical claims with 6. As we will see, I will further identify four types of ethical claims,
each having a corresponding area of research concerning practical justification (labeled 7–10).
For this reason, I label the domain concerning the justification of legal-political claims 11.

(the seventh) concerns Categorical Imperatives in general.[8] A further area of justification (10) concerns ethical *principles*.[9]

Research is sometimes done on the practical justification of the Categorical Imperatives, but sometimes more emphasis is put on the justification of ethical principles. As before, considerable work has been done on issues, which require research beyond one particular area, but the identification of these various areas is, as I said, somewhat artificial and meant to give some orientation in the literature. One could also further identify an area of research concerned with rules. As Kant puts it, each principle has under it several practical rules and work in, say, applied ethics could focus on the justification of such rules. I am not emphasizing this area, however, since it has not been traditionally a major area of research (and some contemporary Kantians even claim that Kant's philosophy does not intend to be relevant for this type of work), but more and more work on this is currently emerging.

The second distinction I would like to mention here is that between the various formulations of the Categorical Imperative and, in particular, between the Formula of the Universal Law (*"act only in accordance with that maxim through which you can at the same time will that it become a universal law"*; *GMS* 4: 421)[10] and the Formula of Humanity (*"so act that you use humanity, whether in your own person or in the person of any other, always at the same time as an end, never merely as a means"*; *GMS* 4: 429). There is also a third famous formulation, the Formula of the Kingdom of Ends, and, according to Kant, the relation between these formulae is the following:

> The above three ways of representing the principle of morality are at bottom only so many formulae of the very same law, and any one of them of itself unites the other two in it. There is nevertheless a difference among them, which is indeed subjectively rather than objectively practical, intended namely to bring an idea of reason closer to intuition (by a certain analogy) and thereby to feeling. (*GMS* 4: 436)

---

[8] I use capital letters to refer to the various formulations that Kant puts forward, for example in the *Groundwork*, and that are supposed to express conditions that a maxim must meet in order to be morally permissible. Sometimes, in the literature, maxims that turn out to be obligatory are also called categorical imperatives. So I capitalize the expression that refers to the tests of the maxims (for instance, the Formula of the Universal Law or the Formula of Humanity), rather than the tested maxims.

[9] I count this area as the tenth, rather than the eighth, since two further domains of investigation of practical justification (8 and 9) can be identified depending on whether the Categorical Imperative considered is given by the Formula of Universal Law or by the Formula of Humanity; see Diagram 1.

[10] There is some controversy in the literature about the various formulae of the Categorical Imperative—how many they are and which ones are equivalent. As a result, there may be variations in the ways commentators identify them. For the formula above (*"act only in accordance with that maxim through which you can at the same time will that it become a universal law"*), I use Paton's name—the Formula of the Universal Law. (Kant 1991: 96)

When work has not focused on the seventh area of research I identified above (the area having to do with the justification of the Categorical Imperatives in general), but has focused on a particular formula, most of the time this has been the Formula of Universal Law. More recently, there has been some published research also on the Formula of the Kingdom of Ends, but it seems that many commentators have started again to look quite closely at the Formula of Humanity. I have identified therefore only two main areas of research here, partly for contingent reasons: the eighth area is related to the Formula of the Universal Law, whereas the ninth, to the Formula of Humanity.

As I have mentioned, I would like now to return to the initial distinction I introduced in this section, between theoretical and practical cognition. I have so far mentioned areas of research concerning practical justification of practical cognition, and perhaps one could think this is enough, since the notion of justifying practically theoretical cognition does not make much sense anyway. There is, however, as we will see in chapter 1, a set of theoretical claims that Kant thinks can be justified only practically, and these are the practical postulates. The practical justification of these claims is an area where, again, commentators have done a considerable amount of research.[11]

The final distinction I would like to introduce concerns these postulates. Starting from some of Kant's assertions, commentators sometimes distinguish between the postulate of freedom, on the one hand, and, on the other, the postulates of the existence of God and immortality of the soul. The former seems to play for Kant a more fundamental role. As he puts it in the second *Critique*, "whereas freedom is indeed the *ratio essendi* of the moral law, the moral law is the *ratio cognoscendi* of freedom...[W]ere there no freedom, the moral law would *not be encountered* at all in ourselves" (*KpV* 5: 4n). Hence, freedom seems to ground the moral law, whereas the claims concerning immortality and the existence of God are grounded in the moral law (even if only indirectly).

I think, however, that this relative priority of freedom over the other two ideas of reason (immortality and God) is apparent. It is true that, for Kant, the moral law depends ontologically on freedom, but, first, he also says that freedom depends epistemologically or cognitively on the moral law;[12] second, moreover, the moral law seems to be in a certain sense dependent ontologically both on God and on the immortality of the soul, and the practical postulates are epistemologically dependent on the moral law.

Be that as it may, these postulates have attracted a lot of attention and they are central for the final two areas (the twelfth and thirteenth) that I would like

---

[11] I label this area 14, rather than 12, since chapter 14, which illustrates this topic is a commentary on chapter 13, which discusses predominantly issues related to Kant's account of the practical postulate of the existence of God.

[12] "...had not the moral law *already* been distinctly thought in our reason, we should never consider ourselves justified in *assuming* such a thing as freedom (even though it is not self-contradictory)" (*KpV* 5: 4n).

to mention in connection with practical justification. In the next section of this introduction, I would like to illustrate some of the debates in these areas.[13] In the final section, I offer some concluding remarks.

III. Debates

As I have mentioned, one possible debate in area 1 concerns precisely Kant's notion of practical justification in general and, in particular, whether or not it is an epistemic process. I will discuss these and other related topics in chapter 1 of this volume. Thus, first and paradoxically, although an examination of Kant's justification of various (especially practical) norms is under way in the literature and most of the Kantians have something to say about this topic, not much has been written on Kant's view of justification (*Rechtfertigung*). Second, what has been written on Kant's *Rechtfertigung* suggests that practical *Rechtfertigung* in Kant is a nonepistemic notion and, hence, a notion that cannot be placed within an account of Kant's moral or practical epistemology. Third, Kant makes use of the notion of *Rechtfertigung* in many ways and many contexts, so much so that it sometimes looks like we are dealing with more than one concept under the same name. I argue that Kant's view of practical justification is unitary and coherent, that it is significant for practical epistemology and that it overlaps with the contemporary notion of justification in a way that makes it relevant for the numerous current debates.

Concerning practical justification of "ought" claims in general, we can raise questions about the famous Kantian implication from "ought" to "can." Kant seems to take this implication to hold for all types of practical claims.[14] Hence, an account of this implication will bear results for the practical "ought" in general. The attempt to account for, or contribute to the justification of, this implication can thus be placed as central for area 2.

One way to understand the claim that "ought implies can" (even for the conditional "ought" introduced by the hypothetical imperative) is moral: the point here would be that it is not morally permissible to make a requirement (whether moral or nonmoral) on an agent who cannot perform it; hence, to say that "ought implies can" would be a moral truth. Yet, there is also a theoretical and, moreover, a metaphysical way of understanding this implication.

---

[13] In this way, I am also introducing the following chapters of this volume.

[14] Most of Kant's claims are about moral reason. But the definition of the Hypothetical Imperative shows conclusively that the dictum is supposed to apply to practical reason generally: "Now, all imperatives command either *hypothetically* or *categorically*. The former represent the practical necessity of a possible action as a means to achieving something else that one wills (or that it is at least possible for one to will)" (*GMS* 4: 414). It seems to be clear that the "ought," which applies to the means to a certain end, presupposes the possibility of the means to that end; hence, the "ought" of the instrumental action also presupposes its possibility.

According to this theoretical approach, we can take the "ought implies can" dictum to describe a necessary connection between knowing yourself to be under the moral law and knowing yourself to be able to act as the moral law commands. This, according to Sebastian Rödl, is the best way to make sense of Kant's famous "ought implies can" claim.[15]

Of course, in general, according to Kant, one way to account for a necessary connection is logical: if there is a logical contradiction between the practical "ought" and the physical "cannot," "ought" does imply "can." In the case of the "ought implies can" dictum, this may seem less obvious, since the "ought" and the "can" are of different kinds—one practical, the other one, physical.

The other way in which Kant usually tries to account for a necessary relation between two notions is transcendental, through a synthetic relation, which holds a priori, and which is granted by a causal link. The a priori character of the relation makes necessary a metaphysical account. According to Rödl, we can offer such an account if we regard practical reason as deriving an action from the representation of the "ought": the recognition by practical reason that a certain action is derived from the "ought" is the cause, which brings the action about. This kind of causality, however, seems to be missing from contemporary accounts in the philosophy of action.[16]

Further questions can be raised at this point: can we be in a situation, where we think we can reach an end and, then, discover that, in fact, we cannot? Or is failing to act as the practical "ought" requires sufficient to prove that my thought that I should act in such and such a way does not manifest my power to act according to the representation of the moral law? As we have seen, Rödl's account refers mainly to moral reason and the moral law, but it should be possible in principle to extend his account also to nonmoral practical reason and the Hypothetical Imperative, insofar as the focus here will be on elements, which are common to these Imperatives.[17] By contrast, the attempt to explore the differences between the three types of rationality and to address questions that are specific for one or two of these particular types of reason, but not for all three, will move the discussion on the level of the areas 3, 4, or 5 (see Diagram 1).

One question we can adequately raise in these areas is precisely whether we can convincingly maintain the distinctions between instrumental, prudential, and moral reason. A possible objection starts from Kant's view that instrumental and prudential claims have in fact their normative force in theoretical reason—they describe the best means to given ends on the basis of the laws of nature. Yet, if we follow the classical Humean argument, according to which practical reason is reducible to instrumental and prudential reason, and if these are indeed only forms of theoretical reason, then not only is there no distinct

---

[15] See chapter 2 of this volume.
[16] Rödl refers here to Davidson (1980) and Korsgaard (1997).
[17] For the reason why I capitalize this expression, see note 8 above.

practical reason, but the differences between the three types of practical reason mentioned so far become insignificant.

According to Allen Wood, however, practical reason is not reducible to theoretical reason and, moreover, even instrumental and prudential reason go beyond theoretical reason and, hence, are not reducible to it.[18] One reason why Kant thought prudential reason, like instrumental reason, is guided by the Hypothetical Imperative is precisely that he regarded it as a distinct type of reason. If moral reason is guided by the Categorical Imperative, whereas prudential reason by the Hypothetical Imperative, then we have a clear way in which we can distinguish between moral and instrumental reason. What is more, instrumental reason cannot be reduced to theoretical reason. Thus, Wood claims, although we may say that rules of skill are the best means to whatever end a person happens to have, we cannot reduce the practical character of an end to the fact that the agent happens to have it. Agents happen to have many ends, but they endorse and pursue only some of them.

Wood thinks Kant's account of prudential reason is confused; for, we cannot justify counsels of prudence simply by means of the Hypothetical Imperative. Given that happiness, as the greatest achievable total satisfaction of all of that individual's inclinations, is an end which must be constructed to begin with, we cannot justify any counsel as simply the best means to the given end, but need also to prioritize this end of total satisfaction over more immediate ends. Yet, according to Wood, the attempt to justify the pursuit of this end on the basis of moral reason will again bring prudential and moral reason close to each other, and Kant's moral theory, closer to eudaimonism.[19]

Desire-based principles, insofar as we are sensible, and not merely rational, beings, will be a constant presence in our lives. Kant links this fact to the necessary character of happiness, as an end we pursue as part of our essence. From this perspective, a desire-based principle falls more appropriately under the category of a counsel of prudence, rather than under that

---

[18] See chapter 3 of this volume.

[19] In chapter 3 of this volume, Wood also considers another aspect of practical justification, namely, the perspective from which practical justification is undertaken. He rejects the objection that Kant's account presupposes a first-person perspective or a monological approach to justification. Even rules of skill and counsels of prudence, where there is an irreducible subjective element, have in Kant an intersubjective character that is due to the objective nature of the Hypothetical Imperative, Wood claims. Moreover, in the case of moral imperatives, there is a primacy of the standpoint of another. In talking about the recognition of the dignity of other human beings, Kant uses the Fichtean term *Anerkennung*. This leads Wood to a different way of thinking about dignity: an agent recognizes dignity when she realizes that she must not consider a decision only by calculating values from her standpoint, but needs to combine her standpoint with those of others. Moreover, Wood suggests that autonomy can be interpreted not simply as giving law to myself, but as self-legislation understood as the result of being guided by a common rational will, which is shared by all rational beings, insofar as they are ideally rational—the legislator is the community of rational agents as a whole. Obviously, discussion of prudential and moral reason moves Wood's argument into areas 4 and 5.

of a rule of skill, since the latter aims at contingent ends. Yet, given the problem of determining the content of the notion of happiness, a problem Kant himself identifies and attributes to the empirical character of such a notion, the justification of counsels of prudence becomes a difficult problem in area 4.

According to Larry Krasnoff (chapter 4), we can say that such and such an empirical end is justified by *being judged* as necessary for a happy life. This, however, will be only a provisional justification. Krasnoff assumes, however, that the Categorical Imperative can turn this provisional justification into a solid ground, and he investigates the ontological status of this ground. In this way, his argument becomes also relevant for the practical justification of ethical claims in general (area 6).

The standard constructivist interpretation of Kant, which can be traced back to O'Neill and Korsgaard, claims that value does not exist independently from us, but is created or constructed by us.[20] Realism (for instance, Ameriks, Wood, Guyer) asserts that our free and rational nature is good in an independent and objective sense, and all claims about value follow from this fact.[21] Kant seems to be clear that there is a basic standard of moral justification that is objective. Constructivists do not deny this, but realists think that this implies realism about moral value.

Given that the Categorical Imperative, as the fundamental standard of rightness, is the source of value in Kant's account, empirical ends will also have to derive value from the Categorical Imperative. For Krasnoff, in Kant, the Categorical Imperative plays the role of a proxy for justification on the basis of substantive claims. The justification provided by the Categorical Imperative is neither realist, since there is no substantive value put forward through this justification, nor constructivist in the standard sense, since standard constructivism assumes that there is value in the process of reflection, which makes possible value itself. Yet, Krasnoff argues, a condition for the possibility of value may have no independent worth.

He suggests an alternative account, according to which the commitment to the Categorical Imperative is a commitment to the fact that agents' substantive reasons for the desire-based principles cannot be justified, but must ultimately be considered as at least plausible, if I am granted the same by the others. As a proxy for the substantive reasons that might justify the desire-based principles, the Categorical Imperative does not provide substantive reasons for principles, nor does it ignore them by suggesting the value of the principles is given by the agents' choices. We have a reason to respect the others' potentially different reasons, insofar as they are equally committed to respecting ours.

---

[20] Among others, Krasnoff refers here to O'Neill (1996) and Korsgaard (2008; 2009).

[21] References are made here to Ameriks (2003), Wood (2007), and Guyer (1998).

Consider now the issue of the practical justification of moral principles. One question we can raise here concerns the relation of moral principles in general (whether ethical or juridical) to empirical elements. This would place the discussion in the centre of area 5. The issue here would be whether the justification of moral claims in general has to make reference to any empirical factors. According to Kant, there is a need for a pure moral philosophy, which could be separated from all empirical elements. This, however, is a puzzling claim given that some of Kant's most famous examples of unconditional duties involve empirical elements.[22]

Otfried Höffe draws a distinction between the ground of the bindingness of moral duties and the duties themselves, and he claims that only the former is free from empirical elements. This ground is the concept of goodness, which plays only an ontological role, in the sense that it is constitutive of the object of morality. At this point, Höffe's discussion moves in the area of the possibility of ethics. In particular, the deduction of the a priori concept of the good is a metaethical argument, which makes possible ethical theory.

Making this concept of goodness more specific through various empirical elements leads to particular principles and duties. Höffe distinguishes, however, between two sets of empirical conditions—there is first a set of elements that play a role even in the fundamental, normative part of Kant's moral philosophy. Secondly, there are empirical aspects that will be relevant only for the applied part of Kant's moral philosophy.

In addition, at the first level, Höffe distinguishes between three types of empirical factors. The first type refers to human beings as rational beings that are limited and tempted by inclinations; these factors lead to the various formulations of the Categorical Imperative. The second type of empirical factor is given by the fact that human beings have to live in the same world; this, according to Höffe, leads to a fundamental social anthropology. If we add to this the third type of empirical factor, that human beings are embodied and can be injured, we obtain the fundamental principle of right.

Arguments in area 5 concern claims that are equally relevant for ethics and juridical philosophy. For example, Höffe's discussion of the concept of goodness and the deduction of this category are equally relevant whether one focuses on ethics or legal philosophy. Even his discussion of the Principle of Right and of various legal principles, as well as the long section on *The Doctrine of Right*, §§B and C, can also be seen as parts of ethics. This is because, in fact, according to Kant, "all duties, just because they are duties, belong to ethics" (*MS* 6: 219). But Kant also notes that the lawgiving for these duties may be part of ethics. When the issue concerns justification of strictly ethical claims, we are in area 6.

---

[22] See chapter 5 of this volume.

Specific for the ethical domain in Kant are debates around the issue of motivation. Robert Stern (chapter 6) focuses precisely on the debate between internalism and externalism concerning motivation.[23] The issue here is whether, for an agent, it would be possible to judge that she ought to act in a particular way and, yet, claim she had no motivation to act in that way. Externalists regard such cases as possible, although rare, whereas internalists think there is a conceptual inconsistency involved here.

Internalism about motivation seems to go well along a form of antirealism. For instance, according to the expressivist view, what is right or wrong depends on the agent's attitudes, desires, and passions, and if these suggest that something is right then it is indeed impossible to conceive of an agent who would not have motivation to act accordingly. Still, the relation between the realist/antirealist and the internalist/externalist debates is not simple, since realism is not necessarily incompatible with internalism.

On Stern's account, the issue in the realist/antirealist debate is whether moral facts (such as the fact that lying is wrong) hold independently of human attitudes, responses or choices. The realist will claim that such moral facts are independent of those factors, whereas the nonrealist will claim that such facts obtain precisely because of those factors. The constructivist antirealist, for instance, will claim that lying is made wrong by the fact that agents operating under certain conditions would endorse or choose to avoid lying.

Stern attempts to explain away these debates or at least to make them less antagonistic through Kant's metaethical views on the ontology of moral standards and motivation. He thinks Kant can explain in what sense an appropriate moral theory has both realist and antirealist aspects, both motivationally externalist and internalist features. The starting point of the argument is Kant's distinction between holy and human wills, which Stern argues is constitutive of Kant's account of moral obligation.

Now, as we have already seen, according to Kant, there are two aspects of norm-giving: first, norm-giving contains a norm, which "represents an action that is to be done as *objectively* necessary"; secondly, norm-giving has an incentive, "which connects a ground for determining choice to this action *subjectively* with the representation of the law" or norm. (*MS* 6:218) Hence, in giving a norm or in norm-giving, we do not only provide a norm which represents a duty, but also connect this duty to a ground that determines us to act in such a way that the duty is fulfilled by the performance of the action represented by the norm.

The distinction between ethical and juridical norm-giving is drawn in Kant's account by reference to this incentive. Ethical norm-giving has duty as

---

[23] Darwall (1992), Smith (1994), and Superson (2009) are referred to by Stern, but not as representatives of either internalism or externalism. Darwall is supposed to distinguish between various debates related to internalism and externalism. Smith puts forward an argument in support of internalism and Superson discusses the relation between internalism and scepticism.

incentive, whereas juridical norm-giving admits also incentives other than the idea of duty. What this implies is that we can have juridical norm-giving which has duty as an incentive, but we cannot have ethical norm-giving which does not have duty as an incentive. It must also be noted that, in order for a duty to allow enforcement, it must have additional specific features, apart from being objectively necessary. One such feature is externality: juridical duties represent outer actions.[24] But there are other such features.[25]

As I have mentioned in section II, Kant distinguishes between the Categorical Imperative, the principles of action which are tested by the Categorical Imperative, and the rules of action that can be derived from the principles of action. In fact, this is a distinction between first-, second-, and third-order norms, and, depending on which of these three levels of normativity we focus on, we are going to deal with a different type of justificaton. For instance, one issue which is fiercely debated in the literature is that of the justification of the Categorical Imperative. One can focus on those aspects which are common between the various formulations of the Categorical Imperative, in which case the argument develops in area 7.

For instance, in chapter 7, Karl Ameriks examines the question of the dominance of ethical reasons in Kant's moral philosophy and the extent to which this dominance can be justified. His argument focuses on Kant's justification of the authority of the Categorical Imperative from the fact of reason, and he responds to the proposals of two recent commentators who think that Kant's strategy is (and should be) argumentative all the way down on pain of becoming dogmatic.[26] Yet, Ameriks claims, we should perhaps accept that Kant's argument from the fact of reason is a dogmatic claim made from a point already within a substantive moral position. Although the claim has been prepared by the development of a metaphysical system, it is still one with a certain dogmatic character.

We can go even further and try to examine the extent to which particular formulations of the Categorical Imperative are justifiable and the extent to which the metaphysical character of the justifications is due to any dogmatic claims. Until recently, the most discussed formulation of the Categorical Imperative has been the Formula of Universal Law. An examination of its justification would place us in area 8. As mentioned, more recently, commentators have also started to discuss extensively the Formula of Humanity, which seems more intuitive and better able to explain how we can test maxims. The investigation of the justification of this formulation will be central for area 9.

---

[24] Note, however, that some duties which represent outer actions are ethical duties, for instance, generosity; even duties which are enforceable may be ethical, for instance, some of the duties to oneself.

[25] For instance, other features are implicit in Kant's discussion of ambiguous right. In general, juridical duties must refer to other people, must not immediately require a ground for the determination of the will, and must not presuppose the adoption of an end.

[26] Ameriks discusses Sussman (2007) and Kleingeld (2010).

To illustrate debates in these areas, consider Paul Guyer's contribution, chapter 8; he outlines three accounts of the justification of the Formula of Universal Law, each of which is considered to represent a version of constructivism. One type of justification is Rawls's constructivism, which famously starts from a conception of the person and justifies moral standards as those standards agents, who conceive of themselves according to that conception, would adopt.[27] Crucial here is that Rawls assumes, rather than justifies, the conception of the person, which is the starting point of his theory of justice.

A second version of constructivism is Kant's. The starting point for Kant, Guyer thinks, is the moral law, and the principles of justice are derived by Kant with the help of the moral law and of some very general facts about human life. One difference between Rawls's and Kant's forms of constructivism is that whereas Kant claims to have grounded the moral law, Rawls acknowledges that he starts by assuming this conception of the person.

The third version of constructivism, Korsgaard's, seems to aim to narrow the gap between Kant and Rawls through a justification of the conception of the person that would be the ground of constructivism (Korsgaard 2009). Unlike Kant, Korsgaard does not make appeal to transcendental idealism in her justification, but she relies on a metaphysical claim concerning the conditions that make possible a person's self-constitution. Guyer's argument is that Rawls's strategy is to be preferred, since Korsgaard's justification is unsuccessful and Kant's appeal to transcendental idealism is to be avoided. Such an argument is therefore clearly central for area 8.

By contrast, a significant part of Andrews Reath's contribution (chapter 9) is related to the issue of the justification of the Formula of Humanity, a topic that defines area 9. Reath examines a specific type of approach to Kant's Formula of Humanity, which he calls "Formal."[28] He identifies several desiderata that an interpretation of this formula would ideally have to meet, and he concludes that both versions of the formal interpretation that he considers can do quite well when evaluated against the desiderata. The starting point of his argument is that the formal interpretation can account for the unconditional validity of the Categorical Imperative. The question is whether it can also account for six other claims Kant makes.

One of these claims is that the various formulations of the Categorical Imperative that Kant puts forward are normatively equivalent. The second is that rational nature as an end in itself is the substantive value that underlies moral thought. The third claim has two parts: first, that the Formula of Humanity is a formulation of the Categorical Imperative which is more intuitive than the Formula of the Universal Law; secondly, that through the Formula

---

[27] Guyer refers here mainly to Rawls's reprint of the three 1980 lectures on "Kantian Constructivism" (Rawls 1999).

[28] He identifies this position in the works of Korsgaard (2008) and Engstrom (2009).

of Humanity, the overall project of the *Groundwork* is advanced. The fourth claim is about how rational nature as an end in itself is a sufficient condition for a moral principle. Next, in *Groundwork* III, Kant claims that he shows that humanity is an end in itself, so an interpretation of the Formula of Humanity should be able to account for this too. Finally, Kant also claims that rational nature is distinguished from everything else by the fact that it sets itself as an end, and this end is the matter of every good will.

One version of the formal interpretation that Reath considers has the problem of explaining the equivalence with the Formula of Universal Law; yet, Reath thinks there are ways to overcome this problem. The second version that is discussed can easily show the equivalence, but misses the intuitive appeal; again, Reath thinks this problem can be addressed. Reath's argument attempts to determine the degree of accuracy of a particular interpretation of the Formula of Humanity. Given that one of the desiderata is the normative equivalence with the Formula of Universal Law, his argument contributes indirectly to debates in area 8 too.

Going back to the distinction, in Kant, between the Categorical Imperative, the moral principles, and the rules of action, I have mentioned that we can address the question of justification on each of these three levels. In the preceding discussion, I offered some illustrations of arguments, which deal with the justification of the Categorical Imperative—whether focusing on general features or on the specific features of a particular formulation. By contrast, in chapter 10 Houston Smit and Mark Timmons focus on the question of the justification of ethical principles and, hence, develop an argument in area 10.

More exactly, on the basis of the Formula of Humanity, they try to map out Kant's derivation of particular duties in the Doctrine of Virtue. They follow the Kantian distinctions between duties to oneself and duties to others, between duties to oneself qua animal being and qua moral being, and between duties to others of love and of respect. They conclude that Kant is successful in deriving a set of ethical duties from particular conceptions of duty and respect with the help of additional empirical premises.

Smit and Timmons regard the relationship between the Formula of Humanity and the various principles of duty as explanatory. First, they start by taking for granted the Formula of Humanity. Secondly, they explain the deontic status of the various principles of duty (whether they are required, permitted, or forbidden). Moreover, the authors claim, their argument refers to derivations which take place a priori—they do not establish only that certain principles are, say, required, but also how they are required on the basis of the Formula of Humanity.[29] Finally, it

---

[29] Smit and Timmons talk about the issue of determinacy, by which they mean the question whether the moral principle in Kant includes concepts the conditions of application of which are sufficiently determinate to allow us to derive the duties Kant claims can be derived from this law. Here, Smit and Timmons refer to various texts by Thomas E. Hill, Jr. (for instance, 1993 and 1996) and Wood (for instance, 2007).

is worth noting that, for them, the principles that are derived should not already be built into the principle from which they are supposed to be derived.

Derivation in their study is understood as a process whereby, between the general principle and the derived consequence, there is at least one premise about the nature of the maxim being evaluated. Recall now Kant's distinction between the two branches of moral philosophy: ethics and legal or political philosophy. I have so far followed some distinctions Kant offers within ethics. I would now like to go back to area 11, where debates are centred on the justification of legal or political claims.

As an illustration, consider Howard Williams's contribution to this volume (chapter 11). Like Höffe, he emphasizes the importance, in Kant, of the empirical elements and he makes reference both to human beings' neediness and to the crucial significance of a social dimension in the justification of legal norms. In particular, his question concerns the extent to which Kant can be regarded as a libertarian political theorist.

In response to accusations that he had inaccurately portrayed Kant as a libertarian political philosopher, Williams emphasizes the importance, in Kant, of social provisions for those who are unable to meet their basic needs.[30] Thus, the necessary presupposition of a general will, which constitutes the social dimension for the justification of legal norms, assumes that the collective agreement emerges from moral agents. Moral agency, however, presupposes at least the satisfaction of basic needs. Hence, a requirement for the provision of social assistance for those in dire need is an implication of Kant's claim that the idea of general will is presupposed by the specific way in which legal norms are applied in particular cases in societies.

The libertarian aspect Williams thinks can be found in Kant is the separation between ethics and legal philosophy and, in particular, Kant's well-known claim that, in the context of legal philosophy, what counts is the external side of freedom, and, hence, freedom is understood as the absence of constraints. The implication, for Kant, is the dislike of paternalism in politics, which marks another similarity with libertarianism. By contrast, Kant is not suspicious of the state as a matter of principle, he does not think that individual liberty has absolute priority, including over equality and community, and he tries to combine patriotism and cosmopolitanism, a mix which cannot be found in libertarian theories.

Various other issues can be discussed here, but for the purpose of an illustration of debates in this area, the discussion of Williams's contribution to this volume should suffice. At this point, I can return to the distinction between theoretical and practical cognition and examine further the practical justification of theoretical claims, more exactly, of the practical postulates. Recall that the postulate concerning the existence of freedom seems to have a different status than the postulates of the existence of God and of the immortality of the

---

[30] He responds mainly to Holtman (2004) and Kaufman (1999).

soul. This is because freedom is a necessary condition of morality in general, whereas the postulates of the existence of God and of immortality are necessary conditions of the highest good.

Henry Allison (chapter 12) focuses on the practical justification of the theoretical claim concerning freedom. His argument is therefore central for area 12. He begins with Kant's argument in the *Groundwork*, an argument he traces back to Kant's review of Schulz (*RS*). There, Kant draws an analogy between the freedom to think (to reason on the basis of objective rules, rather than to be determined by subjective factors) and the freedom to choose (with an assumption that the choice is based on objective grounds). Assuming the "Reciprocity Thesis" (a free will and a will under moral laws are one and the same), in order to show that we are really subject to the Categorical Imperative, we need to show we are free. But, in the first *Critique*, Kant has demonstrated we cannot show this; the alternative strategy is to show that we have to presuppose freedom.

The argument has two steps: showing that every being that can act only under the idea of freedom is free in the practical sense and showing that to every rational being that has a will we must lend the idea of freedom under which she acts. At any rate, Allison's focus is on the argument for freedom, not for the moral law, so he moves on from the *Groundwork* and Kant's review of Schulz to the second *Critique*.

Allison explores the metaphysical implications of the practical justification of freedom. According to Kant, the fact of reason proves the actuality of freedom, but this is for practical purposes (for the agent concerned with the practical question). According to Allison, the objection to his (nonmetaphysical) version of transcendental idealism, which is most related to the topic of his chapter, is that he cannot show that the nonideal has greater ontological status than the ideal. One problem, Allison says, is to place freedom in the real-ideal metaphysical framework. Within this framework we are forced to choose between: we are really free and only seem to be causally determined or that the noumenal self is free and the phenomenal one is causally determined.[31] The first view undermines Kant's empirical realism, whereas the second commits Kant to the implausible view of two selves and a counterintuitive view of moral responsibility.

The problem in exploring the metaphysical status of freedom is the assumption that there must be a "fact of the matter" regarding freedom. By contrast, he suggests we should accept that we deal with two regulative principles, each with its own sphere of validity. In this way, we do not end up with the ontological thesis regarding freedom or with the fictionalist view of freedom (we act as if we are free, although we know we are not); instead, we end up with warranted assertability from the practical point of view. In other words, qua

---

[31] Allison refers here to Guyer's naturalizing interpretation, in Guyer (1993).

rational agent engaged in a process of deliberation concerning what I ought to do, I must consider myself free from natural determinism (*Groundwork*) and, as bound by the moral law, I must consider myself autonomous (second *Critique*). This is Kant's practical justification of freedom, which is sufficient for practical purposes.

In chapter 13, John Hare raises another question in the area of the possibility of morality, the question of the relation between morality and religion. He starts from Kant's paradoxical claims that morality does not need religion, on the one hand, and, on the other, that morality inevitably leads to religion. The apparent tension can be removed if Kant's first claim is examined carefully—Kant talks about the fact that for us, *insofar as we are free*, morality does not need religion. Yet, as creatures of need, we also have the end of happiness.

There are two implications of this: first, happiness will have to figure somehow in our conception of the good; secondly, moreover, we have to conceive of the possibility of becoming moral in spite of our propensity to evil. In both cases, a belief in the existence of God is the starting point for accounts, which show the possibility of happiness and moral action. This indicates clearly that his argument is in area 13.

What Hare takes to be the fundamental difficulty for Kant is the relation between freedom and temporality. Thus, since a revolution in the disposition requires a noumenal change in the person from being under the Evil Maxim to being under the Good Maxim, one can ask when and where this change will take place. Of course, Kant rejects such questions as unintelligible and his Critical philosophy allows him to do so, but the question is whether the higher degree of intelligibility is not available in a rival theory.

In chapter 14, Adrian Moore focuses precisely on this question, which no longer pertains to a specific postulate, but concerns the practical justification of "is" claims in general. Hence, his argument develops in the final area on Diagram 1, area 14. Moore's text may seem unusual within the economy of this volume: it is a commentary on Hare's article and it is relatively short. Yet, it raises two significant points, both of which are made possible by Hare's text. The first point is that transcendental freedom and perhaps transcendental idealism more generally cannot be faulted simply by the accusation of the unintelligibility of an idea, such as that of noumenal change.

Second, however, Moore raises a question about Kant's idea of practical justification, in the second sense mentioned above (not as justification of practical claims, but as justification of theoretical claims, a justification grounded on the moral law). According to the standard interpretation, Kant thinks we must believe in God, because only God can guarantee a distribution of happiness in accordance with virtue or morality. Yet, Moore asks, is it possible to concede that what we must believe may be false?

On the one hand, Moore says, the fact that we have no alternative, but to believe something does not mean that the object of our belief is true. On the other hand, however, the fact that we have no alternative, but to believe that something is the case means precisely that we cannot believe it to be false. The fundamental question for Kant, Moore suggests, is the nature of the "must," the nature of the necessity, which attaches to the fact that we believe something.

IV. Conclusion

With the discussion of Moore's contribution, all fourteen areas of discussion of practical justification have been illustrated. Each area has been mainly illustrated by reference to a chapter in this volume, and numbers for chapters and research areas are in correspondence. What is important to note in this respect is the unity of the volume, the complementarity of the contributions, and the broad spectrum of themes and positions covered.

Bibliography

Ameriks, K. (2003) *Interpreting Kant's Critiques*. Oxford: Oxford University Press.

Chignell, A. (2007) "Kant's Concepts of Justification," *Noûs* 41(1): 33–63.

Darwall, S. (1992) "Internalism and Agency," *Philosophical Perspectives* 6: 155–74.

Davidson, D. (1980) "Freedom to Act," in *Essays on Actions and Events*, 63–81. Oxford: Clarendon Press.

Engstrom, S. (2009) *The Form of Practical Knowledge: A Study of the Categorical Imperative*. Cambridge, MA: Harvard University Press.

Guyer, P. (1993) *Kant and the Experience of Freedom: Essays on Aesthetics and Morality*. Cambridge: Cambridge University Press.

Guyer, P. (1998) "The Value of Reason and the Value of Freedom," *Ethics* 109(1): 22–35.

Hill, T. E., Jr. (1993) "Donagan's Kant," *Ethics* 104(1): 22–52.

Hill, T. E., Jr. (1996) "Moral Dilemmas, Gaps and Residues," in H. E. Mason (ed.), *Moral Dilemmas and Moral Theory*. Oxford: Oxford University Press.

Holtman, S. W. (2004) "Kantian Justice and Poverty Relief," *Kant-Studien*, 95(1): 86–106.

Kant, I. (1991) *The Moral Law: Groundwork of the Metaphysics of Morals*, Tr. H. J. Paton. London: Routledge.

Kant, I. (1996a) *Critique of Pure Reason*. Tr. W. S. Pluhar. Indianapolis: Hackett.

Kant, I. (1996b) "Groundwork of The Metaphysics of Morals," in *Practical Philosophy*, 37–108. Tr. and ed. M. J. Gregor. Cambridge: Cambridge University Press.

Kant, I. (1996c) "The Metaphysics of Morals," in *Practical Philosophy*, 353–604. Tr. and ed. M. J. Gregor. Cambridge: Cambridge University Press.

Kant, I. (1997) *Prolegomena to Any Future Metaphysics*. Tr. and ed. G. Hatfield. Cambridge: Cambridge University Press.

Kant, I. (2002) *Critique of Practical Reason*. Tr. W. S. Pluhar. Indianapolis: Hackett.

Kaufman, A. (1999) *Welfare in the Kantian State*. Oxford: Oxford University Press.

Kleingeld, P. (2010) "Moral Consciousness and the Fact of Reason," in A. Reath and J. Timmermann (eds.), *A Critical Guide to Kant's "Critique of Practical Reason"*, 55–72. Cambridge: Cambridge University Press.

Korsgaard, C. M. (1997) "The Normativity of Instrumental Reason," in G. Cullity and B. Gaut (eds.), *Ethics and Practical Reason*, 215–54. Oxford: Oxford University Press.

Korsgaard, C. M. (2008) *The Constitution of Agency: Essays on Practical Reason and Moral Psychology*. Oxford: Oxford University Press.

Korsgaard, C. M. (2009) *Self-constitution: Agency, Identity, and Integrity*. Oxford: Oxford University Press.

O'Neill, O. (1996) *Towards Justice and Virtue: A Constructive Account of Practical Reasoning*. Cambridge: Cambridge University Press.

Rawls, J. (1980) "Kantian Constructivism in Moral Theory," *Journal of Philosophy* 77(9): 515–72. Reprinted in Rawls (1999).

Rawls, J. (1999) *Collected Papers*. Ed. S. Freeman. Cambridge, MA: Harvard University Press.

Smith, M. (1994) *The Moral Problem*. Oxford: Blackwell.

Stevenson, L. (2003) "Opinion, Belief or Faith, and Knowledge," *Kantian Review* 7(1): 72–101. Reprinted in Stevenson (2011).

Stevenson, L. (2011) *Inspirations from Kant*. Oxford: Oxford University Press.

Superson, A. M. (2009) *The Moral Skeptic*. Oxford: Oxford University Press.

Sussman, D. (2007) "From Deduction to Deed: Kant's Grounding of the Moral Law," *Kantian Review* 13(1): 52–81.

Wood, A. W. (2008) *Kantian Ethics*. Cambridge: Cambridge University Press.

Kant's *Rechtfertigung* and the Epistemic Character of Practical Justification[1]

Sorin Baiasu

I. Introduction

The attempt to discuss the process of practical justification in Kant encounters several difficulties. First and paradoxically, although an examination of Kant's justification of various (especially practical) norms is under way in the literature, and most of the Kantians have something to say about this topic, not much has been written on Kant's view of justification [*Rechtfertigung*]. Second, what has been written on Kant's *Rechtfertigung* suggests that practical *Rechtfertigung* in Kant is a nonepistemic notion and, hence, a notion that cannot be placed within an account of Kant's moral or practical epistemology. Third, Kant makes use of the notion of *Rechtfertigung* in many ways and many contexts, so much so that it sometimes looks like we are dealing with more than one concept under the same name.

In what follows I hope to answer all these questions in a way which shows that Kant's view of practical justification is unitary and coherent, that it is significant for practical epistemology, and that it overlaps with the contemporary notion of justification in a way which makes Kant's account of practical justification extremely relevant for the numerous current debates. I begin, in section II, with a discussion of Kant's notion of justification; I explore several ways in which he uses this notion in a variety of contexts, and I make reference primarily to the first *Critique*, but also to the *Prolegomena*, *Religion*, and the third *Critique*. I argue that, where the notion seems to break into distinct

[1] I am grateful to an anonymous reviewer from Oxford University Press for very helpful comments. A draft of this paper was presented to the Philosophy Department Research Seminars at the University of Bilkent. I am grateful to Bill Wringe, Lars Vinx, and Varol Akman for the invite and to them and all those in attendance for stimulating discussion.

concepts due to the radically different use of *Rechtfertigung*, we are in fact still dealing with one unitary and consistent, although quite general, notion.

In section III, I examine one of the few discussions in the literature on Kant's *Rechtfertigung*. I focus on the distinction between theoretical and practical justification, and I address primarily the claim that practical justification in Kant is nonepistemic. In the attempt to make room for a notion of justification in Kant's practical epistemology, I refer importantly to Kant's second *Critique*, where Kant explains how practical cognition is able to expand even our theoretical cognition of the unconditioned.

Once I have presented a general account of *Rechtfertigung* and have made room for this notion in Kant's practical epistemology, it will become clear that Kant's account of practical justification is unitary and coherent, and has an important epistemic role to play in practical philosophy. This is sufficient to show the relevance of this account for current debates on practical justification.

II. *Rechtfertigung*

To my knowledge, there is yet no study of Kant's notion of *Rechtfertigung*[2]— the German noun usually translated by "justification" (or, for the equivalent verb, "to justify").[3] So, I will begin with what, in the absence of other literature, seem to me the obvious starting points: a brief note on the term's origin and some of the uses Kant makes of this notion in the first *Critique*. I will however continue with an attempt to present the common core of the various uses he makes of the notion in the first *Critique* and in some other texts, in particular, the *Prolegomena* and *Religion within the Boundaries of Mere Reason*.

Etymologically, both "justification" and *Rechtfertigung* can ultimately be traced back to Latin, and, with some approximation, they mean the same thing: to make right.[4] Although they both come from Latin, they are derived from distinct words in Latin, more exactly, from *jus* and *regula*; yet, they seem to take over the overlapping parts of the meanings of these terms to refer to the process of making right. Of course, the notion of justification is usually employed to mean a process of *showing* that something is right. This suggests that we have the object of justification, the criterion on the basis of which we distinguish between right and wrong, and, finally, the judgment through which, according to the criterion, that thing is right or wrong.

---

[2] The same goes for cognate terms, such as *berechtigen* (to justify).

[3] There is no entry corresponding to this term in Caygill (1995). The notion is, however, included in the forthcoming *Kant Lexikon*, edited by Georg Mohr, Jürgen Stolzenberg, and Marcus Willaschek (Forthcoming). In his "Kant's Concepts of Justification," Andrew Chignell does not claim his notion of justification refers to Kant's *Rechtfertigung*, although he does not distance himself from this interpretation either (2007).

[4] See the corresponding entries in Scott (1772) and Kluge (1891).

Yet, whether these suggestions are correct depends on the account of norms one has in view. On a constructivist reading, for instance, criteria of rightness are constructed, rather than already existing, so, depending on how a criterion is constructed, the object of justification may turn out to be right or wrong. A further complication occurs if we consider the nature of the object of justification. If we regard the object of justification as constituted in some sense by the process of criterion-construction, then a process of justification can literally make something right.

What kind of view of justification does Kant have? Consider the following passage from the *Critique of Pure Reason*:

> If we can prove that only by means of the categories can an object be thought, this will already suffice as a deduction of them and as a justification [*Rechtfertigung*] of their objective validity. (A97)

Kant talks here about the justification of the objective validity of the categories. What such a justification requires is a proof showing that an object can be thought only by means of the categories. Such a proof would be sufficient as a justification of the categories' objective validity. Moreover, Kant seems to suggest a distinction between the notion of deduction and that of justification. At A84/B116, Kant confirms this:

> We consider ourselves justified [*berechtigt*], even without having offered a deduction, to assign to [...] empirical concepts a meaning and imagined signification, because we always have experience available to us to prove their objective reality.

Here Kant talks about "justification" independently of "deduction." What we need for a justification is a proof, which, in this case, consists of an indication that the appropriate experience is in place. Kant's concern is not with the justification of particular instances of assigning to concepts meaning, but with the justification of the general process of meaning-assignment.

It might also be worth emphasizing that, in this context, Kant talks about justification reflectively—"we consider ourselves justified [*halten uns berechtigt*]." What is justified is not even the process of meaning-assignment, but we ourselves in making the assignment. This way of using the term might be motivated by the fact that Kant does not talk here about individual instances of meaning-assignment, but, as I have already said, about the process as a whole.

Further on, Kant also notes that:

> Even if our judgement has no contradiction in it, it may nonetheless link concepts in a way not borne out by the object, or may link them even if no basis justifying such a judgement [*welcher ein solches Urteil berechtigte*] is given to us either a priori or a posteriori. (*KrV* A150/B190)

In this context, the focus is no longer on the justification of the objective validity of categories or on the possibility of a process of correctly assigning meaning to empirical concepts; instead, Kant talks about the justification of judgments. Moreover, he says that such a justification can be either a priori or a posteriori. Interestingly, he also discusses justification as being provided by a basis, and the implication seems to be that not any basis would do.

Still in the first *Critique*, Kant also claims that:

> The previous two principles [the principle of the axioms of intuition and the principle of the anticipations of perception], which I called the mathematical principles because they justified [*berechtigten*] applying mathematics to appearances, dealt with appearances in regard to their mere possibility. (A178/B221)

This seems to be another variation on "justification." Justification now is of the application of mathematics to appearances and is provided by principles. We know from Kant's discussion of the axioms and anticipations that their principles show why we can employ numerical concepts in empirical judgments. Hence, these principles justify in this way the application of mathematics. Again, here, Kant is not concerned with the correct employment of numerical concepts in particular cases, but with the possibility (in principle) of applying them correctly in empirical judgments.

So far, therefore, "justification" has referred to the categories' objective validity, to the appropriateness of assigning meaning to empirical concepts, to the judgments' adequate combination of concepts, and to the legitimate application of mathematics. And there are further interesting examples in the first *Critique*: at A195/B240, succession in the object (something occurs preceded by something else) is justified [*berechtiget*] by a rule; A249 includes discussion of the division of objects into phenomena and noumena, a division that the concept of appearances justifies [*berechtige*]; B315 talks about the impossibility of justifying [*rechtfertigen*] synthetic a priori propositions, if the constitutive concepts are taken to refer to things in themselves, that is, if categories are used in a merely transcendental way; at B368, Kant announces that he will justify [*rechtfertigen*] the use, for the concepts of pure reason, of the designation "transcendental ideas"; at B402, in a note, Kant talks about the expressions obtained by locating the soul in terms of the categories as justified [*gerehctfertigt*]; A396 makes reference to the justification [*Rechtfertigung*] of the arrangement of the paralogisms of pure reason.

Examples can continue. What is common to all these employments of "justification" is a relation between a basis, that for which the basis provides a ground, and the strength of the basis (sufficiency). And, yet, there are various types of basis and various ways to conceive the nature of a basis and its relation to the object of justification. As we have seen, a basis can be provided by a proof (whether a priori or a posteriori), by a certain experience, by principles, or by a concept.

This preliminary presentation of the notion of justification can help us now understand better Kant's use of *Rechtfertigung* in his discussion of sound common sense in *Prolegomena*. In that context, he seems to oppose justification and sound common sense. He contrasts the justification and deduction of the possibility of a priori concepts of understanding in metaphysics, on the one hand, and, on the other, a merely empirical grasp of concepts by sound common sense (*Prol* 4: 370–71). But, whereas the contrast holds very well between an a priori and an empirical grasp of concepts, it is unclear Kant would not talk about justification outside metaphysics:

> ... outside metaphysics, probability and sound common sense can indeed have their beneficial and legitimate use, though following principles entirely their own, whose importance always depends on a relation to the practical. (*Prol* 4: 371)

As long as there is a legitimate use of sound common sense on the basis of certain principles, there is no reason in principle why such use would not need justification at least in some instances. Where justification seems to be missing completely is in the case of those "propositions that are immediately certain, and for which one not only need give no proof, but also for which one need not, in general, be accountable" (*Prol* 4: 370). The existence of such propositions is invoked, according to Kant, by "false friends" of ordinary common sense, as an objection to metaphysics, where Kant thinks every claim must be proved— yet, the objection sounds, the process of proving or grounding one's claims must stop at some point. It is clear, however, that, in fact, Kant contrasts the notion of justified judgment and that of immediately certain judgment. This is not surprising, if we agree that the notion of justification presupposes a sufficient relation between a basis or proof and that which is to be justified.

Perhaps a more problematic use of *Rechtfertigung* occurs in *Religion within the Boundaries of Mere Reason*. There, Kant seems to contrast justification, on the one hand, and, on the other, an appeal to revelation. Thus, he thinks that for a person to believe and profess a mystery, which has been proclaimed (by others) as in some sense revealed, is to do "something contrary to his conscience" (*RGV* 6: 171). This is because, although the person cannot be convinced of the truth of this revelation, he affirms it as his faith, whereas faith is supposed to be "the inner profession of what a human being firmly holds to be true" (*RGV* 6: 171).

And, yet, what Kant says further indicates that, for him, justification is not in conflict with revelation:

> Suppose now that a certain church were to claim that it knows precisely the way in which God makes up for that moral lack in the human race, and were at the same time to sentence to eternal damnation all human beings who do not know in any natural way that means of justification [*Rechtfertigung*]

of which reason has no cognition, and hence also to fail to elevate it to a principle of religion and to profess it as such. (*RGV* 6: 171–2)

In this context, "justification" refers to moral value and is something God does or at least something of which we have no knowledge, but which we attribute to God.[5] A person lacking in moral value can be "justified" in this way by God, that is, can be made morally right. This may seem to suggest that, in *Religion*, although there is no new feature of the notion of justification on account of a contrast with "revelation," still we seem to deal with a distinct notion of justification.

First, what God justifies is a person, whereas our justifications are of various forms of assent. Second, moreover, we justify to a person or another, whereas God justifies absolutely. Finally, in the justification of our claims we have some criteria of justification, we have our assent (to a claim) and, finally, the justification; in the case of divine justification, God does not simply try to show that something, as it is, meets certain criteria of validity; rather, what is justified undergoes a change in the process of justification. Thus, in our example, the person is transformed into a moral agent through God's grace.

These differences, however, turn out to be differences between a general notion of justification and its specific application in a particular case. Thus, according to Kant,[6] divine understanding does not merely present objects given in sensible intuition, but through the presentation of the objects, it produces these objects. Hence, a divine will would present and at the same time create a person as a moral agent. In other words, God's justification of a person can be seen as a justification of a claim (that that person is a moral agent), where the support is provided by the very presentation implicit in the claim, since such a presentation, as divine, also produces the object of representation.

Second, it is true that, when we justify a claim, we justify it as a result of a possible challenge formulated either by others or by ourselves. Yet, there are two ways in which I can provide support for my claim. First, I may try to show that this claim is in accordance with the particular views and interests of the person I am addressing or, second, I may try to show that it is rational to hold

---

[5] According to Kant, "it is always therefore a decree of grace when we are relieved of all responsibility for the sake of this good in which we believe" (*RGV* 6: 76). And, he continues, "it can further be asked whether this deduction of the idea of a *justification* [*Rechtfertigung*] of a human being who is indeed guilty but has passed into a disposition well-pleasing to God has any practical use at all" (*RGV* 6: 76—original emphasis). See also *SF* 7: 43.

[6] I make haste to add, although this is well known in Kantian studies, that, when he talks about God, Kant's only claim is that it is not possible to demonstrate that God does not exist. He does not claim that God exists; on the contrary, he maintains that we cannot demonstrate the existence of God and all we have is a postulate of the existence of God that is justified practically, that is, from the perspective of an already justified moral law. Hence, the position of the theist is less dogmatic than that of the atheist from a practical point of view, but theoretically or scientifically, they are equally dogmatic.

this claim given all the evidence and criteria of justification.[7] So, although as a matter of fact, I am always going to address someone when I justify a claim, I may address her by making appeal to criteria of justification and evidence that I take to be holding for all rational beings, including the person I am addressing. So, in a sense, it is true that our justifications are always made to someone, but they need not address that person as a particular individual with specific interests and views; they may address her as a rational being that shares or can share the experiences and criteria used in the justification with all the other rational beings.[8]

Finally, Kant clearly acknowledges that the idea of divine justification is a speculative one, going beyond the realm of possible experience and, hence, beyond the a priori sensible conditions of experience, including time.[9] From this perspective, therefore, it would make little sense to talk about temporal order of various aspects or even about change.[10] We seem therefore to have the same notion of justification, but applied to the case where God justifies the moral character of a person.

It would be worth adding one further note: I have said that one difference between *Rechtfertigung* in the context discussed in *Religion* and the notion as presented so far in the first *Critique* and the *Prolegomena* is that the former sense refers to the way God justifies a person, whereas the latter has to do with the way we justify our claims. But recall the reflective use of the notion that I emphasized above in the discussion of one of the quotations from the first *Critique*: we consider ourselves justified to do such and such a thing. This can be seen as a bridge between the two notions, which I have just identified as potentially in conflict.

The conclusion I draw at this point is that *Rechtfertigung* refers in Kant to any attempt to offer a sufficient proof in support of what is to be justified. As a further confirmation of this reading, consider two quotations, one of which represents one of the very few places where Kant focuses to a certain extent specifically on the notion of *Rechtfertigung*. Thus, in the first *Critique*, he says:

> The situation is quite different when reason is dealing not with the verdict
> of a judge but with claims of a fellow-citizen, and is expected merely to
> defend itself against them. For these claims likewise seek to be dogmatic,
> although in denying, as the former claims are also in affirming; and

---

[7] Kant expresses this as a distinction between trying to persuade and trying to convince (*KU* 5: 461). I will discuss a bit more this distinction in section III.

[8] We can introduce a complication here on account of the difference between the criteria of justification in theoretical and in practical philosophy. The point, however, is that practical justification, which is my concern here, makes appeal to criteria of justification which are supposed to be valid for all rational beings, not only for human beings.

[9] An example of this is Kant's claim that I quote below from "Religion" that divine justification in this sense is unknown naturally to human reason.

[10] Again, see discussion below (section III).

hence there takes place a justification [*Rechtfertigung*] κατ' 'άνθρωπον. Such justification secures one's claims against any encroachment and provides one with a titled possession that need not fear any pretensions from others even if it cannot itself adequately be proved κατ' 'αλήθειαν. (A739/B767)

Here Kant talks about justification of claims, whereas in the third *Critique* he discusses sufficient proofs of conviction:

> Now proofs that try to convince are, in turn, of two kinds. Such a proof may be intended to decide what the object is *in itself*, or what it is *for us* (human beings as such) according to the principles of reason that we must follow in judging it. (In other words, the proof may be κατ' 'αλήθειαν or κατ' 'άνθρωπον, with the last word taken in a universal sense, for human beings as such). (*KU* 5: 462–3)

Given that justification seems to be a process of providing sufficient proofs for a certain form of assent to particular claims, and given that conviction is the type of assent where it makes sense to talk about justification, we have an additional confirmation of the interpretation of *Rechtfertigung* presented so far.

In the next section, I begin to focus more on practical justification, and I start with one of the few texts in the literature that discuss Kant's view on some of the forms of assent we hold more frequently in our epistemic activities. One distinction in that text may seem to suggest that practical justification in general is nonepistemic and, hence, that it will not be part of a practical epistemology.

III. Practical Epistemology in Kant

Unlike his theoretical epistemology, Kant's practical epistemology seems connected very strongly with contemporary moral theory.[11] For instance, Kantian constructivism and discourse ethics, which incorporate accounts of practical cognition, are some of the most important developments in recent ethics, and they are both formulated with an unequivocal acknowledgment of the continuing influence of Kant's practical philosophy.[12] There is, however, a remaining suspicion that, although Kant has many things to say that are relevant for contemporary moral epistemology, and in particular for the issue of practical justification, when he talks about *Rechtfertigung* he has in

---

[11] According to Andrew Chignell, contemporary epistemologists often find Kant's writings about knowledge foreign to their interests; in addition, those working on Kant's epistemology rarely find any obvious relation to contemporary epistemology (2007: 33).

[12] See, for instance, John Rawls (1980; 1989) and Jürgen Habermas (1984; 1996).

mind a different concept than that standardly referred to by the same term in contemporary philosophy.

The discussion in the previous section should indicate at least that Kant's interest in the concept of *Rechtfertigung* is not very far from our concern with justification. As I have mentioned, the literature on Kant on *Rechtfertigung* is scant;[13] nevertheless, commentators have started to investigate those forms of assent, which can be justified, in particular opinion [*Meinung*], knowledge [*Wissen*], and faith/belief [*Glauben*].[14] This, for instance, is the topic of Chignell (2007), and he in fact entitles his study "Kant's Concepts of Justification," although he does not comment on the relation between his notion of justification and Kant's *Rechtfertigung*.

By "justification," Chignell means *"the evaluative concept that specifies conditions under which a propositional attitude is rationally acceptable with a moderate-to-high degree of confidence"* (2007: 33). Hence, according to this definition, the object of justification is a propositional attitude, the process of justification consists in determining whether the propositional attitude meets the conditions of rational acceptability, and the status of justified propositional attitude is reached when rational acceptability has a sufficient (moderate to high) degree of confidence.

As we have seen, the propositional attitude that Kant considers is assent [*Fürwahrhalten*].[15] If the basis of assent is sufficient objectively, Kant says, then we deal with conviction, which is valid for everyone; Kant contrasts conviction with persuasion, which is an assent with bases only in the particular characteristics of the person who holds it (*KrV* A820/B848). Truth, Kant notes, rests on agreement with the object. This implies that the judgments every understanding

---

[13] There is a series of articles where the word "justification" even figures in the title, but their main focus is on the particular grounding of one claim or another (e.g., Pereboom 1990; McCarthy 1984; Yost 2010) In other words, the idea of justification is more or less taken to refer to the activity of providing some good grounds for a particular claim or set of claims.

[14] Stevenson (2003) and Chignell (2007). It may seem that an opinion does not need justification; nevertheless, according to Kant, although opinion is subjectively and objectively insufficient assent, it requires at least some knowledge (*KrV* A822/B850). If this is the case for opinion, then for faith/belief the situation will be even clearer, since faith/belief requires subjectively sufficient assent. See also note 15 below. I use "faith/belief" for the German *Glauben*, because in English sometimes "faith," sometimes "belief" is appropriate, and some translations use one, others the second, still others vary the terms depending on the context.

[15] Sometimes (for instance, in the *Lectures on Logic*) this is translated as "holding-to-be-true", which is the etymological rendition (Kant 1992). Chignell takes this term to refer to a motivational element—it would not simply be "holding-to-be-true", but "holding-because-true". (Chignell 2007: 38) I doubt this is the case. A discussion of this element would take me beyond the scope of this chapter and may seem anyway to be a narrow issue. But, in fact, it is broader than the question of whether motivation has anything to do with assent; this is because it blocks the possibility of assent, which is not held because it is true, but because it is persuasive. Hence, there is a link here with Chignell's interpretation of Kant's notion of persuasion and the distinction persuasion/conviction. Although broader than it initially seemed, this is still an issue, which is not central for this chapter.

articulates about an object must be in agreement. Hence, one way to test whether assent is conviction or mere persuasion is the possibility of communicating the assent and finding it to be valid for every rational being. Subjectively, that is, as an appearance of his own mind, persuasion cannot be distinguished from conviction, Kant claims. But the bases of the assent that are valid for me can be tested on the understanding of the others to see whether they have the same effect on them. This is a subjective means to detect the private validity of a judgment. If the subjectively particular causes of the judgment are identified, then we expose the status of assent as persuasion (*KrV* A821/B849).

To assert something, Kant says, I must take the judgment I formulate as objectively valid for all and, hence, as conviction. If I know that the judgment is merely valid for me and, hence, as persuasion, I should not try to assert it. Assent marks the subjective validity of the judgment. From what Kant says about persuasion, I infer that, in principle, there may be bases that convince me of the validity of my judgment, but which, although they are not objective, nor are they simply linked to some of my particular characteristics and, hence, not simply persuasion. Therefore, conviction should hold both subjectively and objectively.

Concerning the relation between assent and conviction, Kant distinguishes between opinion [*Meinen*], faith/belief [*Glauben*], and knowledge [*Wissen*]. Opinion is an assent consciously insufficient both subjectively and objectively. If the assent is sufficient only subjectively and is regarded as objectively insufficient, then the assent is called faith/belief. Finally, knowledge is the assent that is sufficient both subjectively and objectively (*KrV* A822/B850).

Now, according to Chignell, Kant employs both epistemic and non-epistemic concepts of justification (2007: 34). The epistemic concept refers to assent under conditions that are sufficient for rational acceptability, and when the object of assent is a candidate (if true and immune to Gettier-type objections) for knowledge. The nonepistemic notion refers to pragmatic or practical conditions, which guarantee for assent sufficient rational acceptability, but not the status of candidate for knowledge, even if the object of assent is true. The rational acceptance licensed in this way is from a *practical* point of view.

A bit further in his text, Chignell distinguishes between forms of assent with regard to which Kant is a direct voluntarist and those in relation to which he is a direct involuntarist. For instance, while I can just decide (direct voluntarism) to adopt the object of opinion (an unproved mathematical theorem that I would like to use as a working hypothesis),[16] I cannot simply decide (direct involuntarism) to adopt that of which we have knowledge. Thus, Chignell says:

> ...there are other species of assent—and in particular those that may (if true and justified) count as knowledge—that are not under our

---

[16] According to Chignell, Kant is also a direct voluntarist about moral faith/belief, that is, about our morally grounded belief in the existence of God and the immortality of the soul.

direct control. Kant typically refers to these knowledge-candidates as "convictions" (*Überzeugungen*). (2007: 36)

Epistemic justification refers to objective conditions of rational acceptability for assent that is also a candidate for knowledge. Since Kant refers to these knowledge candidates as convictions, epistemic justification consists of (objective) conditions of rational acceptability of convictions. Nonepistemic justification, by contrast, includes all practical conditions of rational acceptability. I am going to call this type of justification, which consists of practical conditions of rational acceptability, practical justification. However, if we follow Chignell's distinction between epistemic and nonepistemic justification, the implication is that practical justification is nonepistemic.

But, if practical justification is nonepistemic, then Kant's practical or moral epistemology could not include a notion of justification, since paradoxically, as part of a practical epistemology, this notion of justification would have to be practical, in which case it could no longer be epistemic and, hence, part of an epistemology. And a practical epistemology without a notion of justification would be a strange account of practical knowledge.

Let me briefly restate my worry: according to Kant, there is a distinction between knowledge [*Wissen*] and cognition [*Erkenntnisse*].[17] Some cases of practical cognition do not qualify as cases of knowledge. These are usually taken to be the cases of the postulates of pure practical reason which make claims concerning the existence of God and of a life after death. More generally, however, for Kant, anything with reference to the relation of reason to the will has always a practical character (*KpV* 5: 57). Hence, the justification of the rightness of a principle is precisely a justification of the constraining role of reason on the will. This justification, therefore, seems to take place under the aegis of the practical and, hence, according to the distinction between epistemic and nonepistemic justification, would have to fall in the latter category.

Now, what Kant calls "knowledge" [*Wissen*] is, in fact, theoretical cognition [*theoretische Erkenntnisse*] (as Kant explicitly puts it, in, for instance, *KpV* 5: 56). If the only epistemic justification we can have is that of theoretical cognition (knowledge), then practical justification in general must be classed as nonepistemic. And, then, puzzlingly, by practical epistemology we must understand a domain of philosophy that does not have a viable notion of justification. For justification in practical epistemology is practical, in which case, at least according to the distinction between epistemic and nonepistemic justification, it will be nonepistemic and therefore outside the domain of practical epistemology.

---

[17] This is what motivates the change in the translation of *Erkenntnisse* from "knowledge" to "cognition," for instance, by Werner Pluhar (Kant 1996a).

One clarification is in order. It can be objected that Kant does talk about conviction in relation to practical justification. For instance, in the third *Critique*, in relation to a certain type of proof, he says:

> if it is based on a practical principle of reason (which therefore holds universally and necessarily), then it may indeed claim to convince sufficiently from a pure practical point of view. (*KU* 5: 463)

Hence, if epistemic justification is that which gives rise to conviction, practical justification, which can also generate conviction, may perhaps also be regarded as epistemic.

In response, one can first point to the fact that the initial claim was only that *typically* a conviction is a candidate to the status of knowledge.[18] The implication then is that some convictions need not be candidates to the status of knowledge. Hence, although one may talk about convictions in relation to practical cognition, those convictions are not candidates to knowledge, and, hence, are not epistemic.[19]

The suggestion, then, is to pay attention to Kant's distinction between two types of conviction, only one of which is a candidate for the status of knowledge. Reference here can be made quite easily to Kant's *Lectures on Logic*, in particular the "Jäsche Logic":

> ... we can now draw the universal result that all our conviction is thus either *logical* or *practical*. When we know, namely, that we are free of all subjective grounds and yet the holding-to-be-true [assent—*Fürwahrhaltung*] is sufficient, then we are *convinced*, and in fact *logically* convinced, or convinced on *objective* grounds (the object is certain).
>
> Complete holding-to-be-true [assent] on subjective grounds, which in a *practical relation* hold just as much as objective grounds, is also conviction, though not logical but rather *practical* conviction (*I am certain*). And this practical conviction, or this *moral belief of reason* [*moralische Vernunftglaube*], is often firmer than all knowledge. With knowledge one still listens to opposed grounds, but not with belief [*Glaube*], because here it does not depend on objective grounds but on the moral interest of the subject. (*Log* 9: 72)

According to this distinction, logical conviction is conviction based on objective grounds, which are sufficient without the contribution of subjective grounds.

---

[18] "Kant typically refers to these knowledge-candidates as 'convictions' (*Überzeugungen*)" (Chignell 2007: 36).

[19] Chignell distinguishes between conviction that is knowledge and mere conviction. Both of these, however, are (according to a distinction Kant makes and which I will introduce next) "logical"; there is, in addition, another type of conviction—"practical" conviction.

Practical conviction, by contrast, is based on subjective grounds; one is convinced that something must be the case as a means to a specific end. Consequently, one could explain how Kant can talk about conviction in relation to practical justification: what he has in mind is practical, not logical conviction. Yet, if epistemic justification is given by logical conviction which is, thus, not mere conviction, but also a candidate for knowledge, then practical justification is not epistemic, although it may well ground conviction (that is, practical conviction).

Consequently, epistemic justification concerns logical conviction and sometimes turns such conviction into knowledge, if that which the conviction is about (the claim or assertion) is true. Here, a further clarification is in order. Kant specifies that assent may rest on objective bases, but also requires subjective causes in the mind of the person who is judging (*KrV* A820/B848). This means that, even when epistemic justification can show that an assent is objectively sufficient or sufficient on objective grounds, we still need subjective causes in the mind of the person who has the assent.

According to Chignell, one way to understand the subjective cause for assent when we deal with knowledge is as *recognition* that assent is based on sufficient objective grounds (2007: 44). Subjectively sufficient assent is then defined through a series of conditions: that such assent need not imply reflection, that it should not involve an infinite regress (due to the fact that recognition can be understood as involving subjective assent), that it should make conceptual room for persuasion (subjectively sufficient assent where the grounds for assent may be bad), and that it should avoid a case where assent is not well founded. Since subjectively sufficient assent (SS) depends on objectively sufficient assent (OS), we need both notions. The result is the following:

[OS] S's assent that p is objectively sufficient iff ($\exists g_1$) such that
  (i) g_1 is a ground that S has, and
  (ii) g_1 is a sufficient objective ground for assenting to p. [...]
[SS$_1$][20] S's assent that p is subjectively sufficient iff ($\exists g_2$) such that
  (i) g_2 is a ground that S has,
  (ii) S's assent is based on g_2, and
  (iii) on reflection, S would cite g_2 as a sufficient objective ground for his assent. (Chignell 2007: 46–7)

These two definitions constitute the notion of epistemic assent, which is then contrasted with that of nonepistemic assent. Since my aim here is to make some room for practical justification under the category of the epistemic, I will contrast Chignell's epistemic and nonepistemic assents and I will try to determine where practical justification should be placed. Specific about nonepistemic assent is that it cannot be objectively sufficient, since this would place it under the notion of

---

[20] The number in "SS$_1$" is required because Chignell will introduce two other notions of subjectively sufficient assent.

OS, as defined above. For this reason, we are going to find under this category only assent, which is subjectively sufficient. Chignell identifies two such notions:

[SS_2] S's assent that p is subjectively sufficient$_2$ iff ($\exists m_1$)such that
  (i) m_1 is a merit which assent that p has for S, and
  (ii) m_1 is a sufficient non-epistemic merit for assenting to p.
[SS_3] S's assent that p is subjectively sufficient$_3$ iff ($\exists m_2$) such that
  (i) m_2 is a merit which assents that p has for S,
  (ii) S's assent is based on m_2, and
  (iii) on reflection, S would cite m_2 as a sufficient non-epistemic merit
    for his assent. (Chignell 2007: 55–6)

According to Chignell, knowledge requires OS and SS_1; rational belief requires SS_2 and reflective belief requires SS_3, which is "the counterpart of knowledge in the realm of *Glaube*, and it is the highest state that assent based on non-epistemic merits can achieve" (2007: 56).

If we look at the distinction between epistemic and nonepistemic assent, which is the starting point of my discussion in this section, we can see that the objective grounds of assent give the mark of the epistemic. Whether epistemic or nonepistemic, assent can be subjectively sufficient, but the difference between SS_1, which refers to epistemic assent, and SS_2 and SS_3, which refer to nonepistemic assent, is that the agent (S) would regard the support for assent as an objective ground in the former case and as nonepistemic merit in the latter cases. The best way to understand this distinction further is to clarify the notion of objective ground.

Chignell begins with a quote from the *Blomberg Logic*, which provides a definition of ground as that from which something can be cognized (Chignell 2007: 39; *V-Lo/Blomberg* 24: 42). He then quotes Kant's first *Critique* for a definition of objective ground: that which provides reliable information about the constitution of the object or state of affairs described by some proposition (Chignell 2007: 39; *KrV* A821/B849). This is in line with what Kant says in the *Jäsche Logic*, as already quoted above: unlike knowledge, belief [*Glaube*] "does not depend on objective grounds but on the moral interest of the subject" (*Log* 9: 72). Knowledge [*Wissen*] is here firmly associated with the idea of objective ground, whereas faith/belief [*Glaube*], with moral interests. This, however, seems in tension with other claims Kant makes in the same work and which are also echoed elsewhere.

For instance, in discussing the assent presupposed by faith/belief [*Glauben*], he excludes as possible objects of faith/belief those "objects of cognition by reason (cognition *a priori*), whether theoretical, e. g., in mathematics and metaphysics, or practical, in morals" (*Log* 9: 68; see also *KrV* A822–3/B850–51). This suggests that we can have objective grounds in the case of practical philosophy: insofar as a ground is that from which something can be cognized, practical cognition *a priori* will need grounds; insofar as an objective ground provides reliable information about the constitution of an object, we can have objective grounds in morality, because the grounds we have there can provide reliable information about the constitution of the objects cognized by practical reason.

This shows clearly that the tension is not between Kant's claims, but between the idea that we can have knowledge only in the theoretical domain, an idea that is not Kant's, on the one hand, and, on the other, some of Kant's claims. Once we accept that we can have knowledge in the practical domain, there is no reason to exclude that kind of justification from the category of epistemic justification or from that of ground of epistemic assent. In fact, in the *Jäsche Logic*, Kant explicitly says that we do have practical knowledge: "Nothing could be more ridiculous than, e. g., only to opine in mathematics. Here, as in metaphysics and in morals, the rule is *either to know or not to know*" (*Log* 9: 67; see also *KrV* A823/B851).

The question is, then, how it is possible to have objective grounds in practical philosophy. The problem in practical philosophy is that our claims are about what ought to be the case, rather than about what is the case. Since what is the case may not be what ought to be the case (say, the action I am witnessing is not the action that ought to have been performed), we cannot derive our practical claims from our theoretical claims. If so, our practical claims are a priori and, more exactly, they are claims formulated by practical reason. But a priori claims formulated by reason usually refer to objects of which we can have no knowledge. This is the case for the claims concerning the existence of God or the immortality of the soul, which are theoretical claims which refer to the unconditional and, hence, which we can think only with the help of the ideas of reason. Yet, given that our experience is only of conditioned aspects of the world, we cannot know whether there is anything that corresponds to these ideas. As Kant puts it, "it is intrinsically impossible to exhibit rational ideas in intuition, and hence also intrinsically impossible to prove theoretically that they are possible" (*KU* 5: 468).

There is however one exception: the idea of freedom. Kant makes this claim in various places, but I will focus on what he says in the third *Critique*. In "On What Kind of Assent Results from a Practical Faith", he starts by defining matters of fact as "objects of concepts whose objective reality can be proved" (*KU* 5: 468). He specifies that proving the objective reality of the objects of concepts can be done either by reason (*a priori*) or by experience (*a posteriori*), and, in the former case, either from theoretical or from practical data of reason. At any rate, Kant adds, this proof will be provided by an intuition corresponding to the data.

Now, the reality of the idea of freedom is established through practical laws of pure reason and, if we act on these laws, we can establish the reality of the idea in the actual acts and, hence, in experience. This, Kant says, is possible through the concept of causality, which we think in the idea of freedom. Given the concept of causality and the effects freedom seems to have in nature in the form of moral actions, we can conclude that freedom has objective reality. Moreover, in this way, freedom expands reason beyond the bounds within which any concept of nature would have to remain confined. In other words, nature and our knowledge of nature are related to sensibility; although freedom cannot be the object of a sensible intuition, its effects (moral, free actions) are objects of experience (*KU* 5: 474).

But if the object corresponding to the concept of freedom has objective reality, then claims about this object can be supported with reliable information about the constitution of this object. Yet, this is precisely the idea of an objective ground, which, as we have seen, is the mark of the epistemic. Of course, there are differences between objects of experience and the object corresponding to the idea of freedom, but there are also significant similarities. For instance, according to Kant, we know the object corresponding to the concept of freedom by thinking of it as a cause, and determining it both through its effects (which are objects of experience) and through the laws of this causality (moral principles, which regulate the effects of freedom).

Some entities in the sciences, initially hypothesized in order to account for certain phenomena, may come to be known through their effects and through the laws which regulate the occurrence of those effects, although they may not be perceivable either directly or indirectly through the senses. To be sure, as I said, there are also significant differences. For instance, the reasons why certain causes in the sciences may not be directly or indirectly perceivable through the senses is distinct from the reason why the object corresponding to the idea of freedom is not. In the former case, we may deal with entities that are too small to be directly perceivable, and the instruments of observation may affect their indirect observation. In the latter case, the object is by definition beyond the conditions which make possible sensibility and perceivability.

Although in the case of moral actions Kant says that we can perceive them, what we can perceive are those features which may also characterize evil or morally indifferent actions. Imagine, for instance, an evil person who performs actions that conform to moral standards in order to get the others to trust him. Imagine also a person who performs by accident an action that conforms to the relevant moral standard. The actions we perceive are indistinguishable from the same actions performed out of duty by a moral agent.

Be that as it may, the point is that, if the mark of the epistemic justification is that objective grounds constitute it, then at least certain types of practical justification are epistemic. Specifically, as I have argued so far, justification of certain moral principles is epistemic, since moral principles are items of practical knowledge, as laws of the causality of freedom. Kant famously claims that the existence of God and the immortality of the soul (the postulates of practical reason) are theoretical claims, which cannot be considered knowledge, but are matters of faith or belief. In the remainder of this section I would like to argue that, even if we focus on practical postulates, it can still be demonstrated that the grounds provided in support of the postulates *should* be regarded as constitutive of *epistemic* justification.

To show this, I would like to go back to the second *Critique*, to Chapter VII of the Dialectic of Pure Practical Reason. This chapter examines "How it is possible to think an expansion of pure reason for a practical aim without thereby also expanding its cognition as speculative" (*KpV* 5: 134–41). At the beginning of this chapter, Kant explains how pure cognition can be expanded practically: what we need, he says, is an *a priori* aim or purpose that is presented as practically necessary independently from all theoretical principles. This purpose, he continues, is possible only if three theoretical concepts are presupposed as possible, although no intuition can correspond to them (since they are ideas of pure reason) and, hence, no objective reality can be attributed to them by following the "theoretical path" (*KpV* 5: 134). These three ideas (freedom, immortality, and God) are postulated as possible through the practical law, which presents the purpose as practically necessary.

I take it, however, that the crucial claim Kant makes is the following:

> By this, then, the theoretical cognition of pure reason does of course acquire an increase, which however consists merely in this: that those concepts which are otherwise problematic (merely thinkable), are now assertorically declared to be concepts to which objects actually belong, because practical reason unavoidably requires the existence of these for the possibility of its object [...], which moreover is absolutely necessary practically, and theoretical reason is thereby entitled to presuppose them. (*KpV* 5: 134)

According to Kant's argument here, the justification of the postulates of practical reason does not merely entitle us to a moral faith or belief in immortality and the existence of God, we are also entitled to limited *theoretical* cognition that the concepts corresponding to the ideas of reason are not merely problematic (thinkable), but also assertoric (declarable as concepts to which objects *actually* belong).

Kant hastens to add that we cannot make use of this expansion of the theoretical cognition of pure reason to obtain "an expansion of speculation, i. e., no positive use can now be made of it for a *theoretical aim*" (*KpV* 5: 134). Such a use would allow us to say something about the objects that actually belong to these concepts, and not simply to assert that objects do belong to the ideas of reason. Yet, Kant says, we are not allowed to expand our cognition in this way, but only with regard to the practical use of pure reason. In the same way in which Kant claimed in the third *Critique* that the idea of freedom can acquire objective reality, he claims the same about immortality and God (*KpV* 5: 135).

This discussion is in fact useful also as a qualification of the brief examination of the objective reality of freedom presented above. For Kant now says that the suprasensible objects that correspond to the ideas of reason cannot be further cognized even with the introduction of the practical necessary purpose determined by the moral law.[21] For what is missing for the expansion of pure cognition in the theoretical direction is an intuition of the objects corresponding to the ideas of reason:

> Theoretical cognition, *not indeed of these objects* but of reason as such, has thereby been expanded insofar as through the practical postulates those ideas have after all been *given objects*, because a merely problematic thought has thereby for the first time acquired objective reality. This was, therefore, no expansion of the cognition *of given suprasensible objects*, but still an expansion of theoretical reason and of its cognition with regard to the suprasensible as such, insofar as theoretical reason was compelled to grant *that there are such objects*, even though it could not determine them more closely and hence could not itself expand this cognition of the objects (which have now been given to it on a practical basis and also only for practical use). (*KpV* 5: 135)

This long quotation clarifies some aspects of the status of the claims Kant makes. It seems that it is possible to distinguish between the following three categories of claims. First, there are claims about what there is (theoretical claims), which are made with a view to a theoretical aim (that of creating a unified system of knowledge). Kant is quite clear that we are not entitled to such claims about the objects corresponding to the ideas of reason. Second, there are those theoretical claims which are necessary conditions for the possibility of a practical purpose. It is with regard to such claims that Kant says we are entitled only to moral faith or beliefs and *not* to knowledge. Finally, there are practical claims, which are derived from the practical necessity of the moral law and which lead us to knowledge about what is right and what is wrong. Yet, this knowledge is not acquired with a view to a theoretical, but to a practical aim.

It seems, therefore, that, according to Kant, we cannot talk only about practical knowledge acquired with a view to a practical purpose, but also about some limited practical knowledge acquired with a view to a theoretical purpose, and this is the knowledge of the suprasensible as such. Since in this way we expand theoretical cognition and since we do this on the basis of the justification of our entitlement to belief or faith in the practical postulates, this justification has also an indirect epistemic character. Hence, there is a sense in which even the justification of moral faith or belief has an epistemic character.

This concludes my attempt to make more room for epistemic justification, and this notion includes now reference not only to theoretical claims where

---

[21] I am using Pluhar's translation for *übersinnlich*, namely, "suprasensible." By contrast, Gregor has "supersensible".

access to the corresponding objects through sensible intuition is in principle possible, but reference also to practical claims concerning the objects corresponding to the ideas of reason, but claims made with a practical purpose in view. Finally, epistemic justification can also refer to theoretical claims, which are supported from a theoretical viewpoint in a very limited sense and from a practical viewpoint in a more substantial way, but this leads only to faith or belief.

IV. Conclusion

Following the introductory section, in the second section of this chapter, I offered an account of Kant's notion of *Rechtfertigung*. The conclusion was that, despite the various uses Kant makes of this notion in a variety of contexts, the core meaning of this notion is that of an attempt to offer a sufficient proof in support of that which is to be justified. In section III, I considered the status of practical justification. The question of the status of practical justification was prompted by Kant's claim that we cannot have practical *knowledge* of the postulates of practical reason, although we can justify them practically. This claim may understandably suggest that, on Kant's account, practical justification is not epistemic. I have argued that, granting Kant's claim is not sufficient to deny practical justification the status of an epistemic process, even if this process is taken to fall short of producing knowledge of what corresponds to the ideas of reason.

Kant relies on an account of practical justification, which seems both coherent and unitary. Moreover, this is an account which is compatible with a view of practical justification as epistemic. His view of practical *Rechtfertigung* is therefore highly relevant for current debates on moral and political justification, and it is not surprising to note the dominance, within these debates, of Kantian theories. There is the potential in Kant's account to help us take a step forward in the attempt to provide and apply a consistent and robust model of practical justification in the current context of justification crisis.

Bibliography

Caygill, H. (1995) *A Kant Dictionary*. Oxford: Blackwell.

Chignell, A. (2007) "Kant's Concepts of Justification," *Noûs* 41(1): 33–63.

Habermas, J. (1984) *The Theory of Communicative Action. Vol. 1: Reason and the Rationalization of Society*. Tr. T. McCarthy. Boston: Beacon.

Habermas, J. (1996) *Between Facts and Norms. Contributions to a Discourse Theory of Law and Democracy*. Tr. W. Rehg. Cambridge: Polity.

Kant, I. (1987) *Critique of Judgment*. Tr. W. S. Pluhar. Indianapolis: Hackett.

Kant, I. (1992) *Lectures on Logic*. Tr. and ed. J. M. Young. Paperback ed., 2004. Cambridge: Cambridge University Press.

Kant, I. (1996a) *Critique of Pure Reason*. Tr. W. S. Pluhar. Indianapolis: Hackett.

Kant, I. (1996b) "Groundwork of The Metaphysics of Morals," in *Practical Philosophy*, 37–108. Tr. and ed. M. J. Gregor. Cambridge: Cambridge University Press.

Kant, I. (1996c) "The Metaphysics of Morals," in *Practical Philosophy*, 353–604. Tr. and ed. M. J. Gregor. Cambridge: Cambridge University Press.

Kant, I. (1996d) "Religion within the Boundaries of Mere Reason," in *Religion and Rational Theology*. Tr. and ed. A. W. Wood and G. di Giovanni. Cambridge: Cambridge University Press.

Kant, I. (1997) *Prolegomena to Any Future Metaphysics*. Tr. and ed. G. Hatfield. Cambridge: Cambridge University Press.

Kant, I. (2002) *Critique of Practical Reason*. Tr. W. S. Pluhar. Indianapolis: Hackett.

Kluge, F. (1891) *An Etymological Dictionary of German Language*. London: George Bell.

McCarthy, M. (1984) "Kant's 'Groundwork' Justification of Freedom," *Dialogue* 23(3): 457–474.

Mohr, G., Stolzenberg, J., and Willaschek, M. (eds.) (Forthcoming) *Kant-Lexikon*. Berlin: De Gruyter.

Pereboom, D. (1990) "Kant on Justification in Transcendental Philosophy," *Synthese* 85(1): 25–54.

Rawls, J. (1980) "Kantian Constructivism in Moral Theory," *Journal of Philosophy* 77(9): 515–72. Reprinted in Rawls (1999).

Rawls, J. (1989) "Themes in Kant's Moral Philosophy," in E. Förster (ed.) *Kant's Transcendental Deductions. The Three "Critiques" and the "Opus Postumum"*, 81–113. Stanford: Stanford University Press.

Scott, J. N. (1772) *A New Universal Etymological Dictionary*. Eighteenth Century Collection Online. University of Oxford. Accessed: 12 September 2012.

Stevenson, L. (2003) "Opinion, Belief or Faith, and Knowledge," *Kantian Review* 7(1): 72–101. Reprinted in Stevenson (2011).

Stevenson, L. (2011) *Inspirations from Kant*. Oxford: Oxford University Press.

{ 2 }

Why Ought Implies Can

Sebastian Rödl

I. Introduction

Suppose someone alleges that his lustful inclination is quite irresistible
to him when he encounters the favored object and the opportunity. [Ask
him] whether, if in front of the house where he finds this opportunity a
gallows were erected on which he would be strung up immediately after
gratifying his lust, he would not then conquer his inclination. One does
not have to guess long what he would reply. But ask him whether, if his
prince demanded, on the threat of the same prompt penalty of death,
that he give false testimony against an honest man whom the prince
would like to ruin under specious pretenses, he might consider it possible
to overcome his love of life, however great it may be. He will perhaps not
venture to assure us whether or not he would overcome that love, but he
must concede without hesitation that doing so would be possible for him.
He judges, therefore, that he can do something because he is conscious
that he ought to do it, and he cognizes freedom within himself—the
freedom with which otherwise, without the moral law, he would have
remained unacquainted. (*KpV* 5: 30)[1]

---

[1] Setzet, daß jemand von seiner wollüstigen Neigung vorgibt, sie sei, wenn ihm der beliebte
Gegenstand und die Gelegenheit dazu vorkämen, für ihn ganz unwiderstehlich, ob, wenn ein
Galgen vor dem Hause, da er diese Gelegenheit trifft, aufgerichtet wäre, um ihn sogleich nach
genossener Wollust daran zu knüpfen, er alsdann nicht seine Neigung bezwingen würde. Man
darf nicht lange raten, was er antworten würde. Fragt ihn aber, ob, wenn sein Fürst ihm, unter
Androhung derselben unverzögerten Todesstrafe, zumutete, ein falsches Zeugnis wider einen
ehrlichen Mann, den er gerne unter scheinbaren Vorwänden verderben möchte, abzulegen, ob er
da, so groß auch seine Liebe zum Leben sein mag, sie wohl zu überwinden für möglich halte. Ob
er es tun würde, oder nicht, wird er vielleicht sich nicht getrauen zu versichern; daß es ihm aber
möglich sei, muß er ohne Bedenken einräumen. Er urteilet also, daß er etwas kann, darum weil er
sich bewußt ist, daß er es soll, und erkennt in sich die Freiheit, die ihm sonst ohne das moralische
Gesetz unbekannt geblieben wäre.

Kant says that, recognizing that I must resist the prince, I know that I can. Knowing that the moral law requires that I act in a certain way, I know that I have the power to act according to my knowledge. I shall seek to explain why this is true. I am not aware of an account of this passage in the current literature on Kant that brings out its truth. I suspect this is because, for the most part, contemporary moral philosophy lacks the concept of a practical thought, a concept Kant deploys in the passage. As the thought "I must do this" represents an unconditional necessity, reason is its origin. This shows that reason is practical—as Kant asserts—because the thought is a *practical* thought. This is what Kant presupposes and the meaning and significance of which is not appreciated in the current empiricist environment.

I proceed as follows. First, I present a normative account of the connection of thinking one must do something and being able to do it (section II), and explain why it does not capture Kant's thought (section III). Hence, the connection must be grounded in the metaphysical character of thinking one must do something. Indeed, it resides in the unity of deriving an action from something general and acting according to a general representation (sections IV through VI). It will transpire that the truth of Kant's claim is founded on this: *thinking one must do such-and-such is an act of the power to do it.* I apply this to the moral law (section VII), and then explain why the thought acquires an imperative expression and thus a seeming distance from the action it prescribes (section VIII).

II. The Normative Account of the Nexus of Obligation and Power

The thought Kant expresses in our passage may be encapsulated in the formula "ought implies can": if someone ought to do something, then he can do it. Why should there be such a nexus of obligation and power? What could be its ground?

It may seem that there is no such nexus. Consider a given legal code, or a code of etiquette. Then there is sense of "ought" in which it may be the case that someone ought to do something: the code requires that he do it. Knowing the code, we may judge that someone who is subject to it must do something in this sense. Now, having ascertained that, we have not yet spoken to the question whether he has the power to do what we found he must do. Having determined his obligations, we have not yet determined his powers. An example will make this clear. Imagine a code of etiquette that requires that a man asking a lady to dance graciously kiss her hand. Now you are asking a lady to dance. You must kiss her hand graciously. But you cannot. For reasons we need not enlarge upon, you drool over the lady's hand as you kiss her. Perhaps, if this is your case, you must not ask any lady to dance. But it may be that you had to ask the lady to dance: her position and yours demanded it. You must do something you cannot do. There is nothing incoherent in this idea.[2]

We might say it is not incoherent, but cruel. A code that requires someone to do something even as he cannot do it is cruel. The code should be relaxed: if someone cannot do what it requires, he should be exempt, or be required to do the best he can. This demand may be just. But there is no incoherence in rejecting it: in thinking that he who cannot live up to the code is a weakling and justly despised; that the code must never be relaxed and that relaxing it would be our downfall.

There is no metaphysical connection between a code of conduct and the power of someone subject to it to conform to it. What the code requires of him is one thing; that he can do it is another. As there is no connection, there is space for us to establish one, imposing a *normative requirement* on any given code: we require that a code of conduct contain a provision that, in case its demands exceed the powers of someone subject to it, the demands be suitably weakened. "If someone ought to do something, he can do it" then does not signify a metaphysical nexus of power and obligation. It serves as a rule for adapting obligations to powers: if someone ostensibly must do something he cannot do, he is exempt. He must do it *ostensibly* in the sense that he would have to do it if he could.

I have been speaking of a given legal code or code of etiquette. Now we turn to the moral law. Is it possible that the moral law requires someone to do something he cannot do? We may argue that this is not possible on the following ground. It is cruel to impose on someone a duty he cannot meet. And the moral law bans cruelty. It cannot be a source of cruelty. A given code of etiquette may or may not contain a provision that exempts the weak from its requirements. The moral law *does* contain such a provision.

If this is why we think that the moral law never requires someone to do something he cannot do, then we hold that there is *no* metaphysical nexus that links being subject to the moral law to having the power to act according to it. Rather, we judge it a moral truth that no one should be subject to obligations he cannot meet. This is then part of the content of the moral law, which in this way demands its own adaptation to the powers of those who are subject to it. There may be disagreement on this. Someone may say: it cannot be excluded that some lack the power to live a noble life. This is a moral judgment. If we call it wrong, we, too, pass a moral judgment.[3]

---

[2] Shall I blame you for failing to do what you must? No. "Poor sucker", I think, "can't blame him". Compare the discussion of the relation of blame to "ought implies can" in Stern (2004).

[3] This section does not seek to establish that there is no metaphysical nexus of being under a rule and having the power to act according to it. It aims to bring out that the normative account rests on the presupposition that there is no metaphysical nexus. It may be said that there is, in general, a metaphysical nexus: a rule that governs the comportment of men prescribes things

III. Kant's Topic Is the Metaphysics of the Moral Law

This is how one might interpret the formula "ought implies can" in its application to the moral law. This interpretation does not articulate Kant's thought. It
presents the notion that ought implies can as a part of the content of the moral
law. But Kant's topic is not the content, but the metaphysics of the moral law.
By nominal definition, the moral law determines the will independently of any
inclination: being determined by the moral law, the will is determined by, and
only by, its representation of a course of action as required by the moral law.
The idea of the moral law is the idea of this kind of causality. We may wonder
how such a causality is possible, and how we can know that it is. If this is our
question, we do not make progress by enlarging on the content of the moral
law. But that *is* the question the passage at the start addresses. The passage says
that, being conscious of the moral law, that is, knowing myself to be under the
moral law, I know that I have the power to act according to it. I know that my
will is capable of being determined by the law and by it alone. If this is right,
then consciousness of the moral law provides me with metaphysical knowledge,
synthetic a priori knowledge, about myself: I know that I am the kind of thing
to exemplify the causality of the moral law. I recognize the metaphysical possibility of the law and its causality by being conscious of the law because my
consciousness of the law reveals its *actuality* in me.

Kant describes a metaphysical unity of knowing oneself to be under the
moral law and having the power to act according to it. Such a unity can obtain
only on account of the metaphysical character of the relevant consciousness
of the moral law. Consciousness of the moral law manifests itself in thinking,
on a given occasion, that the law requires a certain course of action. "I must
(must not) do this", I think. My thinking this shows, shows me, that I can do
(or refrain from doing) this. If this is true, then the thought "I must" is of a
special kind. It must be its formal character that it is a thought according to
which its subject acts. That is, *the thought must be an act of a power to act in the
way the thought represents as necessary*. If we call such a thought—a thought
that springs from a power to act according to it, this very thought—a practical
thought, we can put Kant's idea as follows: "I must do this", which represents
doing it as required by the moral law, is a *practical thought*.

Kant conceives of the locution "I must do this", which refers to the moral
law, as expressing a practical thought, a thought according to which its subject
acts, or, equivalently, a thought that is an act of a power to act according to this

---

men can do. There can be no rule that requires that one turn the moon around (Annette Baier's
example in Baier 1970) or jump over Chicago (Rogers Albritton's example in Albritton 1985).
I do not object to this claim. It must be developed. Presumably, its ground is this: a concept that
specifies what a rule requires must be capable of informing the will of those who are under the
rule. They must be able to deploy it in practical thought. If this is right, then developing the claim
will lead into the area explored in the rest of this paper. Following Kant, I go there directly.

thought. If we understand this idea, we understand the quoted passage. For, if my knowing myself to be under the moral law is an act of my power to act according to the law, then my knowledge shows that I possess this power. My knowledge how to act shows my power so to act in the way in which, in general, an act of a power shows the power of which it is an act.

IV. Our Thought is the Conclusion of Practical Reasoning

We need to reflect on a kind of thought, which may be expressed by "I must do this". According to Kant, my thinking a thought of this kind—more precisely, the consciousness of the moral law contained in it—is a fact of reason, which reason, as this is its fact, is practical. As a fact of reason, the thought "I must do this" will be located in practical reasoning. For, reason is the power of inference, practical reason, of practical inference. Indeed, the thought that is our topic is the kind of thought to be the *conclusion* of practical reasoning. It answers the question what to do. "To do" here is a gerundive and belongs to a family of forms that we may call imperatives. English has no synthetic first-person imperative forms, but analytic forms such as, "Let us do that", "We should do it".

It is sometimes said that practical reasoning concludes in a judgment that there is, or that there is most, reason to do such-and-such. If this were right, then practical reasoning would be mince-pie reasoning (as Anscombe famously put it), namely, reasoning distinguished by its subject matter; the special subject matter of practical reasoning would be reasons for doing things. Now, the idea of reasoning about reasons should anyway raise suspicion. And indeed, that the conclusion of practical reasoning cannot be a judgment about reasons for doing something becomes clear as soon as we ask what "reason for doing something" means. And we must not say, a reason for doing something is something that speaks in favor of doing it; we are asking what that is. In fact, a reason for doing something is something from which one may reason *practically* to the conclusion that it is to be done. Hence, the concept of a reason for acting depends on the concept of practical reasoning: it is a formal concept describing what falls under it as a premise of practical reasoning. Hence, we cannot use it to elucidate the practicality of practical reasoning.

What is practical reasoning, reasoning about what to do? It has been said that it is reasoning toward action and concludes in an action. We shall see that this is true. But we must recognize how strange an idea this is. It is not that the conclusion of practical reasoning is doing something *as opposed to* thinking one should do it. A conclusion of reasoning is an act of applying a concept; it is a thought. Something other than a thought could be—perhaps, in some sense—the effect of reasoning, but not its conclusion. *If an action is the conclusion of practical reasoning, then an action is a thought.* And this is a difficult idea to comprehend.

Practical reasoning is reasoning about what to do; its conclusion represents something as to be done, or, equivalently, as something one should do. In saying that the conclusion of practical reasoning is an action, we describe the formal character of this representation: it is a movement, an act of doing what is represented as to be done. Once we understand this unity of thinking one should do something and doing it, it will be a small step to seeing that the thought that one should do it is an act of a power to do it. The unity in question will emerge as we reflect on the ideas of deriving an action and acting according to a representation.

V. Deriving an Action

Everything in nature works according to laws. Only a rational being has the capacity to act according to the representation of laws, that is, according to principles, or has a will. Since reason is required for the derivation of actions from laws, the will is nothing other than practical reason. (*GMS* 4: 412)[4]

We can distinguish two ways of deriving an action from something general: as a means to an end, and as an instance of a law. I say: I am going upstairs because my camera is upstairs. How can the fact that the camera is upstairs explain why I am going upstairs? It can by revealing going upstairs to be a means (a phase, a step) to an end I am pursuing, getting the camera, say. Thinking that my camera is upstairs, I am deriving my action, going upstairs, as a means from my end, getting the camera. In the derivation, my thinking that the camera is upstairs and my wanting to get it play distinct roles: my end, getting the camera, is the measure of my action, and from it I derive it. Deriving it is recognizing the instrumental nexus of going upstairs and fetching the camera, and my thinking that the camera is upstairs is my recognizing this nexus.

An end is general in relation to the means to it. From a given end, a potentially infinite number of means can be derived. An end does not limit the number of actions that may be derived from it in the described manner. Hence, an end is a unity of a potentially infinite number of means; and the idea of the general is the idea of such a unity.

A law is a unity of a potentially infinite number of acts that conform to it. Therefore, deriving an action as means from an end is analogous to deriving an action as exemplifying a law. As the nexus of an end to the means to it is

---

[4] Ein jedes Ding der Natur wirkt nach Gesetzen. Nur ein vernünftiges Wesen hat das Vermögen, nach der Vorstellung der Gesetze, d. i. nach Prinzipien, zu handeln, oder einen Willen. Da zur Ableitung der Handlungen von Gesetzen Vernunft erfodert wird, so ist der Wille nichts anderes, als praktische Vernunft.

analogous to the nexus of a law to its instances, there is a form of deriving an action in which a law takes the position that above was occupied by an end. I say, I am helping my brother to paint his apartment because I promised to do that. It may be that the fact that I promised to help my brother reveals helping him to be a means to an end I am pursuing: I may have a scheme in which my act of fidelity is an element, or I may want to be well regarded by my brother with a view to unspecific advantages. Then "I am helping my brother because I promised to do it" is formally like "I am going upstairs because my camera is upstairs": the fact I give reveals my action to be a means to an end. But it may be different: it may be that the fact that I promised my brother to help him explains my helping him, not by revealing it to be a means to an end, but by showing it to be an instance of a law: one does as one has promised. Or, in imperative form: you must do what you have promised to do.

Kant thinks that the law from which, ultimately, my action derives cannot be "Keep your promises", but rather is the categorical imperative. For, he thinks that the possibility of deriving an action from a law is intelligible only if that law ultimately is the categorical imperative. Unless the categorical imperative stands behind my idea of fidelity as that from which ultimately my action is derived, it will not be true that we have to do with that form: derivation of an action not from an end, but from a law.

This thesis of Kant's is not important to our discussion. The insight into the metaphysical nexus of being subject to a practical law (a law from which one may derive an action) and having the power to act according to this law is independent of this thesis. Indeed, this thesis (that the only practical law is the categorical imperative) may be represented as a consequence of that insight (that being subject to a practical law *is* having the power to act according to it): a practical law must be such as to sustain the nexus of consciousness of it and power to act, and one may argue (it is arguable that Kant argues) that only the categorical imperative sustains this nexus.

VI. Acting According to a Representation

Deriving an action from a law is reasoning to the conclusion that such-and-such is to be done because doing it is exemplifying the law. Analogously, deriving an action from an end is reasoning to the conclusion that such-and-such is to be done as doing it is a means to that end. Now, Kant equates deriving an action from a law with acting according to the representation of that law. For—returning to the passage quoted in section V—from the premise that deriving an action requires reason, that is, from the premise that (practical) reason is the power to derive an action from something general, and the premise that the will is a power to act according to a general representation, Kant concludes that the will is *nothing other than* practical reason. This inference is valid only if deriving an action from something is nothing other than acting according to its representation. Hence, Kant implicitly affirms this equation, which he evidently thinks obvious enough. Our task is to render what is intelligible for Kant—that is, in itself—intelligible for us.

Deriving an action from a law is acting according to a representation of this law. Analogously, deriving an action from an end is acting according to the representation of that end. *Deriving an action is acting.* Reason in general is the power to derive; the power to derive an action is practical reason. If deriving an action is acting, then practical reason, being a power to derive action, is a power to act, namely, the power to act according to a general representation. To form the idea of practical reason, we must see why deriving an action is acting. First we consider acting according to the representation of an end, then acting according to the representation of a law.

A representation according to which someone acts causes her action: when someone is doing A according to her representation of doing B, then *she is doing A because she wants to do B.* But this does not suffice. Someone's wanting to do something may cause all manner of movement on her part, which will not on that account alone be a case of acting according to the representation. For example, someone may be falling ill because he wants to lose weight, in this way: he has been wanting to lose weight for a long time, nothing he tried has worked, at last his anxiety manifests itself in somatic symptoms. As he falls ill, he does not act according to his representation of losing weight. It is obvious what is missing: if he is to act *according to* his representation, he must recognize that his action *accords* with his representation. He must subsume his action under the representation; in the given case, he must see that it serves the represented end. But even with this, we have not yet captured acting according to a representation. It is conceivable that the man recognizes that he is losing weight on account of his illness. Indeed, he may welcome his illness as helping him reach his end of losing weight. Still, he does not act according to his representation.

Acting according to a representation requires causality of the representation, and requires the subject's recognition that his action accords with the representation. But these conditions, taken together, are not sufficient, as our example shows. It would be wrong to conclude that we must seek a further condition. We do not miss some third thing, but the unity of the two given things.[5]

---

[5] In consequence, it is not possible to define acting according to a representation in terms intelligible independently of what they define. As conditions of acting according to a representation, the causality and the subject's recognition of the nexus of its terms are of a peculiar kind, the kind being defined by their unity, which is the unity of acting according to a representation. The idea that the concept of intentional action signifies a unity of causality (the representation causes the action) and agreement (the action satisfies the representation) is developed in depth in Horst (2012).

In the example, causality and recognition have come together *per accidens*: it is not internal to the truth of the explanation, "He is falling ill because he wants to lose weight", that he recognizes that his falling ill accords with his end of losing weight. His recognition is *an independent reality* from the one that the explanation records. Consider by contrast the person who is going upstairs because she wants to fetch the camera. We can concoct a story in which the fact that she is going upstairs because she wants to fetch the camera is independent of her recognition of the instrumental nexus of going upstairs and fetching the camera. But in the usual course of things, the explanation will represent her as acting according to her representation of fetching the camera. And then the explanation is true only if she knows that going upstairs is a way to fetch the camera. She subsumes her going upstairs as a means under this end. Her subsuming the action is an act of *practical* reason and an act of deriving the action, if it constitutes the causality of her representation of the end, the causality represented by the explanation, "She is going upstairs because she wants to fetch the camera".

The concept of action according to a representation signifies a special kind of causality, a causality constituted by the subject's joining its terms in thought. The subject's recognition of the accord of the action with the representation that is its cause is not added to an independently constituted causality; it is *the form of the causality*. Practical reason is not a term in causal relations of a kind that also characterizes the movements of nonrational animals and inanimate substances. Practical reason is *inside* a causality that therefore is characteristic of the movements of a rational subject.

The concept of practical reason designates a kind of causality. Kant says that. Contemporary philosophy lacks the idea of this kind of causality and therefore the idea of practical reason. Donald Davidson writes:

> wanting to do something of type *x* may cause someone to do something of type *x*, and yet the causal chain may operate in such a manner that the act is not intentional... Beliefs and desires that would rationalize an action if they caused it in the *right* way—through a course of practical reasoning, as we might try saying—may cause it in other ways. (1980: 78–9)

We can replace "acting intentionally" by "acting according to a representation"; the formulae are equivalent, at least for our present purposes. Davidson suggests that the difference between someone who is falling ill because he wants to lose weight and someone who is going upstairs because she wants to fetch the camera is a difference in the causal chain—a chain of causes and effects—that joins wanting and doing: in the one case, practical reasoning is among the members of this chain, in the other it is not. But this does not capture the difference. For, even if the subject's subsuming the action as a means under the thing wanted is a term in a chain of causes that links wanting and doing, it is still *external to this causal nexus* that the end points of the chain figure in the content of an act that lies between them.

We can surmise that Davidson sees this from his cautious "we might try saying", which suggests that he understands that saying it will not help. Christine Korsgaard is less cautious. As Davidson, she notes that someone who is doing A because he wants to do B, and thinks that doing A is a means to this end, need not be acting according to his representation of doing B. He is not, she observes, when he is doing A because he is "conditioned" to do A whenever he wants this and thinks that. Korsgaard discusses Nagel's example of someone who "has been conditioned so that whenever he wants a drink and believes the object before him is a pencil sharpener, he wants to put a coin in the pencil sharpener" (Nagel 1978: 33–4).

> Neither the joint causal efficacy of the belief and the desire, nor the existence of an appropriate conceptual connection, nor the bare conjunction of these two facts, enables us to judge that a person acts rationally. For the person to act rationally, she must be motivated by her own recognition of the appropriate conceptual connection between her belief and her desire. We may say that she herself must combine the belief and the desire in the right way. A person acts rationally, then, only when her action is the expression of her own mental activity. (Korsgaard 1997: 221)

The "mental activity" serves the function of Davidson's "course of practical reasoning". The difference between Korsgaard and Davidson is that she says what Davidson imagines we might try saying, suggesting that saying it will be futile. And futile it is. For, how does the mental activity figure in the account? It may be a further cause, another member in the causal chain. Then it does not mark the difference. Action according to a representation differs from action that manifests its subject's being conditioned in a certain way not in that, in addition to belief and desire, there is a further cause of the movement, mental activity. Someone may be conditioned to do A whenever she wants this, believes that, and engages in a certain mental activity. Now, it is clear that Korsgaard wants to use a notion of mental activity that renders the last sentence ungrammatical. But she does not explain that notion; she only gives a further word for what we seek to understand: "activity", "agency", and so on. These words can serve as a preliminary indication of our topic, but they provide no comprehension of it, especially not when prefixed by "mental".

VII. Application to the Moral Law

Action according to a representation does not have special causes, but exhibits a special kind of causality. Someone acting according to a representation derives the action from what she represents. The derivation is an act of practical reasoning in that it answers the question what to do. The subject represents her action as a means to an end she is pursuing and as to be done on that account: "I should do A because I want to do B". Her thinking this is *the causality of her representation*, the causal nexus represented by "She is doing A because she wants to do B". Hence, her thinking she should do A because she wants to do B is *not an independent reality* from her doing A because she wants to do B. It is *the same reality*. If someone is acting according to her representation of doing B, in, say, doing A, then her acting according to this representation is nothing other than her thinking that she should do A for the sake of doing B. Acting according to the representation of an end is deriving the action from this end.

We developed the idea of a thought that is the causality of a representation according to which its subject acts from the case of action according to the representation of an end. Exploiting the analogy noted above we can apply this idea to action according to a law and specifically the moral law. In order for someone to act according to her representation of the moral law, it does not suffice that this representation cause her doing something that accords with the law in any old way. Rather, she must recognize that her action accords with the law. And this recognition cannot be conceived as a further cause, which then would again be operating independently of the subject's consciousness of it. Rather her recognition of her action as conforming to the moral law must be the causality of her representation of the law. So someone acts according to the moral law only if "She is acting in this way because the moral law requires it" and "She knows that she should act in this way because the moral law requires it" describe *the same reality*. By implication, so do, in this case, the statements, "She is acting in this way" and "She knows that she should". That is, her acting in this way is the conclusion of her practical reasoning.

We inquire after the character of the thought that represents acting in a certain way as required by the moral law, with a view to understanding how thinking it manifests a power to act according to the law. Now, action according to a representation involves an act of deriving the action from the representation, which act is the causality of the representation. The derivation concludes in a thought that represents the action as necessary, which thought, if the subject acts as represented, is identical with the action it represents. This applies to acting according to the moral law: it involves an act of deriving an action from the moral law, the conclusion of which derivation, representing the action as necessary, is acting according to the law. It follows that the power to act according to the representation of the moral law is exercised in thoughts representing acting in a certain way as required by the moral law. Consciousness of the moral law is an act of the power to act according to the moral law. This was what we set out to show.

VIII. Instrumental and Moral Reasoning

It may seem that the given account of the nexus of ought and can must be false because it shows too much. It says that the thought that I should do something is an act of a power to do it because it is a practical thought: when I act according to a representation, then thinking the thought, deriving the action from the representation, is acting in the way the thought represents as necessary. This is the general character of action according to a representation, be it of an end or of a law. But while, according to Kant, I know that I have the power to act according to the moral law from thinking that I should, the fact that I think I should do something because it serves an end I am pursuing does not reveal that I can do it. I may overestimate my powers and think I can reach my end in a way in which, in fact, I cannot reach it. While this is true, it shows a difference of action according to an end and action according to a law. It does not show that the nexus of ought and can does not obtain in both cases.

Aristotle explains that reasoning about how to achieve a given end comes to rest in things I can do in the sense of things I can achieve; we may call them poietic powers and final means. In this way instrumental reasoning reveals the end from which it starts to be an end its subject can reach. The validity of any intermediary conclusions, purporting to represent non-final means, depends on this. That the end points of instrumental reasoning are things the reasoning subject can achieve describes the metaphysical character of instrumental reasoning: it is practical, deriving action. A subject of instrumental reasoning is in command of final means; it is a subject of powers to achieve things. Her poietic powers constitute the space of her instrumental reasoning.[6]

Now, a subject's poietic powers, in constituting the space of her instrumental reasoning, constitute the space of her ends. And this is how, here, the inner nexus of thinking one should do something and having the power to do it plays out. It does so in the following way. Instrumental reasoning terminates in things the subject can do. This is not a normative principle requiring that I adapt my ends to my powers. This would presuppose that having an end is independent of having powers by whose exercise it may be reached. Then I could compare my ends with my powers and be called upon, or not, to adapt the former to the latter. (Then we may well wonder what the ground of this imperative might be.) Of course it may happen that I find I have no way to do something I set out to do. I recognize that there is no way of stringing together things I can do in such a way that they add up to my reaching what I thought of as my end. What transpires in this case is not that my end exceeds

---

[6] In the way in which, according to the doctrine of Wittgenstein (1984), the objects constitute the space of possible facts.

my powers (so that the question can be posed whether, in the face of this, I should hold on to that end). Rather, it transpires that my ostensible end is not the kind of thing to be my end. There is no such thing as my pursuing it and, consequently, I never was pursuing it. An end is a starting point of instrumental reasoning. This distinguishes it from the object of a wish. But unless instrumental reasoning reaches a terminus, none of its steps is valid. Hence, if it *cannot* reach a terminus, it *cannot* start.[7]

Acting according to a law is not acting according to an end.[8] In respect of an end, there is a distinction of pursuing and reaching it, expressed in language by the contrast of progressive and perfective aspect: I am doing it, I have done it. I may have been pursuing an end I did not reach. With respect to a law, there is no such distinction: when I am acting according to the law, then I have acted according to the law. In Aristotle's terminology, action according to an end is kinesis, or poiesis, action according to a law is energeia, or praxis. The schematic expressions "doing something", "acting", "action" must be interpreted according to context as signifying either the one or the other.

Acting according to the moral law is not poiesis. Therefore, powers to achieve ends, poietic powers, do not provide the space of reasoning that derives an action from the moral law. Of course, acting according to the moral law will be pursuing certain ends because doing so is exemplifying the law. (In Kant's example, the man before the prince may decide to utter certain words; he may fail; indeed, he may be wrong in thinking that he has the power to utter these words.) Hence, my power to act according to the moral law includes my being a subject of poietic powers, that is, my being a subject capable of pursuing ends. But it is not the office of moral reasoning—reasoning that derives an action from a law—to represent any end as something I can achieve. What I know from thinking I should do something, when this is my recognition that doing it exemplifies the moral law, is not that I can achieve a certain end, but that I can act according to the moral law. It is possible that I fail in exercising *this* power, but then the failure is not one of failing to reach an end I have been pursuing, but a failure to be determined by the moral law.[9]

---

[7] "Start" and "end" here have a logical, not a temporal meaning. In order to develop this, it would be necessary to dislodge the erroneous view that practical reasoning is a mental process. Indeed, the above reflections begin to show why the category of process does not designate the temporality of reasoning. Cf. Boyle (2011).

[8] I am here distinguishing end from law. Of course, one might deploy a more abstract concept of an end, such as Kant's: the object of a concept insofar as the latter is regarded as the ground of the possibility of the former. What I distinguish as end and law then would both be ends, but different kinds of ends. This is a verbal issue. The difference in question is the one marked by the different forms of practical reasoning distinguished above.

[9] I further develop the formal differences of practical reasoning internal to praxis and poiesis respectively in Rödl (2011).

IX. Holy Will and Human Will

It may seem that our account of the nexus of ought and can must be false because it shows too much in a different way. It says that thinking that one should do something is an act of a power to do it because, in action according to a representation, thinking one should do something is identical with doing it. But I may recognize that the moral law requires that I do such-and-such and yet not do it. Kant says as much.

However, it does not follow that, *when* I am doing what I think I should do, my doing it is an independent reality of my thinking I should do it. This would destroy the concept of action according to a representation. And that it is possible to fail to act according to the representation of the moral law cannot entail that there is no such thing as acting according to that representation. Nor does it follow that, when I fail to act according to my representation, my thought that I should act in such-and-such a way, derived from this representation, does not, as it does when I do act according to my representation, manifest my power to act according to this representation. Rather, that I may fail to act according to my representation shows that my power thus to act is fallible: its proper exercise is liable to be thwarted by circumstances that are external to it.

The concept of fallibility does not apply to acts of a power, but to a power. For example, it is nonsense to call an *act* of knowledge fallible. Either it is knowledge, which excludes that it is false, or it is false, in which case it is not knowledge. If it is knowledge, then it cannot be false.[10] A *power* of knowledge may be fallible: liable to be thwarted in its exercise by unfavorable circumstances. However, Kant does not even think it correct to call a power fallible. He does not think *the* power to act according to the representation of the moral law is fallible. Rather, it is fallible *in man* because, in man, it is placed in a circumstance that may thwart its proper exercise. That circumstance is man's sensible nature. But *the same power* is the principle of the acts of a holy will.[11] The holy will is such that there is no space for the idea of circumstances that may interfere with the exercise of the power to act according to the moral law. Therefore, as an act of a holy will, the thought deriving an action from the moral law is not expressed by an imperative. It does not represent the action as to be done, but as good to do. "[Imperatives] say that to do or to omit something would be good, but they say it to a will that does not always do something just because it is represented to it that it would be good to do that thing" (*GMS* 4: 413).[12]

---

[10] One might want to say: it could have been false. This is a misleading way of saying that the act issues from a power that could have been prevented from being exercised properly, although in the given case it was not so prevented. See below.

[11] Compare Lavin (2004).

[12] [Imperative] sagen, daß etwas zu tun oder zu unterlassen gut sein würde, allein sie sagen es einem Willen, der nicht immer darum etwas tut, weil ihm vorgestellt wird, daß es zu tun gut sei.

This does not mean that the holy will thinks a different thought from the one I think, thinking that I ought to do such-and-such, representing it as required by the moral law. The difference in the mode of expression does not signify a difference in the thought expressed. It signifies that, in me, the power of which the thought is an act is liable to be thwarted by external circumstances.

In the holy will, representing doing something as good is doing it. So the holy will knows he can act according to the moral law *by acting according to the moral law*. By contrast, man knows that he can act according to the moral law *by thinking he should*. The difference between the holy will and the human will is not a difference in the thought, nor in the power of which this thought is an act. The difference is that, in man, the power of practical reasoning is trapped in sensible nature.[13]

Bibliography

Albritton, R. (1985) "Freedom of Will and Freedom of Action," *Proceedings and Addresses of the American Philosophical Association* 59(2): 239–51.

Baier, A. (1970) "Act and Intent," *Journal of Philosophy* 67(19): 648–58.

Boyle, M. (2011) "'Making up Your Mind' and the Activity of Reason," *Philosopher's Imprint* 11(17): 1–24.

Davidson, D. (1980) "Freedom to Act," in *Essays on Actions and Events*, 63–81. Oxford: Clarendon Press.

Horst, D. (2012) *Absichtliches Handeln*. Paderborn: Mentis.

Kant, I. (2002) *Critique of Practical Reason*. Tr. W. S. Pluhar. Indianapolis: Hackett.

Kant, I. (1996) "Groundwork of The Metaphysics of Morals," in *Practical Philosophy*, 37–108. Tr. and ed. M. J. Gregor. Cambridge: Cambridge University Press.

Korsgaard, C. (1997) "The Normativity of Instrumental Reason," in G. Cullity and B. Gaut (eds.), *Ethics and Practical Reason*, 215–54. Oxford: Oxford University Press.

Lavin, D. (2004) "Practical Reason and the Possibility of Error," *Ethics* 114(3): 424–57.

Nagel, T. (1978) *The Possibility of Altruism*. Princeton: Princeton University Press.

Rödl, S. (2011) "Two Forms of Practical Knowledge," in A. Ford, J. Hornsby, and F. Stoutland (eds.), *Essays on Anscombe's Intention*, 211–41.Cambridge, MA: Harvard University Press.

Stern, R. (2004) "Does 'Ought' Imply 'Can'? And Did Kant Think It Does?" *Utilitas* 16(1): 42–61.

Wittgenstein, L. (1984 [1921]) *Tractatus Logico-Philosophicus*. Frankfurt am Main: Suhrkamp.

---

[13] I am grateful to Douglas Lavin for enlightening conversations on the topic of this essay.

3

Kant on Practical Reason

Allen W. Wood

Kant's principal thematic discussion of practical reason occurs in one single place: in the Second Section of the *Groundwork for the Metaphysics of Morals,* where Kant proposes to provide a philosophical derivation of the supreme principle of morality by "follow[ing] and distinctly exhibit[ing] the practical faculty of reason from its universal rules of determination up to where the concept of duty arises from it" (*GMS* 4: 412). Since Kant here proposes to investigate the "universal rules of determination" of practical reason, we might expect a complete account of practical rationality. But Kant's chief interest here is in *moral* reason, and specifically in deriving the supreme principle of morality. This narrower aim prevents him from providing a truly complete and "universal" theory, by causing him to slight his treatment of the nonmoral species of practical reason, to give exaggerated emphasis, in certain respects, to what they have in common with moral reason and also to exaggerate, by contrast, their differences from moral reason. So what we get is an account of practical reason which is perhaps not only incomplete but also skewed by the narrower aim which the account is meant to serve.

One consequence of this aim is that because his theory of morality in the *Groundwork* began with the concept of duty as moral *necessitation* (constraint in opposition to recalcitrant inclinations), Kant is concerned with practical reason primarily as a faculty of *self-constraint*—that is, a faculty through which we guide our conduct, and even *require* ourselves to do certain things (for reasons). So he is not thinking mainly about cases where action for reasons is easy and natural, harmonizing with empirical desires. Instead, he focuses on cases requiring explicit self-constraint or reflective rational self-supervision.

Some philosophers nowadays distinguish *pro tanto* reasons for doing something—which might be outweighed by countervailing reasons for doing the opposite—from reasons that strictly require doing the thing. Philosophers also sometimes distinguish *reasons* for doing something (what Christine Korsgaard has recently called "substantive reasons"[1]) from "requirements of rationality" (or "rational principles," such as that to will the end requires you to will the means). Using this distinction, they sometimes argue that (substantive) reasons do not rest on principles, and even question whether requirements of rationality themselves necessarily provide us with any substantive reasons at all (even *pro tanto* reasons) for doing anything (see Broome 2005; Kolodny 2005).

Kant's concern with *necessitation* by principles of reason might tempt us to think that he cannot admit there are any *pro tanto* reasons, only reasons that decisively *require* us to do something. This might also lead us to think that he cannot allow for any reasons at all except principles (requirement of rationality), and is therefore committed to the view that such requirements do always furnish us with reasons (indeed, with the only practical reasons there are). Another way Kant's aim influences his account of practical reason is that since he is looking for the supreme *principle* of morality, he is focused not on the various truths (or facts, or states of affairs) that count for us as practical reasons (in the plural), or on what these reasons may have in common that make them reasons for action, but instead on the general *principles* that underlie these various reasons. This might lead our present-day philosophers of rationality to think that he is interested solely in what some of them call "requirements of rationality," and not at all in the substantive reasons people have for doing things.

A closer examination of Kant's account, however, will enable us to avoid such hasty and erroneous conclusions. Kant does think that (substantive) reasons depend on principles, and he definitely does not think of these principles in the way some philosophers now think of "requirements of rationality." Kant's concern with necessitation by rational principles gave him few occasions to attend to some of the questions that preoccupy present-day philosophical accounts of practical reason, but I do not think he is committed to any errors or questionable positions on them.

I. Reasons and Rational Justification

Yet a third consequence of Kant's aims in the *Groundwork* discussion is that he seems to have been interested primarily in what we may call (following Francis Hutcheson's famous distinction) "motivating reasons" (but Hutcheson called them "exciting reasons") rather than "justifying reasons" (Hutcheson 1971: 217–18). That is, because Kant is interested in the way certain rational principles might constrain our actions, he is concerned with the *rational motivation* of actions, rather than in what agents might say to

---

[1] Korsgaard (2009).

one another (or even to themselves) if asked to give *ex post facto* a *rational justification* what they are doing. Of course under the right conditions, the two kinds of reasons might well be systematically related. If what rationally constrains (and motivates) me to do A is that A conforms to a moral principle or duty, then I can presumably justify doing A, at least to myself, perhaps to others as well, by citing that principle and its rationally (morally) constraining force.

In general, however, *justification* is always justification *to* someone. Owing to the relationships in which people may stand to one another, the considerations that justify an action to one person may not serve to justify it to another. For example, if I take an action that negatively affects your interests, I might justify it to you by showing that it violated none of your rights, and also that in acting I showed due concern for your welfare. But what motivated me in performing the action might be something that has nothing to do with you at all, and considerations of your rights and interests might not play any role in the way I justify the action to some third person. However, if I choose an action because I am aware there are certain reasons to do it, then what motivates me ought always to be at least a central part of what I would offer *myself* as my justification for the action.

Some philosophers other than Kant have held that it is indispensable to moral rationality to consider the specific "second-person" claims that one person may have on another. This has been argued powerfully, for instance, by Stephen Darwall, who has also drawn some critical conclusions regarding Kant's own arguments in the *Groundwork* (Darwall 2006: 213–42). Darwall rightly cites J. G. Fichte, as anticipating much of his argument and as providing an insightful account of the role of second-person reasons, both in our thinking about people's rights and about moral reasons generally (Fichte 2000: 29–52). Adam Smith, another great figure in the history of moral philosophy (whose importance, like Fichte's, has been greatly underestimated), also in effect argued for the indispensability to morality of considering the standpoint of others on the reasons why agents do what they do. On Smith's account, the "propriety" of an action depends on the attitudes others may take toward it (either with specific concerns in regard to it, or viewing it from a rational impartial standpoint), and toward the feelings or affections from which the action proceeded (Smith 2000: part I). Kant's moral philosophy has been much better studied than either Smith's or Fichte's. On the topic of *justification*, however, and of practical reason in the form of *justifying reasons*, I think these other two great philosophers offer important insights not present in Kant, so that a satisfactory account of these topics would have to pay attention to matters theorized by them but neglected by Kant. Kant was not altogether unaware of these matters, however. I will conclude this chapter by reflecting on the way Kant's philosophy does in a way take account of the intersubjective dimension essential to all rational justification.

II. Practical Reason as Self-constraint by Objective Value

Kant's aim in the *Groundwork* is to work from a consideration of practical reason in general, and its principles, and proceed upward (or inward) toward the supreme principle of morality, which in his view is reason's supreme use. For our purposes, however, if we are interested in Kant's general account of practical reason, it is best not to concentrate on (or even to think primarily about) moral rationality until we have to. We will make fewer mistakes if we consider first what Kant says about the other kinds and principles of practical rationality, and especially attend to what Kant thinks all the different kinds of practical rationality have in common.

The main thing they have in common, as we have already seen, is that one primary function of practical reason—the function Kant is most interested in—is *self-constraint*. Principles of reason are principles of rational self-government. This means the motivating force of any kind of reason is *internal* to the faculty of reason itself, and the principles on which it operates. It is not drawn from something outside it, such as an empirical impulse or inclination. Rational motivation itself, therefore, is never furnished by empirical impulses or inclinations. These become relevant to practical reason only when we adopt maxims or set ends based on them, and then ask ourselves questions about these ends and maxims relevant to their rational pursuit—such as what actions would serve to achieve our ends, or what rational priority they should have in relation to other ends, or whether (in light of prudential or moral considerations) we should set these ends at all. Empirical desires become relevant to practical reason only when they engage its principles by being taken up in maxims and the pursuit of ends through purposive choices.

Another point, connected to this one, is that rational principles are always universally valid, valid equally for all rational beings. Their ultimate validity is not dependent on anything (such as contingent desires or the choice of ends) that might distinguish one rational being from another. Of course the *applicability* (and specific consequences of application) of any rational principle is going to vary a lot from one rational being to another, based on their differing inclinations, knowledge, and contingent situation. For example, whether the principle that willing the end requires me to will the necessary means applies to this action of mine depends on whether it just so happens that I have willed some end and also need to constrain myself to adopt the necessary means. Similarly, the moral rule that I ought to keep my promise obviously applies to this action only if I have made a promise and this action is required to keep it. But the principles themselves, and the rational grounds for following them, will not vary from one person to another. Kant holds that they belong to the faculty of reason itself, rather than arising out of the data on which this faculty operates. This is what makes them *a priori*, in Kant's usage of the term.

Behind Kant's approach there are some very deep assumptions, no doubt controversial, often not shared by his critics, or even implicitly rejected by them without even realizing what is going on. It may be wise early in this discussion to make some of them explicit. Many familiar (non-Kantian) conceptions of reason treat desires either as implicitly containing basic evaluations or else as the starting point for a reductive naturalistic account of value. Empirical desires (which Kant would call "inclinations"), are thus taken for granted, at least *ceteris paribus*, by practical reason as the foundation of its activity. The function of practical reason, on this view, is to assist in the satisfaction of desires, by managing their economy, so to speak, and by adjusting their pursuit to the resources available for satisfying them. Naturalistic accounts of practical reason treat it as merely a set of mechanisms that have evolved to perform this function.

Kant, however, distinguishes sharply between empirical desires (or inclinations) and desires grounded on reason (especially moral reason) (*KpV* 5: 8n; *MS* 6: 211–14). This distinction is of course well known, and is often attributed by critics either to an arid intellectualism or to a morbid hatred on Kant's part of the natural and sensual. But this common view rests on a serious misunderstanding. Kant's views at this point instead rest on a rich and interesting theory of human nature, which owes much to currents in the Enlightenment going back at least to Hobbes, but including Mandeville, Diderot, Adam Smith, and above all Jean-Jacques Rousseau. This view holds that human beings are fundamentally and irrationally competitive creatures, whose rivalries serve the natural end of developing their faculties.[2] It therefore treats our empirical desires (or inclinations) with distrust, as arising not merely from our nonrational animal nature, but also from our positively irrational social nature.

On this basis, Kant assumes that empirical desire never automatically provides a reason for acting to satisfy it, and it assigns to our faculty of reason the task of critically evaluating all desires, and objects of desire, a function which grounds the guiding and motivating functions of practical reason. The standards for such evaluation are a set of principles proceeding from the faculty of reason itself (hence their a priori status), not to be reduced to natural mechanisms operating on a set of innocent natural desires taken as givens. Reasons must therefore be fundamentally *evaluative* (by purely rational objective standards) in a way that separates them from inclinations (*empirical* desires), which contain no evaluation, or none that is not under deep suspicion of being irrational and self-deceptive. The faculty of reason, historically developed through nature's device of social competition, is therefore destined to turn against the very conditions in human nature through which it emerged, and it stands over against empirical desires as a judge and as a constraining authority.

This helps to account for Kant's emphasis on the critical-evaluative and also the self-constraining function of reason, which is crucial, given Kant's picture of human nature, not only in moral reason but also in prudential and even in

---

[2] I have discussed this side of Kantian anthropology and philosophy of history in Wood (1999, chapters 6–9).

instrumental reason. It is beyond the scope of this chapter to evaluate Kant's Enlightenment theory of human nature, or to decide how far its assumptions about the relation of reason to evaluation, desire and motivation might be preferable to the ones that tend to be assumed in non-Kantian accounts of practical reason. My hope is that by bringing into view the tip of the iceberg of Kant's theory of human nature, we can at least begin to appreciate the real grounds for his distinctive approach to the whole topic of practical reason.

But the primary thing to keep in mind here, I believe, is that Kant accepts the idea that there are *objective reasons* for doing or not doing some things, that these are distinct from desires (though they might create desires, or give rational support to already existing desires). Kant does not hold, as some have thought, that the mere appreciation of reasons or practical principles can or should bring about an action or omission. He thinks human actions always presuppose desires and feelings of certain kinds, though what *rationally* motivates them is never merely a desire. I think Kant's views on this important point have much in common with many of the positions defended at length by Derek Parfit in his wonderful book *On What Matters*[3]—in fact, more in common than Parfit himself realizes.

III. Basic Principles and Intermediate Principles

As Kant expounds the practical use of reason, for every basic principle grounding a distinct kind of practical reason, there are intermediate principles, independent of this basic principle, through which the fundamental principle must be applied. For instance, the principle that if you will the end you must will the necessary means has to be applied through "rules of skill" telling you specifically what are the indispensable means to a given end (*GMS* 4: 415). Likewise, the principle of morality has to be applied through moral rules or duties, which Kant makes the subject of part I: "The Doctrine of Elements in the Doctrine of Virtue" (*MS* 6: 417–74). These intermediate principles are not *deduced* from the rational principle, though it is the rational principle that gives them their practical significance—their motivating (or constraining) force.

For instance, it may be a rule of the medical art that the only way to cure a patient of disease D is to administer medication M (cf. *GMS* 4: 415). This rule is logically independent of the principle of instrumental reason that tells you

---

[3] Parfit (2011, especially chapters 1–7 and 24–30). I don't mean to say, of course, that Kant agreed with Parfit's position on some of the metaethical issues Parfit discusses in volume 2 of his book (or even thought much about these issues). But Kant seems to me much closer to Parfit on many topics than he is to Rawls or "Kantian constructivists" who follow Rawls. It is appropriate that Kant plays a big role in the position that Parfit develops, though I do think Parfit at times misunderstands Kant in some of his critical discussions of him (for instance, in chapters 12–14 and especially appendices F–I). But these are topics too large and too far afield to talk about here.

that if you will the end you are required to will the means. But that principle, together with the rule of medical art, constrains a physician who wants to cure her patient of disease D to administer medication M. Likewise, in light of the fact that people need the voluntary participation of others in order to be happy, Kant holds that the only way to universalize your maxim of willing your own happiness is to recognize a duty to give others voluntary help. The moral law tells us that we must adopt this maxim of self-love only in a universalized form, so it tells us that we must constrain ourselves (that we have a duty to) give voluntary help to others who need it (*MS* 6: 393, 453). We will see presently that, although Kant himself at times seems confused about some of this, there are analogous intermediate rules ("counsels of prudence") which are related in a similar way to the basic principle of prudential reason.

Because Kant is considering practical reason chiefly as a faculty of self-constraint (or "necessitation"), he thinks of principles of reason mainly as *imperatives*. "The representation of an objective principle, insofar as it is necessitating for a will, is called a 'command' (of reason), and the formula of a command is called an **imperative**" (*GMS* 4: 413). We probably think of "imperative" first as a grammatical term (characterizing the syntactic form of a certain kind of sentence). But Kant's conception of an imperative here is part of a philosophical theory of practical reason, so it is not grammatical or linguistic in import. An imperative in his sense is whatever plays the role in deliberation of constraining us by grounding what we do in a rational principle. Kant says that imperatives are expressed by an "ought" (*sollen*) (*GMS* 4: 413), but this too is obviously not true if taken as a linguistic remark. Any linguistic formula used in this way counts as an imperative, whatever its grammatical form. Many imperatives (in Kant's sense) are normally best expressed in indicative sentences from which the auxiliary verb "ought" is wholly absent. As we will see later, for Kant the most natural linguistic form for an *imperative* (in his sense) would be an indicative sentence whose subject is an expression referring to an action and whose predicate is "... is (practically) good" (cf. *GMS* 4: 413, 414).

Kant famously distinguishes two kinds of imperatives: hypothetical and categorical. The difference between them is that an action represented as necessary by a *hypothetical* imperative presupposes, for its rational necessity, the setting of some end independently of the imperative. A *categorical* imperative rationally necessitates independently of any such pre-given end. It is a conceptual truth for Kant, however, that all action involves the setting of an end to be produced by the action. In fact, an *action,* properly speaking, is whatever performance we may rationally represent as a means to an end. It is crucial that this last sentence applies every bit as much to actions that follow categorical imperatives as to those that follow hypothetical imperatives. The difference is not whether an action aims at the production of an end (for Kant all action does that) but whether, in relation to the rational requirement to perform the action, the end in question is already given to reason independently of the rational imperative under consideration. In the case of hypothetical imperatives, it is; in the case of categorical imperatives, the imperatives themselves involve the setting of the end, by specifying the end to be set.

Kant even argues that if there were no ends to be produced that are necessarily connected with the concept of a categorical imperative ("ends that are in their concept duties"), then a categorical imperative itself would be impossible (*MS* 6: 384–5). He holds that there are two general kinds of ends to be produced that are rationally required by categorical imperatives: our own perfection and the happiness of others. To these necessary moral ends Kant gives the name "duties of virtue" (*MS* 6: 382–4, 385–8). In the case of hypothetical imperatives, however, the imperative always presupposes some end given independently of the imperative—either by contingent, discretionary choice or by prudential reason.

IV. The Three Kinds of Practical Reason

Kant distinguishes three species of practical reason: (1) technical (or instrumental) reason, which involves a hypothetical imperative with a contingently given end; (2) pragmatic (or prudential) reason, which involves an end necessarily given but dependent on something outside reason itself (namely, the end of happiness); and (3) moral reason, which gives us rational laws in the form of categorical imperatives. Let us consider each in turn—but especially the first two. This is not only because they are de-emphasized in Kant's own discussion, but also because (perhaps partly for this reason) some of what Kant says about them is problematic and even confused. We will have to interpret, supplement, or perhaps even modify what he actually says about them if we are to arrive at a coherent Kantian account of these kinds of practical reason.

Instrumental reason. According to Kant, a hypothetical imperative that specifies the means to a contingent or "discretionary" end is called a "problematic" (or "technical") imperative.[4] Kant introduces instrumental reason by citing the many "imperatives of skill" that belong to all arts and sciences, and which parents teach their children in the hope that it may enable them to achieve whatever ends they may choose to set later in life (*GMS* 4: 415). (His examples of such rules are drawn from medicine and from geometrical construction, *GMS* 4: 415, 418.) Nearly all rules of skill (certainly the medical ones, though not the geometrical ones) are based on merely empirical connections of cause and effect, often connections holding only for the most part or with reasonable probability. Few such rules, if any, specify the *only possible*

---

[4] Kant eventually rejected the term "problematic imperative," holding that in its most natural interpretation, the term even contains a contradiction. In the *Critique of the Power of Judgment*, he insisted that it should be replaced with the term "technical imperative" (*KU* 5: 172–3, see First Introduction to *KU* 20: 200n).

way to reach their end; thus few can represent an action as strictly *necessary* for its achievement. If an *imperative* is the formula of a command of reason that strictly *necessitates* the actions falling under it—and moreover, a command that is universally valid a priori for all rational beings—then actual rules of skill are virtually never imperatives. So Kant cannot coherently mean to say that "imperatives of skill" are themselves typical examples of technical imperatives. In fact, the content of a rule of skill is never anything but the *theoretical* proposition that a certain result is caused (perhaps even merely for the most part) by a certain kind of action. This point, put together with the idea that all practical reason may be reduced to instrumental reason, is the chief argument sometimes used to provide a pretended defense of the titillating (but silly) Humean paradoxes that there is really no such thing as *practical* reason at all, that I can have no *reason* not to prefer the destruction of the world to the scratching of my finger, and that reason is and ought to be only a slave of the passions (Hume 1967: 413–16).

Principles of reason are universal in the sense that they apply in the same way to all rational agents. Kant thinks that even rules of skill may be considered "universally valid" at least in the sense that they propose tell *anyone who has the end in question* what they must do to achieve it. His intent, however, is apparently not to say that rules of skill are themselves hypothetical imperatives in the sense he means, but rather to suggest that they rest on a single such imperative as their common ground. Thomas Hill calls this general imperative "the Hypothetical Imperative" (Hill 2002: 172–3). Kant famously formulates it in this way: "Whoever wills the end, also wills (insofar as reason has decisive influence on his actions) the means that are necessary to it that are in his control." Further, Kant regards this proposition as not only true a priori but as *analytic* (*GMS* 4: 417). Rules of skill, however (even those, drawn from mathematics, which may be considered a priori) are obviously not analytic:

> For in the volition of an object, as my effect, is already thought my causality as an acting cause, i.e. the use of means, and the imperative extracts the concept of actions necessary for this end out of the concept of a volition of this end (to be sure, synthetic propositions belong to determining the means themselves to the proposed aim, but they have nothing to do with the ground, with making the act of the will actual, but rather with how to make the object actual). That in order to divide a line into equal parts in accordance with a secure principle I must draw two arcs from its endpoints—this mathematics obviously teaches only through synthetic propositions; but that if I know that the specified effect can occur only through such an action, I would also will the action that is required for it—that is an analytic proposition; for to represent something as an effect possible through me in a certain way and to represent myself, in regard to it, acting in that way—those are entirely the same (*GMS* 4: 417).

If we think that the principle of practical reason involved in technical imperatives (or even hypothetical imperatives generally) is the theoretical proposition
that a certain state of affairs can be caused in a certain way, then we have already
fundamentally misunderstood the way *practical* reason might bear on the situation. Practical reason is not what is employed in coming to know which action
I must perform in order to achieve an end (that is purely a matter for *theoretical*
reason). *Practical* reason is rather needed to constrain myself to perform that
action *when I already know the theoretical truth* that it is the necessary means to
my end that is in my power. (If we think it is not the office of reason, but rather
the function of rationally unmotivated desires, sentiments, or passions, to exercise this motivating function, then we are well on the way to the folly of uttering
such nonsense as that reason is and ought to be only a slave of the passions.)

Suppose, for instance, that I have set myself an end—for example, to make a
good impression on my first day at a new job by showing up on time. Suppose
further that I know the theoretical truth that in order to do this, I must get
out of bed as soon as my alarm clock goes off. It is not the office of practical
reason, in the form of the Hypothetical Imperative, to provide me with this
knowledge. That belongs to the theoretical understanding. The job of practical reason is rather to constrain me, in light of this knowledge, to rise on time,
overcoming through reason my slothful inclination to stay in bed.

If this point is misunderstood, however, it may lead to a new attempt to
reduce practical reason to theoretical reason—this time, to a set of theoretical
claims about my psychology. It is often said about instrumental reason that you
can avoid rational criticism not only by taking the action necessary for your
end, but also by giving up the end. It may be analytic, so the argument goes,
that if I will the end, I will the action that counts as an indispensable means,
but this analytic proposition holds equally whether I take the action or give up
the end. Therefore, it is claimed, the real question here is still only a theoretical
one: namely, whether I do as a matter of fact truly have the end (of making a
good impression the first day on the job). If I stay in bed an extra half hour
and show up late, then that shows only (so the argument goes) that I did not
really have the end I thought I had; and if I do get up, then I find out that I did
after all have the end—which theoretical truth is demonstrated by the fact that
I took the necessary means to it. In either case, no distinctive claim of "practical reason" seems to be involved here at all, only some theoretical truths, one
way or another, about my psychology.

This argument, however, gets things entirely wrong about instrumental
reason. To begin with, it misunderstands the nature of the proposition Kant
takes to be analytic. This is not a theoretical but a practical proposition. It is
not the proposition that he who (really and truly) wills the end also does in
fact will the means, but rather the practical proposition that in performing the
rational act of setting the end, I have thereby subjected myself to the practical
norm that I *ought* to will the necessary means, thus giving myself a practical

(instrumental) *reason* for doing so. The error here may arise from the empiricist assumption that motivation is entirely a matter of states (desires, sentiments, passions) to which we are passive. But setting an end is not something that simply *happens* to you (like being seized by a rationally unmotivated desire). It is something you *do*—it is a rational act, an act of freedom (*MS* 6: 381). Its immediate consequences are not causal but normative.

Nonrational animals, in Kant's view, cannot set ends, or devise means to them; for them, he thinks, this is all mechanically determined by instinct, perhaps modified by empirical conditioning (*MAM* 8: 111–12). With rational agents, he believes, things are different. Setting an end is an act of *volition*, and volition is a normative activity, both in the sense that it can create (subjective) norms (maxims) and in the sense that it is subject to (objective) norms (practical principles of instrumental and prudential reason or moral laws). The concept of an end contains the concept of an action *to be performed* as a means, and therefore lays down the subjective norm that you should perform that action— which norm is, in turn, grounded on the Hypothetical Imperative, the objective (analytical) norm that you should perform whatever action in your power is required as a necessary means to the end.

T. M. Scanlon here follows Broome and Kolodny all the way to the misguided conclusion that the so-called "requirements of rationality"—including those of instrumental reason—are not properly speaking normative at all (Scanlon forthcoming; cf. Broome 2005; Kolodny 2005). He thinks that when I choose to perform the action which is a necessary means to my end, my *reason* is not the Hypothetical Imperative (or anything like that) but only the reason I have for pursuing the end. And Scanlon thinks the rationality of my action depends on there actually *being* a genuine or good reason for pursuing the end; it is not sufficient that I *think* there is one. All these claims seem to me erroneous. As a rational agent, I have a *reason* to conform to the Hypothetical Imperative, and this reason is (at least sometimes and in some respects) distinct from my reason for setting the end that makes the Hypothetical Imperative applicable to me. My reason for setting the end of making a good impression on my first day is quite distinct from my reason for getting out of bed in order to do this.

In adopting the contrary view, Scanlon is moved by the thought that I do not ultimately *have a reason* (or at least a *genuine* or *good* reason) to perform an act necessary for my end if I am mistaken in my belief that I have a good reason to set the end. He may be right about this if by a "good" or "genuine" reason we mean something like a "decisive reason all things considered." Yet I think we should at least say that as long as I *think* I have a good reason for pursuing the end, which gives me a good or genuine *pro tanto* reason for taking the necessary means to it. Instrumental rationality is made relevant to my present action based on that *pro tanto* reason.

Kant, at any rate, is crystal clear that *instrumental* reason does not require that the end in question should be good in any way. "Whether the end is rational and good is not the question here, but only what one has to do to achieve it" (*GMS* 4: 415). That is why abandoning my end is not a way of *complying* with the requirements of instrumental reason, but only a way of making them *irrelevant* (to me, at present, regarding the action that was necessary to an end it turns out I do not have). Abandoning an end is a different way of avoiding rational criticism from taking the required means to it. Only the latter is relevant to the question whether I am complying with the demands of *instrumental* reason. As to the former, whether I have a *reason* to abandon my end is obviously not settled by the fact that I have an inclination not to take an action rationally required for it. For instance, my inclination to stay in bed (simply as such and all by itself) constitutes *no reason at all* (not even a *pro tanto* reason) for me to give up the end of making a good impression on my first day on the job. It could become such a reason, but only in a larger context—such as the determination by *prudential* reason that practicing lethargy in the morning is more conducive to my long-term well-being than holding down a job, or the determination by *moral* reason that losing this sleazy job through tardiness would be a fulfillment of my duty. Even if, in light of my overall ends, my desire to stay in bed turned out to be such a reason, that would still have nothing whatever to do with the requirements of *instrumental* reason relative to my end of making a good impression by being on time.

Because Kant's attention is focused on rational constraint, and the uses of nonmoral practical reason that are most analogous to the concept of duty in the case of moral reason, his account of instrumental reason is more limited in scope than seems justified even by the spirit of what he says about instrumental reason. Kant's Hypothetical Imperative, for instance, tells us only that we must take any action that is an absolutely indispensable means to an end that we set. Clearly instrumental reason demands something broader than this—though obviously far less easy to formulate in the brief space Kant allows himself in the *Groundwork*. To set an end is not merely to lay down a norm to the effect that you should refrain from anything whose omission would absolutely preclude attainment of your end. It also involves some more positive norm to the effect that you ought, *ceteris paribus*, to develop some plan for achieving the end, and either take the feasible steps that belong to the plan or perhaps modify the plan along the way, so as to work persistently at achieving the end for as long as you continue to have it. But this is only a rough formulation, which it would be hard to make more precise, and only in a very specific context could it yield precise constraints on your actions of the form "You absolutely must do this." We would surely be selling Kant short if we thought that his conception of instrumental reason must preclude such more vaguely specified and more flexible reasons for action. His very limited discussion of instrumental reason in the *Groundwork* is designed to bring out only some of the basic points, especially those leading to illuminating parallels with moral reason, whose fundamental principle is his sole concern there.

Prudential reason. A second kind of practical reason distinguished by Kant is "pragmatic" reason, whose imperatives constrain us in the interest of our own happiness. I think that what Kant says about instrumental reason, if understood along the lines just presented, constitutes a consistent and cogent account. The same cannot obviously be said for his remarks on prudential reason, which require some careful—perhaps even selective—interpretation, if they are to amount to an even minimally coherent story.

Kant is aware of a powerful tendency in the ethical theories of the past to reduce moral reason to prudential reason. He is determined to resist this tendency, and therefore in the *Groundwork* he is motivated to draw as sharp a distinction as he can between prudential and moral reason. For this reason, I think he may exaggerate this distinction at times, even as he himself sees it. This, together with the very limited space he provides himself in discussing prudential reason (again, on his way to his main topic, which is moral reason), creates serious difficulties for anyone trying to develop a defensible Kantian account of practical reason based on this brief discussion. The situation is further complicated by the fact that Kant's views about human happiness and its pursuit themselves, from the side of empirical psychology or anthropology, contain some insightful and intriguing perplexities and paradoxes, including certain suggestions that the human desire for happiness itself may be in certain respects not entirely rational, or even internally incoherent. These views, precisely because they are of interest in their own right, and challenge conventional opinions, are bound to complicate further any theory of prudential reason that Kant may propose.

To put the problem briefly, Kant faces a dilemma: on the one side, there is the danger of separating prudential reason so far from moral reason (and so aligning it with instrumental reason) that it ceases to be a distinctive kind of practical reason at all; and on the other side, the danger of recognizing its distinctiveness in a way that opens the door to important questions about prudential reason for which Kant's official account provides no (or no explicit) answers. Resolving this dilemma is an unavoidable task for a reader of the *Groundwork* who is interested in developing a Kantian account of prudential reason for its own sake. This was not a task Kant set himself in the *Groundwork*, and what he says explicitly in that work is clearly not adequate to it.

Kant's treatment of the end of happiness in relation to prudential reason is characterized by three main claims:

The actuality claim: Happiness, as distinct from all other empirical ends, may be presupposed a priori without exception as an *actual* end for every finite rational being, an end "belonging to his essence" (*GMS* 4: 415–16; cf. *KpV* 5: 25; *Anth* 7: 326).

The totality claim: Happiness is an idea, framed by the reason and imagination of each individual, of the greatest achievable total satisfaction of all that individual's inclinations (*GMS* 4: 418; cf. *GMS* 4: 393, 399; *KpV* 5: 124; *KU* 5: 430).

The indeterminacy claim: No individual's idea of happiness is ever determinate or, ultimately, even coherent; it varies over time, often capriciously, and even at any given time no individual can form a precise and consistent idea of what he wishes and wills under the heading of his own happiness (*GMS* 4: 417–19; cf. *KU* 5: 430–31; *Anth* 7: 233–5).

An important conclusion Kant draws from the indeterminacy claim is that there are, strictly speaking, no imperatives of prudence. There is no action which, for all rational beings, is necessarily required for happiness. At most there are "counsels (*consilia*)," rules that result, generally speaking and for the most part (but not unexceptionably), to happiness for most people (*GMS* 4: 418–19). The class of "imperatives of prudence" is necessarily empty.

Kant's attempt to integrate prudence into his conception of practical reason, however, appears to begin with the actuality claim: Happiness is not merely a possible end (such as the ends involved in rules of skill) but an end that may be presupposed as actual for all human beings as belonging to their essence (*GMS* 4: 416, cf. *MS* 6: 387). Therefore, the hypothetical imperative with regard to it is one whose antecedent, so to speak, always holds. This makes imperatives of prudence "assertoric" rather than merely "problematic" (or technical), but not yet "apodictic" (or categorical), because they still rest on a pre-given end (that of happiness) (*GMS* 4: 415).

From this last point, Kant appears to draw the conclusion that imperatives of prudence—if there were any—would be merely hypothetical imperatives, that prudential reason is simply instrumental reason—but distinguished by the fact that the end in question is in fact always *actual* (not contingent or discretionary).

This official account, however, breaks down in incoherence as soon as we ask even a few simple questions and consider Kant's own explicit answers to them.[5] Human beings have many empirical desires, and many different ends based on them. At any given time, some of these ends, or even a single one of them, are given priority over others and acted upon. Is the actuality claim limited to saying that for every human being, happiness is always in fact one such end among others? Surely there are other ends besides happiness that belong among everyone's ends—the end of having sufficient food and sleep, a comfortable surrounding temperature, and many others too. The priorities among such ends—and their relative priority in relation to other, discretionary ends (ends not all people have)—vary greatly from time to time and person to person. If all the actuality claim amounts to is that happiness is one end among others

---

[5] Patrick Kain provides a stalwart exposition of the official account in Kain (2003). But he concludes by admitting (Kain 2003: 250–51) that the account is "incomplete." I think this rather innocent word underestimates the problems with the official account, which seems to me threatened with hopeless incoherence unless modified in something like the way I am suggesting here.

that we all have, then it claims no unique status for happiness among human ends, and therefore the actuality claim does not justify treating assertoric (pragmatic or prudential) imperatives any differently from many other hypothetical imperatives. This way of taking the actuality claim, therefore, is incompatible with the idea that prudential reason is a distinctive species of practical reason. It involves either the collapse of prudential reason into instrumental reason, or else it places prudential reason alongside many other possible (or bogus) "species" of practical reason—such as what we might call "alimentary reason," involving the (always actual) human end of having enough to eat, or "soporific reason," involving the (also always actual) human end of getting enough sleep, and so forth.

The special and distinctive character of prudential reason therefore seems salvageable only if the actuality claim is understood as involving also what we may call the *unique priority claim*: That among an agent's empirical ends, happiness enjoys a unique priority—perhaps this is what Kant means by saying that it "belongs to [every human being's] essence." On the basis of Kant's totality claim, it might be held that happiness, as idea of the greatest sum total of empirical satisfaction, is an end having absolute priority over all other empirical ends, an end to which every other must give way in cases of conflict, or even the single end lending a unique (prudential) reason-giving force to the inclinations that go to make it up. For instance, from prudential reason we may temporarily postpone even eating or sleeping if we think our overall happiness is best promoted by doing so. Kant says that "as far as our nature as sensible beings is concerned, all that counts is our *happiness*, if this is appraised, as reason especially requires, not in terms of transitory feeling but of the influence this contingency has on our whole existence and our satisfaction with it; [from the standpoint of practical reason as a whole, of course,] happiness is not the only thing that counts," but this is only because it can be overridden by morality (*KpV* 5: 61).

The unique priority claim itself, however, might be taken in either of two senses: First, it might be understood as

> The *empirical priority claim*: that as a matter of fact, human beings do always give their happiness priority over all inclinations or other empirical desires.

Or second, it might be taken as

> The *rational (or normative) priority claim*: that practical reason requires them to give happiness this unique priority, and—at least as far as prudence is concerned (and leaving aside the claims of morality)—practical reason commands that they always prefer their happiness to any other, merely momentary pleasure or partial empirical interest with which it might come into conflict.

Kant's presentation of the actuality claim as if it were merely a fact about human nature which could be presupposed to hold of all rational beings, seems to favor the empirical priority version of the actuality claim over the rational priority version. Something like this was even maintained by John Locke, when he said:

> All other good however great in reality, or appearance, excites not a man's *desires*, who looks not on it to make a part of that happiness, wherewith he, in his present thoughts, can satisfie himself. Happiness, under this view, every one constantly pursues, and desires what makes any part of it: Other things, acknowledged to be good, he can look upon without desire; pass by, and be content without. (Locke 1975: II.XXI.§43, 259)

The problem with the empirical actuality claim, however, is that it is a claim about empirical human psychology that is plainly *false*. People often overeat, oversleep, or indulge in pleasures that are bad for them in ways they know are are counterproductive to their happiness. Locke misses this point because his attention is captivated by the thought that we can think things good without necessarily desiring them (which is true). But it is not true that whatever we desire we desire only as part of our happiness. Moreover, Kant himself knows this very well, and even explains it, on the basis of his indeterminacy claim:

> The precept of happiness is for the most part so constituted that it greatly infringes on some inclinations and yet the human being cannot make any determinate and secure concept of the sum of satisfaction of them all, under the name of "happiness"; hence it is not to be wondered at that a single inclination, which is determinate in regard to what it promises and the time in which its satisfaction can be obtained, can outweigh a wavering idea; and the human being, e.g. a person with gout, could choose to enjoy what tastes good and suffer what he must, because in accordance with his reckoning, here at least he has not sacrificed the enjoyment of the present moment through expectations, perhaps groundless, of a happiness that is supposed to lie in health. [So] in this case...the general inclination to happiness does not determine his will. (*GMS* 4: 399)

So we don't in fact always pursue our happiness consistently, or always prefer it to the satisfaction of particular inclinations. Still less are our inclinations effective in getting us to act, as Locke asserts, only when we understand them to be directed to our happiness. Our inclinations are frequently strong desires that are independent of, even directly opposed to, our end of happiness.

If, therefore, the end of happiness is to have a unique priority sufficient to mark prudential reason off decisively from instrumental reason, then the actuality claim must be understood *normatively*, as the *rational priority claim*. That Kant at least tacitly accepts the priority claim in this sense is also indicated by a passage just quoted, in which he says that with regard to our sensible desires, "all that counts is our *happiness*," adding that this is what "reason especially requires" if happiness is understood not as momentary contentment but the sum total of empirical satisfaction with our "whole existence" (*KpV* 5: 61).

If prudential reason is grounded on the rational priority claim, however, then this has some direct consequences that seem impossible to reconcile with some of the other things Kant says. It also raises some vital questions about prudential reason that he does not answer (and it is not obvious how he would answer). For then it becomes clear that the basic issue of prudential reason is not how to constrain oneself to take the means to an end already given; the issue is rather the rationality of one's ends among themselves, of the priorities among them. Kant's imprudent gout sufferer (*GMS* 4: 399), for instance, knows perfectly well the *means* to open the liquor cabinet and get at the brandy he desires, and also the *means* to keep his gout from acting up—namely, to leave the liquor cabinet alone and lay off the brandy. What he needs to constrain himself to do, through the exercise of prudential reason, is to give priority to the *end* of his happiness (satisfaction with his life as a whole) over the short-term end of satisfying a momentary impulse the indulgence of which will later leave him much unhappier. So it gets prudential reason basically wrong to focus, as Kant does, on the possible hypothetical imperatives that might be involved in pursuing the end of one's happiness.

Kant is distracted from all this not only by his haste to put prudential reason under the same heading as instrumental reason (the heading of hypothetical rather than categorical imperatives), but also by the parallel he sees between rules of skill, on the one hand, and counsels of prudence on the other—precepts of "diet, frugality, politeness, restraint, of which experience teaches that they most promote welfare on the average" (*GMS* 4: 418). For these look like rules that would lead you to perform actions that are, by and large, means to happiness (in whatever you might take your happiness to consist), in something like the same way that the actions falling under a rule of skill would promote the contingent end of the science or art to which it belongs.[6] But we have seen that in the case of instrumental reason, the real imperative of practical reason is not to be identified with any of these rules, but rather with a more basic, universal and a priori principle (Hill's Hypothetical Imperative) that rationally constrains

---

[6] Kant's main contrast between rules of skill and counsels of prudence seems to be based on his indeterminacy claim about happiness, which leads him to the conclusion that there are, strictly speaking, no assertoric imperatives, but only "counsels" that tell us what promotes happiness for most people on average (but allowing for many exceptions). Here he seems not only to be running together the rational imperatives of reason (instrumental and prudential) with the empirical rules falling under them, but also greatly exaggerating the difference between rules of skill and counsels of prudence. It may be that the ends of the arts and sciences are clear and determinate in the way that the end of happiness cannot be for us human beings (though that too is questionable for many arts), but however determinate the ends of an art may be, since there is virtually always more than one way to achieve any end, few rules of skill, if any, apply necessarily and in all cases, so rules of skill are like counsels of prudence in this respect.

us, once we have set an end, to take the necessary means to it. If we attempt
to formulate an analogous principle for prudential reason, it will not concern
means–ends relations at all, but rather the relation of priority between the rational end of happiness and all the other contingent ends that are based on inclinations or empirical desires. What is prudent about the gout sufferer's observing
his diet is that it places the end of his happiness ahead of the momentary satisfaction obtainable from an imprudent indulgence; what is prudent about your
observing the counsel of politeness is not really that you have chosen the correct
means to an already given end, but rather that you discreetly put your long-term
self-interest ahead of the momentary impulse to pursue a competing end by
blurting out an angry insult at someone who will then become your enemy and
go on to do you harm.

The first task shows how the concept of happiness itself is in
In his lectures, Kant distinguishes two tasks of prudential reason: determination of the end (of happiness) and determination of the means to it (*V-Mo/
Collins* 27: 246).[7] The first task shows how the concept of happiness itself is in
a way twofold for Kant: It is the concept of the greatest whole of satisfaction
of our inclinations, which at the general level is the same for everyone, and it is
also a more specific concept of those particular ends that I take to constitute
this greatest whole of satisfaction *for me*.

The first task, of determining the end, is the task of moving from the general concept, valid for everyone, to a more specific one, valid for me, that permits of a rational choice of means (the second task). The question naturally
arises here whether Kant understands this "totality" to include all my inclinations, or whether I might decide for good reasons to limit my conception of
my happiness to the satisfaction of only some of my inclinations—excluding
the satisfaction of others from my idea of happiness, even if the inclinations
go on existing in me. I think between these two alternatives, Kant clearly
opts for the second. For he thinks of happiness as the name for an idea (of
reason or imagination) that I make for myself, so that my framing of this
idea determines the content of my happiness—it is not determined solely by
whatever inclinations I happen to have. In framing my idea of happiness,
I must consider not only the strength of my various inclinations but also my
resources for satisfying them. Kant realizes that some ends we may take to
be part of our happiness might have unfortunate consequences connected
with them that we did not anticipate, so that we might more prudently have
excluded these from our idea of our happiness and have decided to leave them
unsatisfied or at least to satisfy them only if resources permit, or when bad
consequences would not result (see *GMS* 4: 418–19). Moreover, as is clear
from Kant's indeterminacy claim, he does not think our idea of happiness is
ever at any point in time entirely determinate in these respects, and it may also

---

[7] I am grateful to Grant Rozeboom for calling my attention to this passage, and to the role
played in Kant's conception of prudential reason by the task of "determining the end."

involve various errors, illusions, or incoherences. There might even be rules or maxims of prudential reason to the effect that our idea of happiness should be coherent, that it should include the satisfaction of inclinations whose frustration we know would make us miserable, and that it should not include inclinations for whose satisfaction we have no hope of obtaining the means. Kant never states any such maxims, though it does not seem contrary to the spirit of his conception of prudential reason to do so. The maxims just stated would have to be conditional or *ceteris paribus*, however, since for many of us they might not all be jointly satisfiable.

The rational principle of prudence relates in the first instance to the general concept of happiness, making it a precept of reason to pursue happiness (whenever this does not conflict with duty). But in consequence it also enjoins the task of making our concept more determinate, and thus an object of practical pursuit (even though, following his indeterminacy claim, Kant thinks we can never do this finally, or perfectly, or even, perhaps, entirely coherently). Only when (and insofar as) the concept of my happiness has been made determinate, can the question arise of choosing the correct means to it (by way, perhaps, of a hypothetical or technical imperative).

The basic principle of prudential reason, therefore, cannot possibly be a principle that tells us how take the best means to the end of happiness. Kant holds, as we have seen, that owing to the indeterminacy claim, there are no imperatives of prudence, but only "counsels." However, there might be a basic *principle of prudence* that could be formulated roughly as follows: "Use your reason, understanding, and imagination to form for yourself a more determinate idea of the greatest attainable total satisfaction of your inclinations (under the name of 'happiness'); and give first priority, among all your nonmoral ends, to happiness, preferring it to all other nonmoral ends when they conflict with it." But now we need to ask (as Kant does about both hypothetical and categorical imperatives): How is this prudential principle possible? And it is not clear how Kant will answer this question. For we now see that the basic principle of prudential reason is not a hypothetical imperative, telling us how to achieve a presupposed end; it is a principle rationally directing us to form an end of a certain kind and also to give it unique rational priority over all competing empirical ends. And such a principle is plainly not analytic, as Kant takes the Hypothetical Imperative to be.

At times, Kant suggests that we form the idea of happiness in order to compare our condition as a whole with that of other people, with the aim of judging ourselves superior to them (*RGV* 6: 27). Arrogance and self-conceit, however, do not look like a rationally creditable basis for prudence. Of course, the principle of morality also says we do have a duty to make the happiness of others our end, which rests on regarding humanity in their person as an end in itself (*GMS* 4: 430, *MS* 6: 387–8, 393–4). We have no *direct* moral duty to make our own happiness an end, but this is only because Kant thinks we need no direct moral constraint to make happiness an end (*MS* 6: 388).[8] We might base the *prudential* constraint of reason to give priority to our happiness over other ends of inclination on the fact that we rationally regard our own existence as an end in itself, and prudence constitutes rational regard for our humanity in the same way that the duty to promote the happiness of others constitutes moral regard for their humanity. But such an account of the rational basis of prudence is nowhere spelled out by Kant, and the general dependence of prudential or even instrumental reason on moral reason, though it has been suggested by some Kantians, does not seem to be part of his explicit position.[9] If it were, Kantian ethics would be closer to eudaimonism than he seems to want it to be. In fact, Kant's account of prudential reason seems conspicuously confused, and the confusions, occasioned by his haste to align it with instrumental reason under the heading of a hypothetical imperative, lead him to distort the nature of prudential reason, preventing him even from asking the questions he needs to ask in order to give a defensible account of the rational basis of prudence.

Moral reason. Kant says of the three principles of practical reason—instrumental, prudential and moral—that they are "distinguished by a *difference* [*Ungleichheit*] in the necessitation of the will" (*GMS* 4: 416). The term *Ungleichheit* here might also be translated as "inequality" (the term in German certainly suggests something comparative, something more than mere nonidentity). That is, we might take Kant as saying that prudential reason trumps or overrides instrumental reason, and moral reason trumps or overrides prudential reason. If we do this, and if we also understand both instrumental and prudential reason as I have already suggested, then we get a fairly complete and coherent Kantian account of practical reason. Reason in its practical use concerns the setting and pursuit of ends. At the most basic level, as instrumental reason it enjoins us to take the means to whatever ends we may have set. But it also imposes rational constraints on which ends we set, commanding us not to set ends based on our empirical desires that are

---

[8] It is not clear that Kant is being entirely self-consistent here. For he says that we have a duty to perfect our skills, based on the fact that self-perfection makes us "worthy of our humanity," even though "technically practical reason also counsels" us to develop the skills we need (*MS* 6: 387). He might equally have argued that along with prudential reason, moral reason might command us to act prudently—to avoid a bad diet, for instance—as a way of honoring our humanity. This would be a direct and not merely an indirect duty to pursue our happiness, exactly analogous to our duty of self-perfection.

[9] Christine Korsgaard has presented an interpretation of Kant on which the independence of instrumental reason is called into question, and instrumental reason itself is held to be unintelligible on its own, apart from its foundation in moral reason (Korsgaard 1997: 215–54). I toyed with a similar idea in Wood (1999, 55–70), and have done it again just now regarding prudential reason in note 8. But I do not think Kant actually makes any claims of this kind. I don't think his insistence on an *Ungleichheit* (in the sense of unequal status, or even lexical order) between the claims of the three species of practical reason directly commits him to hold that the normativity of instrumental or prudential reason must rest on the normativity of moral reason. On the contrary, it would sooner commit him to the reverse.

at odds with the end of our happiness, and to limit our pursuit even of our happiness when that is overridden by moral duty.

Moral reason, however, though not based on any pre-given end, does set certain ends, which is our duty to have. These are our own perfection and the happiness of others. Kantian theory, however, does not conceive these obligatory ends as admitting of summing or maximizing: it requires that we include various ends falling under the general concepts "our own perfection" and "the happiness of others" among the ends we set, and it forbids us from making our own imperfection or anyone else's unhappiness (or any part of these) an end (though under many circumstances it might permit us to cause another's unhappiness as a permissible means or by-product of fulfilling some duty, or even of the permissible pursuit of our own happiness). But it does not require that we place "the greatest happiness" (of any individual) or "the general happiness" (of the whole sentient world) among our ends. (It is consistent, in fact, with regarding these expressions as nonsensical or nonreferring, and therefore "the greatest happiness" and "the general happiness" as not possible ends at all.)

V. Kantian Reasons and Practical Good

Many contemporary accounts of practical reason are concerned not only with rational principles or "the requirements of rationality," but even more with the nature of reasons, and with such notions as *pro tanto* reasons. Kant's account in the *Groundwork* is not concerned with such notions, but I think it would be a mistake to suppose that Kant in any way denies that there are *pro tanto* reasons in the sense used by contemporary philosophers. From what we have seen, in fact, I think we can even begin to develop a Kantian account of what reasons of this kind would consist in.

An important element in developing such an account, I think, is Kant's interesting formulation of the idea of "practical good": "The will," he says, "is a faculty of choosing *only that* which reason, independently of inclination, recognizes as practically necessary, i.e. as good" (*GMS* 4: 412). "Practical *good*, however, is that which determines the will by representations of reason, hence not from subjective causes but objectively, i.e. from grounds that are valid for every rational being as such" (*GMS* 4: 413). I take Kant's notion of practical good to be a somewhat technical one, narrower in application than the way the term "good" is generally used in less precise theoretical contexts (even by Kant himself). Objects or states of affairs we pursue as ends, for instance, are often considered *good*, and Kant himself speaks of them in this way, for instance, in talking about "the highest good" (*summum bonum*) (which includes the satisfaction of our inclinations or our happiness, when we have made ourselves worthy of it) (*KrV* A810–12/B838–40, *KpV* 5: 110–13, *KU* 5: 448–50). In the strict sense, however, "practical good" refers only to a *way of acting* (*KpV* 5: 60), namely, one that is necessitated by, and grounded on, representations of reason that are objective, valid for all rational beings as such.

The concept of practical good is in place whenever an action is in any way required by an imperative of reason—whether of instrumental, prudential, or moral reason, since all imperatives formulate objectively valid principles. Practical good is what reason requires or grounds, independently of inclination, in the sense that an action's being practically good is a reason for doing it that deserves to prevail over against the mere inclination not to do it. This is true equally of actions that fall under instrumental, prudential and moral reason. It is *not true*, however, that Kant regards actions performed from reason as actions done without interest or desire. This is because he thinks that reason of itself creates an interest in actions and a desire to perform them (*GMS* 4: 413n; *KpV* 5: 9n; *MS* 6: 211–13). These desires would be, in Thomas Nagel's sense, "motivated" desires (Nagel 1970: 29), and also, in John Rawls's sense "principle-dependent" rather than "object-dependent" desires (Rawls 2000: 45–8, 151–2).

Practical good may be regarded as the form of *any* practical reason. A fact constitutes a reason for me if, under one of the three basic principles of reason, this fact makes a certain action practically good for me. Thus if I have set an end Z, and it is the case that performing action H is an indispensable means for me to attain Z, then following the principle of instrumental reason (the Hypothetical Imperative), I am constrained by reason to perform H, which makes H is practically good (for me under the circumstances), and constitutes a reason for me to perform H. If, as I have suggested, we allow a somewhat more flexible and capacious view of instrumental reason, so that it enjoins not merely the performance of actions indispensably necessary to our ends but also grounds the performance of actions that in one way or another bring our ends about, then the fact that H tends to promote Z would also make H practically good in a looser sense, and give me at least a *pro tanto* reason for performing H. Likewise, if G is a state of mine that belongs to my conception of my happiness, then according to the principle of prudential reason, I have at least a *pro tanto* reason for bringing about G, and also a *pro tanto* reason for performing any action H that is required for G or tends to bring about G. Of course, all reasons furnished by either instrumental or prudential reason are never more than *pro tanto* reasons in the sense that they can be overridden by moral reasons.

Even morality, however, provides me with some *pro tanto* reasons. Morality gives rise, Kant says, to many distinct "grounds of obligation" or "obligating reasons" (*Verpflichtungsgründe, rationes obligandi*), some of which may be stronger than others (*MS* 6: 224). To the extent that any obligating reason can be overridden by a still stronger one, that obligating reason is always a *pro tanto* reason. Morality commands us to make the happiness of others an end, and therefore to include all the elements of every rational being's happiness among our ends. This gives me a *pro tanto* reason for contributing to the happiness of any person, or to any part of that happiness. But of course the duty to perform any action that contributes to any part of another's happiness is only a wide or meritorious duty (unless special circumstances turn it into more than this). For instance, if you are a stranger to me, and in no special need of my help, then I need not give your happiness any priority among my ends, and there is nothing blamable or contrary to duty in my preferring some portion of my own happiness to it, unless I thereby violate some perfect or strictly owed duty toward you, such as a duty of right.

VI. "Virtue" Theories of Practical Reason

Kant allows, then, that morality gives rise to different reasons, even *pro tanto* reasons. But he regards them as reasons of a single distinctive kind, based on a rational principle which is fundamental and overriding in relation to all the other reasons we may have to do anything. This view is controversial, and it would be beyond the scope of this chapter to give it anything like a full defense here. But it may help to compare it to fashionable competitors. For example, there are a number of views of practical reason according to which there is no distinctively moral reason that all responsible agents have for doing what they morally ought to do (for doing their "duty," as Kant would put it). Some of these views, usually associated with the names of Hobbes and Hume, hold that all reasons are either theoretical or merely instrumental. Others, even closer to the real Hume, and associated with what is now called "virtue ethics," hold that practical reasons, especially those associated with morality, are grounded in the agent's character. (Such a view has been recently articulated with sophistication by Kieran Setiya (Setiya 2007).)

The main trouble with all these views seems to me that they cannot explain how—or even consistently allow that—a morally bad person, or a person who happens not to have set any moral ends, could ever have a good and compelling reason to do the right thing. If I am such a person, how can I then be expected to do the right thing, or blamed for not doing it? Perhaps this might be done by applying the notion of virtue normatively—though why one should be *blamed* for not acting as the virtuous person would is not adequately explained.

These theories say we can take negative attitudes toward morally bad people, or even blame them for moral badness, but it is not clear how they can consider us justified in doing so if by their own lights these people have no reason not to behave in morally bad ways. Suppose I am a callous or cruel person and treat others' rights and welfare with contempt. How can you be justified in blaming me for behaving this way, or in calling me by various bad names (the names of various vices), if you admit I have no reason to behave any other way? If you yourself say that I have no reason not to behave cruelly or callously, then why should I care what nasty names you call me when I behave in these ways? And where do you get off abusing me for doing what you yourself think I have no reason not to do? It seems, by your own lights, that you and not I are the person open to rational criticism.

Further, on this theory what counts as virtue has to depend simply on how we feel about people: the "virtuous" person is simply the kind that this person and others like, and there can be no reason (beyond these contingent likings) why anyone should admire such a person, want to be one, or want to act like one. Some people happen to like and admire cruel and arrogant people, who refuse to respect the rights of others and care nothing for their welfare. On this "virtue" theory, it would seem that if more people were like them, then the cruel and arrogant would be the "virtuous," and there would be no reason to be kind or respectful of the rights of others.

Some philosophers seem to find these consequences acceptable; they exhort us to have the wisdom and modesty to admit that there is, or can be, nothing more to reasons, normativity, and so forth, than what people contingently and empirically happen to like, approve of, and so forth. It seems relevant, on such views, that I find their assertions filling me only with scorn and indignation, since they think we have no objective reason to care about morality, and seem to regard all moral exhortation as nothing but an attempt to coerce or manipulate one another using irrational feelings. Shouldn't it count against this kind of "virtue" theory, just in its own terms (and its account of reasons, rationality, and so forth) if many of us find that we regard it with disapproval and even contempt?

Present-day virtue theorists often appeal to Aristotle, but if they do so on behalf of the view just mentioned, then they get him wrong in an important way. For Aristotle, if you are a virtuous person, you are virtuous *because* you act for good reasons: You "follow right reason," as he puts it; and Aristotle repeatedly insists that virtue accords with right reason, *not* the reverse.[10] In other words, it is the fact that you follow right reason that makes you virtuous; it is *not* the case that this or that is a reason (for you) because you happen to be a virtuous person. Reasons come first, virtue comes second. You have to explain what virtue is in terms of reasons; you can't explain what reasons are in terms of virtue. When you ask what you should do, you are inquiring what there is good reason for you to do *whatever sort of person you might happen to be*. Obviously, in asking what you should do, and looking for reasons for doing one thing rather than another, one thing you are always asking (directly or indirectly) is *also* what kind of person you should be, which sometimes also includes asking what a virtuous person is like. Reasons are what have to decide that for you, and they can't satisfactorily perform this office if they are treated as mere by-products of a theory of virtue.

---

[10] Aristotle (1999: 1103b31, 1107a2, 1115b12, 1117a8, 1119a20, 1125b35, 1138a10, b20–34, 1144b23–8, 1147b3, b31, 1151a12, a22): cf. *Eudemian Ethics* 1220b19, 1222a8, b5.

Aristotle's "right reason," like Kant's motive of "morality" or "duty," may show itself in a plurality of ways, but it seems to be fundamentally unitary and closely associated (for Aristotle) with the rational part of the soul, which is the supreme human faculty.[11] It is reason that makes us aware of the practical good, as distinct from the merely pleasant. A "virtue theory" that is authentically Aristotelian would involve a conception of reason that is very close to Kant's.

Let's sum up. From the account we have given, we can see that on Kant's theory of practical reason, the ways actions can be practically good, and therefore the reasons we can have to perform actions, are extremely varied. Inclinations are never simply in and of themselves reasons, but they can give rise to reasons as soon as we set their objects as ends, or include their satisfaction in our idea of our happiness. Facts about how to reach our ends, or the ends of others, are also reasons, sometimes only instrumental reasons, sometimes prudential reasons, sometimes even moral reasons. Moral reason has systematic priority over prudential reason and over hypothetical imperatives about how to reach merely contingent ends, but since some moral duties are imperfect, wide, or meritorious, the moral reasons we have for actions are often merely *pro tanto* reasons, which may often be overridden by prudential or even merely instrumental reasons.

VII. Rational Justification

It remains to say something about the relation of Kant's account of practical reason to the topic of *justification*. Rational justification, as I said before, is always justification *to* someone, if only to the agent herself whose action is to be justified. A theory of rational justification that might be based on Kant's explicit account of practical reason would probably take the agent's own point of view as primary, and consider justification to others as consisting in getting them to see the action from the agent's point of view, and how it is rationally justified from that point of view.

This "first-person" or self-oriented justification seems to work perfectly well when the only kind of practical rationality involved is instrumental or prudential rationality concerning my own ends or my own happiness. But I can also offer another a rational justification for my action by getting the other to understand my end and to understand my action as the necessary, or the best, or at least a rationally acceptable means to it, or getting the other to see my action, and its end, as contributing to my happiness, according to my idea of it. Here the rational justification, to others as well as myself, consists in showing how the action is practically good according to the Hypothetical Imperative or according to the basic principle of prudential reason. It may even work for

---

[11] Aristotle (1999: 1095a10, 1098a3, 1102b15, 1111b12, 1119b11, 1147b1, 1150b28, 1169a1, a5, 1170b12).

some kinds of moral justification, such as the fulfillment of duties to myself, or even the promotion of some other-regarding but impersonal good, such as the utilitarian end of the general happiness (assuming that notion makes sense). Instrumental reason may also have intersubjective uses when people share an end in common, and reason to one another about the best way for each of them to contribute to their shared end.

Prudential reason might work the same way if we could formulate an idea of the collective happiness of a group, and promote it in preference to the partial happiness of its individual members. From a Kantian point of view, utilitarianism looks like a misguided attempt to reduce morality to merely a collective prudential reason. For Kant, however, there is also an essential element of intersubjectivity in rational justification even when it starts from the standpoint of the agent. For one thing, as we have seen, all the principles of reason (instrumental and prudential as well as moral) are conceived by Kant as objective principles, valid for all rational agents. Even my rational justification of actions—to myself and from my own practical point of view—must rest on principles that are valid even for me only to the extent that they can be seen as valid for others as well. And Kant regards it as an empirical fact that human beings are capable of grasping what is universally valid only by communicating with others and embracing their point of view by understanding their own expression of it.

This is why Kant thinks that "the very existence of reason depends on freedom [of communication]" (*KrV* A738/B766) and the use of the judgment of others as a *criterium veritatis externam* (*Anth* 7: 128). Kant therefore formulates the principle of enlightenment—"thinking for oneself" as asking oneself, "whenever one is to accept something, whether one could find it feasible to make the ground or rule on which one accepts it into a universal principle of reason" (*WDO* 8: 146n). And this in turn, is why the maxim of thinking for oneself leads inevitably to the maxim of thinking from the standpoint of everyone else, which one can do only by entering into rational communication with them (*KU* 5: 294–5; cf. *Anth* 7: 200, 228, 25: 1480: *Log* 9: 57; *Refl* 1486 15: 715).

Justification on the basis of instrumental and prudential reason, and some forms of moral reason, starts with the agent's standpoint and becomes justification to others by getting them to adopt that standpoint. Rational justification cannot work in the same way, however, when the issue is another's rights, interests, or other claims on me. Then things are turned around, and my rational justification of the action to myself consists in my coming to see my action from the standpoint of the other who is affected by it, and showing how the action respects that other's rights or satisfies the other's legitimate claims or interests. Even in relation to my pursuit of an apparently impersonal good, such as the public interest or the general happiness, justification cannot take place only from my point of view unless we assume that I am entitled (all by myself) to determine the content of these ends, as if I were entitled to choose for others which ends we should pursue in common. Obviously this is not the right way to think about the ends that are objects of common pursuit by a community of agents. Moral ends, in Kant's view, belong to a "realm of ends." An end is an object that a rational being must freely choose for itself: "I can indeed be constrained by others to perform *actions* that are directed as means to an end, but I can never be constrained by others to have an end" (*MS* 6: 381). A "realm" is a systematic unity of ends shared by rational beings, regarded as a universal community standing under a common moral legislation (*GMS* 4: 433–4; cf. *RGV* 6: 96–102). In a realm of ends, the laws I am to obey harmonize my ends with a system of ends shared by all rational beings. In that sense, moral justification, following this formulation of the moral law, always has implicit reference to the standpoint of others as well as the agent's standpoint.

VIII. Mutual Recognition and Community

The primacy of the standpoint of another in Kantian ethics is even clearer when we are talking about moral justification in terms of a person's *rights*, or what we owe to them by duties of respect. "The respect that I have for others or that another can require of me (*observantia aliis praestanda*) is therefore the recognition (*Anerkennung*) of the dignity (*dignitas*) in other human beings, that is, of a worth that has no price, no equivalent for which the object evaluated (*aestimii*) could be exchanged" (*MS* 6: 462; cf. *GMS* 4: 434–5).

It is not accidental that Kant uses the same term here (*Anerkennung*) that was (at about the same time, yet quite independently) coined by Fichte to capture the essential and reciprocal relation any rational subject must have to other rational subjects, constituting the relation of right (Fichte 2000: 39–52). But there is something a bit awkward and opaque in Kant's way of formulating the distinction between dignity and price, which focuses on the kind of value something has for an individual agent (and from its own point of view). We are told that something has a *price* if it admits of an equivalent for which it might be rationally exchanged. The *dignity* (of another person, or the moral law, or something whose value is grounded on theirs) is defined only negatively—as that value which cannot be estimated in this way. To determine the price of something is to be given information that can be used in rational deliberation about what you should do regarding it— how much it is to be valued in your deliberation relative to other things having a price. To be told that something has dignity is to be told only that it has no place in *those* kinds of calculations. Common interpretations of Kant's notion of dignity hold that what has dignity is something having *infinite* value, so to speak, in such calculations. The dignity of humanity would then imply that any act that fails to treat a human being as having infinite value would be forbidden. This invites the objection that this makes it impossible to relate that value to others, and leads

naturally to the thought that Kantian ethics must be a system of irrationally strict
moral rules, closed to all deliberation based on comparing the consequences of
different alternatives.

Let me suggest a way of thinking about dignity that might open the way to
a better interpretation. Price is the kind of value that may be used by practical
reason in deciding what to do from the standpoint of some agent for whom the
factors relevant to a decision may be assigned prices and weighed, by instrumental or prudential reason, relative to them. Dignity, however, is the kind of value
that tells the agent that she must not consider the decision only by calculating
values from this standpoint, but that she needs also to combine her standpoint
somehow with that of others, and abandon (or at least conditionalize) the whole
procedure of deciding what to do by weighing and calculating values from any
single standpoint. For a rational agent to appreciate dignity as a value is for that
agent to recognize the necessity of shifting from the orientation of providing
rational justification to herself (and giving it to others by getting them to see
her point of view) to the orientation of including the standpoint of another, or
integrating different standpoints into the process of making the decision.

This would mean making the decision not merely by calculating relative to
a set of values (prices) attached to factors in it and weighing the overall utility
of outcomes, but by including in the process also a set of cooperative relationships between different agents who are regarded as parties to it—and to all of
whom it must be rationally justified if it is to count as rationally justified to any
of them. The idea of the dignity of every rational being also contains the thesis
that these cooperative relationships must proceed on terms of the fundamental
equality of all persons and mutual respect between them.

There are some grounds for seeing such an interpretation of the positive content of the Kantian notion of dignity as already present—at least implicitly—in
Kant's own account of it. The dignity of personhood is the value that for Kant
belongs to autonomy, the capacity for self-legislation. The Kantian conception
of autonomy might be seen, and often has been seen, in terms of this standard
conception of practical rationality, as the giving of moral law to *myself*. But this
is not actually how Kant describes autonomy when he first introduces the idea.
He presents it instead as "the idea *of the will of every rational being as a will giving universal law*" (*GMS* 4: 431). In other words, I legislate to myself to precisely
the same extent that I legislate for all other rational beings, and conversely, they
legislate to me in exactly the same way that I legislate to them. My will may be
regarded as self-legislative precisely to the degree that it is a common rational
will shared by all rational beings to the extent that they are ideally rational. The
autonomous legislator is not myself as an individual agent, but rather each of
us ideally legislating for ourselves and all the others. But perhaps the best way
of thinking of this ideal legislation is to think of the legislator as the community
of rational agents as a whole legislating for all its members through their reciprocal rational interaction. If we think of it that way, then we have transcended

the idea of rationality as deliberation from a single agent's point of view, and opened ourselves to considering intersubjective relations between different agents and different standpoints as constitutive of rationality.

Most traditional theories of practical rationality take the standpoint of a single agent. Even those that want to calculate the good of a collective, or make decisions relative to a common good, such as the general happiness, have operated from the standpoint of a single agent (whether individual or collective in constitution) that simply takes this common good as its own end. The terms of communication and cooperation between agents are then seen as merely instrumental to achieving either the good of individuals or some common good which is the end of the single agent (individual or collective) that is supposed to be calculating the value of utilities and means with a view to achieving it. On this view, rational justification is always justification to that single agent, from its point of view, in achieving whatever ends it has adopted. Kant's official theory of practical reason as presented in the *Groundwork* looks like a theory of this kind, oriented exclusively to the standpoint of any individual rational being. But if we adopt the interpretation I have suggested of the Kantian notion of dignity, then Kant's conception of moral value, especially the idea of humanity in the person of every rational being as an end in itself and the dignity of every person as a value surpassing any price, pushes this whole ("first-person," "individualistic," or "monological") conception of practical reason to its limits, and even invites us to transcend them.

Kant may thus be seen as the Moses of the moral world, who leads us to the borders of traditional (monological) conceptions of practical reason, and even points us toward what might lie beyond them, but never quite himself sets foot in the promised land.

Bibliography

Aristotle (1999) *Nicomachean Ethics*. Tr. and ed. T. Irwin. 2nd ed. Indianapolis: Hackett. Cited by Bekker number.

Aristotle. (2011) *Eudemian Ethics*. Tr. and ed. A. Kenny. Oxford: Oxford University Press. Cited by Bekker number.

Broome, J. (2005) "Does Rationality Give Us Reasons?" *Philosophical Issues* 15(1): 321–337.

Darwall, S. (2006) *The Second-Person Standpoint: Morality, Respect, and Accountability*. Cambridge, MA: Harvard University Press.

Fichte, J. G. (2000 [1796]) *Foundations of Natural Right*. Ed. F. Neuhouser, tr. M. Baur. Cambridge: Cambridge University Press, 2000.

Fichte, J. G. (2005 [1798]) *System of Ethics*. Tr. D. Breazeale and G. Zller. Cambridge: Cambridge University Press.

Hill, T. E., Jr. (2002) *Human Welfare and Moral Worth: Kantian Perspectives*. Oxford: Oxford University Press.

Hume, D. (1967 [1739]) *A Treatise on Human Nature*. Ed. L. A. Selby-Bigge. Oxford: Clarendon Press.

Hutcheson, F. (1971 [1742]) *An Essay on the Nature and Conduct of the Passions and Affections. With Illustrations on the Moral Sense*. Ed. B. Peach. Cambridge, MA: Harvard University Press.

Kain, P. (2003), "Prudential Reasons in Kant's Anthropology," in B. Jacobs and P. Kain (eds.), *Essays on Kant's Anthropology*, 230–65. Cambridge: Cambridge University Press.

Kant, I. (1992–) *The Cambridge Edition of the Works of Immanuel Kant*. Cambridge and New York: Cambridge University Press.

Kolodny, N. (2005), "Why Be Rational?" *Mind* 114(455): 509–63.

Korsgaard, C. M. (1997) "The Normativity of Instrumental Reason," in G. Cullity and B. Gaut (eds.), *Ethics and Practical Reason*, 215–54. Oxford: Oxford University Press.

Korsgaard, C. M. (2009) "The Activity of Reason," *Proceedings and Addresses of the American Philosophical Association* 83(2): 23–43.

Locke, J. (1975 [1690]). *Essay Concerning Human Understanding*. Ed. P. Nidditch. Oxford: Oxford University Press.

Nagel, T. (1970) *The Possibility of Altruism*. Princeton: Princeton University Press.

Parfit, D. (2011) *On What Matters*. Oxford: Oxford University Press.

Rawls, J. (2000) *Lectures on the History of Moral Philosophy*. Ed. B. Herman. Cambridge, MA: Harvard University Press.

Scanlon, T. M. (Forthcoming) "Reasons and Rationality," *Philosophy*.

Setiya, K. (2007) *Reasons without Rationalism*. Princeton: Princeton University Press.

Smith, A. (2000 [1759]) *The Theory of Moral Sentiments*. Amherst, NY: Prometheus Books.

Wood, A. W. (1999) *Kant's Ethical Thought*. New York: Cambridge University Press.

4

Constructing Practical Justification

HOW CAN THE CATEGORICAL IMPERATIVE JUSTIFY DESIRE-BASED ACTIONS?

Larry Krasnoff

I. Introduction: Kant as Realist and Constructivist

Interpretations of Kant's practical philosophy influenced by John Rawls have stressed a nonmetaphysical or even antirealist account of value. According to this "Harvard reading," defended by Onora O'Neill (1989; 1996) and especially by Christine Korsgaard (1996b; 2008; 2009), Kant holds that value does not exist in any external or independent sense, but instead is created or constructed by us. For Kant, this interpretation suggests, the good is the object of a rational will, and a rational will is one that wills laws of its own. Outside of the principles we will for ourselves, then, nothing is good in any independent or objective sense.

Recently this constructivist account of Kantian ethics has come under steady criticism by interpreters such as Karl Ameriks (2000; 2003), Patrick Kain (2004; 2006), Eric Watkins and William FitzPatrick (2002; see also FitzPatrick 2005), Alison Hills (2008), Robert Stern (2012), and to a lesser extent, Allen Wood (2008) and Paul Guyer (1998). The criticisms of course vary, but their emphasis is constant: the Harvard reading is overly subjective and unfaithful to Kant. The critics maintain that Kant's claims about the priority of the moral law and the unconditional value of autonomy fit better with a more traditionally realist or metaphysical account of value. According to the realist reading, Kant holds that our free and/or rational nature is good in an independent and objective sense, and all his claims about value follow from this basic normative fact.

The issue that divides these interpretations seems clear enough, but evaluating the debate between them turns out to be especially complicated. For one thing, since Kant's practical philosophy exerts a continuing influence in contemporary moral and political thinking, it is virtually impossible to sort out the textual from the philosophical issues in the debate. When Korsgaard speaks of grounding obligations in claims to identity, and O'Neill speaks of a recursive vindication of reason, they are trying to tell us that Kant has something surprisingly radical to say to us today, that he is already responding to the kind of skepticism about independent claims to rationality that animates contemporary postmodernism. For someone like Ameriks, especially, this updating of Kant is textually and historically suspect; the very attempt to insert Kant into a conversation about postmodernism suggests that something has already gone wrong in the reading of an eighteenth-century Prussian who was quite familiar with Pietism and Christian Wolff but totally unfamiliar with Nietzsche or Lyotard. On the other hand, it is perfectly clear that Ameriks is not at all attracted to these antirealist forms of "post-Kantian" thought, so that Kant's practical philosophy is all the more plausible for holding to an old-fashioned realist perspective. Hence when the realists make a plea for a more traditional reading, their motivations are just as philosophical as they are textual or historical, just as philosophical as Korsgaard's or O'Neill's are.[1] With both sides making both textual and philosophical claims at the same time, it is not easy to understand what the debate is finally about. In one sense, everyone involved is trying to do the same thing: to make the best philosophical sense of Kant's most basic claims. But since there can be, and is, disagreement both about what makes philosophical sense and what Kant's basic claims are, the dispute is doubly complicated.

Even if we could agree on the claims to be evaluated, though, what follows from them in a metaphysical or ontological sense is still not clear. On the one hand, it certainly seems right to say that Kant holds that there is a basic standard of moral justification that holds for all rational agents. This standard of justification is in an important sense objective; any agent who departs from it can be said to be morally wrong. That much Korsgaard or O'Neill would clearly grant, but according to Wood (2008), this basic sort of objectivity already implies a realism about moral value: the supreme principle of morality is independent of what anyone wills. And this is precisely what Korsgaard, especially, wants to deny. On the other hand, since Wood's Kantian candidate for an independent normative entity is the rational will (1999: 129–30), he has to grant that the objects of our choices have a kind of derivative value that comes only from the will itself. That is, even the realist Kantian has to grant that Kant holds that our (permissible) empirical ends have no independent value, and that any value they have is constructed by us as rational agents who will them.[2] What Ameriks and Kain, especially, object to in the constructivist interpretation is the idea that humans can simply will value

---

[1] As is nicely emphasized in Breazeale (2003; see especially 239–41).

[2] It is for this reason that Hills (2008) classifies Wood, along with Korsgaard, as a constructivist, not a realist. Both Wood and Korsgaard, contends Hills, endorse a "conferral modal" of nonmoral value that is opposed to realism. This reading is based on Wood (1999). But Wood later insists (2008) that his understanding of Kant is clearly realist. Wood's case thus illustrates the complicated nature of this entire debate.

into existence, but if it is true that the rational will is what has value in itself, then the choices of the rational will do in fact bring value into existence.

What this means is that Kant's practical philosophy has what seem to be both realist and constructivist elements, and that any successful interpretation needs to acknowledge this. It is not clear how the realist Kantian can object, in any very general way, to the claim that our choices create value, because that claim seems to follow directly from Kant's account of our empirical ends. But the constructivist seems hard pressed to say that we create the standard of moral justification out of our own willing, because the Kantian standard of moral justification is supposed to remain the same no matter what anyone wills. In response to this last objection, Korsgaard (1996b) seems to be saying that all of us accept a particular identity, that of rational agents, so that we all will the same moral principle with our (rational) wills. On this kind of constructivism, the basic Kantian moral principle is what our rational identities all will. But this claim looks like it requires the further claim that our rational identity has a priority over our other identities, so that only its willing is fully justified. And this further claim looks like it requires a (realist) claim about the value of our rationality over other aspects of our nature.

Hence the debate between realist and constructivist interpretations of Kant is particularly complicated. At the same time, we can see from our discussion of these complications that we would understand the metaphysical implications of Kant's practical philosophy much better if we could understand one distinctive but puzzling Kant claim: that the supreme principle of morality, the categorical imperative (abbreviated hereafter as the CI), somehow creates or confers the value of our (permissible) empirical ends. How can we make sense of this? What ontological or metaphysical sense does it make, or need to make? Just what is it about the moral principle that allows it to perform this value-conferring operation? How and why should we understand our moral or rational willing as somehow constitutive of value? Why should we see the categorical imperative not simply as a principle of moral justification, but as one that somehow justifies our empirical ends?

This paper seeks to address these questions in several stages. I will begin by considering several possible interpretations of the claim that a desire-based principle is rationally justified when it conforms to the CI. After identifying what I take to be the most plausible of these interpretations, I will turn to the question of how, on this view, we should understand the rational status of the CI itself. Finally, I will assess what this understanding of the CI means for the interpretation of Kant's practical philosophy as realist or constructivist. My conclusion will be that some version of the Harvard, constructivist reading has to be correct, though my favored version may look somewhat different from O'Neill's and especially from Korsgaard's. Throughout the chapter, my primary focus will be philosophical rather than textual; the goal here is to make the most philosophical sense of a Kantian account of practical justification.

Like most everyone else in the debate, I too think that the account I will favor is also the one that has the best grounding in Kant's texts. But the task of showing that will have to be left for another time.

II. Desires as Reasons

Again, the view that we are trying to understand is the following: for Kant, an action prompted by a desire or an inclination is rationally justified when it conforms to universal law, when the maxim of acting on the desire could be willed by all rational agents. I am going to approach this thesis as divided into two parts: first, the negative claim that desires are not in themselves reasons for action, and second, the positive claim that the conformity to the CI makes them into reasons, thereby conferring value on the satisfaction of our desires.

In defense of the first, negative claim, much recent writing on Kant has stressed the self-conscious, reflective, or deliberative nature of our agency, for which the mere fact of a desire does not automatically move us to action (Allison 1990; Hill 1992: 76–96; Korsgaard 1996a: 159–187). At least within the subjective, first-person perspective of the deliberating agent, we act on a desire only when we choose to endorse it as a reason, thereby affirming, at least implicitly, a principle of action that says that the desire is good to satisfy. Henry Allison's term (1990: 5–6) for this claim is the "incorporation thesis": a desire can be a reason only if it has been incorporated into a maxim, an at least implicit principle that endorses the satisfaction of the desire as valuable. Until a desire has been incorporated into a maxim, it is, as Kant's terminology suggests, simply something we are inclined to do, a candidate for a reason rather than a reason in itself.

Allison and others have also pointed out that a maxim, although in itself only a rule endorsed by a particular agent, always has a general form that speaks, at least potentially, to all rational agents: it says that something is good for at least all similarly situated agents to do. This kind of generality, however, falls well short of the universality required by the CI; to say that my maxim must imply a claim about what is good for any rational agent to do does not yet imply that I must will that my maxim become, or even that it could become, a law for all rational agents (Allison 1990: 204–7). There is no theoretical or practical inconsistency in my acting on a maxim that I take to be rational, and my hoping or even willing that others do not act on that maxim, on what I take to be rational. There is thus no way to get from the bare reflective or deliberative nature of our rational agency to the moral requirement that we respect rational agency in ourselves and all others. Reflective endorsement, to use Korsgaard's terminology, is a necessary condition of our valuing things, not yet something we must necessarily value in itself. (How Korsgaard wants to get us to the second, stronger claim is a matter to which I will return, later on in the discussion.)

Even the claim that reflective endorsement is a necessary condition of our valuing something, however, can be understood in two different ways, one stronger and one weaker. On the stronger understanding, reflective endorsement is at least a part of what can make a desire into a reason for us. On the weaker understanding, by contrast, reflective endorsement is simply something we must do if a desire is to become a reason for us. The stronger understanding sees reflective endorsement as at least part of the content of our reasons for action, while the weaker understanding sees reflective endorsement as simply part of the activity of practical reasoning, one that has little effect on the content of our reasons for action.

Which understanding is correct? It might seem that the fact of reflective endorsement has to have some effect on the content of practical reasoning, because we have already granted that our reflective nature makes it impossible for us to regard the mere fact of our having a desire as itself a reason for action. But even if we must reflectively endorse our desires, nothing in the nature of reflective endorsement itself prevents us from endorsing a principle like "Do what you strongly desire to do." I do not regard that principle as particularly plausible, at least as a general rule, but its implausibility is a substantive matter of practical reasoning, not a failure of or a confusion about the nature of reflective endorsement. Still, it is important to see that the need for reflective endorsement does drive us toward a deliberative engagement with the substantive reasons that might justify our acting on our desires. Even though it is perfectly possible to reflectively endorse the fact or the strength of a desire as a reason for acting on that desire, the attitude of reflection is inherently one in which desires appear as subjective tendencies about ourselves, tendencies that are then assessed as candidates for objective claims about what is good for human beings. In reflection, we do necessarily have to distinguish between the subjective fact of our desires ("I am hungry") and the objective or substantive claim that the desire points to, the claim that would justify our wanting what we do ("My body needs food in order for me to be healthy and function well"). Even in a case where what we reflectively endorse is simply doing what we feel like, the reflective endorsement is going to imply a claim about the value of simply acting on certain desires in our lives. If I choose chocolate ice cream over strawberry, I might not be committing myself to the substantive claim that chocolate is the truly superior form of ice cream. I might well just choose chocolate because I feel a craving for it today. But even that choice, viewed in the light of reflection, looks like it implies that the substantive, if negative, claim that settling on the truly superior ice cream is no big deal, that nothing particular important turns on my simply indulging the craving that I happen to have. And to say this is to do more than to appeal to the fact of the desire.[3]

---

[3] This kind of example is at issue in an exchange between Ginsborg (1998) and Korsgaard (1998).

If these considerations are correct, things look like this. We have so far seen no reason to affirm the stronger thesis that reflective endorsement is part of the content of justified reasons for action. On the other hand, reflective endorsement does, contrary to the weaker thesis, have an effect on the content of what counts as a practical reason. Desires, regarded simply as facts about our individual psychologies, do not count as reasons for action; rather, to be regarded as reasons, they need to be converted into substantive claims about what it is good for agents like ourselves to do. The negative thesis that desires do not count as reasons in themselves is itself the product of reflection's demand for a stronger kind of reason.

III. The Indeterminacy of Happiness

This should seem like an awkward conclusion for a Kantian account of practical reasoning, because it is precisely what I have called substantive practical reasons that occupy the most of awkward of places in Kant's thinking. Indeed they often seem to have no place at all. For while Kant endorses a general principle of instrumental rationality ("the Hypothetical Imperative," instructing us to take the necessary means to the ends we have willed[4]) and a general principle of pure practical reasoning (the CI), he says very little about substantive principles about what desires are truly worth satisfying. Such substantive principles are going to be Aristotelian claims about the nature of human flourishing, and beyond some remarks about developing our rational capacities, it is exactly these claims that Kant seems to say virtually nothing about. A main reason that Kant's account of practical justification strikes many people as unhelpful is that it says little or nothing about the substantive choices that really structure our lives. Substantive practical reasons are located in the very large psychological space between desires as idiosyncratic urges, on the one side, and abstract, universal principles, on the other. To the extent that Kant seems to describe our choices as governed only by these stark alternatives, his account of practical reasoning seems especially unconvincing. If the negative thesis that desires are not reasons seems to imply a demand for substantive practical reasoning, we need to give this kind of practical reasoning a firmer grounding in Kant's account.

In fact Kant does take the demands of substantive practical reasoning seriously, and he does build claims about it into his larger account. But few interpreters have given much weight to these claims, since they seem too general or too negative to have much of any force, or to disconnected from the claims of pure practical reason to play a significant role in Kant's practical philosophy. The claims I have in mind are these: first, that every human being has the end

---

[4] *GMS* 4: 417; see the account in Hill (1992: 17–37).

of happiness; and second, that no human being can say with any determinacy what will make any of us happy.

To appreciate the force of these claims, we can start with the point that, for Kant, the idea of happiness is not simply a kind of additive collection of all the desires we happen to have, or of the collective satisfaction of all of those desires. Rather, the idea of happiness is the special construction of a rational being, who can imagine, as animals who satisfy their desires by instinct do not, the idea of a completely contented life (*GMS* 4: 418). That is, our idea of happiness extends out into the indefinite future, beyond the desires of the present moment, and thus eventually toward the question of what we should desire at all. In both the *Groundwork* and especially in the neglected but important little essay "Conjectural Beginning of Human History," Kant describes human happiness as a kind of task, a problem that we are asked to solve through planning and design (*GMS* 4: 418; *MAM* 8: 111–14). The goal of the task is the feeling of satisfaction, but our experiencing the task as a task means that full satisfaction is always receding into the haze of an always imaginary future. If how to be happy is a problem we must solve, then the question of whether we are truly happy is always in danger of intruding upon any particular feeling of enjoyment. This is the sense in which Kant often remarks that animals or simpler, less reflective sorts of human beings seem happier than more cultivated men (*MAM* 8: 114 and 8: 122; *GMS* 4: 422). The more one reflects on what happiness is, the more types of pleasures one tries out, the harder being happy can come to seem. For Kant, the dissatisfaction of having to plan for happiness is not a merely contingent feeling; it is the necessary result of our reflectiveness on our feelings of satisfaction. Substantive practical reasoning is for Kant the application of our rational powers to the satisfaction of our animal desires, and the result is a conflict between the freedom of reflection and the determinacy of any particular desire. Because we can always raise the reflective question of whether any particular sort of life is truly satisfying, the conclusions of substantive practical reasoning are always indeterminate, or as I will prefer to say, provisional: they can never finally be justified. As I understand it, Kant's claim about the indeterminacy of happiness is not simply a contingent observation about human psychology, but a philosophical conclusion about the nature of substantive practical reasoning. Together, our reflective and empirical natures are such that we must have happiness as an end, but will never be able to say what happiness finally is. We must engage in substantive practical reasoning, and yet that reasoning will never reach an end.

Let's summarize the argument so far. The claim that desires are not reasons is for Kant a consequence of our reflective or deliberative nature. The openness or freedom of reflection does not impose any particular conclusion on our practical reasonings, but it does shift the form of that reasoning from quasi-factual appeals to one's own desires toward substantive, Aristotelian claims about the nature of a happy life. And next, the same openness of reflection means that we will never be able to give any sort of final justification to those substantive practical claims.

IV. The CI as Principle of Practical Justification

All of this preparatory work has been necessary if we are to make the transition to Kant's positive claim that the CI serves as a principle of justification for our empirical ends. This claim should seem in one sense quite puzzling, because the formal, universal structure of the CI implies nothing about the content of those ends. So how can those ends be justified by the CI itself? To understand that claim, we first needed to understand the full implications of the negative claim that desires are not reasons. What we learned in our discussion of the negative claim was that Kant has ruled out certain prominent and seemingly quite plausible principles of practical justification for our empirical ends. For instance, given such an empirical end, E, one might well hold:

   1. I am justified in willing E because I desire it.

That claim, we have seen, cannot be justified in reflection. To endorse the desire invoked in 1, one must in fact endorse the substantive claim set out in:

   2. I am justified in willing E because it is part of what is necessary for a happy life.

But that claim, we also saw, cannot finally be justified. Still, I also argued that claims of the form set out in 2 are unavoidable for us. It is not as if we can escape from the task of substantive practical reasoning, to replace the Aristotelian claims of the sort made in 2 with some other kind of practical reasoning. Having ruled out any claims of type 2 as principles of practical justification, Kant tends to raise the skeptical possibility that:

   3. There is no justification for willing E at all.

But since he also thinks we cannot avoid substantive practical claims, it turns out that for us, in practice, possibility 3 really means:

   4. I am justified in willing E because I willed it, because I have judged that it is part of what is necessary for a happy life.

Now 4 really is in one sense equivalent to the skeptical possibility 3, because it ultimately replaces justification with the arbitrary imposition of the agent's will. But in another sense, 4 is more plausible than 3, because it does incorporate the idea of the agent's judgment, which is meant to be at least putatively rational. It is fairly easy to make 4 look respectable by adding some crucial references to rationality:

5. I am justified in willing E because I rationally willed it, because I have rationally judged that it is part of what is rationally necessary for a happy life.

This seems entirely plausible, but its plausibility turns out to trade on an ambiguity in the notion of "rational judgment." Sometimes that phrase refers to the content of the judgment, meaning that it really is based on reasons. But other times the phrase refers only to the source of the judgment in the agent's rationality. This ambiguity is very clear when we say, as we often do, that an agent's reasons for doing something were bad ones, which means that in another sense they were not really reasons at all. 5 turns out to be ambiguous between the quite plausible:

5a. I am justified in willing E because there are in fact reasons to believe that it is part of what is necessary for a happy life.

and the not nearly as plausible:

5b. I am justified in willing E because I believe that there are in fact reasons to believe that it is part of what is necessary for a happy life.

5a turns out to be plausible because it invokes the existence of substantive reasons for the agent's judgment. But 5b refers only to the fact of the agent's judgment, which retains the subjective and hence potentially arbitrary nature present in 4 and 3.

Now compare Kant's own preferred principle of justification:

6. I am justified in willing E because I would will that it become a universal law, because I judge that everyone is free to endorse and act on my judgment that E is part of what is necessary for a happy life.

It should be quite clear that in a crucial sense, 6 is more like the weaker and more subjective 5b than the stronger and more objective 5a. Like 5b, the Kantian principle 6 says nothing about the substantive reasons for choosing E; it refers only to the agent's willing of E as a candidate for a universal law. At the same time, it is important to see that 6 is in another sense stronger than 5b, because it includes the agent's internal but legislative commitment to permit all others to act on the rational judgment that E is worth pursuing. We have seen this point before, because we have already noted that an agent's own judgment that an end is worth pursuing does not yet imply the further judgment that others ought to achieve, or even be able to achieve, that end. Even if we act on reasons, this does not itself imply that we see those reasons as candidates for universal laws, so that we would reject the reasons if not everyone could act on them. Putting these points together, we can specify the distinctive feature of a Kantian account of practical reason in a fairly precise way: we are asked to take an agent's private commitment to a principle as a candidate for public legislation as a substitute for the substantive reasons that would justify the principle on its own terms. This does not mean that we must endorse the principle or adopt it for ourselves, but it does mean that we should see the agent as having a real justification for the principle that goes beyond her own private judgment that it is good.

V. A Practical Proxy for Fully Rational Justification

Then the obvious question is: why? Why should we accept the universalizability of a maxim, its availability as a piece of public legislation, as a kind of proxy for the agent's having substantive reasons for adopting that maxim? Why should we regard such an agent who acts on a universalizable maxim as justified, particularly if we are not convinced that we should adopt that maxim for ourselves? If this is the distinctive claim of a Kantian theory of practical reasoning, then the substance of such a theory should do the work of explaining why the claim makes sense.

One suggestion that might seem plausible here is that an agent's commitment to public legislation, to universalizability, serves as some sort of *evidence of the existence* of the substantive reasons that would justify the agent's commitment to his or her maxim. That evidence could not be evidence of the *nature* of the substantive reasons, since the formal property of universalizability says nothing about the particularities of those reasons. But perhaps we might say that the agent's dutiful commitment to the CI suggests that he or she is the sort of reflective, deliberative agent who would not act without good reasons. We may not be able to see the details of those reasons, but we can perhaps argue from the rationality of the CI to the rationality of the agent, which would then suggest (though not affirm) the rationality of the agent's substantive reasons. This line of thinking becomes more plausible when coupled with Kant's views about the indeterminacy of happiness, according to which our substantive practical reasonings can be only provisional. That means that our rejection of other people's different conclusions about how to live can be only provisional too; there is equally no way to say that we have found the right, or the wrong, account of human happiness. When faced with a different claim about how to live, then, I cannot simply point to my own substantive views in response; I have to take seriously the possibility that my own views might be wrong, and that the other person's views might be right. And to grant that is in fact granting some substantive plausibility, even if only presumptive, to the other agent's reasons, by virtue of the mere fact of the agent's rationality.

Something about this connection between substantive practical skepticism, or pluralism, and the plausibility of the CI seems exactly right to me. But before we can make full sense of this connection, we need to see that there is nonetheless something quite implausible about the model of evidence that is invoked in the line of argument I have just sketched. On this line of argument, we should take an agent's reflective commitment to the CI as proof of a broader rational capacity, which in turn suggests the existence of potentially good substantive reasons for his or her maxim. But in fact the distinctive feature of commitment to the CI is not the fact of the dutiful agent's rational capacity; that could be directed to any number of principles that the agent hopes rationally to affirm. The distinctive feature of commitment to the CI is the affirmation of the fact of *all other agents'* rational capacities, such that the thwarting of their ability to adopt the agent's preferred maxim counts as a reason against the adoption of the maxim, substantive reasons notwithstanding. A dutiful agent is not just one who exercises a capacity for substantive practical reasoning; he or she is one who values that capacity equally in all agents. So if we are inferring something about the plausibility of the agent's substantive reasons from a commitment to the CI, we need to base that inference not on the agent's use of his or her own rationality, but on his or her commitment to the equal rationality of all agents.

How might that kind of inference work? The key point here is what the CI affirms is a kind of *reciprocity*: my granting justification to another agent's (potentially different) substantive reasons is part of a normative framework that includes his or her recognition of my capacity for practical reasoning, which entails his or her granting justification to my (potentially different) substantive reasons, again accompanied by my recognition of his or her rationality as well.[5] So when another agent acts on the CI, I do not simply infer the existence of his or her substantive reasons. Rather, I note his or her commitment to a scheme of reciprocity in which we all accord respect to the substantive practical choices of others. In the same way that the other (normatively committed) agent has affirmed a commitment to respect my substantive reasonings, I in turn regard his or her substantive reasons as at least presumptively plausible, even if I do not affirm (or even fully understand) them myself. That is what understanding the CI as a principle of practical justification means.

Now, this revised line of argument depends essentially on the thought that it is crucial for me that others, who might not agree with me, nonetheless regard my substantive practical reasonings as worthy of respect, as at least potentially plausible. If this reciprocal understanding is not of crucial value to me, then the line of argument falls apart; there is no reason to employ the CI as a principle of practical justification. In that case, I would simply base my practical reasoning on the substantive values that appealed to me. When other agents appealed to other values, I would be inclined to say just that they were wrong. They would be equally inclined to say that I was wrong, but I would not be

---

[5] As Korsgaard (1996a: 100–101) has pointed out, this is the reason Kant has such trouble with cases in which someone has already acted wrongly, like the notorious murderer at the door; his whole framework of justification presumes a reciprocity that the wrongdoer has already destroyed.

deterred by this, because by hypothesis, I do not need their acknowledgment; all that matters is the substantive considerations that are in question. Nothing in this opposing picture conflicts with the thought that my substantive practical claims might turn out to be wrong, and the different claims of others to be right. I might well have good reasons to take those different claims very seriously. But in such a case, the justification for my or anyone else's claims would depend only on the truth of substantive principles, not on anything any agent affirmed or did. Nothing in this opposing picture is in any way incoherent, and in this sense, the CI really is not rationally required. Adopting the CI as a principle of practical justification means using it as practical surrogate for a fully justifying principle of practical reason.[6] The CI is a practical surrogate because it neither is nor depends on some sort of true principle. Its value depends on an agent's commitment to the idea of public legislation, and our commitment to the value of public legislation depends on our commitment to the idea that we want others to grant legitimacy to our potentially different conceptions of substantive practical reasoning.

VI. Options for Realism

These last remarks should sound quite antirealist, and so it is now time for me to explain just what is wrong with a realist account of Kantian practical justification. The distinctive thesis of the realist Kantians is that the unconditional value of our rational nature is a basic normative fact, and that the value of anything else follows from this fact. An important advantage of this approach is that because it assumes the existence of a normative fact, there is no problem about how to argue from a particular agent's own rational commitments to the legislative commitment to universalizable principles. Indeed realist Kantians have criticized constructivists, especially Korsgaard, for even trying to provide an argument of this kind, for trying to derive the value of other agents from the value of one's own agency. Such a derivation, the realists have claimed, is fundamentally at odds with the claims of morality, for which every rational agent has an equal and unconditional value. If this value is just a basic normative fact, then it should be clear that any justified principle must be capable of being a universal law. On this kind of view, the goodness of my adoption of E as an empirical end must derive from the fact that my choice of E was a product of my rational nature. And if rational nature is unconditionally good, then it is good in all of its instances, which means that my

---

[6] This is why I have argued that the CI should itself be understood as a constructed principle, and that Kant's derivations of the CI should be read not as the search for the unique principle of pure practical reason, but for the unique practical expression of the idea that there ought to be a principle of pure practical reason. See Krasnoff (1999: 402–3).

adoption of E cannot be good if it prevents any other agent from employing their rational agency to adopt E as an end. The goodness of my choice of E, if it is to derive from the value of the rational nature which chose it, cannot be in conflict with rational nature anywhere. Otherwise the justification of my choice of E would be self-undermining. If we assume the unconditional value of rational nature in general, it certainly follows that we must respect the rational natures of every agent.

The difficulty for realism comes in the explanation of the prior claim that rational nature has unconditional value.[7] Of course realists will hesitate to provide explanations for what they take to be basic normative facts. But still the realist must be clear about what it is that is of basic normative value, and the claim that rational nature has unconditional value is not yet clear about the feature of our rational nature that entitles it to its special status. When we respect rational nature, what is it that we are respecting? Kant himself seems to suggest two different answers, corresponding to the negative and positive senses of freedom. The first is, once again, just our reflective or deliberative capacity, the negative freedom from instinct that allows us to evaluate our desires as potential reasons. The second is our positive capacity for legislation, which Kant understands as our capacity to propose and then to act on universal laws. The problem is that neither of these candidates can really do the job that the realist Kantian needs it to do.

Let's take the second proposal, that what makes our rational capacity worthy of respect is that we have the capacity for acting on universal laws, that is, on moral principles. If this were the realist claim, then Kantian realism starts to look empty or dogmatic, because the argument we sketched above would be entirely circular. We could not derive the requirement of universalizability from the unconditional normative value of our humanity, because the value of our humanity would consist in our fidelity to universal laws. This looks like an argument that universal laws are good in themselves, not an argument that our rational natures are good in themselves. In the *Groundwork*, when Kant suggests that autonomy is the ground of the categorical imperative, he seems to be telling us that the normative force of the principle of universal law comes from our rationally willing principles for ourselves. The force of Kantian morality, it seems, derives crucially from our freedom as self-legislators. But if what is of

---

[7] This is an explanation that Hills (2008) does not even attempt to provide. To the extent that her "Kantian value realism" is supposed to be justified, it is because this value realism turns out to cohere with our existing moral intuitions (see especially 108–110). But this ignores a main task of Kant's practical philosophy, which is to provide a rational response to the thought that our existing moral intuitions might turn out to be chimerical, a kind of "phantom of the brain" (*GMS* 4: 445). It is as if Hills thinks that there need only be two chapters in *GMS*, not three. This same gap can be found in Stern (2012), which also treats moral obligation as a kind of intuitively valid fact, ignoring the question of how moral obligations are to be rationally justified (as opposed to simply explained).

basic normative value is the moral will, then the situation is reversed: freedom or autonomy are really good only insofar as they allow us to will according to moral or universal laws.

In contemporary debates, the most consistent and uncompromising defender of this position has been Karl Ameriks (2000 and 2003; see also Kain 2004 and 2006). The goal of Ameriks's work is not just to stake out a realist interpretation of Kant's practical philosophy, but to discredit a whole subsequent tradition of post-Kantian Continental philosophers who took themselves, even as they disagreed with Kant, to be completing the project that he began: to criticize metaphysics in the name of human freedom. For Ameriks, this post-Kantian tradition—which runs from Fichte, through Kierkegaard and Nietzsche, all the way to more contemporary philosophers like Richard Rorty and Robert Pippin—is based on an early but persistent German idealist misreading of Kant, whose own commitments were far more traditional and metaphysical than the post-Kantians (or contemporary Kantian constructivists) would allow (Ameriks 2000: 1–33). Though I will not be able to engage with the range of Ameriks's readings here, I can say something about, and against, his realist claim that what has basic value is not our willing or our autonomy, but our willing according to moral laws.

This kind of view must begin with Kant's claim that we have an inherent consciousness of the moral law, a sense that we are required to conform to unconditional duties. But for these commands to be valid for us, they have to be commands of reason, which means that a realist like Ameriks must show that the moral principle with which he and Kant take us to be familiar is rational in an independent sense. By an independent sense, I mean that no appeals are possible here to any claim that the moral principle is "our own" in the sense that it stems from the nature of our wills. This is the kind of view that Ameriks is ruling out: he argues instead that our wills are truly "our own" only insofar as they are truly conform to rational standards (Ameriks 2003: 193–211 and 263–82). The problem now is that, as I have argued elsewhere and as is implied in the account of the CI that I have sketched above, the principle of universal law cannot be shown to be a fully rational principle, because it expresses only a formal, necessary condition that fully rational principles must meet: that they could be willed by every rational agent (Krasnoff 1999: 402–3; see also Krasnoff 1998: 276–83). There is a gap between what Kant sometimes calls a practical law, a principle valid for every rational agent, and a universalizable maxim, which is really only a candidate for a practical law. If the principle of universal law is valid, we should take someone who acts on a candidate for a practical law, or more precisely, on the consciousness that he or she is acting on a candidate for a practical law, to already be acting on a practical law, and indeed to be acting on the only valid practical law. But it is hard to see why this should be so. Such an agent seems committed to the idea that there *should be* practical laws or fully rational principles, but this is very different from the claim that

Ameriks's realism needs, which is that the agent has grasped the truth of a fully rational principle, and is committed to following it. An agent committed to following any truly rational principles is not yet committed to acting on candidates for rational principles until a fully rational principle comes along, much less to taking this further commitment itself to be conformity to the truly rational principle.[8] Simply to take Kant's moral principle, without assuming any further practical commitments, as fully rational, would amount to a kind of dogmatism.[9]

If this is the consequence of locating the source of value in the moral will, we seem driven back to the first candidate for the value of our rational nature, to the view that what is of unconditional value is our reflective or deliberative capacity. The problem with this answer, though, is that it is basically a return to one or both of the problematic claims 4 and 5b above. It locates the source of value in the subjective fact of the agent's choice, not in anything more objective or substantive that would justify that choice. Once again, if we do take an agent's choices to be of independent value, the requirement of universalizability does follow, because the value of my own choices is no different from the value of everyone else's, so that I must respect the freedom of all other agents to will as I seek to do. But it is still not yet clear why our choices have unconditional value. Again, a stubborn realist could simply point to the existence of a normative fact. But it looks like this alleged normative fact makes little normative sense, because it is not clear why anyone should regard anyone's choices as justified simply because they were chosen. It may be that from the first-person perspective, I regard my own choices as justified, simply because I arrived at them through my own deliberations. But it is hard to see why I should find similar justification in the product of anyone else's deliberations, which fall outside of this first-person perspective. A realist who locates basic normative value in our reflective or deliberative capacity seems to need exactly the argument that contemporary Kantian realists have criticized Korsgaard for trying to make, the attempt to derive the value of others' agency from the value of our own.[10]

---

[8] What is wrong, in general, with Ameriks's work is just this: he takes it as a premise that Kant thinks that we are able to grasp fully rational or metaphysical principles, when in fact Kant's view is that we think that there ought to be rational or metaphysical principles, and so we are always imposing them onto the foreign territory of experience. Traditional metaphysics is about grasping the nature of reality, but what Kant is interested in is the critique of metaphysics, which is about understanding the metaphysical urge as something about ourselves, and thus understanding ourselves as rational agents who demand things of the world and of each other. That's why Kant really is closer to Nietzsche than he is to Leibniz.

[9] For a different version of this criticism that Ameriks's realism would amount to a kind of dogmatism, see Bagnoli (2009).

[10] It is not only realists who have criticized Korsgaard on this account; see also Darwall (2006).

VII. The Failure of Realism

In fact I think it is wrong to read Korsgaard as attempting such a derivation, and it is worth turning explicitly to her argument here, because it helps to clarify what the realist account needs to explain. Despite what many readers have suggested, Korsgaard does not try to argue that one can derive the moral requirement to respect the agency of others from the bare fact of our own rational agency. She does not argue that one cannot rationally will anything without also willing the formula of universal law. These kinds of readings give no real weight to her appeal to the notion of identity, or to the Wittgensteinian claims about our social and linguistic natures that occupy the last part of *The Sources of Normativity*. What Korsgaard wants to argue is that there is no real gap between valuing our own agency and valuing the agency of others, because our valuing any identity means understanding ourselves as just one member of a larger community of others like ourselves, a community in which all of the members understand themselves as obligated by each other and by the ideals that the particular identity implies. Korsgaard's starting point for the derivation of Kantian moral values is not the thin notion of an agent who chooses or judges rationally, but the thicker notion of an agent who values his or her identity as an agent who chooses.[11] It is only from this thicker perspective that we can understand the appeal to Kantian moral obligation, or indeed, Korsgaard suggests, to any kind of obligation at all. By appealing to the notion of a basic normative fact, the realist is trying to eliminate the gap between first-person perspective of one's own deliberations and the moral perspective of conformity to universal law. Rational agency, the realist is saying, is worthy of respect in all of its instantiations. But that claim, Korsgaard is right in saying, makes sense only if rational agency is conceived of as a kind of shared identity, a valuable feature that links us in community with others. And it is that kind of understanding that the realist appeal to the value of our rational agency needs to explain. For that, the bare fact of our reflective nature, the first-person perspective of our own deliberations, is not enough. There must be some shared, valuable feature of our agency that is worthy of our respect.

For Kant's arguments for the value of humanity to make sense, the value of our rational agency must be located not in our fidelity to universal laws (which would amount to a dogmatic assertion of Kantian morality), nor in the bare fact of our reflective nature (a first-personal fact which would then require a dubious argumentative transition to valuing the reflections of others). There

---

[11] I am convinced this is so in Korsgaard (1996b); I am less clear whether it remains true in Korsgaard (2008 and 2009). In these later texts Korsgaard sometimes does seem to want to proceed from an analysis of rational agency, taken generally. Still, I do not see that her "constitutive" arguments about agency amount to any retraction of the distinctive thesis from *The Sources of Normativity* under discussion here: that obligations are grounded in practical identities.

must be some third option here, some feature of our rational agency that makes it immediately valuable in ourselves and others. This feature must be located in the space between the fact of reflectiveness and the principle of universal law that we are trying to justify. And what is located in this space, our earlier discussion has already suggested, is the activity of substantive practical reasoning. That is, the only remaining option for explaining the value of our rational agency is to suggest that it helps to improve our lives, by allowing us to reason about what is truly good. On this kind of view, our rational agency is valuable insofar as it is good at grasping what is good to do. What we are really respecting in respecting the agency of others is respecting their substantive reasonings about how they should live.

The problem with this answer, as we have also already seen, is that it cannot justify an unconditional respect for our rationality, because Kant holds that the conclusions of substantive practical reasoning can be no more than provisional. Any rational judgment about how it is best to live is potentially subject to criticism and revision, which means the most we can ever say about anyone's practical judgment, our own or that of others, is that it is an attempt to grasp the truth about how to live. To the extent that a person's willing is a sign of his or her power to reason about what is truly good, that willing is worthy of respect, but not of the unconditional respect that Kant's moral philosophy seems to demand. We cannot yet say that they are justified in willing what they do, just because that willing conforms to universal law. What somehow happens, if Kant's principle of universal law is right, is that the provisional respect we can allow a person's judgments about how to live somehow gets converted into unconditional respect. But there is no way to explain away this conversion by pointing to some feature of our rationality that has unconditional value, in itself. That is what realism is ultimately trying to do, by making the unconditional goodness of our rationality into a basic normative fact. But there is no such fact, because the fact is that our rationality is really only provisionally good. If we are to regard our rationality as good in itself, that goodness has to be constructed.

On the account I sketched in section V above, we construct our unconditional respect for the rationality of all human beings out of our desire for others, who may draw very different substantive practical conclusions, to accord legitimacy to our own practical conclusions. The threat to our own agency from what Rawls has called the fact of reasonable pluralism, and that also follows from Kant's account of the indeterminacy of happiness, is that others may impose their own conclusions on me without providing what I would take to be a rational justification. Under these conditions, it makes sense for me to accord unconditional respect to the choices of others, in a normative framework in which my and others' choices are accorded the same respect. This respect means allowing a commitment to the universalizability of practical principles, to their suitability for public legislation, as a proxy for the substantive reasons that would justify those principles.

Is this the sort of constructivist derivation that the realists criticized in Korsgaard, one that ignores the independent force of morality by seeking to derive a commitment to the objective value of all agents' rationality from the subjective value of our own?[12] To answer this question and this criticism, let's return to our discussion of Korsgaard's argument.

VIII. Options for Constructivism

I have said that Korsgaard wants to derive our moral obligations not from the bare notion of a reflective agent, but from the thicker notion of an agent who values his or her identity as a reflective agent. And the thicker notion of identity already includes an essential reference to all others who share the identity. The question, then, is why we must value this reflective identity, and it is here that Korsgaard's argument is most clearly constructivist. Rather than pointing to the value of this identity as a kind of normative fact, she derives or constructs its value from the other, more substantive identities that we might happen to value. We cannot value these, she argues, without coming to value our reflectiveness as the supreme value. Why is this so? Korsgaard's answer is that reflective endorsement is a necessary condition for having and valuing any substantive identity. To regard any identity as valuable, to be truly committed to it, we must not simply conform to certain standards of conduct that are associated with the identity, but affirm the identity and the standards of conduct as truly worth following.

Earlier, I suggested that the fact that reflective endorsement was necessary for affirming a desire as a reason did not determine anything positive about what we need to affirm as a reason. Korsgaard's argument seems to conflict with this claim, but it is important to understand, once again, that she is appealing to something more than the bare notion of reflective endorsement here. On her view, reflective endorsement is something more than what we must do if we are to affirm an identity as our own; it is a part of the valuing of the identity itself. That is, Korsgaard thinks that when you value an identity, you value it as your own, so that choosing it for yourself is part of what makes it so important or good. This is so even if the identity is one that you are "born" or socialized into; your valuing of the identity really begins when you have consciously affirmed it as worth following.

The problem with Korsgaard's argument is not in her claim that we must value our reflectiveness, but in the further, moral claim that we must value our reflectiveness more deeply than any other valuable features of any of our

---

[12] Though Bagnoli's version of constructivism (2009) claims to avoid not just realism but also the weaknesses of anti-realism, it may be that the "subjective" nature of her interpretation makes her more, not less, vulnerable to this sort of realist criticism.

identities, such that those other values must yield when they conflict with reflectiveness in ourselves and in others. Ultimately, Korsgaard must say more than that reflection is something we must do to value an identity, and more even than that reflection is something we must value in valuing an identity. In the end, her claim must be that our reflectiveness is itself a kind of independent identity, an identity that has a kind of priority over all our other identities.

To see the differences between these claims, suppose that you value playing tennis. It's clear that a certain level of health and physical vigor is necessary for participation in the sport. But it also seems right to say that if you enjoy playing tennis, part of what you enjoy is the activity of vigorous exercise. The first of those claims is analogous to the weaker claim about reflection that we discussed earlier: reflection is necessary for having an identity, in the sense that cardiovascular function is necessary for playing tennis. Korsgaard's view about reflection is really analogous to the second claim: reflection is a necessary part of the value of an identity, in the sense that enjoying cardiovascular exercise is part of enjoying tennis. The problem is that her conclusion needs to be the even stronger claim that reflection is itself an independent identity that we value above all others, in the sense that my enjoying tennis would reveal that what I really enjoy, above all else, is getting cardiovascular exercise.[13] But that isn't right: it's certainly possible to think that cardiovascular exercise, in itself, is boring, unless it's part of a larger and more interesting activity.

The point here is that being a necessary condition of valuing something and even being a necessary part of what is valued are not enough for having an independent value. I take Korsgaard to have shown, correctly, that you cannot regard any substantive practical claims as justified unless you also value the reflective capacity that allows you to carry out the task of justification. But it does not follow that you must value your reflectiveness as an independent entity, as something that has substantive value in itself.

Korsgaard wants to coopt the communitarian critique of Kantian liberalism by arguing that reflectiveness is just as substantive an identity as the more situated conceptions of human beings favored by the communitarians themselves, and then by going on to argue that reflectiveness is the supreme form of identity, because it is a necessary part of the value of any identity at all. The problem is that the second part of the project seems to undermine the

---

[13] Interestingly, Hills (2008: 194) uses this very analogy to illustrate her claim that on a realist Kantian view, the value of desire-based actions is that they are exercises or expressions of our rational natures. (The present chapter was first drafted and read at a conference in 2007.) But Hills's account assumes, in contrast to the view offered here, that a Kantian gives no real weight to substantive practical reasons; that is, in arguing for the (dubious) conclusion that our empirical ends are valuable simply as expressions of rational nature, her treatment of the analogy makes exactly the kind of claim I am saying is implausible here: that what is really of value in playing tennis is simply the exercise.

first. By arguing that reflectiveness is a part of any substantive identity, she deprives it of the status as an independent identity that could compete with the communitarian's favored sorts of identity. As I have already noted, many readers of Korsgaard have simply ignored the first part of her argument, and then gone on to criticize the second for not making the connection from valuing our own agency to valuing the agency of others. It is the first part of the argument, the claims about identity, that are supposed to guarantee that connection, but those claims seem hard to sustain when the identity in question, our reflectiveness, is no longer a shared or reciprocal value but a necessary feature of individual valuing. In this sense, the realist Kantians (and Darwall 2006) are right to criticize Korsgaard, or at least the part of her argument that they focus on, for trying to derive the value of others' agency from the value of our own.

It is important to see, however, that it is not the constructivist nature of Korsgaard's argument that undermines the reciprocity of Kantian respect for the rationality of all agents. A constructed identity is still an identity that can be fully shared, so long as the construction does not reduce that identity to the activity of a single agent. The construction of the CI I have defended here meets this standard, because it makes an essential reference to others: what motivates our valuing of rational agency, in itself, is the desire to have others respect our own substantive practical conclusions. In this sense, I prefer O'Neill's version of constructivism (1989; 1996), which emphasizes the search for shared and public norms of reason, to Korsgaard's, which emphasizes the individual act of valuing. But O'Neill says rather little about why the shareability or publicity of reasons should be taken to be their most central feature. As I see things, without telling a story about the irreducible plurality of more substantive conceptions of reason, the appeal of a merely formal or public standard of reason remains obscure.[14] But if one is impressed with such a story, then one can go on to affirm our shared, constructed identity as substantive reasoners, whose conclusions ought to be accorded respect.

IX. Conclusion: Justifying Desire-based Principles

I have argued that the distinctive feature of the CI, and thus of a Kantian conception of practical justification, is that it serves as a kind of proxy for the substantive reasons that might justify desire-based principles. The CI does not justify those principles directly, by providing those substantive reasons. But nor does it simply ignore those reasons by suggesting that what is truly of value is an agent's choice, or an agent's willing according to moral or

---

[14] See Krasnoff (1998 and 2010). For the specific point about O'Neill, see Krasnoff (2010: 678).

universal laws. It makes little sense to argue that we should value something merely because someone has chosen it, without any reference to how or why that person chose it.[15] Kant's view, of course, is that we should regard as justified not whatever an agent has chosen, but only what the agent has chosen according to universal law. As for the view that what is truly of value is our willing according to universal law, the view that has been defended by strongly realist Kantians like Ameriks, this view could make more sense, if we could understand why the CI made moral or rational sense without any independent appeal to the value of our substantive practical conclusions, to the value of our desire-based principles. But the CI does not follow from the bare idea of an unconditional duty or a purely rational principle: the principles it justifies are candidates for principles of duty or fully rational principles, not principles of duty or reason in themselves. As for why we should regard the CI itself as the fully moral or rational principle, why we should treat individual agents' candidates for fully rational principles as fully justified, realism has nothing to say, and in this sense its defense of Kantian morality is entirely dogmatic.

What needs to be explained is why we would want to say that someone's desire-based principles were rationally justified, and particularly when we would not endorse them ourselves. The right answer here seems not that they were simply chosen or that the person is simply moral, but because we presume that they were chosen on the basis of substantive practical reasons that could justify them. And why should we presume that? My answer has been that since there is no final end to the activity of substantive practical reasoning, since we must regard all substantive practical conclusions as merely provisional, we have reason to respect others' potentially very different reasons, insofar as they are equally committed to respecting ours.

Is this kind of construction of the CI consistent with the objectivity of the moral law? Clearly I mean to maintain the view that the CI is the supreme principle of practical justification. As for whether the principle is independent of our willing, though I have argued that we create the principle of universal law, and in a sense, even our independent identity as rational agents, I believe that there is still a sense in which my constructivist view retains an appeal to an independent moral law. As I have described it, we accord respect to the substantive conclusions of others because we see the threat, under conditions of pluralism, of others' imposing their different conclusions on us. That sort of coercion, not just in Kant but in the whole liberal tradition, is the central moral wrong; generalized, that wrong becomes a world of unlimited, unjustified coercion, a state of war. Call this the moral law, then, as Kant puts it at the close of the *Rechtslehre*: what moral/practical reason finally says is that there shall be

---

[15] This is a familiar criticism of the idea of autonomy; for a reply, see Krasnoff (2010).

no war (*RL* 6: 354).[16] That much is independent of our willing: that there be a lawful settlement that puts an end to war, by providing a standard that could justify the substantive principles that we have no choice but to adopt, and that otherwise could not be fully justified.

A standard criticism of Kantian ethics is that it gives no real weight to our desires and inclinations, and ultimately to the things that agents truly care about. The realist account makes this criticism worse, by detaching the moral law from the rest of our willing. On a view like Ameriks's, the value of a desire-based principle depends entirely on its being an occasion for acting out of duty, and acting out of duty consists entirely in fidelity to abstract, rational principles. It makes far more sense to locate the Kantian shift to abstract, rational principles in a practical response to a practical problem that confronts our wills—where that means our wills as finite rational agents. That we will the solution to this problem does not make that solution arbitrary. The fact of pluralism and the threat of war are not subjective or constructed facts. That we need a practical way to understand our empirical willing as justified in response to these facts, and that Kant's ethics is that practical response, does not mean that there is no such thing as an independent morality. Rather it helps to explain how that morality speaks to us, how we can come to understand our desire-based principles as not subjective and arbitrary, but rationally justified.[17]

Bibliography

Allison, H. E. (1990) *Kant's Theory of Freedom*. Cambridge: Cambridge University Press.
Ameriks, K. (2000) *Kant and the Fate of Autonomy: Problems in the Appropriation of the Critical Philosophy*. Cambridge: Cambridge University Press.
Ameriks, K. (2003) *Interpreting Kant's Critiques*. Oxford: Oxford University Press.

---

[16] It might be objected that this formulation makes my version of Kant's CI into a hypothetical and not a categorical imperative: if you want to avoid war, you should affirm the formula of universal law. But this objection ignores the essential connection between Kant's understanding of war and his understanding of reason itself. What is to be avoided in war here is not the dangers of injury and death, as terrifying as those are. What is to be avoided to is the rejection of practical justification that the violence of war implies: the thought that one can do anything to another person without offering any sort of justification. As the main argument of the *Rechtslehre* makes clear, even if my intentions are entirely nonviolent, I cannot know that my actions (which always make use of objects and of space on the earth) have not wronged another person without some shared scheme of justification under which my actions (and hence my use of the objects and the space) can be understood as rightful. (See the very clear account in Ripstein 2009.) To avoid war is to have some sort of scheme of public justifcation that we can understand as rational; to fall into war is to lack that scheme entirely. The command to avoid war is thus not hypothetical but categorical: it concerns the possibility of practical reason itself.

[17] I am grateful to Sorin Baiasu and all the other participants at the University of Manchester conference where the original version of this chapter was first presented, for their feedback on the paper, and in particular to Robert Stern for sharing his work on Korsgaard with me, and to Howard Williams, who commented on the paper at the conference.

Bagnoli, C. (2009) "Practical Necessity: The Subjective Experience," in B. Centi and W. Huemer (eds.), *Value and Ontology: Problems and Perspectives*, 23–43. Frankfurt: Ontos-Verlag.

Breazeale, D. (2003) "Two Cheers for post-Kantianism: A Response to Karl Ameriks," *Inquiry* 46(2): 239–59.

Darwall, S. (2006) *The Second-Person Standpoint: Morality, Respect, and Accountability*. Cambridge, MA: Harvard University Press.

Fitzpatrick, W. (2005) "The Practical Turn in Ethical Theory," *Ethics* 115(4): 651–91.

Ginsborg, H. (1998) "Korsgaard on Choosing Nonmoral Ends," *Ethics* 109(1): 5–21.

Guyer, P. (1998) "The Value of Reason and the Value of Freedom," *Ethics* 109(1): 22–35.

Hill, T. E., Jr. (1992) *Dignity and Practical Reason in Kant's Moral Theory*. Ithaca, NY: Cornell University Press.

Hills, A. (2008) "Kantian Value Realism," *Ratio* 21(2): 182–200.

Kain, P. (2004) "Self-legislation in Kant's Moral Philosophy," *Archiv für Geschichte der Philosophie* 86(3): 257–306.

Kain, P. (2006) "Realism and Anti-realism in Kant's Second *Critique*," *Philosophy Compass* 1(5): 449–65.

Kant, I. (1998) *Groundwork of the Metaphysics of Morals*. Tr. M. J. Gregor. Cambridge: Cambridge University Press.

Kant, I. (1963). "Conjectural Beginning of Human History," in L. W. Beck (ed.), *On History*, 53–68. Tr. E. L. Fackenheim. New York: Macmillan.

Korsgaard, C. M. (1996a) *Creating the Kingdom of Ends*. Cambridge: Cambridge University Press.

Korsgaard, C. M. (1996b) *The Sources of Normativity*. Cambridge: Cambridge University Press.

Korsgaard, C. M. (1998) "Motivation, Metaphysics, and the Value of the Self: A Reply to Ginsborg, Guyer, and Schneewind," *Ethics* 109(1): 49–66.

Korsgaard, C. M. (2008) *The Constitution of Agency*. Oxford: Oxford University Press.

Korsgaard, C. M. (2009) *Self-Constitution: Agency, Identity, and Integrity*. Oxford: Oxford University Press.

Krasnoff, L. (1998) "Consensus, Stability, and Normativity in Rawls' Political Liberalism," *Journal of Philosophy* 95(6): 269–92.

Krasnoff, L. (1999) "How Kantian is Constructivism?" *Kant-Studien* 90(4): 385–409.

Krasnoff, L. (2010) "Autonomy and Plurality," *Philosophical Quarterly* 60(241): 673–91.

O'Neill, O. (1989) *Constructions of Reason: Explorations of Kant's Practical Philosophy*. Cambridge: Cambridge University Press.

O'Neill, O. (1996) *Towards Justice and Virtue: A Constructive Account of Practical Reasoning*. Cambridge: Cambridge University Press.

Ripstein, A. (2009) *Force and Freedom: Kant's Legal and Political Philosophy*. Cambridge: Harvard University Press.

Stern, R. (2012) *Understanding Moral Obligation: Kant, Hegel, Kierkegaard*. Cambridge: Cambridge University Press.

Watkins, E., and FitzPatrick, W. (2002) "O'Neill and Korsgaard on the Construction of Normativity," *Journal of Value Inquiry* 36(2–3): 349–67.

Wood, A. W. (1999) *Kant's Ethical Thought*. Cambridge: Cambridge University Press.

Wood, A. W. (2008) *Kantian Ethics*. Cambridge: Cambridge University Press.

5

Anthropology and Metaphysics in Kant's Categorical Imperative of Law

AN INTERPRETATION OF *RECHTSLEHRE*, §§ B AND C[1]

Otfried Höffe

According to orthodox Kant interpretations, the two concepts in the title, Metaphysics and Anthropology, are mutually exclusive. In the Preface to the *Groundwork* Kant strictly distinguishes between a pure philosophy and an empirical philosophy. He calls the empirical part of ethics a "practical anthropology" (*GMS* 4: 388, 13) and for short "anthropology" (4: 389, 9); the pure part, however, he calls "metaphysics of morals," or "moral wisdom" (4: 389, 9) or "pure moral philosophy" (4: 389, 8). There, because of this strict methodological distinction he intends "to work out for once a pure moral philosophy, completely cleansed of everything that may be only empirical and that belongs to anthropology" (4: 389, 8f.). The second section of the *Groundwork*, the "Transition to Metaphysics of Morals," restates this intention and underlines its theoretical and practical significance, namely the undertaking of "a completely isolated metaphysics of morals, mixed with no anthropology" (4: 410, 19ff.).

My heterodox, perhaps even heretical thesis, which is the main idea behind the following considerations, is that Kant overstretches himself here; the opposition between metaphysics and anthropology is either exaggerated or misrepresented. Why? Because Kant's moral philosophy cannot make it without anthropological elements. Kant wants to exclude all empirical factors, but both the "nature of the human being" and "the circumstances of the world" have roles to play (*GMS* 4: 389, 17).

Now, these elements could indeed be impurities that a truly, and not simply supposedly, pure moral philosophy could filter out. In fact, however—and this is my main thesis—these elements are indispensable. This does not imply

---

[1] I want to thank the participants attending the Kant on Justification conference (Manchester, September 20–21, 2007) for their comments and especially my discussant, Peter Niesen.

though that Kant's moral philosophy now belongs to anthropology instead of metaphysics. Indeed, my supplementary thesis is that this does not compromise Kant's concern, which motivates and justifies his talk of metaphysics: in the case of moral laws, the ground of obligation is still to be found "a priori simply in concepts of pure reason" (*GMS* 4: 389, 18f.).

According to the Preface of the *Groundwork*, Kant intends to strictly oppose every empirical ethics. According to my supplementary thesis Kant does live up to this design, though not in some of his overstated formulations. The reason is provided by my supplementary thesis: in this decisive respect, that is, because of the distinctiveness of his object, Kant formulates a resolutely antiempirical ethics. It is however the nature of morals that is primarily antiempirical, and only secondarily and subsidiarily the relevant philosophical discipline. In the first instance, his main thesis quoted above only has an "ontological" meaning, one that pertains to its object, not a disciplinary one. And the metaphysics which is responsible for it is not a theoretical but a purely practical metaphysics—so my second supplementary thesis.

My heterodox thesis does not therefore revise the core of Kantian moral philosophy, but rather specifies its methodological status. It is only the ground of obligation in Kant's moral philosophy that is actually free of all empiricism and of all (practical) anthropology. Whereas pragmatic imperatives have a motive that is, in the end, empirical—for instance, one's (own) happiness—moral or categorical imperatives are free of such motives and for precisely that reason have an a priori and also a metaphysical character.

Because it is not Kant's moral theory, but rather morals themselves, that are metaphysical, there is no methodological reason not to include empirical and thus anthropological elements in the moral theory. The connection I make in my title between metaphysics and anthropology is possible, in a certain sense necessary, which is why—and this is my "complexity theory"—Kant's ethics is methodologically more complex than it would appear from the Preface. This then assumes that the anthropology does not contaminate the core, the ground of obligation.

One more comment should be made concerning the concept of an anthropology: One could suppose that Kant balks at using the term because he is not concerned with the specifics of a given biological species but rather with features that could apply to other species. Indeed, the characteristic, even essential elements of Kant's ethics do not only apply to the biological species *homo sapiens*. But that is not what Kant is concerned with in the quoted passage of the Preface. The object of the field Anthropology, an "earthly being endowed with reason" (*Anth* 7: 119), is admittedly restricted to our species through the reference to the earth. Yet, if we were to use a slightly more formal description, and instead of "earthly being" say "a being living on a planet," then we would see what Kant is actually getting at: impure beings endowed with reason of which we so far only know one kind: our own species.

In order to indicate what place anthropology has in Kant's philosophy of law, I sketch in a first section the complexity thesis with respect to the *Groundwork*. In the second section I examine the first *Critique*'s thesis that there can be a transcendental philosophy only for theoretical but not for practical reason. In the third section I distinguish three levels of anthropology that are indispensable for Kant's ethics. The fourth section discusses the *Rechtslehre, The Doctrine of Right*, and specifically the decisive paragraphs B and C (see Höffe 1995: part I, chapters 4–5). At the end I point to the scope of the matter: that Kant's ethics of right is a fundamental theory of society.

I. A Critical Look into the *Groundwork*

Empirical elements already appear in the *Groundwork*'s examples. They are admittedly uncontroversial, and because they are of a general nature they can be classified as empirical elements of anthropological scope. The "story" that Kant tells about the prohibition against false promises—that a person can fall on hard times and be saved out of them by someone else—has an empirical character, as does the knowledge that it is possible to cause somebody (force their) to help against his own free will: you make a promise that you do not intend to keep.

Now, these examples given by Kant could be relegated to a secondary level, applied ethics, and therefore one could speak of an "applied ethics anthropology," thereby retaining only fundamental ethics as free of anthropology. But this too will lead to disappointment. The fact that the moral law has for human beings the character of a duty, and thus becomes a categorical imperative, further assumes some, even a double, experience. Namely, we assume that beings exist, to whom we can ascribe a capacity to desire along with the relationship to themselves that is called "practical reason" or "will" or, with respect to morals, "pure practical reason" and "autonomous will." Further, we assume that the will stands "under certain subjective limitations and hindrances" (*GMS* 4: 397, 7f.). According to this second "fundamental ethical anthropology" human beings are natural—one can also say finite—rational beings who can be seduced by desires and inclinations; according to *Religion* (*RGV*: part 1), they even have an ineradicable propensity to evil.

This fundamental ethical anthropology, this seducible rational being, is thus applied in the examples to types of situations that put practical reason to the test. And because these types of situations are found across times and cultures— they are indeed aspects of human nature—they are relevant to anthropology: In the case of the prohibition against suicide, it is to be overcome by feeling sick of life; in the case of the prohibition against false promises, it is the need into which one can fall in combination with the ability to lie convincingly; in the case of the duty to help, it is an ability to help given another's need; and for the duty to cultivate oneself, it is the danger of complacency.

On both levels Kant thus fails to achieve his goal of a pure metaphysical ethics: in applied as well as in fundamental ethics. This observation could otherwise be to the advantage of Kant's ethics and rebut the widespread reproach of formalism: Instead of completely freeing morals of all empirical contamination, Kant's ethics draws on a variegated set of empirical elements. As a result, his ethics appears more plausible than would have been expected, though at the cost of falling short of the programme he had set for himself: his supposedly pure moral philosophy is in fact interfused with two levels of anthropological elements.

Luckily, these elements do not go so far as to affect moral obligation, so that Kant's main, antiempirical intention is preserved. On the foundational level of a fundamental ethics, they simply establish the fact that the moral law does not present itself as law but as (categorical) imperative. Even the question whether people can be determined through practical reason is not exclusively, but certainly in part, an empirical one. Experience is included even more in the concept of practical reason that serves one's well being. It is only when you take to the level of the (final) ground of determination, and free yourself of your duty towards your own well-being, that (from this and only this motivational point of view) you leave the realm of experience behind. You then enter into the realm of metaphysics, namely of being worthy of your happiness.

On the subordinate level in turn, that of applied ethics, the anthropological elements simply define the conditions of application without which the moral imperative would remain unemployed. The questions regarding which types of situations should be taken into account and what typical responses are possible—these require experience, and even a creative imagination to be answered. Empirical, even anthropological, elements are not only actually, but necessarily, present in the categorical imperative, the plural form of which is moral duties such as the prohibition against false promises or the duty to help. However, the decisive, moral ground of determination remains of a non-empirical nature. It is one task to find maxims, and another to determine which of them are moral maxims, in order to live your life according to them. In the first case you require only experience; only in the other case is a metaempirical, and thus a metaphysical moment required. The criterion for this moment, by the way, has been established since the first *Critique*; it is the "strict universality" which for Kant is the "secure indication" of the a priori that characterizes pure knowledge (*Kr V* B4).

A critical question for Kant's ethics is whether this indication, this criterion applies to real-life maxims. Herein lies the fundamental difference between a practical and theoretical metaphysics: the a priori and thus metaphysical character in question does not actually show up during the universalization thought experiment, but rather during the act, under the condition that universalizable maxims are being followed.

"Moral anthropology" is the name I give to the essential anthropological elements that make up the conditions of application of morals. Its two levels, the applied and the fundamental ethics anthropologies, do not correspond to that research area that Kant accepts as "the other member of the division of practical philosophy," as the "counterpart of a metaphysics of morals" (*MS* 6:217, 9ff.). Its counterpart, anthropology, is concerned with the secondary task that is part of a "moral education." As such it assumes that moral principles are already established and examines only the subjective conditions that hinder or promote carrying these principles out. Nor do the two levels correspond to the wealth of material and ideas that make up Kant's *Anthropology from a Pragmatic Point of View*. The moral anthropology introduced here for the first time and *against* Kant is an indispensable element of a moral philosophy. It is not the counterpart to, but an integral part of, a metaphysics of morals; its importance is not subsidiary but primary.

My interim conclusion is: though Kant rightly stipulates that ethics has a metaphysics, he overestimates its reach. The programme that he develops in the Preface to the *Groundwork* and which he reaffirms in section II, the "Introduction to the Metaphysics of Morals," turns out to be lacking in necessary detail. The rational domain must indeed, following Kant, be strictly separated from the empirical one in order to maintain the purity of morals and to prevent foreign elements from besmirching moral obligation, that is, the autonomy of the will, and its criterion, universalization. This does not, however, imply that the philosophy of morals, ethics, must on the whole be grounded in reason alone. It is only the ground of determination of morals, but not their complete theory, that can do without experience—not the entire theory of morals. Moral philosophy cannot avoid being contaminated by experience; morals themselves however can—actually, they must.

II. A Transcendental Philosophy of Praxis

The project of a novel philosophy, critical transcendental philosophy, is according to section VII of the introduction to the *Critique of Pure Reason* only possible as a "philosophy [*Weltweisheit*] of pure, merely speculative reason." The other area, "everything practical," relates to feelings which belong to "empirical sources of cognition." Kant does not contradict the Preface to the (later) *Groundwork* because he allows that "the supreme principles of morality" are somewhat free of experience. But this a priori knowledge also includes, he claims, "the concepts of pleasure and displeasure, of desires and inclinations, etc., which are all of empirical origin." These empirical concepts do not underlie moral prescriptions, though they do appear "in the concept of duty, as the hindrance that must be overcome," and hence one "must necessarily include them in the composition of the system of pure morality" (*KrV* B29). This downgrades the corresponding element to a nonpure a priori, which renders it an unfit object for a transcendental philosophy.

Contrary to Kant's point of view, there is a moment within his type of philosophical ethics that is a suitable object for a truly practical and not simply theoretical or speculative transcendental philosophy. He deals with a completely pure a priori, as the text quoted above requires. This purely a priori and yet practical object is the concept of a good as such, that is, without limitation. This moment which compromises the purity of the a priori, that is, feelings, does not yet appear in his text, though the practical and not the theoretical realm is discussed.

The concept of the good as such represents the highest way to evaluate (human) praxis. Because it alone within the realm of the practical has the status of a pure a priori, it constitutes the object of that part of ethics that deals with a pure a priori and is thus metaphysical in the strong sense of the term. The truly first step in the argumentation of moral philosophy is not, as commonly assumed, the general categorical imperative: act in accordance with universalizable maxims. This step does not consist in the purely good will, but rather in the concept of the good as such, which Kant draws upon as if it went without saying in the initial sentence of the *Groundwork*, but which he does not justify there.

A real first or final justification would have to show that whenever praxis is evaluated, a question is raised that can only be finally answered with the idea of a good as such, good without limitation. Following the idea of a transcendental critique, this justification, like the deduction in the first *Critique*, would thus be carried out in two parts. The first, strictly speaking metaphysical argument would have to show that an evaluation that was good as such must rise above all empirical motives. The second, transcendental argument would have to prove that the idea of the good as such is a condition of practical objectivity (contra Fulda 2006: 188, an amazingly sweeping critique; see Höffe 2007: chapter 2).

The beginnings of such a justification can by all means be found in Kant. For example, he lets the thought of a practical reason begin, but not end, with technical and pragmatic levels. Concerning the third and last level, he maintains that it cannot be surpassed inasmuch as it is a presuppositionless, and thus categorical, obligation. On the one hand, since such an obligation transcends all empirical motives (which are, in the end, concerned with one's own well-being), it has a pre-empirical, thus metaphysical character. On the other hand, only it can ensure that the corresponding praxis remains objectively (i.e., without exception and necessarily) valid. The "one hand" suggests the metaphysical and the "other hand" the transcendental argument.

A widespread opinion would have it that a metaphysics is impossible, or at least has been long rendered obsolete. Kant, for his part, considers it as necessary as breathing itself (*Prol* 4: 367). Though this comparison looks at first, for ethics, like an immoderate exaggeration, it appears here to be no more than an at most moderate overstatement: a rhetorical device. The concept of the good as such, which is indispensable to the strict concept of morals, is an element of a practical metaphysics. In the strictest and narrowest sense, a practical meta-physics consists of nothing else than this concept. The moral philosophy which Kant worked out, however, connects the idea of the good as such with moral anthropology, precisely with its fundamental ethical part. It consists hence of an impure or relative a priori and a likewise impure or relative metaphysics.

As is well known, Hegel described the categorical imperative as a "produc-tion of tautologies" in his writing on natural law (1970 [1802–3]: 460). Max Scheler later spoke of "Kant's empty and sterile formalism" (1966: 15). In order to found a material ethics with Kantian means which sidesteps these often repeated criticisms, one often resorts to the material formula of the categorical imperative, that of humankind as an end in itself. However, that formula does not suffice for a true material ethics because it too still requires anthropological elements. But if these elements are to be made use of, then a material ethics can also be arrived at with the help of the formal formula of the categorical imperative, the universalization or natural law formula. We can even phrase the issue more accurately with Hegel: "is" and "ought" are, in categorical duties of right and virtue, gathered together in an original oneness. And because the doctrines of right and virtue have no other object than this oneness, they must consider both aspects together, the purely normative and the anthropological aspect.

III. Three Levels of Anthropology

Let us move on to Kant's systematic ethics of law, the *Metaphysical First Principles of the Doctrine of Right*, or *Doctrine of Right* for short. Without a doubt, my corrections to the *Groundwork* must also be carried through here. Indeed, Kant does not speak broadly of "metaphysics," but more modestly of "metaphysical first principles" as only the principles are metaphysical; the spe-cifics are left to empirical legal practice. But even with this assessment he over-estimates the reach of metaphysics and at the same time underestimates the weight of experience, which is already present in the principles. Altogether, the doctrine of right contains three "levels" of anthropology, one more level than in the moral anthropology that has been introduced so far:

The *first* level consists in the already mentioned fundamental ethical anthro-pology, which precedes the difference between right and virtue and approaches human beings as finite rational beings who can be seduced by their inclinations. It is because of this level that morals generally and their two basic parts, right and virtue, in particular are characterized by duty and imperative. The pre-liminary concepts in the "Introduction to the Metaphysics of Morals" speak of a "sensibly affected" choice (*Willkür*), and explain that this choice "often opposes" the "pure will," which is why moral laws are "categorical (uncondi-tional) imperatives" (*MS* 6: 221). This imperative, which is due to the sensuous nature of humankind, is something we might miss in the general concept of law. But right at the beginning of the pertinent second paragraph, this section speaks of "obligation" (*MS* 6: 230, 8), which in turn is defined as "the necessity of a free action under a categorical imperative" (*MS* 6: 222, 3f.). Despite the indicative mode, Kant has had the imperative in mind from the beginning, and that is why the "person" in paragraph 9 is a being for whom morals present themselves as imperative—to the finite, sensibly affected, and therefore seducible rational being. Kant does not pose the question whether the concept of law can do without this sensibly affected moment. When applied to seducible rational beings, morals, both generally and in the area of law, present themselves as an unrestricted obligation—generally as the categorical imperative, as well in its basic form of universal lawfulness as in its three subforms, natural lawfulness, humanity as an end in itself, and the Formula of the Kingdom of Ends.

The *second*, new "level" is to be inserted between the first and second levels of the above-mentioned moral anthropology. It is necessary because of the new distinction between right and virtue that had not played a role in the *Groundwork*. Each part has its own level: a legal-anthropological and a virtue-anthropological one. For the level specific to the *Doctrine of Right* Kant requires the general ethics of right that he develops in sections A–E of the "Introduction to the Doctrine of Right." This new level is necessary to Kant's basic moral principle of right, namely for the first principle of justice: the singular categorical imperative of right, the principle of the compatibility of freedom that is formulated as a commandment. It constitutes the general part of the legal anthropology, and enumerates the conditions under which the law can appear as that kind of imperative which is characteristic for humanity. This new level consists in a general social anthropology and thus has the rank of a fundamental social philosophy. To it corresponds in the *Doctrine of Virtue* the general part of the virtue anthropology: but instead of a general social anthropology here is to be found an equally general anthropology of people who are responsible towards themselves. The social-anthropological fact presupposed by the singular categorical imperative of right is uncontroversial: rational beings affected by the senses—that they are affected by the senses is presupposed, as already mentioned, by the concept of obligation—these beings who appear in numbers in the outside world. Though this is an empirical presupposition, it nevertheless does not call into question the categorical character because it has no legitimatory weight. Should rational beings endowed with senses fail to coexist, the categorical imperative of right in sections B and C will not become any less obligatory, but certainly less applicable. (In this context neither private right nor public right have a role to play, nor in any case does doctrine of virtue.)

The *third* "level" is the specific anthropology of right and belongs to the plural categorical imperative of right, that is to that special ethic of right that Kant develops in two parts, as private right and as public right. From a systematic point of view we can assign this third level of the doctrine of right to the second level of the above-mentioned moral anthropology. It namely pulls the elements specific to the doctrine of right out of the anthropological elements of the applied ethics.

The systematic beginning consists in an element that is too quickly dealt with in the *Doctrine of Right* for idiosyncratic reasons: the corporeality of human beings as well as the fact that this corporeality can be injured by others. Only such presuppositions allow us to meaningfully speak of a right to life and limb. Because Kant has addressed the theory of innate rights in the "Introduction to the Doctrine of Right" since it was so short, the *Doctrine of Right* begins itself with the external mine and yours. Its legitimation, however, presupposes corporeality and some specifications about it. The institution of private property makes sense only because "corporeal" human beings need living space and goods in order to satisfy their needs and interests. Kant's marriage law draws on human sexuality and his family law on the fact that newborns are needy beings "that don't leave the nest" and that have not put themselves in this position of need.

These and other empirical elements are indispensable to categorical principles of law. Nevertheless, they do not determine more than the conditions of their implementation. Moral obligation, however, is based on a metaphysical element, on the motivational and nonempirical requirement that anthropological conditions be crafted so as to be absolutely valid.

The three levels of an ethics of right, the yet legally unspecified fundamental ethics, the universal, and the specific ethics of right, are not distinguished by their ground or their degree of moral obligation. This never changes. Conceptually or metaethically, there is a highest level of obligation; criteriologically or from the point of view of a normative ethics, it is the ability to universalize that is of import. The difference lies only in increasing amounts of empirical elements.

IV. *The Doctrine of Right*, §§ B and C

Kant does not employ the term "categorical imperative of right." What is meant by this term is, however, present in the *Doctrine of Right*, and in three guises at that. First in the indicative as a universal concept of right (§B), then as an again indicative universal principle of right (§C; see the Appendix, *RL* 6: 371, 20f.), and finally as a universal law in the imperative (§C).

Unlike mathematics, philosophy cannot start out with definitions. Philosophy must generate its concepts from the matter in question. In the case of the moral concept of right or the categorical imperative of right, the matter has two moments. "Formally" it has to do with moral obligation: with legitimacy, as opposed to positive validity, that is, (juridical) legality. The moral moment is well known from the *Groundwork* and from the second *Critique*. Moreover, it is recalled in the general section of the *Metaphysics of Morals*, the Introduction that precedes the specific sections of the *Doctrine of Right* and the *Doctrine of Virtue*. Kant can thus begin in the "Introduction to the Doctrine of Right" with the second, "material" moment that corresponds to a universal anthropology of right. The question as to what the law is responsible for is therefore answered by its conditions of application.

The question aims either at a permitted, at a doable, or finally at a necessary responsibility. Though Kant does not formulate such a distinction, he does nevertheless develop a necessary responsibility, though in a very thetic and concise manner. As stated in the transition from private to public right, it is grounded in an "unavoidable togetherness" (*RL* 6: §42). In the general ethic of right, that is in a part that systematically precedes private and public right, Kant develops it in three steps:

The moral concept of right, which relates to its own corresponding obligation, is concerned *first* "only with the external and indeed practical relation of one person to another, insofar as their actions, as deeds, can have (direct or indirect) influence on each other" (*RL* 6: 230, 9–11). Three moments can be emphasized with respect to this complex definition:

1. The first moment is valid for ethics as a whole. Be it an external lawgiving as in the *Doctrine of Right* or an internal one as in the *Doctrine of Virtue*, it makes sense to speak of moral obligation with respect not to things but only to persons—which Kant understands to be accountable subjects (*RL* 6: 223, 24f. and 32). It is only experience that can tell us (a) that accountable beings exist, and (b) that humans are such beings. Despite the book's title, the "first principles" of the *Doctrine of Right* are not entirely metaphysical. They require experience—knowledge of an invariant feature of the human condition. The missing argument could be supplemented by pointing out that because human beings are capable of thought and speech, we can credit them with accountability and freedom of action.

It is just as important for Kant's concept of right that he is content with accountability. Whereas freedom of the will belongs to the concept of virtue, the law is satisfied with a more modest concept of freedom, that is, with freedom of action. He is thus content with a negative concept of freedom—that is, being free to do or refrain from doing what you want—to which, according to Isaiah Berlin's famous reproach (1969: 37ff.), Kant was supposedly hostile. The consequence is not without importance: even if the multifaceted critique of Kant's idea of freedom of the will were justified, it would not affect his ethics as a whole.

2. Even though someone can experience internal conflict with him- or herself, one accountable subject is not enough to create a problem of rights. Such problems appear—and this is the next empirical presupposition—only when more than one person is involved. Moreover,

  these people must not stand in an aesthetic or a theoretical relation,
  but in a practical one.
3. Two further empirical conditions ensure that the relation is never
  purely aesthetic or theoretical. First, the exterior world is bounded
  as "the earth's surface is not unlimited but closed" (*RL* 6: 230, 23f.).
  Second, people are not pure intellects; they have bodies that lay claim
  to a part of the common world if only because they have extension.
  In addition, corporeal beings have needs and interests for the satisfaction of which they require goods. And in order to acquire them
  people intervene in the common world.

These three elements taken together constitute the first condition of application of the law, the practical coexistence of accountable subjects. With this
Kant underscores that which matters with brilliant clarity, thereby rendering
all additional questions superfluous. The dispute that was ignited by Hobbes
around the questions as to why people influence one another, whether this
influence is friendly or hostile, and what the grounds of potential hostility
are: all of these additional, partly anthropological, partly social and partly
theoretical-historical problems are excluded by Kant from the moral concept
of right. He does not, however, set aside all of experience. He rather con-
centrates on that which an anthropology of right comprises: the unavoidable
social relationships that result from the invariant conditions of human being.
At the same time he avoids the type of objection that was always raised against
Hobbes, from the early Hobbes reception through Rousseau's second essay, to
Borkenau (1973) and Macpherson (1962), namely the (supposed) dependence
of the economic and social conditions of a competitive bourgeois society.

A second type of objection also becomes pointless: that a specific view of
humankind is required in order to justify the idea of right. Were this the case,
(legal) anthropological relativism would have the last word. An objective justification of the idea of right would not be possible.

According to Kant's second condition of application, the law is not concerned with "the relation of one's choice to the mere *wish* (hence also to the
mere need) of the other, ... but only a relation to the other's *choice*" (*RL* 6:
230, 12–15). That the doctrine of right emphasizes choice, that is, freedom
of action and not of will, agrees with its taking accountability as a starting
point. Moreover: whereas you can wish for something that is unattainable,
such as omnipotence or immortality, choice concerns only that which you
actually can, or which you believe you can, achieve through your actions.
Kant does well to take freedom of action as a starting point since the law is
concerned with actions as facts and how these influence one another, whereas
mere wishes remain inward. Heterogeneous inner worlds can exist side by
side without a problem; it is the shared external world that first creates an
unavoidable task for the law.

Under the concept of wish, which he excludes, Kant subsumes needs (*RL* 6: 230, 12f.) and thereby happiness, the implied fulfillment of those needs. He thus turns against a utilitarian theory of right, for example, against Wolff (1969 [1754]) and Mendelssohn (1968 [1783]), who hold the law and the state responsible for the *officia humanitatis*, that is the duty of neighborly love and of solidarity, or for the "advancement of the happiness of the human race" (see Wolff's complete title: 2004 [1736], e.g., §§11, 215, 227, and 476). Morality does demand that we see to the well-being of fellow human beings, but for Kant it is only virtue and not also right that is responsible for "actions of beneficence" (*RL* 6: 230, 13f.).

It is not the matter but only the form that is of import in reciprocal relations of choice, according to Kant's third condition of application (*RL* 6: 230, 16f.). The example that is given clarifies what this ambiguous formulation actually means. Someone who purchases a good is not asked if he or she will gain by the transaction. In this case the choice lies in purchasing or selling, the reciprocal relation in the exchange of goods and money, the matter of the choice in the intention of the two people, and the form of the reciprocal relation in the fact that the exchange is conducted on both sides—without coercion or cheating—consciously and freely.

One could try to use the moral perspective to justify the fact that the matter of choice is not of concern to the law, for according to Kant it is excluding the matter and concentrating on the form that is constitutive (see *KrV* 5: §§2–4). But the fact that an exchange that took place under duress is not moral speaks against such an attempt. Kant uses a different concept of form in section B of the *Doctrine of Right*; the reason for his thesis lies in the premoral element of the concept of right: Inasmuch as they are not the type of action that affects others, intentions can be ignored because the categorical imperative of right relates to the unavoidable part of the social relationship.

To tie the second anthropological level of the *Doctrine of Right*, legal anthropology, to the genuinely metaphysical part of the *Doctrine of Right* is to judge the coexistence of accountable people according to Kant's criterion of morals (universal lawfulness); you thereby attain to Kant's oft-quoted moral concept of right: "Right is therefore the sum of the conditions under which the choice of one can be united with the choice of another in accordance with a universal law of freedom" (*RL* 6: 230, 24–6).

This supplement—when Kant speaks of a "universal" law—should not be taken as explanatory. It is much too obvious that every law formulated without proper nouns possesses a certain degree of universality for Kant to go over this twice (*RL* 6: 230, 22 and 25f.). Kant is rather referring to his general moral criterion, strict universalization, with which the moment of practical metaphysics appears. The moral concept of right thus fulfills the model of legitimation that is "practical metaphysics plus anthropology of right." Metaphysics thereby restricts itself to the genuine moral element of universalization. No further metaphysical elements appear, and particularly no assumption of a theoretical metaphysics. The metaphysics included in the categorical imperative of right is thus only practical, not theoretical, and thus does not pose much of a problem.

The concept of a universal compatibility of freedom of action has two aspects. According to the negative aspect, everyone's freedom of action must be restricted. The reason is not metaphysical, but in a further sense empirical, specifically legal anthropological. As long as *several* people share the same external world, no one can claim living space for him- or herself without ipso facto restricting the living space of all others. Whenever there is only *one* spatially restricted world but several people, a restriction of freedom is in principle inevitable. This restriction gains moral importance only by its specific form: a restricted freedom that follows the law of universalization provides as such the positive aspect of a mutual contract: a safeguarding of freedom. Whenever freedom is limited through a universal law, it is at the same time for everyone and equally safeguarded.

From this moral *concept* Kant infers a (once again moral) *principle* of right (§C), which deals with the same subject matter as the concept, only from another point of view. The concept of right deals with objective right, whereas the principle of right deals with the corresponding subjective right, i.e. all actions to which one is entitled according to one's objective right (*RL* 6: 230, 29–31). This principle accords with the criterion of human rights. Kant expresses this himself in the Introduction under the heading "There is Only One Innate Right": "Freedom (independence from being constrained by another's choice), insofar as it can coexist with the freedom of every other in accordance with a universal law, is the only original right belonging to every man by virtue of his humanity" (*RL* 6: 237, 27–31).

Finally, Kant introduces a yet third variant for the morality of right, the universal and once again moral *law* of right (§D). Because the same content of the concept of right and the principle of right is now however formulated as an imperative, we are actually dealing with the specific categorical imperative of right: "so act externally that the free use of your choice can coexist with the freedom of everyone in accordance with a universal law" (*RL* 6: 231, 10–12). But since the matter—the compatibility of freedom of action according to a universal law—is already addressed in the concept and the principle of right, these too can (with a change of modality) serve as formulations of the categorical imperative of right.

V. Ethics of Right as a Fundamental Social Theory

The philosophers of postmodernity tend to fancy a radical pluralism that legitimizes a variegated set of lifestyles and social formations. We need not rehearse here the arguments in favor of diversity; but we must wonder how far diversity can go. Can it ever be truly radical, reaching all the way down to our roots? The categorical imperative of right suggests we be wary.

In order that plurality not only be presupposed, but also be actually lived, we must assume a right according to which people and groups may live according to their own distinctiveness. The categorical imperative of right provides the standard for precisely this type of right: each person and each group is entitled to their distinctiveness and even intransigence—so long as this claim remains reciprocal and valid for everyone. The categorical imperative of law is founded on the interplay between anthropological considerations and a moral and (in a practical sense) metaphysical assessment. Both the anthropological as well as the practical-metaphysical aspects refer to oneness and universalism, two things a theory of radical pluralism cannot even conceive of.

It is often feared that both sides, that the anthropological as well as the metaphysical elements show an undue preference for certain forms of life over against others. This is not the case for those anthropological and metaphysical elements which together constitute the categorical imperative of right. They rather make explicit the conditions without the acknowledgment of which the desired pluralism would not even be viable. In this Kant's ethics of right takes on significance that is greater than what most usually acknowledge. Whereas a moral principle usually has only a normative role, the categorical imperative of right assumes a supplementary, constitutive role. It is charged with structuring human coexistence according to law. A Kantian ethics of right is consequently much more than a partial social ethics: it has the rank of a fundamental social discipline.

Within the bounds of such an ethics of right, a first, strictly speaking metaphysical argument addresses the moral concept of right as a categorical imperative and, regarding its obligation, as a purely rational concept. A second, transcendental argument shows that the social world can constitute itself as an objectively valid world only on the basis of a categorical imperative of right. However, we are not here concerned with the well-known theoretical objectivity, but with a practical one: not with the truth about a natural world of objects, but with the justice of a world that emerges out of human coexistence. The metaphysical argument defines a counterpoint to the current prevailing empirical legal culture; this counterpoint has a constitutive function in the transcendental argument: it is fundamentally and morally legitimate to establish legal force among humans; it is furthermore morally necessary to institute an enforceable system of laws in order to allow everyone freedom of action.

Bibliography

Berlin, I. (1969) "Two Concepts of Liberty," in *Four Essays on Liberty*. Oxford: Oxford University Press.

Borkenau, F. (1934/1973) *Der Übergang vom feudalen zum bürgerlichen Weltbild. Studien zur Geschichte der Philosophie der Manufakturperiode*. Reprint. Darmstadt: Wissenschaftliche Buchgesellschaft.

Fulda, H. F. (2006) "Notwendigkeit des Rechts unter Voraussetzung des Kategorischen Imperativs der Sittlichkeit," *Jahrbuch für Recht und Ethik* 14: 167–213.

Hegel, G. W. F. (1970 [1802–3]) "Über die wissenschaftlichen Behandlungsarten des Naturrechts…," in *Werke in 20 Bänden*. Vol. 2. Frankfurt am Main: Surkamp.

Hegel, G. W. F. (1999) "On the Scientific Ways of Treating Natural Law…," in *Political Writings*. Tr. H. B. Nisbet. Cambridge: Cambridge University Press.

Höffe, O. (1995) *Kategorische Rechtsprinzipien. Ein Kontrapunkt der Moderne.* 3rd ed. Frankfurt am Main: Suhrkamp.

Höffe, O. (2002) *Categorical Principles of Law. An Counterpoint to Modernity.* Tr. M. Migotti. University Park: Pennsylvania State University Press.

Höffe, O. (2007) *Lebenskunst und Moral. Oder Macht Tugend glücklich?* Munich: C. H. Beck.

Höffe, O. (2009) *Can Virtue Make Us Happy?* Tr. D. McGaughey. Evanston, IL: Northwestern University Press.

Kant, I. (1992–) *The Cambridge Edition of the Works of Immanuel Kant.* Cambridge and New York: Cambridge University Press.

Macpherson, C. B. (1962) *The Political Theory of Possessive Individualism. Hobbes to Locke.* Oxford: Clarendon Press.

Mendelssohn, M. (1968 [1783]) *Jerusalem oder über die religiöse Macht und Judenthum.* Brussels: Culture et Civilisation.

Mendelssohn, M. (1983) *Jerusalem, or On Religious Power and Judaism.* Tr. A. Arkush. Hanover, NH, and London: University Press of New England for Brandeis University Press.

Pufendorf, S. (1934 [1672]) *De iure naturae et gentium.* Latin–English ed. tr. C. H. & W. A. Goldfather. Oxford: Classics of International Law.

Scheler, M. (1966) *Der Formalismus in der Ethik und die materiale Werteethik.* 5th ed. Bern: Francke.

Scheler, M. (1973) *Formalism in Ethics and Non-formal Ethics of Values.* 5th ed. Evanston, IL: Northwestern University Press.

Wolff, C. (1969 [1754]) *Institutiones juris naturae et gentium: in quibus ex ipsa hominis natura continuo nexu omnes obligationes et jura omnia deducuntur.* Ed. M. Thomann. Hildesheim: G. Olms.

Wolff, C. (2004 [1736]) *'Deutsche Politik': Vernünftige Gedanken von dem gesellschaftlichen Leben der Menschen und insonderheit dem gemeinen Wesen.* 4th ed. Ed. H. Hofmann. Munich: Beck.

6

Kant, Moral Obligation, and the Holy Will

Robert Stern

O Duty,

Why hast thou not the visage of a sweetie or a cutie?

—Ogden Nash, "Kind of an Ode to Duty"

Compared to many other aspects of his rich and complex practical philosophy, Kant's discussion of the holy or divine will, and the distinction that he draws between that will and one such as our own, has been little discussed. In some ways this is surprising, as it is a distinction that Kant draws frequently, and which he uses to do important work in his ethical theory. On the other hand, this neglect in the literature on Kant is also readily explicable—for in a context where the predominant mood of ethical theorizing is secular, talk of "the holy will" may in itself cause misgivings; and at the same time, at the core of Kant's discussion seems to lie one of those notorious "Kantian dualisms" (here between reason and desire), where sympathetic commentators have been perhaps understandably wary of making too much of the notion as a result. It may seem best, then, to treat this distinction as of no great significance both to Kant and to philosophy in general, and to pass over it in somewhat embarrassed silence.

In this paper, by contrast, I want to argue that this attitude is mistaken, and that in fact there are valuable insights to be gained by reflecting on the distinction in the way that Kant does, so that when it comes to Kant's practical philosophy, it should be given as much prominence as the related distinction in Kant's theoretical philosophy between the intuitive and discursive intellects.[1] I begin by setting out the way in which Kant conceives of the distinction between the holy will and our own, and what work he uses it to do (sections I to III), and then try to settle some misgivings that may arise concerning it (section IV). I then explain how, when it comes to familiar debates in ethics between realism and antirealism, and between externalism and internalism, we can see Kant's distinction as enabling him to combine

---

[1] Lewis White Beck makes this comparison: see Beck (1960: 50).

elements of both sides in a way that may fruitfully resolve these controversies, and so contribute to the contemporary discussion (sections V and VI). Thus, I try to show, far from being an element in his thought that we would do best to ignore, Kant's conception of the holy will is one that deserves to be taken seriously, as well as being integral to a proper understanding of his ethical views.

I. On Kant's Distinction between the Divine and the Human Wills

Kant draws a distinction between the holy will and a will such as ours throughout his ethical writings and in his lectures on ethics. The actual difference he points to is in essence a simple one, and obviously relates to standard theological conceptions of our "fallen" nature: whereas a divine will acts only in line with the good, and has no inclinations to do otherwise, we have immoral desires and inclinations, that mean we find ourselves drawn to adopt immoral courses of action. As Kant puts it: "The dispositions [*Gesinnungen*] of the deity are morally good, and those of man are not. The dispositions or subjective morality of the divine are therefore coincident with objective morality" (*V-Mo/Collins* 27: 263),[2] but ours are not.

While the contrast Kant draws is itself perhaps not unusual, however, the way Kant uses it is considerably more distinctive. For, he deploys it in order to explain the particular force that morality has for us, which takes the form of a *command* or *imperative*, as telling us that there are things that we *must* or *must not* do—what Kant calls "constraint" or "necessitation" (*Nötigung*). In many passages, Kant explains this obligatoriness in terms of the distinction between the holy will and our own, arguing that it is because we have dispositions to do things other than what is right, that the right for us involves a moral "must"; but for a holy will, which has no inclination to do anything other than what is right, no such "must" applies. A typical statement of Kant's view is the following from the *Groundwork of the Metaphysics of Morals*:

A perfectly good will would, therefore, equally stand under objective laws (of the good),[3] but it could not on this account be represented

---

[2] Cf. also *V-Mo/Mron* 27: 1425: "[T]he divine will is in accordance with the moral law, and that is why His will is holiest and most perfect...God wills everything that is morally good and appropriate, and that is why His will is holy and most perfect"; and *V-Mo/Mron II* 29: 604: "In the Gospel we also find an ideal, namely that of holiness. It is that state of mind from which an evil desire never arises. God alone is holy, and man can never become so, but the ideal is good. The understanding often has to contend with the inclinations. We cannot prevent them, but we can prevent them from determining the will"; and *V-Phil-Th/Pölitz* 28: 1075: "A holy being must not be affected by the least inclination contrary to morality. It must be *impossible* for it to will something that is contrary to the moral law. So understood, no being but God is holy. For every creature always has some needs, and if it wills to satisfy them, it also has inclinations which do not always agree with morality. Thus the human being can *never* be *holy, but of course* [he can be] *virtuous*. For virtue consists precisely in *self-overcoming*."

[3] The "good" here can be broader than the moral good as it may include things that are good qua means; on the other hand, as Timmermann observes (2007: 62–3, note 27), "[i]t is most likely

as *necessitated* to actions in conformity with law since of itself, by its subjective constitution, it can be determined only through the representation of the good. Hence no imperatives hold for the *divine* will and in general for a *holy* will: the 'ought' is out of place here, because volition is of itself necessarily in accord with the law. Therefore imperatives are only formulae expressing the relation of objective laws of volition in general to the subjective imperfection of the will of this or that rational being, for example, of the human will. (*GMS* 4: 414)

Thus, the principles that determine what it is good and bad to do apply to the holy will, where these principles are laws because they hold of all agents universally, and of such agents independently of the contingencies of their desires and goals, and thus necessarily.[4] However, because the holy will is morally perfect, these laws lack any necessitating force for it, whereas our lack of moral perfection means that they possess such force for us.[5]

This, I take it, is the basic outline of Kant's position; but before adding some complexities to the discussion, let me next set out what issues Kant was concerned to address in putting it forward.

II. Explaining the Moral "Must"

In making the distinction he does between the holy will and one like our own in the way we have outlined, Kant is offering part of a solution to a fundamental transcendental or "how possible?" question in ethics: namely, how are categorical imperatives possible?[6] Unless we have a convincing answer to this question, Kant fears, we may doubt the intelligibility of the moral, where an aspect of the problem is that it can be hard to see what gives the commands

---

that Kant first and foremost has the *moral* law in mind when he says that the same objective laws of the good hold for both kinds of will [viz. human and holy] alike."

[4] On universality, see *GMS* 4: 412: "moral laws are to hold for every rational being as such." On necessity, cf. Kant's distinction between *principles* and *laws*, where the former are what govern "what it is necessary to do merely for achieving a discretionary purpose," and so can be "regard[ed] as in [themselves] contingent and we can always be released from the precept if we give up the purpose," whereas a moral law "leaves the will no discretion with respect to the opposite, so that it alone brings with it that necessity which we require of a law" (*GMS* 4: 420). Cf. also *GMS* 4: 389.

[5] Cf. *MS* 6: 222: "An imperative is a practical rule by which an action in itself contingent is *made* necessary. An imperative differs from a practical law in that a law indeed represents an action as necessary but takes no account of whether this action already inheres by *inner* necessity in the acting subject (as in a holy being) or whether it is contingent (as in a human being); for where the former is the case there is no imperative. Hence an imperative is a rule the representation of which *makes* necessary an action that is subjectively contingent and this represents the subject as one that must be *constrained* (necessitated) to conform with the rule."

[6] I say "part of a solution" because the problem is not just that categorical imperatives are imperatival, but also that they are *categorical* and not merely hypothetical, where this is not an issue that concerns us here.

of morality their special imperatival force, and thus what makes them necessitating: for, if we explain the source of the demand by appeal to a demander, such as God, then we would seem to undermine our freedom as moral agents, in making moral obedience into obedience to the will of another, whilst also making morality conditional;[7] but if we treat the world in itself as exerting an obligatory force, we would seem to attribute to it a mysterious capacity for exerting authority over us. Thus, just as in the theoretical case, where Kant is concerned that worries about metaphysical necessity might lead us (as it did Hume) into doubting that synthetic a priori knowledge is possible, so in the practical case, Kant is concerned that doubts about the necessitation involved in the moral "must" might lead us into doubt concerning the moral law. As Kant puts it: "This question does not inquire how the performance of the action that the imperative commands can be thought, but only how *the necessitation of the will*, which the imperative expresses in the problem, can be thought [or conceived, or made sense of: *gedacht*]" (*GMS* 4: 417, my emphasis).[8] If the "must" in "you must not tell lies" is not explained, therefore, this can leave us wondering how there can be any such necessity[9]—just as in the case of metaphysical necessity, we can be left wondering how it can be the case that every event *must* have a cause.

It can therefore be seen how Kant's distinction between the holy will and ours is designed to resolve this puzzle, by appeal to the fact that our will is divided between reason and inclination in a way that the will of the divine being is not, a division that Kant characterizes in the terms of his transcendental idealism as mapping onto the distinction between the noumenal and phenomenal realms (or the "intelligible world" and "the world of sense"):

And so categorical imperatives are possible by this: that the idea of freedom makes me a member of an intelligible world and consequently, if I were only this, all my actions *would* always be in conformity with the autonomy of the will; but since at the same time I intuit myself as a

---

[7] Cf. *GMS* 4: 443. The extent to which this passage shows Kant to be opposed to divine command theories in this way has been disputed recently by John Hare, however. See Hare (2000a; 2000b; 2001: 87–119; 2007: 122–75). Whilst I believe that Hare's position is mistaken, I do not have space to challenge it here, and will simply follow what I take to be the more orthodox line without any further defense. I respond to Hare at greater length in Stern (2012: 58–67).

[8] For a helpful discussion of the background to this issue in Wolff and Baumgarten, see Schwaiger (2009).

[9] Cf. Garner (1990: 141 and 143): "How could *any* feature of something outside us make it the case that we are objectively required to do something?...It is the peculiar combination of objectivity and prescriptivity...that makes moral facts and properties queer...It is hard to believe in objective prescriptivity because it is hard to make sense of a demand without a demander, and hard to find a place for demands and demandingness apart from human interests and conventions. We know what it is for our friends, our job, and our projects to make demands on us, but we do not know what it is for *reality* to do so." Garner is of course here explicating one aspect of J. L. Mackie's famous "argument from queerness."

member of the world of sense, they *ought* to be in conformity with it; and this *categorical* ought represents a synthetic proposition a priori, since to my will affected by sensible desires there is added the idea of the same will but belonging to the world of the understanding—a will pure and practical of itself, which contains the supreme condition, in accordance with reason, of the former will . . . The moral "*ought*" is then [the person's] own necessary "*will*" as a member of the intelligible world, and is thought by him as "ought" only insofar as he regards himself at the same time as a member of the world of sense. (*GMS* 4: 454–5)[10]

Kant thus uses his transcendental idealism, and his dualistic picture of the will, to help address the transcendental question he raises concerning the imperatival nature of morality, in order to explain hereby how that is possible. Kant's distinction between the holy will and ours therefore forms a crucial part of his answer to the problem of accounting for the moral "must," in a way that explains its possibility (unlike a view that simply treats the "must" as a feature of the world), but without recourse to the problematic notion of a divine legislator as the source of that "must" (thus avoiding any need to adopt a divine command theory).

III. Analyzing the Distinction

Having shown the way Kant sets out the distinction, and indicated the role he gives it within his practical philosophy, I now want to examine it in a little more detail. For, although in some ways Kant's position is fairly straightforward, it is nonetheless not without its ambiguities.

One issue concerns what it is about the holy will, exactly, that makes it the case that there is no moral obligation for a will of this kind. The simplest answer to this question, which I have largely adopted in sketching Kant's position above, is to think that morality lacks any obligatory force for the holy will because it has no *resistance* to morality: unencumbered as it is by any nonmoral desires

---

[10] Cf. also *V-MS/Vigil* 27: 510: "Although the obligation is established by reason, it is nevertheless assumed that in the performance of our duty we have regard to ourselves as passive beings, and that another person must be present, who necessitates us to duty. Crusius found this necessitating person in God, and Baumgarten likewise in the divine will, albeit known through reason, and not positively, and on this principle a particular moral system has been erected. If, however, we pay heed to self-regarding duties, then man is presented in his physical nature, i.e., insofar as he is subject to the laws of nature, as the obligated, and rightly so; but if the obligator is personified as an ideal being or moral person, it can be none other than the legislation of reason; this, then, is man considered solely as an intelligible being, who here obligates man as a sensory being, and we thus have a relationship of man *qua* phenomenon toward himself *qua* noumenon. The situation is similar in obligations toward others." For a closely related passage, see *MS* 6: 417–18.

and inclinations, it feels no *constraint* in acting morality, because nothing in its will fights against the moral course of action as determined by reason, and so no part of its will has to be restrained or held back in any way. This picture fits with many passages from Kant, such as when he says that if we had a holy will "the [moral] law would finally cease to be a command to us, since we would never be tempted to be unfaithful to it" (*KpV* 5: 82); or characterizes a "*holy* (superhuman) being" as one "in whom no hindering impulses would impede the law of its will and who would thus gladly do everything in conformity with the law" (*MS* 6: 405); or states that "[God is] unlimited only in this, that no moral necessitation can be supposed in Him, in regard to the determination of His will, since he lacks the limitations imposed on human nature, of an inclination to contravene the laws" (*V-MS/Vigil* 27: 547).

However, as well as this way of characterizing what is distinctive about the holy will, as being a will that lacks any nonmoral inclinations, Kant also characterized the holy will in terms that deploy more of his technical machinery, particularly the idea of a *maxim*. Unfortunately, however, there is some ambiguity in Kant's account of what maxims are, where this is then reflected in apparently contradictory claims Kant makes about how the holy will stands in relation to maxims—for, Kant sometimes states that the holy will (unlike us) has *no* maxims,[11] and sometimes that it has maxims, but unlike us, its maxims always coincide with the moral law.[12]

The difficulty here arises, because of an underlying unclarity in what Kant means in characterizing maxims as "subjective principles of acting."[13] At times he seems to mean by this nothing more than the idea that a maxim is a principle on which an agent acts or proposes to act, in which case there is no difficulty for him in attributing maxims to the holy will, and claiming that the principles on which it acts will always be ones that conform to the moral law. However, Kant also characterizes the "subjective" nature of maxims in a further way, not just as principles employed by subjects in acting, but as principles that have merely subjective *validity*, in contrast to the objective validity of the practical law, where the subjectivity of a maxim in *this* sense means that it holds for the subject only in so far as it relates merely to his or her "conditions," such as what he or she is inclined to do, and thus does not apply to those whose "conditions" are different. So, out of concern for my health,

---

[11] Cf. *KpV* 5: 79: "All three concepts, however—that of an *incentive*, of an *interest* and of a *maxim*—can be applied only to finite beings. For they all presuppose a limitation on the nature of a being, in that the subjective constitution of its choice does not of itself accord with the objective law of a practical reason; they presuppose the need to be impelled to activity by something because an internal obstacle is opposed to it. Thus they cannot be applied to the divine will."

[12] Cf. *GMS* 4: 439: "A will whose maxims necessarily conform with the laws of autonomy is a *holy*, absolutely good will"; and *KpV* 5: 32: "a *holy* will...would not be capable of any maxim conflicting with the moral law."

[13] Cf. *GMS* 4: 420 note, and also *GMS* 4: 401 note.

I might make it my maxim to drink less coffee because I think drinking coffee leads to insomnia; but this is merely a subjective rule, as it does not profess to be valid for anyone else, relating as it does to my particular inclinations, and my views about the effects of coffee on my sleep and insomnia on my health. By contrast, on this picture, a moral principle has an objectivity that maxims lack, because they do indeed apply to others, where here the relevant grounds or conditions are not confined to the individual subject.[14] Thus, while in both cases, because they are general principles, maxims and practical laws are determined by reason, in the former case it is reason working on the basis of the particular agent's particular preferences and so framing principles with limited applicability, while in the latter it is reason arriving at genuine laws that apply to all, independent of these circumstances. Now, given *this* conception of maxims, as having only subjective validity in this sense, it is understandable why Kant might come to say that the holy will lacks them altogether: for, if none of the "conditions" that give merely subjective validity to maxims apply to the holy will, and if instead the only principles that guide it are the principles of the objectively valid practical law, then it becomes clear why Kant might claim that we cannot think of the holy will as having maxims—but it also becomes clear why, given the *other* way in which the notion of a maxim is also used by Kant, he might allow that the holy will can have maxims, and speak of the holy will in these terms.[15]

Having resolved the apparent contradictions in Kant's position with regard to the holy will on the issue of maxims, we can now turn to another area where there also might appear to be some ambiguity: namely, on what basis does Kant claim that the holy will cannot be obligated to act, or stand under a duty? In the first section, I suggested that Kant's reason for this claim is that he thought that for these notions to apply to an agent, what it is right for them to do must exert some necessitating force, which is impossible in the case of a holy will, as

---

[14] Cf. *KpV* 5: 19: "Practical *principles* are propositions that contain a general determination of the will, having under it several practical rules. They are subjective, or *maxims*, when the condition is regarded by the subject as holding only for his will; but they are objective, or practical *laws*, when the condition is cognized as objective, that is, as holding for the will of every rational being." Cf. also *V-MS/Vigil* 27: 495: "The *maxim* of an action differs, that is, from an objective principle in this, that the latter occurs only insofar as we consider the possibility of the action on certain rational grounds, whereas the former includes all subjective grounds of action whatsoever, insofar as they are taken to be real. N.B. The principle is always objective, and is called a maxim *quoad subjectum* [as to the subject]. It is understood as the rule universally acknowledged by reason, while the maxim is the subjectively practical principle, insofar as the subject makes the rule by which he is to act into the motive of his action as well."

[15] Cf. Paton (1967: 61): "Kant speaks at times as if all maxims are grounded on sensuous inclinations, and consequently as if a divine or holy will could have no maxims. A holy will would have no maxims which were not also objective principles; but to say this is not to deny that it acts in accordance with maxims, if we interpret 'maxims' to mean principles manifested in action. It is all-important to recognize that while maxims are commonly based on inclinations...it may nevertheless be possible to act on maxims which are not so based."

it lacks the inclination to do anything other than the moral action; but there is another way of taking Kant's position here that should be considered.

On this alternative view, the reason why the holy will has no duties or obligations is that duties and obligations require the agent to be able to *fail* to act as they are obligated to do, so that in this sense "ought implies might not." Kant's position has been presented along these lines by Samuel Kerstein, who writes that

> [a]ccording to Kant, one can be obliged to do something only if there is some possibility that he will fail to do it. Yet some beings, for example, God, might be such that they cannot fail to obey the supreme principle of morality. It would thus make no sense to say that they have an obligation to obey it. (Kerstein 2002: 2)

Kerstein cites evidence that Kant believed in the "ought implies might not" principle by pointing to a passage in the *Metaphysics of Morals*, where Kant is discussing whether we could have a duty to pursue our own happiness, which Kerstein reads as saying that "an agent cannot have an obligation to promote the end of his own happiness, since each agent unavoidably has this end" (Kerstein 2002: 193 note 4).

Now, the principle "ought implies might not" is perhaps plausible, and there is some additional textual evidence that Kant held it as a necessary condition for obligatoriness.[16] But in fact the passage Kerstein cites seems to suggest that Kant also believed that more was required to account for obligatoriness as it applies to us; for here Kant says that we cannot have the duty to pursue our happiness because this happiness accords with our desires, and thus there is no experience of *resistance* in aiming at happiness as an end (in contrast, say, to our own perfection, where we do experience resistance from desire, and where therefore it makes sense to speak of a duty to self):

> *[H]is own happiness* is an end that every human being has (by virtue of the impulses of his nature), but this end can never without self-contradiction

---

[16] See for example: *V-MS/Vigil* 27: 486: "In God the nature of action is likewise that it accords with the moral laws which are formed by the concepts of the highest reason; save only that since no subjective possibility of contravening such laws is possible in His Case, His actions being morally necessary both objectively and subjectively, no imperative is appropriate to Him either, since however He acts, He does so in accordance with the moral laws, and will at all times act freely and unconditionally"; *GMS* 4: 414: "Hence no imperatives hold for the *divine* will and in general for the *holy* will: the 'ought' is out of place here, because volition is of itself necessarily in accord with the law"; *GMS* 4: 449: "... this 'ought' is strictly speaking a 'will' that holds for every rational being under the condition that reason in him is practical without hindrance; but for beings like us—who are also affected by sensibility, by incentives of a different kind, and in whose case that which reason by itself would do is not always done—that necessity of action is called also an 'ought,' and the subjective necessity is distinguished from the objective"; and *MS* 6: 222: "An imperative differs from a practical law in that a law indeed represents an action as necessary but takes no account of whether this action already inheres by an *inner* necessity in the acting subject (as in a holy being) or whether it is contingent (as in the human being); for where the former is the case there is no imperative."

be regarded as a duty. What everybody already wants unavoidably, of his own accord, does not come under the concept of *duty*, which is *constraint* to an end adopted reluctantly. Hence it is self-contradictory to say that he is *under obligation* to promote his own happiness with all his powers. (*MS* 6: 386)[17]

Here Kant clearly seems to make the conceptual claim that I am interested in, and not just the one attributed to him by Kerstein, namely that "*duty . . .* is *constraint* to an end adopted reluctantly," where it is precisely this lack of "reluctance" and hence constraint that seems to make the concept of duty "self-contradictory" in this context—and thus, equally contradictory in the case of the holy will.[18] In the light of this textual evidence, I think it is reasonable to conclude that there is more to Kant's position here than just an appeal to the "ought implies might not" principle, and that the account I offered in the first section should be allowed to stand.

IV. Concerns about Kant's Distinction

Having further clarified Kant's position on the distinction between the holy will and our own, and how this relates to his account of duty and obligation, I now want to briefly consider concerns that might be raised about it, and about the work that Kant uses it to do.

---

[17] Cf. also *KpV* 5: 37: "A command that everyone should seek to make himself happy would be foolish, for one never commands of someone what he unavoidably wants already." Of course, "foolishness" is a weaker notion than self-contradictoriness, but is a negative mark against such a command nonetheless.

[18] Kant seems to have this view in several other passages, e.g., *MS* 6: 379: "The very *concept of duty* is already the concept of a *necessitation* (constraint) of free choice through the law. This constraint may be an *external constraint* or a *self-constraint*. The moral *imperative* makes this constraint known through the categorical nature of its pronouncements (the unconditional ought). Such constraint, therefore, does not apply to rational beings as such (there could also be *holy* ones) but rather to *human beings*, rational *natural* beings, who are unholy enough that pleasure can induce them to break the moral law, even though they recognize its authority; and even when they do obey the law, they do so *reluctantly* (in the face of opposition from their inclinations), and it is in this that such *constraint* properly consists"; and *V-Mo/Mron II* 29: 616–17: "*Necessitas actionis invitae* [necessity of action against one's will] is a compulsion. For this it is required, not only that our will be not morally good, but also that it have hindrances. A compulsion always presupposes a hindrance in the will. A man often has inclinations which conflict with the moral law. So duty we regard as a compulsion. A compulsion occurs when we have an inclination to the opposite of an action. The necessitation to an action, such that we have an inclination to its opposite, is therefore compulsion." Cf. also *KpV* 5: 32; 5: 83; *V-Mo/Mron II* 29: 605; 29: 611; *V-MS/Vigil* 27: 519; 27: 623.

1. THE HOLY WILL AND THE GOOD WILL

A first such concern might be to wonder whether Kant can in fact make the idea of the holy will, as he conceives it, consistent with his own philosophical position, and in particular with his conception of the good will. For, in the *Groundwork* and elsewhere, Kant famously characterizes the good will as a will that acts out of duty; but if the holy will cannot act in this way, how can it be good?

I think this worry underlies H. A. Prichard's claim, in his unpublished lectures on the *Groundwork*, that "[Kant's] idea of a holy will is untenable" (Prichard 2002: 55). Prichard argues that Kant must explain how the holy will is moved to action, where (Prichard states) the mere goodness or rightness of some state of affairs cannot explain this in itself. However, Kant has ruled out using a "sense of obligation" as the explanation for action by the holy will, as this will is not supposed to have any such sense. Thus, Prichard argues, Kant is forced to say that the holy will acts out of a "good desire." But then, it seems, Kant has contradicted his own analysis of the good will, which is a will that acts out of a sense of duty, not inclination, no matter how beneficent: "For though it is possible to perform duties from some good motive other than a sense of obligation, e.g. a desire arising from affection or public spirit, and though such an act will manifest goodness, the goodness manifested will not be moral goodness" (Prichard 2002: 55–6). The question Prichard is pressing, therefore, is the internal coherence of Kant's position: "having formulated the spirit in which a moral being will act, viz. the sense of obligation" (Prichard 2002: 56), but having deprived the holy will of any such sense, how can the holy will be a moral being?

While interesting and prima facie plausible, I think however that Prichard's concern can be allayed.

A first point to note, regarding Kant's conception of the good will itself, is that it is a mistake to think that Kant *identified* the idea of the good will with the will that acts from duty, as if goodness must always involve dutifulness. In fact, when introducing his conception of the good will at the beginning of the *Groundwork*, Kant says that dutifulness characterizes the good will only when thought of "under certain subjective limitations and hindrances"; he just wants to stress that these "subjective limitations and hindrances" do not take away its goodness altogether—indeed, "far from concealing it and making it unrecognizable, [they] rather bring it out by contrast and make it shine forth all the more brightly" (*GMS* 4: 397). These "subjective limitations and hindrances" are obviously the nonmoral inclinations that prevent us from being holy wills, but where we can still display goodness through acting out of duty: but it is clear from the outset of the *Groundwork* that Kant did not *identify* being a good will with acting out of duty, but merely thought of this as a way of being good, under special constraints and conditions. There thus seems to be no incoherence, from a Kantian point of view, in holding that the holy will acts from the thought that doing this act would be good, and not from the thought that it is its duty.

Second, there are two possible responses one might give to Prichard's worry concerning the actions of a holy will, where Prichard thinks this is a worrisome issue because such actions cannot be explained as arising from a sense of duty (as a holy will has no such sense) or from desires (because a holy will has none). One response is to accept that Prichard is right to be puzzled here, but to argue that Kant would have not have seen anything problematic in such puzzlement; rather, it is just what we would expect, given our limited understanding of any such will (where, of course, this kind of response would fit with Kant's more general emphasis on our cognitive limitations regarding questions of this sort). Even if this kind of reply is in some ways unsatisfying, it is not clear why this still doesn't allow Kant's conception of the holy will to do the work he requires of it, namely to provide a contrast class to a will such as our own.

A more positive response, however, would be to challenge Prichard's claim that the holy will is a "being without desire" (Prichard 2002: 55) in *any* sense. For, of course, while holy wills must lack any desire to do what is wrong, we might still think of the holy will as having inclinations that are in accord with what is right, in a way that would explain the contrast with our own case, while making the agency of the holy will less inchoate than on the first response. So, if we first consider what moral action involves in our own case, Kant's account seems to be that we have various inclinations (such as the desire to commit suicide, or keep some money that has been borrowed), but where conscience then leads us to question such inclinations, and test their associated maxims, where the various formulae that Kant proposes are the tests we use to determine the rightness or wrongness of the actions we feel inclined to perform.[19] We can therefore think of the holy will as also having inclinations,[20] which are what lead it to act, but only inclinations that are moral; but when it acts on them, it does so because they have been assessed in accordance with the formulae and thus in moral terms, so it is not acting *merely* out of feeling or on the basis of inclinations. However, unlike us, because the holy will has no *non*-moral inclinations, these formulae do not constitute imperatives, or what it *ought* to do, but rather what it *will* do, in a way that makes the holy will exempt from duty and obligation, as Kant claims.

I will not attempt to adjudicate between these responses to Prichard here, but both seem available to Kant in ways that suggest the Prichardian worry can be defused. In fact, although Kant does not introduce this distinction very often or with much emphasis,[21] he might be said to draw the contrast between us

---

[19] Cf. *GMS* 4: 421–4.

[20] For a defense of the view that we should see the holy will as having inclinations, see Willaschek (2006: 130–32).

[21] Cf. *MS* 6: 383.

and the holy will in *both* these ways, when he distinguishes between the human will on the one hand, and two *types* of holy will—namely *finite* holy wills and *infinite* ones. The former seem to have inclinations arising from their sensuous natures, but where these inclinations (unlike ours) are always in harmony with reason or at least offer no temptation to it, where the infinite holy will then appears to contrast with the finite holy will in having no inclinations at all. One might then worry, in a Prichardian manner, how such an infinite holy will could operate—but where again it may seem plausible to respond that such understanding is beyond us, while pointing to the finite holy will as a perhaps more intelligible but no less significant contrast class to the human case, on whom the imperatival force of morality still falls.

2. THE HOLY WILL AND "KANTIAN DUALISM"

A second concern to consider is one that was mentioned at the outset: namely, that Kant's account of obligatoriness as it relates to a will that (like ours) is not holy, seems to be symptomatic of the sort of dualistic picture which his critics in the idealist and romantic traditions imputed to Kant, and which so troubled them—this time between reason and desire, duty and inclination. In searching for a more unified picture of the human agent, and in their unwillingness to accept any stark differentiation between the human and the divine, it is unsurprising that this issue of the holy will proved a sticking point for Kant's contemporaries and successors, from Schiller to Hegel.

Now, in order to get this issue into focus, it is important not to exaggerate or misidentify the concerns of Kant's critics here: in fact, there were significant areas of agreement. Thus, both Schiller and Hegel accepted that we are not immediately or spontaneously inclined to moral action, in the manner of the holy will, and that to acquire these moral inclinations requires effort and work for us, through the results of education and habit-forming, in a broadly Aristotelian manner.[22] Indeed, Schiller was prepared to follow Kant in

---

[22] For Schiller, see Schiller (1967: 15), where he characterizes man's "natural character" as "selfish and violent"; and pp. 173–9, where he characterizes man's natural state in amoral terms: "Unacquainted as he is with his *own* human dignity, he is far from respecting it in others; and, conscious of his own savage greed, he fears it in every creature which resembles him" (1967: 173). For Hegel, see Hegel (1991b): §151, p. 195): "But if it is simply *identical* with the actuality of individuals, the ethical [*das Sittliche*], as their general mode of behaviour, appears as a *custom* [*Sitte*]; and the *habit* of the ethical appears as a *second nature* which takes the place of the original and purely natural will and is the all-pervading soul, significance, and actuality of individual existence [*Dasein*]"; and §18 Addition, p. 51: "The Christian doctrine that man is by nature evil is superior to the other according to which he is good. Interpreted philosophically, this doctrine should be understood as follows. As spirit, man is a free being [*Wesen*] who is in a position not to let himself be determined by natural drives. When he exists in an immediate and uncivilized [*ungebildeten*] condition, he is therefore in a situation in which he ought not to be, and from which he must liberate himself. This is the meaning of the doctrine of original sin, without which Christianity would not be the religion of freedom."

taking this process to be one of endless striving, while even for Hegel it would require the coming into being of the rational State to be properly achieved.[23] Moreover, both Schiller and Hegel fully appreciated and sympathized with the motivations behind Kant's position, as required to redress the balance in ethics in favor of rationalism and notions of duty, and against feeling and eudaimonism.[24] It would be wrong to say, therefore, that Schiller and Hegel rejected the very distinction between the holy will and our own, and treated us simply as equivalent in moral character and dispositions to such a perfect moral agent.

However, while accepting the distinction, and even while accepting this makes it hard or even impossible to say that we could be compared to a will that is divine, by going without any nonmoral inclinations, Schiller and Hegel nonetheless disagreed with Kant about the *difficulty* that a properly brought up human moral agent will find in resisting his or her nonmoral inclinations, and thus Kant's tendency to make the idea of *struggle* and *resistance* central to his account of moral obligatoriness, and of human moral experience. Thus, while Schiller accepts that (unlike the holy will) we have nonmoral inclinations, and these may always be part of our nature, he thinks we are also capable of "inclinations to duty," of the sort that he associates with "grace."[25] And likewise, Hegel holds that while human beings are susceptible to "natural drives" that go against morality, they are also capable of gaining emotional and affective

---

[23] See Schiller (1962: 289; 1967: 111; and 2005: 154): "Human beings do have the task of establishing an intimate agreement between their two natures, of always being a harmonious whole, and of acting with their full human capacity. But this beauty of character, the ripest fruit of humanity, is only an idea that they can valiantly strive to live up to, yet, despite all efforts, can never fully attain." Cf. also Schiller (1962: 293; 2005: 158): "In the emotions, agreement with the law of reason is only possible by contravening the demands of nature. And since nature, for ethical reasons, never withdraws her demands, and therefore everything on her side remains the same, no matter how the will behaves in relation to her, so here there is no agreement possible between inclination and duty, between reason and sensuousness; so humans cannot here act with their whole nature in harmony, but only with their reason."

[24] Cf. Schiller (1962: 282; 2005: 148): "In common experience…pleasure is the reason for acting rationally. We have to thank the immortal author of the Critique, to whom fame is due for having reestablished healthy human reason out of philosophical reason, for the fact that morality itself has finally stopped using this language"; and cf. Hegel (1991b: 15–17; and 1991a: §54 Addition, p. 101): "This prevalent moral theory [prior to Kant] was, generally speaking, the system of *Eudaemonism* which, in response to the question of the vocation of man, imparted the answer that he must posit his *happiness* as his aim. Insofar as happiness was understood to be the satisfaction of man's particular inclinations, wishes, needs, etc., what is accidental and personal was made into the principle of his willing and its exercise. In reaction against this Eudaemonism, which lacked any firm footing, and opened the door to every sort of caprice and whim, Kant set up practical reason; and by so doing he expressed the demand for a determination of the will that is universal and equally binding upon all."

[25] See Schiller (1962: 297–308; 2005: 160–70). Schiller's position is made more complicated, however, by his equal (and perhaps more Kantian) insistence of the significance of *dignity*, which consists in a greater degree of self-overcoming. For a fuller discussion of Schiller's position than I can give here, see Stern (2012: 103–35).

satisfaction in moral action, and thus experiencing no necessary exertion in exercising the will when acting ethically.[26]

It might be said, however, that if this is the issue that underlies their residual worries concerning Kant's apparent "dualism," it is an exaggerated one and does not really apply: for, it could be argued, nothing in Kant's picture of obligation actually *requires* any such struggle of this sort. Instead, it could be claimed, all Kant needs and all he is appealing to is a weaker notion, namely the idea that nonmoral action is always *possible* for us in a way that it is not for the holy will; this means that morality serves to constrain us to the extent that it prevents us from taking this option, but where this need not involve any great inner battle between the forces of duty and inclination, reason and desire. That this is the best way to understand Kant's position has been argued by Philip Stratton-Lake:

> The moral law appears to us as an imperative because we do not necessarily will in accordance with it. It appears, therefore, as a *constraint* for a finite rational will. It is easy to take the notion of a constraint as implying that our natural inclinations are in some way essentially opposed to the requirements of the moral law. But Kant thinks that the moral law appears to us as necessitating, or constraining, not because our natural inclinations are intrinsically immoral, but because of the *contingency* of the connection between what we are inclined to do and what we ought to will. The notion of a constraint should not, therefore, be understood as presupposing a conception of inclination as essentially opposed to morality (a view that Hegel and Hegelians are fond of ascribing to Kant), but as expressing the fact that the moral law places a rational *limit* on the practical possibilities open to us in certain circumstances, and is recognised as such. The moral law does not appear to a perfectly rational being as a rational *constraint* because it does not limit the possibilities open to such a will. This is because such a being does not have possibilities open to it which can conflict with, and hence can be limited by, the moral law. (Stratton-Lake 2000: 37–8)[27]

On this sort of account, therefore, we can explain why Kant used the language of constraint and necessitation, in so far as morality limits our options in a way

---

[26] Cf. Hegel (1991b: §151 Addition, p. 195): "Education [*Pädagogik*] is the art of making human beings ethical: it considers them as natural beings and shows them how they can be reborn, and how their original nature can be transformed into a second, spiritual nature so that this spiritual nature becomes *habitual* to them," and §124, p. 152, where Hegel (mis)quotes Schiller, and objects to the way in which "abstract reflection ... produces a view of morality as a perennial and hostile struggle against one's own satisfaction."

[27] Cf. also Stratton-Lake (1996: 50): "I do not, however, think Kant did conceive of morality as essentially opposed to sensibility. The main textual evidence in support of the view that he did is his conception of duties, or obligations as constraints. Duty, according to Kant, is essentially a constraint for a finite will, and a finite will is a sensible will. But what can morality be constraining

that it does not for the holy will, but not in a way that introduces the sort of dualistic picture that so concerned Schiller, Hegel, and many others.

However, while this reading of Kant might make his position more palatable to some tastes, the textual evidence is against it. Stratton-Lake cites in his support the following sentence from *The Metaphysics of Morals*, which may indeed seem to make nothing more than the point he attributes to Kant, that morality constrains us merely to the extent of limiting the various options proposed to us by our inclinations: "The very *concept of duty* is already the concept of a *necessitation* (constraint) of free choice through the law." However, Kant immediately continues:

> This constraint may be an *external constraint* or a *self-constraint*. The moral *imperative* makes this constraint known through the categorical nature of its pronouncement (the unconditional ought). Such constraint, therefore, does not apply to rational beings as such (there could also be *holy* ones) but rather to *human beings*, rational *natural* beings, who are unholy enough that pleasure can induce them to break the moral law, even though they recognize its authority; and even when they do obey the law, they do it *reluctantly* [*ungern*] (in the face of opposition from their inclinations), and it is in this that such *constraint* properly consists.[28]

Kant seems unequivocal here in emphasizing the element of struggle and consequent reluctance involved in obligation, and so exactly the element in his view that Schiller and Hegel found so problematic. And this is by no means an isolated passage, so that while he may have thought we could develop inclinations to be moral, Kant also seems to have held that where we are conscious of a duty, we must invariably experience reluctance, resistance, and a sense of hindrance—not just an awareness of the existence of possible nonmoral options, but also the thwarted desire to take them.[29] For Kant, it seems, the concept of duty only makes sense in this context.

Moreover, if we downplay these aspects of Kant's view, we also arguably lose much of the explanatory power of Kant's position, which is to account for the

---

if it is not our sensible nature? And, it may be asked, what does it mean to say that morality is essentially a constraint on sensibility unless sensibility is conceived of as essentially opposing it?

But moral constraint need not be interpreted as overpowering the opposing force of sensibility. Moral constraint may be interpreted as a *rational limitation* of the possibilities open to one in certain situations... It is for this reason that duty is inapplicable to a holy will. Such a will is not constrained, or limited by morality because it necessarily wills what is right. Since it is not possible for a holy will to set itself to bring about anything other than a moral end, morality cannot be conceived of as a limitation on the possible courses of action open to it. It is, however, *possible* for a finite will to set itself to bring about some end other than the one required by morality. On this interpretation, then, Kant's view does not commit him to the view that morality and sensibility are essentially opposed, but only to the view that they *may* be opposed."

[28] *MS* 6: 379.

[29] Cf. the passages cited above, note 18.

felt necessity of morality, the way it exercises a certain authority or control over us—where Kant seems to rely on the "clash" between the forces of reason and desire, duty and inclination, to account for this experience.[30] If we go too far in depriving Kant of his "dualism," therefore, we will arguably lose this aspect of his account, which is required if he is to do justice to what he is setting out to explain.[31] Conversely, Kant's critics such as Schiller and Hegel are not in a good position to make sense of this feature of our moral life, and so attempt to downplay it or do away with it altogether: but it is arguable that this leaves them failing to leave room for the demandingness that ethics must require, if it is not to become complacent and ask too little of us. Thus, while Kant can be accused by Schiller and Hegel of seeming to make morality go against the grain of our dispositions, Schiller and Hegel can in their turn be accused of compromising the critical force of morality and potentially radical nature of its demands, by trying to prevent morality from going beyond them in this way.[32]

3. ACCOUNTING FOR NECESSITATION WITHOUT THE DISTINCTION

However, even if it is accepted that it is important for an account of obligation to explain the imperatival force that morality has for us as a feature of our moral experience, it might be said that alternative and better ways of doing this can be found, that can do without Kant's distinction between the holy will and our own.

---

[30] Cf. Sidgwick (1907: 77; my emphasis): "Such cognitions [of the rightness and wrongness of conduct], again, I have called 'dictates,' or 'imperatives'; because, in so far as they relate to conduct on which anyone is deliberating, they are accompanied by a certain impulse to do the acts recognised as right, *which is liable to conflict with other impulses.*" As Sidgwick makes clear on pp. 34–5 (to which he is referring here), it is this conflict which he makes crucial to the commandingness of morality, and which he sees as distinctive to us as moral agents, much like Kant—where also much like Kant (I argue in section V) he treats this picture as compatible with a realism about what is right: "In fact, this possible conflict of motives seems to be connoted by the term 'dictate' or 'imperative,' which describes the relation of Reason to mere inclinations or non-rational impulses by comparing it to the relation between the will of a superior and the wills of his subordinates. This conflict seems also to be implied in the terms 'ought,' 'duty,' 'moral obligation,' as used in ordinary moral discourse: and hence these terms cannot be applied to the actions of rational beings to whom we cannot attribute impulses conflicting with reason. We may, however, say of such beings that their actions are 'reasonable,' or (in an absolute sense) 'right'." Cf. also Schneewind (1992: 317): "[For Kant] The term 'ought' is central to our moral vocabulary because the tension between reason and desire is central to our moral experience."

[31] Cf. Kant's response to Schiller in *RGV*, where Kant makes clear that he is unwilling "to associate *gracefulness* with the *concept of duty*...For the concept of duty includes unconditional necessitation, to which gracefulness stands in direct contradiction" (*RGV* 6: 23 note). Some commentators have taken Kant's subsequent talk of the joyous temperament that should go along with duty as a sign that he is in fact closer to Schiller's model of grace than this first comment suggests. But it is important that the joy taken is in the successful doing of one's duty and hence in the self-mastery that this has involved, not a joy that will somehow take this element of mastery away, in the manner of Schiller's model of grace.

[32] For further discussion of this and related issues, see Stern (2012: 247–52).

An alternative strategy of this sort has been put forward recently by Christine Korsgaard. On the one hand, she has little sympathy with attempts to downplay the role of necessitation as a psychological force in our moral lives,[33] and to replace it with what she calls the "Good Dog" picture of the virtuous agent, as someone "whose desires and inclinations have been so perfectly trained that he always does what he ought to do spontaneously and with tail-wagging cheerfulness and enthusiasm" (Korsgaard 2009: 3). On the other hand, she does not think necessitation can be accounted for by adopting the opposite model of the "Miserable Sinner," which treats human beings as "in a state of eternal reform, who must repress [their] unruly desires in order to conform to the demands of duty" (Korsgaard 2009: 3). Korsgaard claims that "[t]he opposition between the two pictures is shallow, for they share the basic intuition that the experience of necessitation is a sign that there is something wrong with the person who undergoes it," and thus they both "denigrate the experience of necessitation" (Korsgaard 2009: 3–4). She also argues that both pictures fail to give an adequate account of how we are necessitated, or how it is we come to be bound to what is right or good (Korsgaard 2009: 4–7).

Now, Korsgaard sees Kant's attempt to offer an account of necessitation which employs the contrast between us and the holy will as fitting into the flawed "Miserable Sinner" model; and though she accepts that therefore Kant in part adopted this model, she thinks he was wrong to do so, for the reasons outlined above.[34] But she thinks we can use different Kantian materials to develop a better and less shallow way of understanding necessitation, which traces the issue back to the struggle for self-constitution, and what is involved in that:

> I believe that these theories [associated with the "Good Dog" and "Miserable Sinner" models] both underestimate and misplace the role of necessitation in our psychic lives. There is work and effort—a kind of struggle—involved in the moral life, and those who struggle successfully are the ones whom we call "rational" or "good". But it is not the struggle *to be rational* or *to be good*. It is, instead, the ongoing struggle for integrity, the struggle for psychic unity, the struggle to be, in the face of psychic complexity, a single unified agent. Normative standards—as I am about to argue—are the principles by which we achieve the psychic unity that makes agency possible. The work of achieving psychic unity, the work that we experience as necessitation, is what I am going to call *self-constitution*. (Korsgaard 2009: 7)

---

[33] Cf. Korsgaard (2009: 3): "[T]he normativity of obligation is, among other things, a psychological force. Let me give this phenomenon a name, borrowed from Immanuel Kant. Since normativity is a form of necessity, Kant calls its operation within us—its manifestation as a psychological force—*necessitation.*"

[34] Cf. Korsgaard (2009: 4 note 5), and Korsgaard (2008: 52 note 39), where she states that "the view that the will's imperfection is what makes us subject to an *ought* . . . is a red herring here."

Korsgaard thus develops what she still thinks of as a Kantian account of necessitation, but one that makes no appeal to his conception of the holy will, and the contrast that conception allows Kant to draw with a finite will such as ours.

It is not possible here to work through Korsgaard's position in any detail, as she offers a complex view that requires extensive consideration to do it justice. However, I think there is an obvious potential difficulty for it, which does not seem to afflict the Kantian position that she rejects as based around the "struggle to be good." For, that position locates duty and obligation as arising from the way in which the goodness and rightness present themselves to us, and thus as residing in the moral situation, so that it is what is right and good that obligate and necessitate; but, by contrast, the worry about Korsgaard's account is that it puts this necessitation in the wrong place (so to speak), where it is the struggle of the subject to unify itself that is responsible for this as a "psychic force," where this would seem to lack any underlying connection to anything normative. Someone might well think, therefore, that if there is any degree of struggle in morality, and if this is to be used to explain its obligatory force, then this struggle should revolve around the good and the right, not on the difficulties faced by the self-constituting subject—and this is more readily available on the picture of Kant's position that Korsgaard rejects, than on the one with which she replaces it.

Having now tried to clarify Kant's account of obligation, and shown how it rests on his distinction between the holy will and our own, and having responded to possible objections to my reading of that account, and to the account per se, I now want to go on to suggest two respects in which the account can be used to do some useful work, in enabling us to find a way out of two seemingly intractable disputes in ethics: those between realism and antirealism, and between externalist and internalist accounts of motivation.

V. Applying the Distinction: Realism and Antirealism

It is scarcely surprising that the dispute between realists and antirealists in ethics is long-standing and ongoing, as both sides have their clear attractions, while also having their drawbacks, where each is often mirrored in the views of the other. In the recent literature on Kant, these respective advantages and disadvantages have been highlighted in competing interpretations of Kant himself, where both realist and antirealist constructivist accounts have emerged.[35] Very broadly speaking, the contrast here is that the realist claims that moral facts

---

[35] On the constructivist side, these readings originate with John Rawls's seminal article Rawls (1980), and can be found in work by (for example) Korsgaard, O'Neill, and Reath. On the realist side, see for example, Hare (2001: 87–119), Kain (1999; 2004; 2006), Ameriks (2003), Irwin (2004), Langton (2007), Hills (2008). There is also a realist aspect to Allen Wood's reading of Kant: see Wood (1999: 157, and 374–5, notes 4 and 5); this is even clearer in Wood (2008: see e.g., 112–14).

(such as the fact that lying is wrong) hold independently of human attitudes, responses, or choices (for example, of whether we disapprove of lying, or would reject lying in a contractual situation, or would in some way be irrational to adopt lying as a form of behavior), while the antirealist claims that these facts obtain precisely *because of* these attitudes, responses, or choices—where for the *constructivist* antirealist, what matters is that agents operating under certain real or ideal conditions would endorse or accept or choose some behaviors or outcomes over others, thereby making them right or good.

Now, given these contrasting views, there is then a familiar dialectical back-and-forth between them. On the one side, the realist will argue that the constructivist cannot avoid endorsing realism at some point, for unless some moral facts are taken to obtain *prior* to the choices we make as agents, where these choices are then governed by these facts, then the constructive procedure will be utterly unconstrained and its results morally arbitrary and relative. On the other side, the constructivist will argue that any such independent moral facts are too mysterious to be treated as explanatorily basic but are not in any way explained by the realist, while their independence from us makes them a threat to our autonomy as agents. Each side thus raises concerns (of emptiness and relativism on the one hand; and of "queerness" and heteronomy on the other) that appear genuine and serious, but which neither can wholly address left to itself.

At this point, therefore, it is natural to look for a way out of the impasse: and I would argue that Kant's account of obligatoriness using his position on the holy will provides us with such a way forward. For, this account can be viewed as having two levels, and thus as a kind of "hybrid" position that combines elements of realism with elements of antirealism, to the advantage of both.

The realist level concerns the content of morality, what is right and wrong, and the value of freedom on which this rests. Kant is insistent in many passages that not even God can determine by an act of will or choice what this content is to be, as this is not contingent and chosen but fixed and necessary, and so obtains independently of any relation to an agent.[36] He also speaks in many passages as if he conceives of the value of the free rational agent in

---

[36] Cf. *V-Mo/Collins* 27: 282–3: "The lawgiver is not always simultaneously an originator of the law; he is only that if the laws are contingent. But if the laws are practically necessary, and he merely declares that they conform to his will, then he is a lawgiver. So nobody, not even the deity, is an originator of moral laws, since they have not arisen from choice, but are practically necessary; if they were not so, it might even be the case that lying was a virtue. But moral laws can still be subject to a lawgiver; there may be a being who is omnipotent and has power to execute these laws, and to declare that this moral law is at the same time a law of His will and obliges everyone to act accordingly. Such a being is then a lawgiver, though not an originator; just as God is no originator of the fact that a triangle has three corners." Cf. also *MS* 6: 227: "A (morally practical) *law* is a proposition that contains a categorial imperative (a command). One who commands (*imperans*) through a law is the *lawgiver* (*legislator*). He is the author (*autor*) of the obligation in

realist terms.[37] However, as we have seen, Kant does not treat the *obligatoriness* of what is right and wrong as independent in this way, for we give the content of morality its obligatory form, in so far as this depends on our limitedness as finite creatures, so that this obligatoriness is just the way in which what is right and wrong presents itself *to us*, from our human (all too human) perspective; from the perspective of a divine will, and so from the "absolute standpoint," there *is* no duty and obligation, but only what is right and wrong, because the divine will has none of the nonmoral inclinations which (as we have seen) mean that what is right is represented to us in the form of duties and obligations, and thus as the moral "must."[38] Kant is thus able to side with the realist about the right, and thus avoids the specter of emptiness and arbitrariness that threatens constructivism; but he is able to side with the antirealist about the obligatory, and thus avoid much of the "queerness" associated with the idea that the world in itself makes *demands* on us, and also avoid the threat to our autonomy that any such purely "external" demand might seem to imply. Kant thus offers us a hybrid view, that is neither fully realist nor fully antirealist "all the way down," but combines elements of both to the advantage of his position as a whole.[39]

To a significant degree, therefore, I would argue that the basic structure of Kant's ethics resembles that of his theoretical philosophy, which equally employs a form/content distinction to combine realism with idealism. Thus, while Kant rejects an idealism that goes "all the way down" and leads to a Berkeleyan subjectivism that would be unconstrained by the world, he also

---

accordance with the law, but not always the author of the law. In the latter case the law would be a positive (contingent) and chosen law. A law that binds us a priori and unconditionally by our own reason can also be expressed as proceeding from the will of a supreme lawgiver, that is, one who has only rights and no duties (hence from the divine will); but this signifies only the idea of a moral being whose will is a law for everyone, without his being thought of as the author of the law." Cf. also *V-Mo/Vigil* 27: 544: "Were we to conceive of the legislator as *auctor legis*, this would have reference only to statutory laws. But if we ascribe an *auctor* to laws that are known, through reason, from the nature of the case, he can only be an author of the obligation that is contained in the law. Thus God, too, by the declared divine will, is *auctor legis*, and precisely because natural laws were already in existence, and are ordained by Him." For further discussion of this material and related passages, see Hare (2001: 94–7), Kain (1999: 177–99), Irwin (2004), Timmermann (2007: 106–7), and Acton (1970: 38–9).

[37] Cf. *GMS* 4: 428: "But suppose there were something *the existence of which in itself* has an absolute worth, something which as *an end in itself* could be a ground of determinate laws; then in it, and in it alone, would lie the ground of a possible categorical imperative, that is, of a practical law. Now I say that the human being and in general every rational beings *exists* as an end in itself, *not merely as a means* to be used by this will or that will at its discretion."

[38] Cf. *KU*, 5: 403–4: "...it is clear that it depends only on the subjective constitution of our practical faculty that the moral laws must be represented as commands (and the actions which are in accord with them as duties), and that reason expressed this necessity not through a **be** (happening) but through a should-be..."

[39] I think Irwin also sees Kant as adopting this sort of hybrid view: "[Kant] recognizes intrinsic rightness without any acts of commanding or obligating...In Kant's view, commands and act of binding are relevant [only] to finite rational agents, who are also subject to other incentives and so have to be instructed and urged to follow the moral law" (Irwin 2004: 149).

rejects a full-blown realism that aims to treat all our experience of that world as if it conformed to reality as it exists in itself, wholly independent of our perspective on it. And equally, of course, Kant hoped that this would enable us to escape the fruitless oscillation between empirical idealism on the one hand, and transcendental realism on the other. In ethics, it can therefore be argued, Kant could use his distinction between the divine will and our own to settle a similar kind of impasse, in a way that promises some of the similar dividends of his "Copernican revolution" in theoretical philosophy.

VI. Applying the Distinction: Externalism and Internalism

I now want to turn to a second area where again I believe that Kant's account of obligation also enables him to take a distinctive "middle path," this time between externalism and internalism concerning the relation between the normative status of certain actions and the motivations of agents.[40]

This terminology is used in a number of different ways, but at the heart of the dispute I am interested in here is the question whether (as the internalist claims) for someone's actions to possess the moral status they have (of being right or wrong, or good or bad, or a duty, or an obligation, or something they ought to do, and so on) it is necessary for the agent to have (actually or dispositionally) a motivation so to act, so that the former depends on the "internal states" of the latter; or whether on the other hand there is no such link or dependence, as the externalist claims. Thus, on the internalist view, the moral features of actions are said to be essentially related to considerations concerning motivation, thereby bringing in the motivational states of agents, not just features of the action that stand outside the agents concerned and are "external" to them (for example, whether the action would maximize happiness, or is divinely commanded, or is "fitting," or whatever).

One's stance on this dispute can be influenced by a variety of considerations, but perhaps three are central: the relation between cases of moral judgment and action; the threat of moral skepticism and how to deal with it; and the relation between this issue and metaethical disputes concerning realism and various forms of antirealism.

---

[40] This is to be distinguished from a different debate in ethics where the vocabulary of externalism and internalism is also used, which centres on *reasons*, where the internalist argues that for an agent to have a reason to act, that action must in some way relate to the agent's desires, interests and concerns, in a way that the externalist denies. The debate I will discuss is also to be distinguished from another more closely related internalism/externalism dispute, which concerns motivations, but which focuses on whether making a positive moral judgment about an action can in itself give one a motivation to so act (internalism), or whether it can only do so in conjunction with some additional factor (such as a desire to act morally). Following Darwall, this position is often called *judgment internalism*, whereas the one I will discuss is called *existence internalism*: see Darwall (1992).

On the first issue, internalists have been struck by the fact that in making a positive moral judgment concerning some action, it then seems very curious not to act or to at least admit to some inclination to doing so: surely, the internalist argues (absent weakness of will and other complicating factors[41]), in these circumstances we would be forced to conclude that the agent did not really have the moral concept in the first place or had not genuinely made a judgment involving it[42]—where this then suggests (the internalist will claim) that what makes the moral judgment true partly concerns their motivational state and not just some fact "external" to this. By contrast, externalists have thought that such cases, while in fact (thankfully) rare in practice (perhaps because most of us possess an antecedent disposition to act on our moral judgments, or because these judgments bring about such motivations in themselves), nonetheless do not involve any conceptual incoherence as such, as they would if to make a first-personal moral judgment about an action is to already attribute to oneself some motivation to so act.

On the issue of moral skepticism, internalists have taken it as an advantage of their view that a certain sort of moral skeptic is ruled out, namely a skeptic who makes a moral judgment concerning some action ("this is right," "this is what I ought to do"), but denies any motivational connection to the action, and so still asks to be given some motivating reason to act in this way. In so far as dispensing with the threat of skepticism is always desirable in a philosophical position, internalists have therefore claimed it as an advantage of theirs that it does so.[43] Against this, however, externalists have claimed that the internalist position is in fact implausibly strong when it comes to skepticism, in seeming to make amoralism of this kind incoherent, when in fact it is not—the amoralist, the externalist argues, is a perfectly conceivable creature, and we are not guilty of any conceptual error in taking him seriously as a threat.[44]

And on the background metaethical issue, philosophers have often been attracted to internalism because it seems most naturally to go along with an antirealist position in ethics, as this most easily explains why the truth of a moral judgment depends on the motivational status of the agent: for example, on an expressivist view, moral facts are themselves grounded in the attitudes, desires, and passions of agents, where these are states that motivate the agent to act, so it is clear why the internalist claim might hold. On the other side, therefore, realists have generally been wary of accepting internalism in this form, fearing that to do so will push them into an antirealist stance.

---

[41] For example, that there is a greater obligation to do something else.

[42] Cf. Smith (1994: 67–71).

[43] For a thorough discussion of the relation between internalism and moral skepticism, see Superson (2009: 127–59).

[44] Cf. Brink (1989: 46–50).

Here, then, we again have a debate where it is possible to be pulled both ways. For, even if the externalist is right to claim that there is not something wholly inconceivable in a person forming a moral judgment about an action and yet not being moved to do act, on the other hand the internalist seems right to point out that there is *something* curious in this situation that needs to be explained. And even if the externalist is right that amoralist moral skepticism is not incoherent in every respect, on the other hand it would be good to have something to say to such a skeptic along internalist lines. And while the realist might be right to be wary of internalism, this does not in itself count as an argument against it, so that to anyone who is *not* a realist, it might instead count in its favor.

Now, from the perspective of Kant's position as I have characterized it, I think we are in a position to diagnose this debate, and see how it is that there is something plausible in both sides. This diagnosis hinges on the distinction we have drawn between rightness or goodness on the one hand and obligatoriness or duty on the other, a distinction which (as we have seen) relates closely to Kant's contrast between the holy will and a will such as ours. For, I will argue, this enables Kant to be an internalist at the level of obligation and duty, while being an externalist about the right and the good, and thus once again allows him to combine elements from both positions, and so resolve the impasse between them.

When it comes to obligation or duty, as we have seen, Kant holds that these arise for wills such as ours because our nonmoral inclinations are in some sort of tension with our moral motivations, in a way that does not happen for a holy will, which is only ever motivated to act morally. It follows from this account, therefore, that for a person to have an obligation or duty to φ, they must have at least some motivation to φ, as otherwise no such tension could arise. Kant's position on obligation and duty is therefore at least weakly internalist, in the sense that it is committed to there being at least some degree of motivation to φ in the agent who has φ-ing as their duty or obligation, whether or not that motivation will always ultimately be the one that wins out. To this extent, therefore, the Kantian can agree that there is something indeed incoherent in acknowledging a duty or obligation and failing to acknowledge any motivation to do it, which fits with the internalist's intuitions about some of the cases; and he can agree about the absurdity of the skeptic who claims to see that he ought to φ or that φ-ing is his duty, but not to have any motivation to φ: to grasp the former, he must have the latter, for the former involves a tension between *that* motivation, and some other.

On the other hand, Kant can also accommodate externalist concerns that embracing internalism can take us too far: for, as we have seen, Kant's hybrid account allows him to distinguish between moral notions like duty and obligation on the one hand, and notions like the right and the good on the other, and so to hold that while the internalist may be right about the former, the externalist is right about the latter. For, while the internalist's position might well fit with imperatival concepts like duty and obligation, for Kant it is possible also to conceive of moral concepts that do not take this imperatival form, so that judgments involving such concepts need assert or imply nothing about the agent's motivations, but can be employed and made true in an externalist manner. This, then, allows room for an externalist treatment of actions that are right and good for the agent to do, while combining this with an internalist treatment of actions that are obligations or duties for the agent. Moreover, this means that Kant can respect internalist intuitions about the skeptic who ascribes moral properties like duty and obligatoriness to her actions, as such properties would seem to have motivational considerations "built in"; at the same time, however, it can also make space for externalist intuitions concerning the skeptic who only ascribes to them properties like rightness or goodness: for nothing in the moral properties of the right or the good involves this internal relation to motivational forces, in the way that it does for obligatoriness and duty, on Kant's picture. And Kant need not therefore claim that the amoralist about the right and the good, who accepts that an act has these features but lacks any motivation to so act, can be ruled out on the grounds of misusing the relevant concepts or failing to make a judgment.

Moreover, we can also see how Kant can offer a more complex treatment of the relation between internalism and externalism on the one hand, and antirealism and realism on the other. For, just as his antirealism operates at the level of obligatoriness but not at the level of the right and the good, so too his internalism operates only at that level and not the second; he therefore shows how the realist can safely embrace internalism about some aspects of the moral, in so far as this does not in itself force him to become an anti-realist all the way down.

In these respects, it is interesting to compare Kant's position with that of W. D. Falk on such issues. Falk, of course, is generally credited with first crystallizing the whole externalism/internalism debate, both in terms of the distinction itself, and also how it relates to wider metaethical issues, such as the contrast between realism and antirealism. However, it has less often been noted that Falk seems to adopt a view that, like Kant's, operates at different levels and so is equally hybrid in defending an internalism and antirealism about obligation and duty, and an externalism and realism about the right and the good. This has been obscured, I think, because the subsequent debate has often focused on moral properties or judgments in general rather than on duty and obligation in particular, in a way that means this distinction of levels gets lost—so that it is not properly appreciated that when Falk talks about internalism, it is really an internalism about *obligation* that he is speaking about, not about *all* moral properties.

This feature of Falk's position comes out particularly clearly in his article "Obligation and Rightness" (Falk 1945).[45] In this paper, Falk's basic aim is to question whether Ross (and to a lesser degree Prichard), in providing an account of rightness, can also claim to have accounted for moral obligation.

---

[45] This is one of Falk's earliest papers—and perhaps for this reason it was not included in his collection of papers Falk (1986)—and therefore is correspondingly little discussed.

Falk does so by contrasting rightness and goodness as states of affairs external to the subject, with duties and obligations, which involve the subject feeling "*internally constrained* to do the act in question" (Falk 1945: 138). It is for this reason that Falk thinks that "when we try to convince another that he ought to pay his bills, we expect our argument if accepted to affect a change of heart in him, though it may still not change his outward actions" (Falk 1945: 141). Falk therefore argues that the good and the right can be no more than the *ground* of what is obligatory, and should not be confused with obligatoriness as such:

> The nature of the things which we are obliged to do contains only the *grounds*, but not yet the *essence* of moral obligation. What alone can render a prospective action obligatory is that an agent is in some manner impelled to do it, or that he thinks he would be so impelled if he reflected... Hence what makes the good act a duty is not the bare fact that it would be good when done, but the fact that the thought of it is related to ourselves in a special manner; and even if it were the case that ultimately none but good acts were obligatory, their goodness would be no more than the *ground* of a separate obligation to do them... The same argument applies to rightness or fittingness. (Falk 1945: 145)

In distinguishing the right and the good from duty and obligation in this way, Falk like Kant appears to adopt a hybrid view; and this means his position can contain both internalist and externalist elements.

Thus, Falk is willing to accept an externalist position like Ross's and Prichard's when it comes to the right and the good. He argues, however, that this should not be confused with obligation and duty, which have a different logical form from the right and the good, which involve taking into account the motivations of the agent when attributing to them any obligation and duty:

> Here it is interesting to note that the belief that obligations are independent existents is in some manner fostered by the suggestiveness of language. "Having an obligation" or "being under an obligation" suggests a state of affairs existing for an agent, yet not merely in relation to him. But to "have an obligation" is not like "having money in the bank"; to be "under an obligation" is not like being "under a shower" or "in the water." If anything it is like "having an impulse," "having an obsession," or "being in trouble." For the second set of expressions we can substitute assertions about individual states of mind, like "being impelled," "being obsessed" or "being troubled," for the first we cannot. I have no doubt that "having an obligation" ranks with the second. The possibility of substituting for it the expression "being obliged" is a clear clue to this. Strictly speaking, there is nothing that can be called *an obligation*. What we think of when

we use the term is *that agents are obliged by the thought of them*, or *that the thought of actions obliges agents to do them*. We think not of an *entity*, but of a *relation* between agents, the thought of actions, and the doing of actions. (Falk 1945: 143)

Falk therefore argues that "To oblige is to affect, to be obliged is to be affected" (Falk 1945: 143). But it is important to note that he is talking *only* about obligation here, not the right and the good as such, where he raises no objection to the realist accounts of this offered by Ross and Prichard; his objection is just to treating the two normative levels in the same manner, and so treating law and duty as if they were inherent "in the nature of things" (Falk 1986: 180). Falk rightly (on my view) characterizes his position as Kantian, both to the extent that "[t]o Kant the very existence of a duty was inseparable from the existence of a motive," as providing "some real check on [a person's] freedom to act otherwise" (Falk 1986: 29), and because like Kant he traces the "must" of obligation back to the conflict between reason and desire, and the limitations of the human will.[46] Thus, when Falk comes to argue in his later papers that there is a certain incoherence in moral skepticism that the externalist cannot acknowledge, and that the externalist cannot account for the absurdity of being faced with someone who accepts that φ-ing is their duty but questions whether they have any motivation for doing so, it is important to remember that Falk (like Kant) is pressing the force of these internalist considerations just at the level of duty and obligation, so that nothing here commits him to internalism about the "ground" of obligation, which is the right and the good; and in so far as internalism has any affinity with antirealism, nothing commits him to antirealism about this "ground" either.

VII. Conclusion

My aim in this chapter has been to explicate Kant's distinction between the holy will and one like our own, and to show how that distinction plays a significant role in his account of duty and obligation. I do not here pretend to have resolved or anticipated all the objections that might now arise to this position, both as an explication of Kant, and as a position in its own right—indeed, much like the empirical realism/transcendental idealism combination adopted in Kant's theoretical philosophy, to which I have compared it, one can anticipate comparable puzzlements and expressions of dissatisfaction about the overall coherence and stability of the view. However, much as that view in Kant's theoretical philosophy has proved remarkably durable and attractive in the face of such puzzlement and dissatisfaction, so, perhaps, it might in the end turn

---

[46] Cf. Falk (1986: 184 and 168–9).

out similarly here in Kant's practical philosophy, by reflecting a higher wisdom than either of the sides it tries to steer between.[47]

Bibliography

Acton, H. B. (1970) *Kant's Moral Philosophy*. London: Macmillan.

Ameriks, K. (2003) "On Two Non-realist Interpretations of Kant's Ethics," in *Interpreting Kant's Critiques*. Oxford: Oxford University Press.

Beck, L. W. (1960) *A Commentary on Kant's "Critique of Practical Reason."* Chicago: Chicago University Press.

Brink, D. O. (1989) *Moral Realism and the Foundations of Ethics*. Cambridge: Cambridge University Press.

Darwall, S. L. (1992) "Internalism and Agency," *Philosophical Perspectives* 6: 155–74.

Falk, W. D. (1945) "Obligation and Rightness," *Philosophy* 20(76): 129–47.

Falk, W. D. (1986) *Ought, Reasons, and Morality*. Ithaca, NY: Cornell University Press.

Garner, R. T. (1990) "On the Genuine Queerness of Moral Properties and Facts," *Australasian Journal of Philosophy* 68(2): 137–46.

Hare, J. E. (2000a) "Kant on Recognizing our Duties as God's Commands," *Faith and Philosophy* 17(4): 459–78.

Hare, J. E. (2000b) "Kant's Divine Command Theory and its Reception within Analytic Philosophy," in D. Z. Phillips and T. Tessin (eds.), *Kant and Kierkegaard on Religion*, 263–77. New York: Palgrave Macmillan.

Hare, J. E. (2001) *God's Call: Moral Realism, God's Commands, and Human Autonomy*. Grand Rapids, MI: William B. Eerdmans.

Hare, J. E. (2007) *God and Morality: A Philosophical History*. Oxford: Blackwell.

Hegel, G. W. F. (1991a) *The Encyclopaedia of the Philosophical Sciences*, Part I: *The Encyclopaedia Logic*. Tr. T. F. Geraets, W. A. Suchting, and H. S. Harris. Indianapolis: Hackett.

Hegel, G. W. F. (1991b) *The Philosophy of Right*. Tr. H. B. Nisbet. Cambridge: Cambridge University Press.

Hills, A. (2008) "Kantian Value Realism," *Ratio* 21(2): 182–200.

Irwin, T. (2004) "Kantian Autonomy," in J. Hyman and H. Stewart (eds.), *Agency and Action*, 137–64. Cambridge: Cambridge University Press.

Kain, P. (1999) *Self-legislation and Prudence in Kant's Moral Philosophy*. PhD. diss. Notre Dame University.

Kain, P. (2004) "Self-legislation in Kant's Moral Philosophy," *Archiv für Geschichte der Philosophie* 86(3): 257–306.

Kain, P. (2006) "Realism and Anti-realism in Kant's Second *Critique*," *Philosophy Compass* 1(5): 449–65.

Kerstein, S. J. (2002). *Kant's Search for the Supreme Principle of Morality*. Cambridge, Cambridge University Press.

---

[47] I am grateful to the following people who provided me with helpful comments on previous drafts of this paper: Karl Ameriks, Sorin Baiasu, Daniel Elstein, Paul Franks, Charles Larmore, Oliver Sensen, Philip Stratton-Lake, Oliver Thorndike, and Marcus Willaschek.

Korsgaard, C. M. (2008). "The Normativity of Instrumental Reason," in *The Constitution of Agency: Essays on Practical Reason and Moral Psychology*, 27–68. Oxford: Oxford University Press.

Korsgaard, C. M. (2009) *Self-constitution: Agency, Identity, and Integrity*. Oxford: Oxford University Press.

Langton, R. (2007) "Objective and Unconditional Value," *Philosophical Review* 116(2): 57–85.

Paton, H. J. (1967) *The Categorical Imperative*. 6th ed. London: Hutchinson.

Prichard, H. A. (2002) "Kant's *Fundamental Principles of the Metaphysic of Morals*," in *Moral Writings*. Ed. J. MacAdam. Oxford: Oxford University Press.

Rawls, J. (1980) "Kantian Constructivism in Moral Theory," *Journal of Philosophy* 77(9): 515–72.

Schiller, F. (1962) "Über Anmut und Würde," in *Nationalausgabe der Werke Schillers*. Vol. 20. Weimar: Böhlau.

Schiller, F. (1967) *On the Aesthetic Education of Man in a Series of Letters*. Tr. E. M. Wilkinson and L. A. Willoughby. Oxford: Oxford University Press.

Schiller, F. (2005) "On Grace and Dignity." Tr. J. V. Curran in *Schiller's "On Grace and Dignity" in its Cultural Context*. Rochester, NY: Camden House.

Schneewind, J. B. (1992) "Autonomy, Obligation, and Virtue: An Overview of Kant's Moral Philosophy," in P. Guyer (ed.), *The Cambridge Companion to Kant*, 309–41. Cambridge: Cambridge University Press.

Schwaiger, C. (2009) "The Theory of Obligation in Wolff, Baumgarten, and the Early Kant," in K. Ameriks and O. Höffe (eds.), *Kant's Moral and Legal Philosophy*, 58–76. Cambridge: Cambridge University Press.

Sidgwick, H. (1907) *The Methods of Ethics*. 7th ed. Indianapolis: Hackett.

Smith, M. (1994) *The Moral Problem*. Oxford: Blackwell.

Stern, R. (2012) *Understanding Moral Obligation: Kant, Hegel, Kierkegaard*. Cambridge: Cambridge University Press.

Stratton-Lake, P. (1996) "In Defence of the Abstract," *Bulletin of the Hegel Society of Great Britain* 33: 42–53.

Stratton-Lake, P. (2000) *Kant, Duty and Moral Worth*. London: Routledge.

Superson, A. M. (2009) *The Moral Skeptic*. Oxford: Oxford University Press.

Timmermann, J. (2007) *Kant's "Groundwork of the Metaphysics of Morals": A Commentary*. Cambridge: Cambridge University Press.

Willaschek, M. (2006) "Practical Reason: A Commentary on Kant's *Groundwork of the Metaphysics of Morals* (GMS II, 412–417)," in C. Horn and D. Schönecker (eds.), *Groundwork for the Metaphysics of Morals*, 121–38. Berlin: Walter de Gruyter.

Wood, A. W. (1999) *Kant's Ethical Thought*. Cambridge: Cambridge University Press.

Wood, A. W. (2008) *Kantian Ethics*. Cambridge: Cambridge University Press.

7

Is Practical Justification in Kant Ultimately Dogmatic?

Karl Ameriks

I. Introduction: A New Phase in an Old Dispute

One way to begin to evaluate Kant's theory of morality as autonomy is to distinguish the four major components of the theory, namely, its account of morality's possibility, content, motivation, and authority.[1] With respect to all four of these components, worries can arise about Kant as a dogmatic philosopher. His account of morality's possibility rests on a controversial metaphysics of transcendental idealism and transcendental freedom, his account of content rests on a formalism that invokes controversial claims about the adequacy of a pure universalization procedure and a nonnatural conception of persons as "ends in themselves," and his theory of motivation invokes a metaphysical account of the feeling of respect, as well as pure postulates involving traditional notions of God, immortality, and a nonnatural highest good.

Elsewhere I have already offered some defense of Kant on these first three issues,[2] so my concern here is primarily the fourth topic, the issue of morality's claim to authority. This claim can be divided into a number of subclaims, including what I call morality's claims to "feasibility," "pure authority" (or "authority proper"), and "dominance" (or "authoritative dominance"). By morality's "feasibility," I mean an allowance that the moral law "holds" in that it provides a recognizable principle that is understood to be in *some* significant way applicable to human beings. Like the rules of chess, etiquette, or positive

---

[1] All these topics are intertwined and addressed in Kant's concern with showing that pure practical reason has "reality," and that reason proves itself "in der Tat praktisch" (*KpV* 5: 42).

[2] See Ameriks (2000: 311 n. 4; 2003: chapters 8 and 11; 2006: chapter 4). Ameriks (2000: chapter 7), stresses some problems in Kant's theory of motivation and radical evil, but recently Kant's views even here have been given a strong defense by many scholars. See especially work by John Hare and Patrick Kain, e.g., Hare (2001) and Kain (2006).

law, this kind of "holding" involves a limited but successful objective as well as subjective de facto aspect. That is, it implies both that there are well-structured rules that normatively govern the relevant area, and also that human beings have relevant access to them, that is, some kind of not entirely unsympathetic way of making use of them. Feasibility is a minimal condition, still far short of what I generally mean by "pure authority." I take "authority," in this central sense, to require, in addition, a recognition by agents that there is a special and deep *de jure* aspect to the rules of morality, in that that these rules (unlike those of chess, etc.) are understood to have at least some kind of legitimate claim on *everyone's attention* as beings with practical reason. Like feasibility, pure authority has a subjective as well as objective aspect, although the objective aspect has primacy, since something can be "recognized" only if it is really there to be recognized.[3]

Recognizing morality's authority in this sense still does not amount to accepting its "dominance," however, for this requires, in addition, a submission in principle to the *overriding* status of moral rules, that is, to the thought that not only do they always merit some of our attention but they also categorically should play at least a trumping role in all maxims for action.[4] The conditions of what I call pure authority and dominance are easily conflated because, from *within* Kant's own moral perspective, conceding morality's authority without accepting its dominance can appear incoherent; however, for those who are not already Kantians, the distinction is obviously crucial in argumentative contexts.

I will be approaching the question of dogmatism in Kant's moral theory as primarily a problem concerning the *justification* of his belief that morality has authoritative dominance for us. It is still often objected, by proponents as well as opponents of Kantian thought, that the final position of his practical philosophy leaves even his Critical system with a disturbing "dogmatic" character in this regard.[5] In earlier work, I have noted that Kant himself allows in his late writings that his philosophy can be called "dogmatic" (*practico-dogmatisch*).[6] This is not at all to deny that Kant generally defines a "Critical" approach as the opposite of a "dogmatic" one, and that he presents his own philosophy largely as a solution to the objectionable features of the earlier phase of modern thought that he calls "dogmatism." These fundamental points do not

---

[3] On this point I am in agreement with the realism defended in Larmore (2008).

[4] These basic distinctions are drawn simply for the purpose of simplifying the interpretation of Kant that follows. For a helpful discussion of further important distinctions concerning rationality in general, see Audi (2001: 221–3).

[5] Kleingeld (2010: 61) cites Guyer (2007: 462), Wood (2008: 135), and Allison (1990: 230–49).

[6] See Ameriks (2003: 184 n. 178; original version, Ameriks 1981); cf. Ameriks (2000: chapter 8). Kant repeatedly uses the term "practico-dogmatic" for his own system in *FM* 20: 297, 305, 309, 311. A philosophical analysis of the pejorative meaning of the English term "dogmatic" is offered in Audi (2008).

prevent Kant from at times understandably endorsing an innocent, rather than perjorative, use of the term "dogmatic" for his own system. This use is grounded in both the general fact that the word "dogma" originally signifies any item of teaching and belief, and the more specific fact that Kant's own system essentially involves substantive practical claims that he usually characterizes as matters of belief (*Glaube*, a term that can have, but need not have, the specific meaning of a kind of religious faith).[7] Kant generally contrasts this kind of belief with what he calls knowledge in a strict sense (*Wissen*), which requires proof that is grounded only on a priori theoretical considerations.[8] The practical instances of belief that Kant endorses are, however, by no means to be understood as matters of a mere arbitrary attitude, for they are said to rest on compelling considerations of pure reason and thus to contrast sharply with the whole realm of mere opinion (*Meinung*).

All this helps to explain why, in allowing that for this reason his own system can be called "practico-dogmatic," Kant does not mean to introduce any kind of weakness into his philosophy. Nonetheless, insofar as Kant's practical philosophy—and in particular the second *Critique*'s introduction of the notion of a "fact of reason"—involves substantive commitments that amount to what I once called "an ultimately unargued-for premise of the validity [i.e., what I now call "authoritative dominance"] of morality,"[9] it is understandable that Kant's readers may continue to worry that his system harbors an *objectionable* form of dogmatism—especially because most of them still tend to come to his texts expecting a system that offers a paradigm of purely *argumentative* certainty.

In more recent essays, I have contended that this common expectation needs to be tempered in interpreting Kant's work in general.[10] Even though there are distinctively disquieting aspects to Kant's practical philosophy and its nonargumentative invocation of a "fact of reason," it should still be conceded that it does "reflect a standpoint that certainly appears widespread" (Ameriks 2003: 260). Moreover, I believe this standpoint fares relatively well when the general argumentative limits of philosophy are kept in mind, and Kant's work is evaluated not in a vacuum but in concrete comparison with other approaches to difficult foundational issues. All the same, there is much more that needs to be said about this standpoint, especially since two very perceptive Kant interpreters, David Sussman and Pauline Kleingeld, have recently asked whether, in moving away from stressing worries about Kant's "dogmatism," I have now gone to the

---

[7] See Chignell (2007).

[8] See Ameriks (2008: 177), for a discussion of how, at the end of *KU* §90, Kant comes very close to calling cognition of the moral law itself a form of *Wissen*. Cf. Hogan (2009: 528).

[9] Ameriks (2003: 176; cf. 254).

[10] Ameriks (2003: introduction; 2006: chapter 5). What I take to be Kant's underlying commonsense and realist stance has some similarities to what Tyler Burge calls Kant's willingness to allow a relation to objects that goes beyond "what can in principle be established by argument, by the individual," Burge (2009: 295).

opposite extreme of being too undemanding and have fallen back, to put it dip-
lomatically, into a position of not "setting the philosophical bar very high" for
success in this area.[11] They pose a significant question, and their well-developed
counterproposals deserve a response.

II. The General Dilemma

There are complex interpretative issues here that need to be gone over very
carefully, but before getting into those issues it may help to spell out a per-
plexing general dilemma haunting the whole discussion of Kant's ethics. The
dilemma can be expressed in terms of obvious problems with attempting either
a "bottom up" or a "top down" approach to the task of vindicating pure reason
as practical, given Kant's own very strict (and noninductive) conception of it.
On a "bottom up," that is "progressive," approach, the basic strategy is to begin
by isolating some very general and indisputable features of practical rationality
as such, features that are not yet understood as specifically moral. The strategy
then culminates in the construction of a deduction that aims to prove that these
features entail that any rational agent (that is, anyone who is consistent and
minimally practical at all) must eventually concede that our practical life has to
be governed by the moral law in Kant's strict sense. The recurrent problem with
such an approach is that any features that can seem genuinely "indisputable"
in this context are also features that, on reflection, appear too thin to yield the
substantive conclusion that every rational agent, just as such, must acknowledge the authoritative dominance of Kant's moral law.

   For this reason, it is only natural to explore getting away from the difficulties
of the basic argumentative gap in the first approach by switching over to the
opposite approach, the "top down" or "regressive" strategy. On this approach,
one proceeds without even attempting a deduction, from the mere notion of
rational agency, to an apodictic conclusion that some kind of strict moral principles must in fact be acknowledgeable by all rational agents as authoritatively
dominant, and instead one simply works out the meaning, implications, and
advantages of being committed to such principles and the basic formula underlying them. This approach has the advantage of a kind of realistic modesty, but
its very modesty can also begin to make it look objectionable. Whereas the first
strategy appears much too ambitious, especially given all that we know about
the history of intractable disputes concerning a strict ethics of duty, the second
strategy can appear too dogmatic and undemanding. It appears too dogmatic
when, like most readers, one contrasts (as I did in my earliest work on Kant)
the second strategy's nondeductive approach—and in particular the appeal to
a mere "fact of reason"—with the strict argumentative expectations of most

---

[11] Sussman (2008: 78 n. 4); cf. Kleingeld (2010: 67).

philosophers, including Kant's immediate successors. These expectations are strongly reinforced by the bold—and tempting—ideal of Kant's own early argument in the *Groundwork*, especially its concluding section III, which appears to be presented as aiming at nothing less than a definitive response to the underlying worry that the moral law may be no more than a "chimerical idea" or "phantom" (*GMS* 4: 445). But even if there are understandable reasons for questioning specific aspects of the bold deductive expectations associated with the *Groundwork*, the alternative move to a merely regressive approach (as on the second strategy, and, as is generally acknowledged now, the second *Critique*[12]) can seem, in contrast, much too undemanding, and so it is only natural that there is a recurrent desire for reconstructing some kind of argument that would show that Kantian morality is rationally necessary after all—at least as a "practical presupposition" for everyone.

My own approach at this point will not be to advance a fundamentally new position but primarily to focus on making more understandable some of the common pressures and difficulties in the tempting strategies involved in reacting to the seemingly inescapable and frustrating options that have just been outlined. In the end I remain sympathetic to the thought that it is not easy, after all, to improve on the regressive and relatively dogmatic approach of Kant's own post-*Groundwork* ethics, and hence, even if such an approach does not seem entirely satisfactory, we may need to learn to live with it. Without necessarily allowing "the bar" to drop too low, progress can still be made by letting go of the common assumption that we must always insist on mere arguments to settle issues "all the way down," especially with respect to the foundational issues of ethics.

III. The Historical Context

Before elaborating on the value of maintaining patience with what I take to be Kant's "reversal" to, at the very least, a more explicitly regressive practical strategy in his second *Critique* and other writings after the *Groundwork*, it may help to explain the broad and somewhat unusual context of my earlier worries about elements of dogmatism in Kant's philosophy. These worries were rooted not in any allegiance to a "Cartesian" model of philosophical methodology but rather in reflections on various strands in the immensely influential reception of Kant's work and, in particular, on the fact that the crucial metaphysical commitments of his system have often been downplayed or misunderstood by readers on all sides. I was especially perplexed by the pattern, found especially in many followers of the German tradition, of carrying on in what can look like a kind of bad faith that tries to "have it both ways" in practical philosophy. That is, many writers in this tradition have, on the one hand, steadily exploited the

---

[12] See Timmerman (2007).

enchanting modern rhetoric of a strong commitment to autonomy, while, on the other hand, they have not faced up to the task of providing a detailed philosophical explanation of how this doctrine can be maintained in our era, after the materialist and determinist repercussions of the Scientific Revolution.

Kant's Critical philosophy, in contrast, sets out a direct and detailed proposal concerning our autonomy. What Kant comes to hold in the Critical era is that a commitment to this notion as central to practical philosophy requires nothing less than a fundamentally new metaphysical system, a doctrine of transcendental idealism that directly engages with modern science and brings with it a striking new conception of knowledge and reality—the only conception, allegedly, that allows us to hold onto the needed assertion of the existence of the transcendental freedom of our pure individual will.[13] Kant comes to this position only after seriously exploring non-Critical efforts to do justice to our practical life without such an absolute notion of freedom. His own pre-1760s writings still appear comfortable with versions of compatibilism, but by the 1760s his reflections exhibit an entrenched anticompatibilist reaction to British as well as continental systems along this line.[14] Upon reading Rousseau in the 1760s,[15] and then moving steadily toward his Critical system of the 1780s, Kant becomes firmly committed to the need to develop a full-scale metaphysical defense of the notion of absolute free choice. His final position essentially insists on a pure notion of causation that can involve causings that are not themselves empirically caused. This notion has been constantly attacked as unhelpful or even incomprehensible, but Kant is hardly the only one to have been committed to it, and its evaluation is not the immediate issue here.[16] The immediate issue is simply the remarkable fact that post-Kantian philosophers repeatedly have presumed that the best version of a Kantian doctrine of autonomy can survive without Kant's own metaphysical notions and specific transcendental methodology.

My concern with this issue does not rest on any partisan presumption that a "nonmetaphysical" alternative is impossible concerning the free causality component of the doctrine of autonomy. In fact, one point in my initial charge that Kant's own Critical system is dogmatic—in a disturbing sense—was that even this system, quite surprisingly, does not provide an adequately detailed argument against common "nonmetaphysical" (i.e., very broadly naturalistic) versions of compatibilism, even though this is a position that Kant is definitely very familiar with and would be expected to discuss at length.[17] The main worry behind my initial charge of dogmatism was rooted, however, in a slightly different point, one that basically goes beyond Kant himself. It concerned the

---

[13] See Pereboom (2006) and Hogan (2009: 532 n. 78).

[14] See Ameriks and Höffe (2009, especially chapters 1 and 2).

[15] See Ameriks (forthcoming); cf. Shell (2009).

[16] On this point, see most recently Hogan (2009).

[17] Ameriks (2003: chapter 6); cf. Ameriks (1982; 2000: chapter 8). Kant's most direct argument against compatibilism is his brief pro-Rousseauian and anti-Wolffian tract, *RS* 8: 10–14.

influential tendency, found especially among those later philosophers who are most identified with the Idealist tradition, to accept the appeal of Kant's rhetorical references to notions such as autonomy or the "primacy of practical reason" without also accepting, from the beginning, the responsibility of backing up their rhetoric with either a detailed defense of compatibilism (here the early Schleiermacher stands out against most of his contemporaries because he clearly did attempt such a defense when distancing himself from Kant) or, instead, a defense of an incompatibilist position that is at least as worked out as Kant's complex argument for transcendental idealism and the assertion of our transcendental freedom.

There are two very different and still influential versions of post-Kantianism that are relevant here. On the one hand, I wanted to draw attention to the fact that the early Fichte and "Fichtean" successors of Kant, can appear so mesmerized by the thought of absolute moral freedom that they fail to defend their incompatibilism by addressing, as directly as Kant does, the post-Newtonian issue of our situation within nature, given the modern discovery of universal causal laws.[18] On the other hand, I also felt a need to draw attention to that fact that Hegel, and "Hegelian" successors of Kant, can appear so mesmerized by their particular version of (what I take to be) a holistic and broadly naturalistic version of compatibilism, that they fail to make clear that the much emphasized doctrine of "autonomy" within their systems cannot truly have the fully independent causal meaning that Kant (like the "mainline" tradition up through Rousseau) insists on attaching to the term.[19]

These worries should not be understood as a matter of simply blaming post-Kantians for no longer addressing the issue in the relatively traditional and metaphysical manner of Kant's complex system. The worries also involve an acknowledgment that Kant himself had a role in fostering the problems in the reception of his work. There is no denying that Kant's own language can encourage, at various times, a moralistic and proto-Fichtean belief in an apodictic proof of absolute freedom of (our individual) will, and yet, at other times, a nonmoralistic and proto-Hegelian belief in a system of rational and intersubjective self-realization, one whose content is understandable independently of a transcendentally defined doctrine of absolute freedom. The first belief stresses individual causal independence above all, whereas the second belief abstracts from a stress on causal considerations and simply focuses on our responsiveness to reasons in a way that does not elaborate—or even leave clear room for—(transcendent) metaphysical grounds of individual actions. Hence the classic problem of Schelling's early work *Philosophical Letters on Dogmatism and Criticism* (1795), which focuses on the basic post-Kantian

---

[18] See Ameriks (2000: chapters 3–5).

[19] See Ameriks (2003: chapter 8), and cf. Brandom (2009: chapter 2, "Autonomy, Community, and Freedom")..

alternative of Spinoza or Fichte.[20] Here the early Schelling, like Hegel later, can be understood as shifting away from Kant himself and trying to transform—all too quickly—Spinoza's hard monistic determinism into a more palatable sociohistorical version of compatibilism that would avoid the "subjective" one-sidedness of Fichte's allegedly too individualist approach.

In the wake of these developments, it is not surprising that many later post-Kantians (e.g., Fichte's son, the later Schelling, and Kierkegaard[21]) espoused going back to a kind of personalist spiritualism and appealed to direct assertions of our absolute freedom in a way that, in its methodology, would no doubt appear too "mystical" to Kant himself, just as Crusius's and Rousseau's and Fichte's claims did—or that others held to advocating autonomy in an even more explicitly mundane sense (e.g., Feuerbach), and in a way that would no doubt appear much too naturalist to Kant, just as (in a broad sense) Leibniz's, Wolff's, Spinoza's, and Hume's systems all did.[22]

My initial worry about Kant's dogmatism was thus never intended as a claim that he ever literally reverted to a bad pre-Critical system. The worry was rooted rather in a concern about the multiple historical consequences, for the "fate of autonomy," of Kant's never saying enough about the Critical doctrine of freedom, and especially about the surprising appearance—which was widely noted at the time—of his seeming to fall back in 1788 on a mere *Faktum* without directly explaining how this was related to the strict deductive strategies explored in his own work just before then. This worry about the incomplete and unusual path of Kant's Critical discussion of freedom does not amount, however, to a concession that Kant's own reversion to a regressive reliance on a *Faktum* cannot in any way be defended. But although I believe that some kind of respectable defense of Kant's final position can be offered, I will be arguing that it is very difficult to give it anything more than an apologetic form, that is, just a clarification of how it remains one consistent and significant possibility among others. To this extent, my interpretation of Kant's position leaves him in a weaker argumentative situation than is presumed in the ambitious and sympathetic reconstructions of the *Faktum* offered most recently by Sussman and Kleingeld. They still want to argue that Kant's final position, when properly understood, is much more than one intriguing rational option among others. They imply it provides a unique standard for our practical life, one whose claim to authoritative dominance can be—and was always meant to be, by Kant himself—put forth in a *rationally irresistible* form.

---

[20] The title of Schelling's work is an indirect reference to Reinhold (2005), which appeared in various versions from 1786 to 1792, and it also is meant to imply that the alternatives of Kant and Reinhold have already been superseded.

[21] See Kosch (2006).

[22] Koselleck (2008: 263–4), captures the common connection here with Kantian autonomy when he remarks that there is a "line of argument [that] runs from the Illuminati via Weishaupt and Fichte to the young Hegelians all the way to Marx and Engels."

IV. Sussman's Interpretation: Initial Problems

The title of Sussman's interpretation reveals the fundamental two-sidedness of his approach: "From Deduction to Deed: Kant's Grounding of the Moral Law." This formulation indicates, on the one hand, agreement with those who say that Kant moves away from the ambitious deductive strategy of *Groundwork* III, while, on the other hand, it is also meant to imply that, by moving on to the notion of morality as a *Faktum*, in the sense of a "deed" rather than a mere "datum" of reason, Kant is still able to provide a sufficient "grounding of the moral law."

After carefully detailing several weaknesses in Kant's *Groundwork* III argument, Sussman contends that Kant implicitly came to appreciate these weaknesses himself and found a better way to present his position, one that provides a "critique of empirical practical reason" that is still "prior to and independent of the authority of the moral law" (Sussman 2008: 53). This new approach of the second *Critique* begins by taking over what Sussman calls the *Groundwork's* "regulative" notion that rational practical agents must employ "the idea of freedom" simply in the sense of having a "standard" for action that could be "appreciated" "independently of alien influences."[23] On Sussman's reading, this passage is not yet about the metaphysical issue of whether the will is actually free in an absolute causal sense. On my reading, the passage is at least ambiguous, for the issue of such freedom is precisely the main question left over after *Groundwork* II, and all that Kant says here about working under the "idea of freedom" is that this involves denial of "conscious" "determination" by "impulse" rather than "reason."[24] The crucial term here is "determination," and since that term can have a causal as well as a formal meaning, it still seems to me that what Kant intends to exclude here can also be causal subjection to "alien" efficient factors and not merely, as Sussman stresses, formal or "regulative" subjection to standards other than pure reason.

In either case, it can be agreed that Kant's exclusion of "impulse" here amounts to only the first step of the kind of argument that is ultimately needed, for it still should be shown that there are not other relevant factors—formal as well as efficient—that are much more complex than mere "impulse" but that are still not the same as pure reason. In fact there is an obvious alternative here, for—as Kant himself recognizes—our prudential interest in sensible happiness on the whole is something that is neither mere "impulse" nor pure reason but is instead a complex intentional project of every sensible agent's

---

[23] Sussman (2008: 55). Sussman (2008: 54) cites Kant, *GMS* 4: 448: "Now, one cannot possibly think of a reason that would consciously receive direction from any other quarter with respect to its judgments, since the subject would then attribute the determination of his judgment not to his reason but to an impulse."

[24] *GMS* 4: 448. See Sussman (2008: 78 n. 9), criticizing Ameriks (2003: chapter 9).

basic practical rationality.[25] Non-Kantians would no doubt add that there are also many significant factors other than prudence or utility that compete for our attention and go beyond mere impulse or pure reason. It therefore remains unclear how, even after granting the importance of an anti-impulsive "idea of freedom," a Kantian can begin to establish—and not merely presume or provide an apology for—the specific claim of the authoritative dominance of his notion of pure moral reason.

At this point in *Groundwork* III Kant repeatedly appeals to the notion of a will that belongs "only" to an "intelligible world" (*GMS* 4: 454), and he takes it to be obvious that the lack of any sensibility in such a being would leave it with only moral reasons for action. Hence Sussman claims, "if the standpoint of such an intelligence is to serve as the norm for our own deliberations, then we would indeed have to assign moral concerns complete priority" (Sussman 2008: 61). This claim by itself, however, is hardly meant to settle matters, because it explicitly begins with a substantive and highly controversial "if" clause. Sussman goes on to confront the problem of how this "if" can relate to our own situation as sensible beings, but he does not raise any question about Kant's strong presumption that a purely intelligible being would always have to be guided by moral reason. This presumption seems to me to correspond to one more instance of a Kantian tendency to move a bit quickly with arguments by exclusion. It is true that it is difficult for us to see exactly why an intelligible being without any sensibility to distract it would ever stray from morality. Nonetheless, if one takes the idea of an absolutely free will seriously, it does not seem impossible to consider that it might make decisions that are disconnected from morality and yet are not mere "impulse." Although these would not be decisions that are driven simply by the light of moral reason, it is not clear that they would have to be crazily irrational, any more than would, for example, a decision by an isolated person to engage in one kind of extended mathematical speculation rather than another (without concern specifically with either moral improvement or acting deliberately against morality). A lack of commitment to furthering pure practical reason need not convict an agent of operating directly against basic rationality. On Kant's own lights, *reason*, as a specific faculty (and not just a generic term contrasting with anything sensible), is fundamentally concerned with the unconditioned,[26] whereas mere "intelligence" or rationality can be found wherever there is some condition that is appreciated by the understanding. This implies that a choice that does not serve reason, in Kant's strong sense, need not amount to an

---

[25] Here Sussman (2008: 59), refers to *KpV* 5: 61 and *RGV* 6: 46 n. The complexity of Kant's account of happiness is well brought out in Engstrom (2009).

[26] This connection between reason and the unconditioned is central both to Kant's notion of theoretical reason (B xx), with its basic concept of a "thing in itself," and his notion of practical reason (*KpV* 5: 3), with its basic concept of an "end in itself."

action that we have to say is not rational at all.[27] Conversely, fulfilling the elementary conditions of mere rationality is not enough to show that one is following pure reason.

Leaving aside for now the problem of a neglected set of incidental options (which serve rationality, but not pure reason, in some not explicitly prudential or slavish way), there remains the basic difficulty of showing why all agents like us must give precedence to "the standpoint of such a [pure] intelligence" in contrast to all other interests, including our very own "sensibility" in the broadest sense. The *Groundwork* notoriously appears to have attempted to meet this problem by a questionable appeal to the mere thought that our intelligible side is "higher" than and "grounds" our "sensible" side.[28] However seriously this line of thought was originally intended, it fortunately is not relied on after the *Groundwork*. This leaves a very significant problem, though, for it is not clear how else one might proceed here, other than by begging the justificatory question and invoking moral considerations themselves as the feature of our "intelligible" side that would ground giving it absolute precedence.[29]

Sussman's innovative strategy at this point is to propose that Kant has a decisive independent argument against the pretensions of "our empirically conditioned use of practical reason" (Sussman 2008: 68). According to this strategy, once this argument is deployed, the result is that the only serious actual opponent of pure moral reason is defeated, and thus the moral law can be rationally "grounded" after all, even without a direct deduction. The argument can be divided into two steps, corresponding to Kant's division of sensible interest into innocent "self-love" and non-innocent "self-conceit." The first step involves pointing out that on Kant's mature view our mere "self-love" does not present a fundamental challenge because it "merely advises,"[30] and hence it is not a direct legislative competitor to the authority of morality, which issues "commands." "Self-conceit," in contrast, has legislative pretensions and

---

[27] The term "rational" is ambiguous in English, and philosophers sometimes use it in such a way that anyone going for less than what is "optimal" is not being rational, whereas, in ordinary language, maintaining one's rationality is compatible with making a wide range of strange decisions. I believe Kant is working with a notion of rationality that is meant to be close to ordinary language, but this is not the same as what he takes to be involved with the demands of reason. Matters are complicated here by the fact that in ordinary German the single term *vernünftig* (which may suggest Kant's pure sense of "reason" but does not entail it, even though it derives from the term *Vernunft*) is used, whereas English has available the contrasting terms "rational" and "reasonable."

[28] See *GMS* 4: 453, Sussman (2008: 63), and Ameriks (2003: 175). A difficult feature of Kant's text here is that he himself raises a worry of circularity in an early stage in his argument, and yet he still appears vulnerable to a similar charge at a later stage.

[29] See the appropriate remark at Sussman (2008: 64), that Korsgaard's stress (Korsgaard 1996) on our identifying with the "active" side of ourselves does not meet this problem in a non-question-begging way. He makes a similar remark (Sussman 2008: 80 n. 23) about the reference to our "pure" side in Allison (1990) and Proops (2003).

[30] Sussman (2008: 72), citing *KpV* 5: 86.

is an empirical form of practical rationality with an honor-obsessed "demand for interpersonal recognition...[that brings it] into systematic conflict with the interests of practical reason" (Sussman 2008: 73).

Although Sussman does not discuss this fact, Kant's division is not a late development but goes back to the key revolution in his thought that occurred with his reading of Rousseau in the early 1760s. Already in his detailed notes from that period, Kant manifests an obsession of his own with character-izing the main opponent of morality precisely in terms of a Rousseauian self-conceit that arises from lack of humility and an overriding "desire to gain worth in the opinion of others."[31] Sussman's strategy is to argue that any such concern with "worth" implies a belief in an "objective standard for the assess-ment of persons" (Sussman 2008: 74) and thereby provides a lever whereby Kant can contend that even self-conceited persons acknowledge "standards for the assessment of persons that properly command the assent of others," and thus they must be "implicitly" subordinating themselves "to the principles of pure practical reason, whatever they might turn out to be" (74). In other words, "The simple juxtaposition of self-conceit with a truly moral form of self-assessment is enough to reveal the fraud implicit in any nonmoral concep-tion of the fundamental worth of a person" (74). Sussman concludes: "This humiliation of self-conceit by morality does not presuppose that we already accept the authority of morality. It is enough that we simply entertain the idea of moral self-evaluation seriously."[32]

This last claim is especially difficult to endorse. While it is true that what Kant calls the experience of proper moral humiliation does not require that one "accept" morality in the sense of turning oneself into a person immediately engaging in moral actions, it appears to require that, in the most significant sense, one does already accept the standard of the moral law as authoritatively dominant. The passages in which Kant speaks of our self-conceit being prop-erly struck down come only after, and not before, he speaks of our accepting the "fact of reason," that is, the full authority of the moral law and its impera-tive. The key "strike down" passage that Sussman cites[33] is many pages after the *Faktum* passage (*KpV* 5: 31), and it explicitly says that the humiliation occurs because of a recognition that "certainty of a disposition in accord with this [moral] law is the first condition of any worth of a person."

I conclude that Kant does not take himself to have a route to defeating the claims of self-conceit that proceeds independently of presuming an acceptance of the moral law's authoritative dominance—and on this point he is only being sensible. Even if one is understandably concerned with looking honorable

---

[31] Sussman (2008: 73), citing *RGV* 6: 27. Regarding Rousseau and Kant on humility and self-conceit, see also Ameriks (2012), Neuhouser (2008), and Grenberg (2005).

[32] Sussman (2008: 73; cf. 76).

[33] Sussman (2008: 73), citing *KpV* 5: 73.

in the eyes of others, and it is conceded that seeking this value involves the recognition of some genuine objective standards, it does not follow that one is thereby even on the road toward subordinating oneself to the specific standards of pure practical reason. (Kant holds a similar view with respect to aesthetic value: even though one can define a kind of objective standard of taste that consists in the empirical agreement of one's peers, this does not amount to moving toward genuine pure appreciation of beauty, and it can even be a major obstacle to such appreciation.) There are standards of honor that may be relatively pure in the sense that they are understood not to rely on mere individual whim, but they are not thereby independent of empirical facts about culture and human sensibility, and there is no reason yet to say that appreciating them must lead us to standards that are based on, or must lead to, an acceptance of pure reason. The empirical standards of honor—which Kant himself would acknowledge have in fact been regarded as supreme by generations of "honorable" persons—do not by themselves demonstrate, or even inevitably provide some ground for supposing, the presence of some kind of necessary or unconditional value.

Furthermore, even if it is conceded that only something like Kant's notion of moral law can bring with it something like the notion of unconditional value, it does not immediately follow that persons, simply by being rational and *also* having, through their faculty of pure reason, the *notion* of unconditional value, must concede that for them a concern with unconditional value must actually have absolute priority. Of course, if we somehow do *know* that there exists some value that truly is unconditional, then we can see that in a sense it is higher than anything conditioned, but this still is not sufficient for concluding that we must believe there truly is such an unconditional value *prior* to accepting the dominance of morality in Kant's strict sense. (What does follow, and what I believe gives Kant's position something of an understandable privilege, is that, *insofar* as one considers oneself as being practical primarily because one is at least in part a being of reason—rather than merely a being with basic rationality and a particular natural background, family, tradition of honor, and so forth—then a commitment to the moral law, as the law of pure practical reason, is the clearly "appropriate" way for a being to act when it chooses to act *in light of that* consideration; in this sense Kant's *Faktum* is genuinely and uniquely a fact of *reason*.)

A similar problem arises when one abstracts from the attitude of self-conceit and goes back to the issue of the contrast of self-love and morality. It is true that Kant comes to emphasize that self-love by itself is an innocent orientation that simply needs to be "restricted" by morality (*KpV* 5: 31) when the maxims that it advises happen to conflict with specific moral imperatives. But even though Kant, unlike many other philosophers, does not believe there is an overriding command of prudence or utility, his final position also does not provide a conclusive argument against someone who sometimes prefers to choose mere prudence over the pure moral law. Even if a maxim of prudence appears to go against respecting the dignity of some persons as ends in themselves, agents who are still wondering whether in their own case they absolutely must follow pure morality rather than prudence do not have a neutral or "external" argumentative basis, on Kant's final position, for taking the moral rather than prudent path.[34] Such agents do not even have to allow that they *know* that there are persons in Kant's strict sense, that is, agents who are absolutely free ends in themselves and not at all like "turnspits."[35] Moreover, even if a merely prudent maxim is conceded not to pass the specific requirement of something like Kant's universalization test, this does not mean that an agent who remains devoted to the maxim has opted to forsake rationality altogether. Such an agent still has a variety of understandable considerations within its practical rationality, and it does not have to be classified as nonrational or unkind, let alone a mere wanton or radical skeptic. Without going so far as to say that, even for its own self, prudence has an absolutely commanding privilege, a rational agent can contend that the commands of morality have very substantive and controversial presuppositions, and hence, short of already subscribing to the "fact of reason," it is still permitted, from the perspective of mere rationality, not to take itself to be under strict morality's authoritative dominance.[36]

V. Sussman's Interpretation: Final Problems

It may be with an implicit appreciation of this kind of problem that Sussman, in a concluding consideration, offers what appears to be a rather different line of thought. He proposes that Kant's notion of the *Faktum* as a "deed of reason" refers to a kind of reconstitutive experience: "Pure reason does not reveal the prior validity of the moral law, but instead refashions those who consider its claims into beings who are indeed bound by that law" (Sussman 2008: 77). This is a very interesting proposal, and it need not be denied that this kind of experience can happen with some people, in which case, as Kant says, the "practical a priori concepts" of morality "become cognitions," and "they do not have to wait for intuitions to receive meaning...they themselves produce the reality to which they refer (the disposition of the will)."[37] In such a situation, Sussman's final description could in a sense apply: "were such a being seriously to confront a truly moral understanding of the person, she would be forced to see herself in new ways that would make this conception inescapable for her" (Sussman 2008: 77). This

---

[34] This way of putting the matter was suggested to me by a comment in Bagnoli (2009: 539).

[35] On this point my view differs somewhat from the weight that Hogan (2009), puts on our "knowledge" of other minds. Something more like proper belief may be what Kant needs to say that we have, at least in so far as those minds are characterized as ends in themselves.

[36] Cf. Scheffler (1992).

[37] *KpV* 5: 66, cited at Sussman (2008: 77).

description is understandable to outsiders, however, only if the terms "seriously" and "truly moral" and "forced" simply mean that "such a being" *already* has a Kantian acceptance of the *Faktum* as implying morality's authoritative dominance. And this hardly resolves the argumentative problem for those of us who say we are still wondering how not to appear dogmatic when trying to explain the authority of Kantian morality to agents who do not think that they have had such an experience and are not yet ready to accept the *Faktum* as universally valid, especially when they are still perplexed by the issue even after they feel they have been able to "entertain" all its relevant concepts.

In sum, it can be allowed that in a sense the *Faktum* is a deed "of reason" insofar as, *if* there actually takes place a reconstitutive experience, then this experience can be understood as the product of a faculty, called pure reason, that operates with both executive ("efficient") and judicative ("formal") power. But this faculty still cannot operate as a free-floating metaphysical entity; it can only become actually effective, even on Kant's view, when concrete individuals freely accept the command to endorse its dictates. Hence, the actualization of what one is then, so to speak, "forced to see," in the attitude of committed moral respect, cannot be a matter of sheer "inescapable" force but must involve a prior free commitment to accept the commands of morality as authoritatively dominant—it is as decisive not just abstractly as a "highest" abstract principle, but as truly decisive for oneself, including here and now, given one's total situation (even if one fails to carry through with actions in line with the principle one has genuinely accepted). If agents are not yet ready to make that commitment, then those who are already within the Kantian perspective may say that such agents are in effect condemning themselves (as immoral). For someone not within that perspective, however, there is still no lever for saying that merely being a rational agent is enough by itself to force one to heed the call of "reason" in Kant's strict sense—and this means that the moral law does not get the kind of progressive "grounding" that those who are not yet Kantians (and their neo-Kantian would-be persuaders) have been seeking.

VI. Kleingeld's Interpretation: Initial Problems

Pauline Kleingeld has provided an even more recent treatment of this issue that goes beyond Sussman's discussion in at least two significant respects. First, she critically reviews recent hypotheses that have been offered as to whether Kant's notion of a fact of reason should be understood primarily as a fact, a deed, or just a reference to having a proper a priori origin.[38] Her clarifications here lead to a qualification of the special emphasis by Sussman

---

[38] Kleingeld (2010: 62–4), on Proops (2003) and Henrich (1994). Quotations of Kant cited by Kleingeld use her own translations.

and others on the notion of a deed.[39] Second, and more in line with Sussman, she also presents an argument of her own that even in the second *Critique* Kant offers considerations that do not presuppose acceptance of the moral law specifically but require only an appreciation of pure practical reason in a non-question-begging broad sense.

On the latter point, Kleingeld begins by observing that Kant starts his discussion in the second *Critique* with a search for what is at first simply called the "fundamental law of pure practical reason."[40] In other words, "it is the consciousness of the fundamental law of pure practical reason that is called a fact of reason. This law is subsequently called the moral law—not the other way around."[41] This terminological point is relevant to one (mistaken) way that some readers might be tempted to take my statement that the *Faktum* discussion dogmatically presumes the "validity [i.e., full authority] of morality."[42] As Kleingeld points out, this way of expressing the matter "creates the risk that 'morality' is read in terms of the readers' own 'material' conception of morality instead of in terms of Kant's formal conception of it" (Kleingeld 2010: 66). Terminological issues aside, however, Kleingeld realizes full well that the basic objection of dogmatism can still be raised in slightly adjusted terms. Hence she still feels the need for a "nondogmatic" argument that would "ground the consciousness of moral obligation in the structure of practical reason so as to reach conclusions that apply universally" (Kleingeld 2010: 67).

Kleingeld's strategy at this point is to focus, like Sussman, on Kant's discussion of the general deliberative situation of rational agents. This situation is said to include an ability always to conceive of themselves as being able to act on reasons that are "independent from empirical conditions" and "unconditional," presumably because they involve the thought of a "pure will...determined *by the mere form of the law*."[43] It is only after claiming that this situation brings with it the thought of a rule that commands "one ought absolutely to proceed in a certain way," that Kant draws his remarkable conclusion in *KpV* §7 that the "consciousness of this fundamental law may be called a fact of reason." (*KpV* 5: 31). It is then only in the following Corollary of this section that Kant explicitly claims that pure practical reason provides a "universal law which we call the moral law." (*KpV* 5: 31). There immediately follows Kant's "Remark to this Corollary," cited by Kleingeld in its entirety: "The fact mentioned above is undeniable. One need only analyze the judgment that people pass on the lawfulness of their actions: one will always find that their reason, whatever [their]

---

[39] Kleingeld (2010: 63–4), on Willaschek (1992) and Franks (2005). A somewhat similar position is also impressively developed in Wolff (2009).

[40] Kleingeld (2010: 66), citing *KpV* 5: 29. Cf. *MS* 6: 221.

[41] Kleingeld (2010: 66), cf. *KpV* 5: 31.

[42] Kleingeld (2010: 66), citing Ameriks (2003: 176).

[43] Kleingeld (2010: 69), citing *KpV* 5: 31.

inclination may say to the contrary, nevertheless, incorruptible and coerced by itself, always compares the maxim of the will of an action to the pure will."[44]

This final quotation contains a number of substantive claims that are worth pausing over. Initially the *Faktum* may appear to be described in such a way that it could be an occasional and merely conceptual event. That is, the quotations from *KpV* 5: 31 can seem to amount to little more than the thought that people are capable of imagining a certain very high standard of action, but a standard that might be little more than something like a utopia. Such a standard could be interesting for some people, but its universal relevance is not immediately clear. In *KpV* 5: 32, however, Kant makes explicit, under the heading of the *Faktum* that he had just discussed earlier, a stronger-sounding claim, namely that *whenever* "people pass on the lawfulness of their actions" they will be using this standard to *judge* their own action. There are, of course, objections that can be raised concerning this claim. It makes a very controversial assertion about how people actually go about passing on the "lawfulness" of their actions. Humeans might respond that, apart from the distortions of ideology, there never is anything more to say about "lawfulness" here than just familiar empirical facts concerning higher-level preferences that merely reflect lower-level regularities of natural desire, and hence any insistence that ordinary people should and do (always!) use the standard of a "pure will" is as confused as the traditional claim that ordinary perceptual judgments truly involve perceptions of necessity.

Suppose we leave this controversial issue aside, however, and allow that Kant is making a plausible enough point in insisting, as Kleingeld says, that if people are "serious and push this process [of deliberation] far enough," they can "ask themselves whether to act on their inclinations at all."[45] The problem remains that, even if all this is conceded and a general merely comparative "judgment" is made,[46] it is still not clear that a rational agent *has* to agree that, all things considered, it should always choose to *heed* this judgment by committing to an unconditional law, one that could lead to its acting on some occasions not on any inclinations or anything else other than "the mere form of the law." The resistance of such a rational agent at this point could have a number of understandable grounds. The agent could allow that it has some general understanding of the notion of an unconditional law, and is intrigued by it, and yet insist that it cannot determine how to apply the notion in relevant particular cases. Or, the agent might allow that it can understand the implications of the pure

---

[44] Kleingeld (2010: 69), citing *KpV* 5: 32, from her own translation.

[45] Kleingeld (2010: 68); later she shifts to saying "one realizes that one could act against *all* of one's inclinations" (71). This is a much more dogmatic claim, and the most relevant backing that she gives to it here goes back to *GMS* 4: 448, an argument from 1785 that it is not clear that Kant endorses by 1788.

[46] See *KpV* 5: 29 and Kleingeld (2010: 68): "the very moment agents consciously reflect on possible maxims of action, they "immediately" become conscious of the fundamental law."

will in detail and can even "appreciate" how the "pure will," from its perspective, would claim priority for its unconditional standard over the conditional values of the agent's actual maxims—and yet the agent might still decide to favor its own conditioned ends (especially those that seem central to its particular identity), and understandably believe that when it does so it is still not altogether forsaking its own rationality.[47]

The obvious—and, I believe, interpretatively most appropriate—way to respond to such worries is to say again that by the experience of the *Faktum* Kant means to include not merely an ever possible and obligatory reflective state of comparative judgment but an attitude of commitment that *already* includes an actual acceptance of the authoritative dominance of the moral law. It certainly appears that Kant himself holds to this richer understanding of the *Faktum*, because he immediately goes on to describe it as something that is experienced as a genuine categorical "imperative" (*KpV* 5: 32), and not a mere analytic account of what moralists purport. This reference to a personal activity of responding to an imperative as such also fits the stress that several interpreters have put on speaking of the term *Faktum* as originally involving a kind of deed rather than a mere fact. The language of deed (*Tat*), rather than fact (*Tatsache*), has the advantage of implying that what is relevant here is not just any kind of truth, but a truth that has to do with an activity that (it is presumed) we can be responsible for, and in particular with the responsive activation on our part of a faculty of pure reason that in a crucial sense is internal to us.

This "imputative" aspect of the *Faktum* is important but it cannot be used to explain all aspects of the text. As Kleingeld properly notes (2010: 66), Kant also often speaks of the *Faktum* as simply the moral law itself, and this law is not, as such, a matter that is literally the imputable deed of any active agent. It is true that the law of moral reason is internal to us in the sense that it cannot be defined (either formally or efficiently), for example, as a *brute* imposed fact of nature, the supernatural, history, or convention, that is, in a way not rooted in the essence of rational agents as such. But this still does not mean that the law, or even its authority, is simply a product of actual finite agents, as would be required if it is to be understood just as *literally* "our" deed.

Kleingeld moves on from making this point to allowing that, even if the *Faktum*, as law, should not be said to be literally our deed, that is, the deed of ordinary finite persons, it can still be called a "deed of reason" in the sense of being also, as a fact, a *product* of *reason* itself, just as a decision can be "a decision of [i.e., authoritatively produced by] a king" (2010: 65). This can at first seem to be an appealing way of speaking, but in the end I believe that it too can be misleading, even though it is a proper reminder that the pure authority of morality's law is essentially a matter of the force of necessary principles within pure practical reason as such, and not a mere accidental result of individuals

---

[47] See Ameriks (2000: 337; 2003: 209–11).

as such. Nonetheless, reason does not exist on its own as a free-floating causal power but has actuality only as a faculty of concrete agents. Granted that such agents do not literally make a pure law, or its validity, with their actions,[48] it is crucial that they can become conscious of it, trace it out as reflecting what is also in their own essence, and, above all, endorse it, and then, perhaps, act for its sake, and so on. Hence, to speak of the moral law as a fact "of reason" cannot be to speak of a law that reason itself literally makes. At most, it can only be to speak of a law that agents like us would be agreeing "necessarily" to submit themselves to because they endorse reason's dominance within themselves and take the law to be the kind of thing that reason would literally make if it were a force acting on its own.

All this still leaves unsettled whether "we," simply as finite individual, rational, and sensible agents, might not also *consistently* proceed *without* agreeing to submit to this law. Given the way Kant discusses the *Faktum*, it seems to me that he is not directly answering this question but is rather describing a situation in which the agreement has actually taken place.[49] His description may well strike many people (as it does me) as the description of a highly rational event that often can and truly should happen. But this is not to say that here Kant is offering, or even trying to offer, anything that proves that the mere rationality of agents can "force" this agreement in real commitment to occur.

According to Kleingeld, the key passage cited above from *Kp V* 5: 32 should be read in this way: "In other words, agents who regard themselves as having a will regard the fundamental law of practical reason as the normative principle guiding their choice of maxims ... in attributing a will to themselves, agents implicitly acknowledge this principle as the normative standard for the assessment of maxims. This fact ... is exactly what Kant calls a fact of reason" (2010: 69). This formulation is unobjectionable as long as it is not taken to imply (as Kleingeld appears to believe) that there is still a proof—and that Kant here believes there is such a proof—that requires one to go from the mere situation of being a will reflecting upon its maxims to the situation of accepting a law of practical reason as such as "the normative standard" for oneself, that is, as authoritatively dominant. It remains fundamentally unclear how the movement from the one situation to the other can be necessitated by any deduction or mere argument. The most that the description of the first situation can yield is a set of facts about a reflective attitude, and this does not amount to any standard having to be "accepted" by anyone as "the" exclusive standard, rather than as just a demanding principle, one that has one deep "hook" in our essence but still contrasts in striking ways with other principles that are connected to what also seems to be part of our essence. Matters make

---

[48] Cf. Sussman (2008: 81 n. 32), on Kantian "non-reductive realism." Cf. Kain (2006).

[49] On this point Kleingeld (2010: 61 n. 9) and Sussman (2008: 81 n. 31) refer to Lukow (1993) and O'Neill (2002).

most sense here if we read Kant not as suggesting a direct argumentative path but as just describing a committed situation, a situation that occurs in the specific context of what Kant *fully* means by the *Faktum* and that already involves a genuine acknowledgment of the law as a categorical imperative, that is, a taking of it to be authoritatively dominant.

By itself, advocating being in this situation need not amount to a bad form of dogmatism, but from the perspective of those who are looking for an argumentative bridge forcing them into the moral point of view, it must appear as a kind of dogmatism nonetheless, and the fact that the specific phrase "moral law" is not yet explicitly invoked here should not make a difference. Kleingeld emphasizes that the "core argument can be crafted entirely without using moral terms, and no parochial set of moral intuitions or values is presupposed" (2010: 69). But again, however one characterizes the terms involved, the key point is that there still fails to be any strict "argument"—rather than just many layers of illuminating description—that puts one into the situation of being able to maintain one's rationality only by acknowledging the pure practical law as compelling for oneself.

VII. Kleingeld's Interpretation: Final Problems

In a final consideration (reminiscent of Sussman's appeal to a "reconstitutive experience") aimed at still reaching a kind of compelling conclusion, Kleingeld characterizes her line of argument in terms that rest on the popular and supposedly irresistible notion of an agent perspective: "This argument is convincing only from the agent perspective, but in so far as this is a perspective which is inescapable for us as humans and which cannot be undermined from a theoretical perspective, it is for us . . . fully convincing."[50] Leaving aside the issue of whether there is such a simple thing as "the" agent perspective, the main problem here is that there still remains at least one perspective too many. That is, even this kind of reformulation concedes that *we* each have something like *both* an "agent perpective" and a "theoretical perspective." Once a person recognizes that it itself is still one and the same person with at least these two competing perspectives, it can surely step back and properly ask which of them, if any, has to be given an absolute preference. Once the possibility of such a reflective step is conceded—and it is hard to see how Kantians, of all people, can insist on denying that possibility—then any notion of having found a "fully convincing" argument for morality's dominance still seems doomed.

---

[50] Kleingeld (2010: 72). I have elided her words "in Kant's view" since I take it she endorses the view herself.

I conclude that, rather than trying to bolster Kant's position "from below," even contemporary Kantians should rest content with understanding Kant's *Faktum* in a regressive way, that is, as a kind of admittedly dogmatic claim made from a point already fully within a very substantive moral position, albeit one that at least has been prepared for by the development of an extensive and appropriate metaphysical system. This is a conclusion that may continue to disappoint many of Kant's most sympathetic readers, but it may also reflect a hard-won insight on his part, one that can be accepted even if there remain worries that the complicated manner in which he expresses his final position can easily lead to misunderstandings and questionable developments among his followers.

This conclusion is also consistent with my proposals elsewhere to read Kant in general as having a regressive approach.[51] Advocating such an approach in the practical realm turns out to be especially complicated, however, because in this case there appear to be so many quite different nonargumentative starting points that ordinary people can and do understandably espouse. But here the main problem may lie not with any particular philosophy but simply in the extraordinarily complex character of our practical life itself. Even for those who are firmly convinced by Kant's strict ethics, the thought that here pure reason might be a "chimera" after all presents a thought that is a very different kind of philosophical threat than, say, extremely radical skeptical speculations about the external world or the truths of elementary mathematics. The most general lesson, then, is that the assumed "facts" that regressive arguments may start from need not be all at the same dialectical level. No wonder, then, that Kant chooses to speak here not simply of a *Faktum* but of a unique fact "of *reason*."[52]

Bibliography

Allison, H. E. (1990) *Kant's Theory of Freedom*. Cambridge: Cambridge University Press.

Ameriks, K. (1978) "Kant's Transcendental Deduction as a Regressive Argument," *Kant-Studien* 69(2): 273–85. Reprinted in Ameriks (2003).

Ameriks, K. (1981) "Kant's Deduction of Freedom and Morality," *Journal of the History of Philosophy* 19(1): 53–79. Reprinted in Ameriks (2003).

Ameriks, K. (1982) *Kant's Theory of Mind: An Analysis of the Paralogisms of Pure Reason*. Oxford: Clarendon Press. Rev. ed. (2000).

---

[51] See Ameriks (2003, especially chapter 1, "Kant's Transcendental Deduction as a Regressive Argument" (original version Ameriks 1978).

[52] For help on several matters regarding this essay I am indebted to Robert Audi, Catherine Wilson, Howard Williams, Fred Rush, Jens Timmermann, Vittorio Hösle, and discussants at Notre Dame and the Paton Lecture in St. Andrews.

Ameriks, K. (2000) *Kant and the Fate of Autonomy: Problems in the Appropriation of the Critical Philosophy*. Cambridge: Cambridge University Press.

Ameriks, K. (2003) *Interpreting Kant's Critiques*. Oxford: Oxford University Press.

Ameriks, K. (2006) *Kant and the Historical Turn: Philosophy as Critical Interpretation*. Oxford: Clarendon Press.

Ameriks, K. (2008) "The End of the Critiques: Kant's Moral 'Creationism'," in P. Muchnik (ed.), *Rethinking Kant*, 165–90. Newcastle: Cambridge Scholars Press.

Ameriks, K., and Höffe, O. (eds.) (2009) *Kant's Moral and Legal Philosophy: The German Philosophical Tradition*. Cambridge: Cambridge University Press.

Ameriks, K. (2012) "Kant, Human Nature, and History after Rousseau," in S. Shell and R. Velkley (eds.), *Kant's "Observations" and "Remarks": A Critical Guide*, 247–65. Cambridge: Cambridge University Press.

Audi, R. (2001) *The Architecture of Reason: The Structure and Substance of Rationality*. Oxford: Oxford University Press.

Audi, R. (2008) "Rational Disagreement as a Challenge to Practical Ethics and Moral Theory: An Essay in Moral Epistemology," in Q. Smith (ed.), *Epistemology: New Essays*, 225–49. Oxford: Oxford University Press.

Bagnoli, C. (2009) "Review of Charles Larmore, *The Autonomy of Morality*," *Philosophical Review* 118(4): 536–40.

Brandom, R. (2009) *Reason in Philosophy: Animating Ideas*. Cambridge, MA: Harvard University Press.

Burge, T. (2009) "Perceptual Objectivity," *Philosophical Review* 118(3): 285–324.

Chignell, A. (2007) "Belief in Kant," *Philosophical Review* 116(3): 323–60.

Engstrom, S. (2009) *The Form of Practical Knowledge: A Study of the Categorical Imperative*. Cambridge, MA: Harvard University Press.

Franks, P. W. (2005) *All or Nothing: Systematicity, Transcendental Arguments, and Skepticism in German Idealism*. Cambridge, MA: Harvard University Press.

Grenberg, J. (2005) *Kant and the Ethics of Humility*. Cambridge: Cambridge University Press.

Guyer, P. (2007) "Naturalistic and Transcendental Moments in Kant's Moral Philosophy," *Inquiry* 50(5): 444–64.

Hare, J. E. (2001) *God's Call: Moral Realism, God's Commands, and Human Autonomy*. Grand Rapids, MI: William B. Eerdmans.

Henrich, D. (1994) "The Concept of Moral Insight and Kant's Doctrine of the Fact of Reason," in *The Unity of Reason*. Cambridge, MA: Harvard University Press.

Hogan, D. (2009) "Noumenal affection," *Philosophical Review* 118(4): 501–32.

Kant, I. (1996) *Practical Philosophy*. Tr. and ed. M. J. Gregor. Cambridge: Cambridge University Press.

Kain, P. (2006) "Constructivism, Intrinsic Normativity, and the Motivational Analysis Argument," in H. Klemme, M. Kuehn, and D. Schönecker (eds.), *Moralische Motivation. Kant und die Alternativen*, 55–78. Hamburg: Meiner.

Kleingeld, P. (2010) "Moral Consciousness and the Fact of Reason," in A. Reath and J. Timmermann (eds.), *A Critical Guide to Kant's "Critique of Practical Reason"*. Cambridge: Cambridge University Press.

Korsgaard, C. M. (1996) *Creating the Kingdom of Ends*. Cambridge: Cambridge University Press.

Kosch, M. (2006) *Freedom and Reason in Kant, Schelling, and Kierkegaard*. Oxford: Oxford University Press.

Koselleck, R. (2008) "The Status of the Enlightenment in German History," in H. Joas and K. Wiegandt (eds.), *The Cultural Values of Europe*, 253–64. Liverpool: Liverpool University Press.

Larmore, C. (2008) *The Autonomy of Morality*. New York: Oxford University Press.

Lukow, P. (1993) "The Fact of Reason: Kant's Passage to Ordinary Moral Knowledge," *Kant-Studien* 84(2): 203–21.

Neuhouser, F (2008) *Rousseau's Theodicy of Self-Love: Evil, Rationality, and the Drive for Recognition*. Oxford: Oxford University Press.

O'Neill, O. (2002) "Autonomy and the Fact of Reason in Kant's *Kritik der praktischen Vernunft* (§§ 7–8, 30–41)," in O. Höffe (ed.), *Immanuel Kant: Kritik der praktischen Vernunft*, 81–97. Berlin: Akademieverlag.

Pereboom, D. (2006) "Kant on Transcendental Freedom," *Philosophy and Phenomenological Research* 73(3): 537–67.

Proops, I. (2003) "Kant's Legal Metaphor and the Nature of a Deduction," *Journal of the History of Philosophy* 41(2): 209–29.

Reinhold, K. (2005) *Letters on the Kantian Philosophy*. Ed. K. Ameriks. Tr. James Hebbeler. Cambridge: Cambridge University Press.

Scheffler. S. (1992) *Human Morality*. New York: Oxford University Press.

Schelling, F. (1795/1980). "Philosophische Briefe über Dogmatismus und Kriticismus (Philosophical Letters on Dogmatism and Criticism)," in *The Unconditional in Human Knowledge: Four Early Essays, 1794–6*. Tr. F. Marti. Lewisburg: Bucknell University Press.

Shell, S. (2009) *The Limits of Autonomy*. Cambridge, MA: Harvard University Press.

Sussman, D. (2008) "From Deduction to Deed: Kant's Grounding of the Moral Law," *Kantian Review* 13(1): 52–81.

Timmermann, J. (2007) "Das Creditiv des moralischen Gesetzes," *Studi Kantiani* 20: 111–15.

Willaschek, M. (1992) *Praktische Vernunft. Handlungstheorie und Moralbegründung bei Kant*. Stuttgart: Metzler.

Wolff, M. (2009) "Warum das Faktum der Vernunft ein Faktum ist. Auflösung einiger Verständnisschwierigkeiten in Kants Grundlegung der Moral," *Deutsche Zeitschrift für Philosophie* 57(4): 511–49.

Wood, A. W. (2008) *Kantian Ethics*. Cambridge: Cambridge University Press.

8

Constructivism and Self-constitution
Paul Guyer

I. Introduction

As John Rawls originally described the metaethical method he entitled "constructivism," its argumentative aims were restricted: his proposal was to begin with "a certain conception of the person," a conception that "regards persons as both free and equal, as capable of acting both reasonably and rationally, and therefore as capable of taking part in social cooperation among persons so conceived," and then, without appeal to any "prior and independent order of objects and relations, whether natural or divine, an order apart and distinct from how we conceive of ourselves," to determine what principles for the organization of the basic structure of society agents who so conceived of themselves would adopt. In other words, the project of Rawls's constructivism was "to articulate a public conception of justice that all can live with who regard their person and their relation to society in a certain way," namely in light of this "certain conception of the person."[1] Constructivism as Rawls defined it here was to make no attempt to argue, on either factual or normative grounds, that all human beings must adopt this conception of the person as their self-conception; it was targeted only at people who do conceive of themselves in this way and aimed only at making clear to such people what principles of justice they need to adopt in order to be able to live a social life that conforms to the conception of a person that each person in a group of such people wishes be realized for all. The aim of constructivism so defined is to justify the principles of justice from a certain conception of the person, not to justify the conception of the person itself by means of some argument or on some grounds that any human being must accept. As Rawls put it,

---

[1] John Rawls, "Kantian Constructivism in Moral Theory," Lecture I: "Rational and Full Autonomy." The three lectures comprising "Kantian Constructivism" were originally published in Rawls (1980); they will be cited here from Rawls (1999). The quotations are from p. 306.

On the...view that I shall present, conditions for justifying a conception of justice hold only when a basis is established for political reasoning and understanding within a public culture. The social role of a conception of justice is to enable all members of society to make mutually acceptable to one another their shared institutions and basic arrangements, by citing what are publicly recognized as sufficient reasons, as identified by that conception. To succeed in doing this, a conception must specify admissible social institutions and their possible arrangements into one system, so that they can be justified to all citizens, whatever their social position or more particular interests...the task of justifying a conception of justice becomes: how can people settle on a conception of justice, to serve this social role, that is (most) reasonable for them in virtue of how they conceive of their persons and construe the general features of social cooperation among persons so regarded?

In particular, Rawls supposed that constructivism would be able to dispel conflict between "different understandings" of the proper interpretation and interrelation of the ideals of "freedom and equality" held by people who share this common conception of a person

> by asking: which traditionally recognized principles of freedom and equality, or which natural variations thereof, would free and equal moral persons themselves agree upon, if they were fairly represented solely as such persons...? Their agreement, assuming an agreement would be reached, is conjectured to single out the most appropriate principles of freedom and equality and, therefore, to specify the principles of justice. (Rawls 1999: 305)

Thus constructivism as so defined is supposed to justify principles of justice by deriving them from a certain conception of the person, in particular to resolve conflicts about principles of justice among people who share that conception of the person by showing them that only one interpretation of the content of and relation among competing principles of justice is fully compatible with their conception of the person, but it is not aimed at justifying that conception of the person itself.

Now as those familiar with Rawls's seminal work will have noticed, I have omitted one word from the first line of the penultimate quotation, namely the word "Kantian": as the title of Rawls's lectures made clear, he conceived of his method as Kantian and called his approach "Kantian constructivism." There certainly seems to be an analogy between the method that Rawls proposed for the justification of the principles of justice in his constructivism and the method that Kant followed in his own derivation of the "metaphysical first principles of justice" (*metaphysische Anfangsgründe des Rechts*) in the first half of the 1797 *Metaphysics of Morals*:[2] for Kant the principles or duties of justice

---

[2] A work that I always thought that Rawls strangely ignored; see Guyer (1998), reprinted in Guyer (2000).

are derived by determining what principles of property rights and social and political organization are required for agents who live in our circumstances—that is, who because of their own embodiment need some control of other physical objects, beginning with land, and the labor of others in circumstances in which, ultimately because of the finitude of the surface of the globe, they cannot avoid interaction with each other—if they are to act in conformity with the moral law. With the moral law in hand, Kant considers only the most general facts about human life in order to derive the principles of justice and, just like Rawls, need not search for any further "moral truth interpreted as fixed by a prior and independent order of objects and relations, whether natural or divine... apart and distinct from how we conceive of ourselves" (Rawls 1999: 306). But there also seems to be one great difference between Rawls's method of justification and Kant's own: while for Rawls the conception of the person from which he begins his justification of the principles of justice is the starting-point of his whole philosophical enterprise, for Kant the validity of the moral law that is presupposed in the *Metaphysics of Morals* as the ultimate constraint on acceptable forms of social and political organization is itself supposed to have been grounded in the appropriately named *Groundwork for the Metaphysics of Morals*.[3] For Kant, the moral law is supposed to be in some sense a "synthetic a priori cognition," something that forces itself upon us, not merely a "conception" that people may adopt. In other words, from Kant's own point of view it would seem that Rawls's entire argument for the principles of justice is *analytical*, beginning with a concept that may or may not be accepted by any actual human being or beings, while for Kant the argument for the principles of justice is supposed to start with a synthetic a priori cognition. And at least in the *Groundwork*, it seems as if Kant supposes himself to be able to argue for the universal and necessary although synthetic rather than analytic validity of the moral law for all human beings from some metaphysical premise, something that is indeed "apart and distinct" from how we *conceive* of ourselves, although it may be a fact about how *we are* rather than a fact about what anything outside of ourselves, whether natural or divine, whether the world or God, orders for us or requires of us. Thus, while Kant's own political philosophy might be a form of "constructivism" as Rawls defines it, Kant's complete system of moral philosophy including political philosophy does not seem to be a version of "Kantian constructivism" as Rawls defines that, but to be a method that goes further to include a justification of the moral law itself.

Of course, Rawls may have been wise to eschew any attempt to demonstrate that actual human beings *must* adopt the conception of themselves from which

---

[3] Translations from the *Groundwork* and the *Critique of Practical Reason* will be from Kant (1996) with occasional modifications (such as in my translation of *zur* in Kant's *Grundlegung zur Metaphysik der Sitten* as "for" rather than the genitive "of").

his constructivist justification of the principles of justice begins, for Kant's own attempt to prove the inescapability of the moral law for all human beings from metaphysical insight into the essence of a human being in the *Groundwork* requires acceptance of his doctrine of transcendental idealism, which very few philosophers in the in the century and a half since the cry "Back to Kant!" was first shouted out have been willing to accept.[4] Nevertheless, Rawls's student and successor Christine Korsgaard has attempted to narrow the gap between Kant and "Kantian constructivism" by constructing an argument that it is indeed necessary for all human beings to conceive of themselves by means of the conception of the person that is the foundation for constructivist justification of the principles of justice, and to do so in a way that avoids the specific doctrine of transcendental idealism but nevertheless starts from a metaphysical claim about the essence of a human being. Korsgaard's foundation of moral philosophy upon the conditions for the possibility of what she has called in her recent work "self-constitution"[5] is, I take it, intended to render Rawls's "constructivism" genuinely "Kantian" by transforming Rawls's analytical argumentation that begins with a mere "conception" of the person into a synthetic argument that demonstrates that it is necessary for each human being to adopt this conception of him- or herself and through this necessary to adopt this conception of all other human beings as well.

Korsgaard's theory of self-constitution certainly avoids the specific doctrine of transcendental idealism to which Kant himself appeals for the proof of the validity of the moral law in the *Groundwork*. Nevertheless, it is still questionable whether it proves that human beings must regard themselves by means of the morally laden conception of the person that she shares with Rawls in some non-question-begging way, thus whether she really succeeds in making Rawls's Kantian constructivism as thoroughly Kantian as she would

---

[4] "Back to Kant!" was the slogan affirmed by Otto Liebmann in the work generally regarded to have initiated Neo-Kantianism, his *Kant und die Epigonen* of 1865. But neither of the two main movements of Neo-Kantianism that followed, the "Marburg" Neo-Kantianism founded by Hermann Cohen and the "Heidelberg" Neo-Kantianism established by Wilhelm Windelband, can be regarded as having accepted Kant's transcendental idealism in any straightforward manner. The works that initiated the great revival of Kant studies in the anglophone world a century later, namely Strawson (1966) and Bennett (1966), both explicitly rejected transcendental idealism while trying to salvage other ideas and arguments from Kant. To be sure, Allison (1983) was subtitled *An Interpretation and Defense*, but the "epistemological" or "methodological" rather than "ontological" interpretation of transcendental idealism defended by Allison has certainly been controversial, and what has been particularly controversial is whether his attempt to defend Kant's moral philosophy on his interpretation of transcendental idealism in Allison (1990) can succeed. On the latter, see Guyer (1992); Allison responded in Allison (1993, reprinted in 1996: 109–28, at 124–8).

[5] This is the title of Korsgaard's most recent book (2009). This book is the published version of Locke Lectures that Korsgaard gave at Oxford University in 2002, and that were widely dispersed before the publication of this book. Korsgaard introduced the concept of "self-constitution" as the foundation for moral theory even before the 2002 lectures, for example in Korsgaard (1999). In this chapter I will consider only the presentation of her theory in Korsgaard (2009).

like. If she does not, that leaves open the possibility that Rawls's strategy for political philosophy might be the best we can hope for in moral philosophy as well, namely beginning from a conception of the person that can be shown to have a variety of normative consequences and that can itself be presented in a very attractive light but cannot be derived from any non-controvertible premise that any human being must accept.

The present chapter will not be able to argue conclusively for this result. But it will diagnose the flaws in both Kant's own attempt to prove the validity of the moral law from transcendental idealism and Korsgaard's attempt to do so from the conditions of the possibility of self-constitution, and thereby at least open the door to the suggestion that Rawls's more modest version of constructivism was the right strategy for moral philosophy after all. Before examining the arguments of Kant and Korsgaard, it will be useful to begin with a brief review of Rawls's "certain conception of the person."

II. Rawls's Conception of the Person

Rawls spells out the "conception of the person" from which the "constructivist" justification of principles of justice is supposed to begin in the first two of his 1980 Columbia University Dewey Lectures on "Kantian Constructivism," entitled "Rational and Full Autonomy" and "Representation of Freedom and Equality." The "members of a well-ordered society" within which there is an interest in converging upon and acting in accordance with principles of justice and to whom Rawls's justification is addressed "are, and view themselves and one another in their political and social relations (so far as these are relevant to questions of justice) as, free and equal moral persons. Here there are three distinct notions," he continues, "specified independently: freedom, equality, and moral (as applied to) person[s]" (Rawls 1999: 309). That is, each person in such a society must conceive of both him- or herself and all other members of the society as free, equal, and capable of morality.

Rawls defines what he means by "moral" first: "once they have reached the age of reason, each has, and views the others as having, an effective sense of justice, as well as an understanding of a conception of their good" (Rawls 1999: 309). One might well think that the introduction of the concept of a sense of justice into the definition of moral which is in turn supposed to be one of the premises for the derivation of the principles of justice threatens to render Rawls's entire procedure circular, so perhaps it would be better to replace this concept with something that avoids direct reference to justice, and say instead that the first condition of conceiving of oneself morally is to conceive of others as having, other things being equal, the same privileges and entitlements one is prepared to claim for oneself, whatever they may be. (The "other things being equal" proviso is necessary to prepare the way for an actual society, in which some may forego their privileges because of their own deeds while others may be granted additional privileges when the whole society sees it as in its interest to do so.) Rawls amplifies what he means by "effective" in his phrase "effective sense of justice" by defining the latter as "the capacity to understand, to apply and to act from (and not merely in accordance with) the principles of justice" (Rawls 1999: 312). This clarification, clearly inspired by Kant, means that the moral person has the capacity to understand and to be effectively motivated by moral considerations, although of course every moral theory has always recognized that there is many a slip 'twixt spoon and mouth and that under certain circumstances the failure to realize a moral intention does not diminish the moral quality of the intention or of the character of the agent. The second part of Rawls's definition refers to "the capacity to form, to revise, and rationally to pursue a conception of the good." What this implies is that moral agents have a reflective relation to their own desires and actions, that they are able to reflect upon, organize, and revise as appropriate their desires and goals in order to be able to act coherently and effectively in seeking to realize them. Moral agents thus exercise control over their own actions in pursuit of their own goals and in light of the first component of the Rawlsian definition of "moral" are disposed to extend to others freedom to exercise the same kind of self-control over their desires and actions.

It has been difficult to expound this definition of "moral" without already using the terms "free" and "equal," which Rawls introduces as separate characteristics of his conception of the "person": what the "effective sense of justice" seems to require of agents who have the capacity to form, revise, and pursue their own conception of the good is that they extend to others a freedom to form, revise, and pursue their own conceptions of the good that is equal to their own. But Rawls adds some content to the conceptions of freedom and equality that may be inherent in his conception of the moral person by emphasizing the implications of those two requirements for the relation of individuals to the institutions of their society rather than directly to each other. "Citizens are equal," he states, "in that they regard one another as having an equal right to determine, and to assess upon due reflection, the first principles of justice by which the basic structure of their society is to be governed," and "the members of a well-ordered society are free in that they think they are entitled to make claims on the design of their common institutions in the name of their own fundamental aims and higher-order interests" (Rawls 1999: 309). These definitions suggest that those who conceive of themselves and others as persons in the Rawlsian sense regard all as having equal freedom to influence the basic principles of their society, or equal rights to political participation (again it would seem as if an explicit reference to justice should be avoided in the definition), and equal freedom to benefit from the institutions of their society. Rawls continues his definition of freedom by saying that "as free persons" the members of a well-ordered society "think of themselves as not inevitably tied to the pursuit of the particular final ends that they have at any given time, but rather as capable of revising and changing these ends on reasonable and rational grounds," that is, grounds that take into consideration both their own other interests (the "rational") and the interests of others (the "reasonable") (Rawls 1999: 309). This seems to bring us back to his original definition of the moral: the freedom he is describing here seems to be nothing other than the freedom to exercise the moral power to reflect upon and revise one's goals, and the requirement that one should be free to revise and change one's ends on both reasonable and rational grounds seems to imply that Rawlsian persons conceive of themselves as having the privilege to revise their ends as they see fit, but also to extend the same privilege to others. Once again, the concepts of equality and freedom at stake here seem already contained in the concept of the moral that Rawls is employing, although perhaps the present separation of the concept of freedom from the original concept of the moral is supposed to suggest that in a well-ordered society individuals not only claim for themselves and extend to others the privilege of reflectively revising their own ends but also expect the institutions of their society to preserve and promote rather than restrict this freedom.

Whether Rawls's three components of the conception of a person are independent of one another or not, a clear picture of the self-conception of such a person emerges: such persons conceive of themselves as having the ability and the right to determine their own ends, extend the same privilege to each other in all their personal relations, and in particular aim to organize their social institutions in such a way as to preserve these abilities and rights for all of themselves, not just for some. The central idea of Rawls's constructivism is just this last, that is, the idea that people who conceive of themselves as persons in his sense will determine and implement the basic principles and structures of their society so as to preserve and promote these abilities and privileges for all, and need no other source, whether natural or divine, to arrive at the principles of justice. In Rawls's complete theory, of course, people who so conceive of themselves are supposed to arrive at the principles of justice through the thought experiment or as he calls it in these lectures "model-conception" of the "original position"; that is, they are supposed to consider what principles they or their "representatives" or "trustees" would choose in a situation in which each has the same moral self-conception, each knows what sorts of goals human beings have in general and what sorts of goods they need in order to realize them, but none knows what their own particular abilities, ends, or resources will be. Under such circumstances, they are supposed to choose principles for the organization of their society that will maximize the benefits to anyone no matter how minimal their abilities and resources might turn out to be. The decision to endorse only principles of justice that would be determined in such a condition is supposed to reflect the underlying commitment of the moral person that differences in ability and resources should not matter to the privileges and benefits every person in a well-ordered society should have. It is of course highly debatable whether it is necessary to go through the exercise of imagining what principles of justice representatives of different people or groups of them would choose behind the "veil of ignorance," or whether it would not just be obvious to anyone who fully understood the requirements of conceiving of themselves and others as persons what the only acceptable principles of social organization should be, that is, whether the work of Rawlsian political theory is not already largely done with the introduction of a clear account of the self-conception of the moral person. I will not enter into that debate here. Leaving aside the necessity of going through the thought experiment of imagining the original position, Rawls's theory is that moral agents who comprehend what sorts of social goods are necessary in order for them and others to be able to pursue their own ends rationally, reasonably, and effectively will understand that equal access to certain "primary goods" is necessary for all. These primary goods, as Rawls enumerates them in "Kantian Constructivism," are (1) "basic liberties" such as "freedom of thought and liberty of conscience" as "necessary for the development and exercise of the capacity to decide upon and revise, and rationally to pursue, a conception of the good" and "of the sense of right and justice"; (2) "Freedom of movement and free choice of occupations against a background of diverse opportunities" as "required for the pursuit of final ends"; (3) "Powers and prerogatives of offices and positions of responsibility" as "needed to give scope to various self-governing and social capacities of the self"; (4) "Income and wealth" as "all-purpose means...for achieving directly or indirectly almost any of our ends"; and (5) "The social bases of self-respect" as "essential if individuals are to have a lively sense of their own worth" (Rawls 1999: 313–14) Recognizing that all of these goods are necessary for the effective pursuit of ends by themselves and others, people who conceive of themselves as persons will then recognize that the institutions or "primary structure" of their society must be governed by the two great principles of justice, the principle of equal liberty that "Each person has an equal right to the most extensive scheme of equal basic liberties compatible with a similar scheme of liberties for all" and the difference principle and principle of equal opportunity that "Social and economic inequalities are to meet two conditions: they must be (1) to the greatest expected benefit of the least advantaged; and (2) attached to offices and positions open to all under conditions of fair opportunity."[6] People who conceive of themselves as free and equal moral persons and who recognize the necessity of the primary goods are supposed to converge on these principles as the only way to distribute the primary goods in accordance with their moral self-conception, whether or not they have to imagine themselves behind a veil of ignorance in order to do so.

It is not my aim here to examine whether Rawls's list of primary goods is complete or whether his two principles of justice are the only ones possible for people committed to managing the distribution of primary goods

---

[6] Rawls (1975), reprinted in Rawls (1999), at p. 258.

in their society in accordance with their moral self-conception. My aim has only been to expound the conception of the person that is supposed to lead to the principles of justice through the list of primary goods. What Rawls's Kantian constructivism amounts to is the argument that persons who adopt the conception of the person he has expounded and the list of primary goods he has enumerated will settle on the two principles of justice he states, without needing to appeal to any further norms. But he makes no attempt to argue for the necessity of human beings conceiving of themselves as persons in the sense he has defined, and famously thought that any attempt to do so would have to appeal to "comprehensive moral" views that had no chance of earning universal agreement. So his version of constructivism can only be understood as working out the implications of adopting a certain self-conception, and in this regard as an analytical exercise, an analysis of the implications of adopting this self-conception in a world in which it is a matter of fact that the primary goods he has enumerated are necessary for realizing the ends that persons so conceived will have.

III. Kant's Metaphysical Foundation for Morality

Rawls's Kantian constructivism, intended as a method for political philosophy rather than moral philosophy in general, does correspond to Kant's procedure in political philosophy to a considerable degree. But of course for Kant himself the doctrine of right is grounded in moral philosophy. In Rawls's terms, Kant's own political philosophy is grounded in a comprehensive moral conception.[7] As originally presented in the *Groundwork*, Kant's moral philosophy in turn argues for rather than merely presupposing its own fundamental principle. Thus, Rawls's Kantian constructivism is decidedly more modest in its ambitions than Kant's own method in practical philosophy, including both moral and political philosophy. Versions of constructivism since Rawls, such as that of Christine Korsgaard, have derived the name for their method from Rawls but have shared Kant's larger ambitions, thus turning constructivism from a particular method for political philosophy into a general method for moral philosophy. Our question is whether the more ambitious version of constructivism, whether in the hands of Kant or in those of a recent writer such as Korsgaard, can be successful, or whether Rawls's more modest conception of constructivism is not also more sustainable.

In the Preface to the *Groundwork for the Metaphysics of Morals*, Kant states that the work is "nothing more than the search [*Aufsuchung*] for and

---

[7] See Rawls (1993). The claim that Kant's political philosophy is meant to be grounded in moral philosophy has been controverted in recent years; see especially the essays by Allen Wood, Marcus Willaschek, and Thomas Pogge in Timmons (2002). For my rebuttal of their arguments and defense of the present claim, see Guyer (2002; and 2005: 198–224).

establishment [*Festsetzung*] of the *supreme principle of morality*" (*GMS* 4: 392). Kant's terms "search" and "establishment" are vague, and it might be supposed that Kant's aims in this work are only to clarify the fundamental principle of morality, which he supposes to be recognized in practice by every normal person beginning early in childhood, and to defend it against various sorts of threats that are also natural in every normal person, such as the tendency to conflate the moral law's indirect prescription of happiness for all with a direct endorsement of one's own pursuit of happiness and the liability to excuse one's failures to live up to the moral law by an appeal to determinism, which is after all a necessary condition of cognitive experience. And there can be no doubt that Kant is concerned to clarify the fundamental principle of morality by distinguishing it from any principle of self-love as expressed in popular moral philosophy and to defend the unremitting demands of the moral law against the necessary truth of determinism by means of a theory of the unrestricted freedom of the noumenal will.[8] But it is also perfectly clear that Kant intends the project of laying the foundation for moral philosophy in the work the title of which announces this project to be more than clarification and defense of the supreme principle of morality; he intends to give this normative principle a metaphysical foundation. He signals this principle in numerous ways, but in particular by repeatedly stating that in the first two sections of the *Groundwork* his argument is *analytical*, deriving the content of the moral law from an analysis of common conceptions such as those of the good will (*GMS* 4: 493–5) and duty (*GMS* 4: 412) and of philosophical concepts such as "the universal concept of a rational being as such" (*GMS* 4: 412) and the concept of the categorical imperative itself (*GMS* 4: 420–21), but that in order to show that morality is "something and not a chimerical idea without any truth" we must go beyond the mere explication of the "generally received concept of morality" and venture into the "*synthetic use of pure practical reason*," starting with a "*critique* of this rational faculty itself" (*GMS* 4: 445). Kant's moral philosophy as presented in the *Groundwork* is not confined to an analysis of the content of the moral law and the duties that flow from it nor to the defense of our awareness of our obligation under that law from various natural obfuscations, but is meant to justify the unconditional normative force of that law itself from a critique of our own faculty of pure practical reason. As expounded in the *Groundwork*, moreover, this critique or "synthetic use" of pure practical reason depends upon an appeal to the metaphysics of transcendental idealism, which is supposed to show that the moral law is nothing less than the causal law of our real, that is, noumenal self: the "ought" of the moral law is to be derived from the "is" of our noumenal self.

---

[8] See Guyer (2000a; 2003).

This is hardly the place for a detailed exposition of either the analytical or the synthetic stages of the *Groundwork*.[9] Here a sketch will have to suffice. Kant's analysis of the concept of duty, which is itself the concept of a good will "under certain subjective limitations and hindrances" are endemic to the human condition (*GMS* 4: 397), is that the fulfillment of duty cannot be motivated by inclination or the objects of inclination, only by respect for the moral law itself, but if the will has been "deprived of every impulse that could arise for it from obeying some law" then the only possible content for the moral law that is to be respected by the agent moved by duty is nothing "but the conformity of actions as such with universal law," thus the moral law is "*I ought never to act except in such a way that I could also will that my maxim should become a universal law*" (*GMS* 4: 402). The analysis of the more philosophical concept of a rational being as such is supposed to lead to the same result: A rational being is one that acts in accordance with its own "*representation of laws*" (*GMS* 4: 412); a law that presents itself to rational beings like us who also harbor inclinations that could lead them to resist that law is an imperative (*GMS* 4: 413); but the only viable candidate for such a law and thus for a genuine imperative is neither the technical (quasi-) imperatives of skill, which tell us what means we must adopt in order to achieve ends that turn out to be discretionary or optional (*GMS* 4: 415), nor the pragmatic (quasi-) imperatives of prudence, which can merely give us indeterminate counsels for happiness (*GMS* 4: 418), but the categorical imperative, which commands us regardless of our discretionary ends and conceptions of happiness; but if such an imperative "contains no condition" of such personal preference "to which it would be limited," then "nothing is left with which the maxim of action is to conform but the universality of a law as such," and "There is, therefore, only a single categorical imperative," namely, once again, "*act only in accordance with that maxim through which you can at the same time will that it become a universal law*" (*GMS* 4: 421).[10] But whether Kant starts from the concept of duty or the concept of a rational being as such, in either case "That this practical rule" that results from the analysis is actually "an imperative, that is, that the will of every rational being is necessarily bound to it as a condition, cannot be proved by mere analysis of the concepts that are to be found in it, because it is a synthetic proposition; one would have to go beyond cognition of objects to a critique of the subject, that is, of pure practical reason,

---

[9] For my account of the analytical stage of Kant's argument, see especially Guyer (2007a, chapters 4–5); for my account of the synthetic, metaphysical stage of Kant's argument, see Guyer (2007a, chapter 6; and 2007), and my response to the comments thereon by Allen Wood, Henry Allison, and Sebastian Rödl in Guyer (2007c).

[10] This (first) formulation of the categorical imperative in section II differs from the formulation reached in section I by mandating that one should act only on maxims that *can* be willed as universal laws rather than mandating that one *should* will one's maxims as universal laws. I do not think Kant means anything by this verbal difference, but I will not attempt to defend that claim here.

since this synthetic proposition, which commands apodictically, must be capable of being cognized completely *a priori*" (*GMS* 4: 440).

Kant's synthetic argument for the synthetic proposition that all rational beings are actually bound by the moral law is presented in section III of the *Groundwork*. It actually takes the form of an argument that presupposes that all genuinely rational beings are bound by the moral law as previously analyzed and then attempts to show that we human beings *really are* rational beings and thus really are bound by the moral law. This is where Kant makes his move from a metaphysical "is" to a normative "ought." Section III begins with a restatement of the analytical results of the previous sections, here presented in the form of an argument that "negative" freedom from the determining influence of inclinations can be achieved only by beings that have "positive" freedom, whose will is "a law to itself," which in turn "indicates only the principle, to act on no other maxims than that which can also have as object itself as a universal law" (*GMS* 4: 446–7). This in turn means that such positive "freedom must be presupposed as a property of the will of all" genuinely rational beings," that is, all genuinely rational beings are subject to the moral law (*GMS* 4: 447). But that does not suffice to prove that *we are* such rational beings, as Kant indicates by raising the threat of a circle or *petitio principii*[11] that we might think of ourselves as free in order to think of ourselves as under the moral law but only think we are obliged by the moral law because we have presupposed that we are free (*GMS* 4: 450). The only way that Kant thinks we can escape from this circle and thus prove rather than merely presuppose that we really are obliged by the moral law is to appeal to transcendental idealism. Kant claims that everyone naturally recognizes the distinction between mere appearance and things as they are in themselves, and moreover applies this distinction to the self, thus everyone distinguishes the self as it appears from the self as it really is (*GMS* 4: 451). He then asserts that every "human being really finds in himself a capacity by which he distinguishes himself from all other things, even from himself insofar as he is affected by objects, and that is *reason*," which is "pure self-activity" (*GMS* 4: 452). In other words, reason is the one faculty that we know we can attribute to our self as it is in itself, not to the self as it merely appears. And because reason characterizes us as we really are, it is not affected by inclinations, which exist in the world of mere appearance, thus we have freedom negatively conceived; but because reason must have its own law, which can be nothing but the moral law, as we really are we must have the positive freedom to act in accordance with the moral law, indeed "the human being can never think of the causality of his own will otherwise than under the idea of" positive freedom and its law, the moral law (*GMS* 4: 452). Thus, "The suspicion that we raised above is now removed, the suspicion that a hidden circle

---

[11] See Schönecker (1999: 329–58) and Quarfood (2006: 285–300).

was contained in our inference from freedom to autonomy and from the latter to the moral law" (*GMS* 4: 453).

This argument has notorious problems. For one, if the moral law were really the causal law of our noumenal selves and our noumenal selves were the *ground* (*GMS* 4: 453) of our appearance to ourselves or our phenomenal selves, then, as was quickly pressed against Kant, it is difficult to see how we could have any inclinations contrary to the moral law or how, if *per impossibile* we did, they could have any real effect on our will.[12] Kant himself does not raise this objection in the *Groundwork*, but at the same time he blithely ignores his own view that as the causal law of our real selves the moral law must also be the ground for everything in our phenomenal selves, even our inclinations, and instead in the remainder of section III he describes our situation as one of *struggle* between ourselves in the world of sense, where our actions "would have to be taken to conform wholly to the natural law of desires and inclinations" (*GMS* 4: 453), and ourselves as "intelligence only,"[13] whose moral law is thus *merely* an imperative for our sensible selves (*GMS* 4: 454). Kant thus speaks of the moral law as an *idea* or ideal held up by our pure reason to our desires and inclinations, but does *not* continue to speak of the moral law as the *causal* law of our real selves. It *would* be the law of or for our "better" (*GMS* 4: 454) selves, but it is not the exceptionless law of our actual conduct. Only in *Religion within the Boundaries of Mere Reason*, however, does Kant finally describe freedom as the "inscrutable" ability to choose *between* the moral law and self-love in the way that is necessary to avoid the problem that arises if freedom is the causal law of our real self.

The other problem for Kant's argument, of course, is simply that it requires the appeal to transcendental idealism to make the distinction between our "real" selves and our merely "apparent" selves in the first place, and specifically that it depends on the claim that we have positive knowledge that our real self is fully rational. As Kant presents the argument, it seems to depend on the further inference that since reason is what distinguishes us from everything else in nature, it is what distinguishes *us* as we are in nature from *ourselves* as we really are, which seems a *non sequitur*. But even if we do not worry about this last step, the argument still depends upon a positive claim about us as we are in ourselves, and such a claim seems proscribed by the epistemology of the first *Critique*. To be sure, the further development of Kant's moral philosophy— the doctrine of the postulates of pure practical reason—allows for what Kant later comes to call "practical dogmatic knowledge," or the assertion of claims

---

[12] The earliest statement of this objection against Kant seems to have been offered by Carl Christian Erhard Schmid, in his 1790 book *Determinismus und Freiheit* (see Bittner and Cramer 1975: 249–50); the criticism was then restated in 1792 by Karl Leonhard Reinhold in the second edition of his *Briefe über die kantische Philosophie* (see Bittner and Cramer 1975: 255).

[13] E.g., Kant, *GMS*, 4: 457.

about our real selves (and God) insofar as they are necessary conditions of the possibility of rationally attempting to carry out the demands of morality; but that phase of his moral philosophy depends on the premise that we are subject to the demands of morality in the first place, and since the point of section III of the *Groundwork* is to prove precisely that, it would not seem that Kant should be able to help himself to practical dogmatic knowledge at this stage of his argument. So Kant's attempt to execute the synthetic phase of his argument and thereby prove that we really are subject to the moral law by the use of transcendental idealism seems deeply problematic.

Perhaps in recognition of this second, methodological problem—there is no suggestion that Kant recognized or attempted to deal with the first problem before the publication of the first essay of *Religion within the Boundaries of Mere Reason* in the *Berlinische Monatsschrift* in 1792—Kant dropped the argument to the synthetic truth of the moral law from transcendental idealism in the *Critique of Practical Reason* and replaced it with an argument *from* the indisputable validity of the moral law through transcendental idealism to the reality of the freedom of the noumenal will (or to the postulate or practical dogmatic knowledge thereof).[14] This shift seems to reflect Kant's recognition that while the fundamental principle of morality can indeed be clarified and thus distinguished from any surrogate and can be defended from being undermined by the truth of universal causation in the phenomenal world, it cannot in fact be derived from any non-normative metaphysical fact. Nor of course can it be derived from any more fundamental normative principle, just because it is the fundamental principle of morality. Instead, once he has analyzed the fundamental principle of morality, Kant can only appeal to the self-knowledge of any human agent for confirmation that we all do recognize the unremitting validity of this principle: "we become immediately conscious" of the moral law "as soon as we draw up maxims of the will for ourselves" (*KpV* 5: 29), and "Consciousness of this fundamental law may be called a fact of reason because one cannot reason it out from antecedent data of reason."[15] And this means that in the end Kant's method in moral philosophy is analogous to Rawls's Kantian constructivism after all. Once the moral law is acknowledged, Kant need only introduce a few basic assumptions about the human condition in order to derive the duties of right and ethics, with no additional normative principles grounded in anything outside our own nature, but the moral law itself cannot be derived—only a clear conception of it can be presented in moral philosophy, although of course that

---

[14] See especially *KpV* 5: 47. The classical treatment of this reversal of direction in Kant's argument is Ameriks (1981).

[15] *KpV* 5: 31. Of course there have been numerous interpretations of what Kant means by the phrase "fact of reason," but Lewis White Beck's conclusion that the primary sense of this expression refers to our consciousness of the moral law or of its binding validity for us remains convincing; see Beck (1960: 166–70). See also Rawls (2000).

clear conception can be presented in an attractive light, one that brings out the nobility, or in Kant's term "dignity," of acting in accordance with this principle. But the fundamental principle of morality itself cannot be "constructed" from anything else.

Constructivists in the wake of Rawls have not settled for the modest version of constructivism advocated by Rawls and finally accepted by Kant himself. They have attempted to construct the moral law itself, to derive its "ought" from some metaphysical "is," although not of course from transcendental idealism. Prominent among such post-Rawlsian constructivists is Christine Korsgaard, who attempts to derive the moral law as the very condition of possibility of being a unified agent at all. Let us now see whether her attempt to expand the scope pf constructivism beyond the limits of Rawls's version and Kant's own version in the *Critique of Practical Reason* succeeds where Kant's attempt in the *Groundwork* failed.

IV. Korsgaard on Self-constitution

Of course Korsgaard does not aim to argue for the binding force of the moral law by an appeal to transcendental idealism. But she does intend to argue for it by means of something satisfying the contemporary conception of a transcendental argument.[16] That is, her aim is to show that acknowledging the binding force of the moral law and striving always to act in accordance with it are the necessary conditions of the possibility of genuinely acting at all, so that as long as one is attempting to act or conceives oneself as attempting to act there is no separate question whether one should try to act in accordance with the moral law rather than some other principle. In this way Korsgaard attempts to derive the normativity of the moral law from something that seems not to be a matter of choice at all: one cannot avoid choosing one action or another when presented with any circumstance calling for choice, for even if one's choice is not to intervene in the course of events that will inevitably ensue if one does not divert it in some way, that is itself an action; but if one is inevitably going to act, and adherence to the moral law is itself the necessary condition of being an agent at all, then there is no separate question to be asked why one should acknowledge and adhere to the moral law. And there can be no further question of whether one has a choice whether to be an agent or not, because of course having such a choice would presuppose that one is an agent. So there is no further moment of choice at which one could have a choice whether or not to accept the moral law. Korsgaard's strategy is thus to derive the "ought" of the moral law from

---

[16] Of course the literature on the idea of transcendental argumentation since Strawson revived the respectability of the project in *The Bounds of Sense* (Strawson 1966) is vast. For some recent discussion, see Stern (1999) and Walker (2006).

the "is" of what it is to be an agent at all. In her words, "the kind of unity that is necessary for action cannot be achieved without a commitment to morality... a commitment to the moral law is built right into the activity that, by virtue of being human, we are necessarily engaged in: the activity of making something of ourselves. The moral law is the law of self-constitution, and as such, it is a constitutive principle of human life itself" (Korsgaard 2009: xii–xiii).

Korsgaard embeds her transcendental argument for the necessity of commitment to the moral law on the part of any human agent at all in a rich matrix of historical and systematic analysis, which obviously cannot be reproduced in a few pages. So I will try to present her core argument in the simplest form possible. Korsgaard's central idea is that to have or better to be a unified will rather than a mere "heap of impulses" a human being must act in accordance with a single principle that is nothing less than the moral law, just as to think rather than have a mere heap of ideas one must think in accordance with the fundamental laws of logic: without "the principles of practical reason... the will... will be a *mere heap*, not of ideas now, but of impulses to act" (Korsgaard 2009: 67). Her complete argument that only the moral law provides a sufficient condition for unified willing is spread over several chapters in her book. She begins by showing that adherence to Kant's principle of the hypothetical imperative—"Whoever wills the end also wills (insofar as reason has decisive influence on his action) the indispensably necessary means to it that are in his power"[17]—is a necessary condition for unified willing and action. To have the desire for an end but then not to will to take some step toward realizing the end that is available to one because at the moment for taking that step one is diverted by "timidity, idleness, and depression" or some other "desire and temptation" or any other distraction is the very paradigm of what it is *not* to have an effective will. In Korsgaard's words,

> if I give in to each claim as it appears *I* will do nothing and will not have a life... The reason that I must conform to the [principle of] the hypothetical imperative is that if I don't conform to it, if I always *allow* myself to be derailed by timidity, idleness, or depression, then I never really *will* an end. The *desire* to pursue the end and the desires that draw me away from it each hold sway in their turn, but *my will* is never active. (Korsgaard 2009: 69–70)

A person who desires some object but who can be distracted from taking the next step necessary to obtain it by whatever comes next is just a heap of impulses, not an agent at all.

This consideration, of course, does not go very far: a person who is committed to taking the next step toward realizing some desire is a far cry from an agent who has a unified will with regard to her own life, let alone someone who

---

[17] *GMS* 4: 417, cited at Korsgaard (2009: 68).

is committed to acting on no maxim for herself unless she can also will it to be a universal law. Korsgaard advances her argument by next introducing what she calls "the argument against particularistic willing" (Korsgaard 2009: 72). Her claim here is that we can see from her argument about the hypothetical imperative that to will is to make oneself the cause of an action, and that "when you determine your own causality you must operate as a whole, as something over and above your parts, when you do so." The argument against particularistic willing is then that you cannot do this if you accept as a reason to act something "that applies only to the case before you, and has no implications for any other case," which would be "particularistic willing." Carrying through on some desire by taking some necessary step or steps toward realizing it, which is what the principle of the hypothetical imperative requires, will still not constitute one a unified agent if the next time that desire appears one does not regard it (other things being equal) as a reason for action at all. In that case, one would still be just a heap of impulses, although perhaps a heap with some short-lived connections among a few impulses. But "If particularistic willing is impossible," Korsgaard argues, "then it follows that willing must be universal—that is, a maxim, in order to be willed at all, must be willed as a universal law" (Korsgaard 2009: 73). Korsgaard's argument is basically that in order to conceive of oneself as the cause of an action, one must conceive of oneself as acting on a principle of choice, but that a principle of particularistic willing would collapse the distinction between a principle and a mere impulse, and thus reduce one to a heap of impulses: "particularistic willing makes it impossible for you to distinguish yourself, your principle of choice, from the various incentives on which you act" (Korsgaard 2009: 75). So anything that is to count as a principle on which one could see oneself as a will or as the cause of an action must be more general than what would in fact be merely the pseudo-principle of particularistic willing, which would be nothing more than the disposition to act on whatever impulse presents itself and thus not a principle after all.

We can readily concede this but still wonder how we are supposed to get to the conclusion that "If a particularistic maxim is impossible, then when you will a maxim you must take it to be universal" (Korsgaard 2009: 76). If I may borrow a phrase made famous in another Kantian context, it looks as if Korsgaard is committing a "*non sequitur* of numbing grossness," that is, inferring from the conceded fact that in order to be a unified will or genuine agent a person must make choices in accordance with some principle that she sees as valid for multiple moments in her *own* life that in order to be a unified will a person must act only in accordance with principles that she sees as valid for *everyone* throughout all their lives. Certainly nothing in the argument against particularistic willing thus far suggests that only principles that are universal in the latter sense will suffice to avoid the fate of being a mere heap of impulses.

Korsgaard signals that she is trying to avoid any such fallacy at the end of the chapter on "Practical Reason and the Unity of the Will" in which she is making the argument against the principle of particularistic willing by saying that her argument thus far "proves both more than and less than . . . Kant thought it did," although I do not think she explains the limits of the argument thus far very clearly. She says it has only proven the necessity of the "categorical imperative," "the law of acting only on maxims that you can will to be universal laws," and not the necessity of the "moral law," "the law of acting only on maxims that all rational beings could act on together in a workable cooperative system" (Korsgaard 2009: 80), but for Kant the difference between the categorical imperative and the moral law is only supposed to be phenomenological, the categorical imperative being how the moral law presents itself to us recalcitrant human beings, and the explications of the categorical imperative and moral law respectively that Korsgaard gives sound awfully much like Kant's first and third formulations of the categorical imperative, the principle of universalizability and the principle of the realm of ends, which are of course supposed to be extensionally equivalent, requiring of us exactly the same things.[18] For Kant the requirement of universalizability is supposed to entail the requirement of working together cooperatively, and it would seem strange indeed to take the categorical imperative to require of one only adherence to maxims valid throughout one's own life but not equally valid for all others.

But none of this matters very much, for in the final chapters of her book Korsgaard does offer a further, extended argument that is designed to show that particularistic willing can in fact be avoided only by accepting the principle of acting only on maxims or reasons that are universal in the full-blown sense of being valid for all persons anytime. This argument is inspired by Plato as well as by Kant, and takes the form of showing that all forms of "constitutions" of the self other than that of acting in accordance with intersubjectively universalizable maxims still leave one a mere heap of impulses rather than a genuinely unified agent. The argument proceeds in two steps distributed over Korsgaard (2009), chapter 8, "Defective Action," and chapter 9, "Integrity and Interaction." In the first step, Korsgaard attempts to show through a Platonic review of defective forms of politically inspired "constitutions" for the soul that only the "aristocratic" constitution, in accordance with which the agent rules herself "for the good of the soul as a whole" (175), constitutes a unified and effective will rather than a mere heap of impulses. In the second step, she appeals to Kant's political philosophy and his account of interpersonal relationships such as marriage and friendship to show that because human beings must always unify themselves in interaction with others, not in isolation, they can render themselves more than mere heaps of impulses only by acting in accordance with principles that others can accept too, or by acting only on reasons that are reasons for all. Thus

---

[18] Once again, there is a huge literature on the question of the extensional equivalence of Kant's formulations of the categorical imperative. For some discussion, see Guyer (1995), with references to the pre-1995 literature on the subject; and Wood (2006).

the necessary conditions for personal integrity are supposed to be sufficient conditions and genuinely moral principles for intersubjective interaction (just as in Kant's transcendental deduction of the categories the necessary conditions for the unity of apperception are also supposed to be sufficient conditions for the constitution of an objective world, with the unified self in interaction with other objects).

The argument begins easily. Korsgaard reviews the "timocratic," "oligar- chic," "democratic," and "tyrannical" souls, and shows that each of these is really nothing but a heap of impulses and not a unified will at all. The timocratic soul is one driven by the "sense of honor and the love of victory" to the point where he can become totally irresponsive to his actual circumstances, so bent on demonstrating a certain kind of glamour in action that he can let everything else he might care about or pretend to care about perish for the sake of this glamour. This is to be driven by just one impulse, and "here, an inco- herence in his will makes its appearance, destroying his efficacy and his agency with it" (Korsgaard 2009: 165). The oligarchic person is one who is driven by the goal of maximizing the satisfaction of his desires, which might seem to be a unifying principle, but since the mere idea of maximizing desires includes no provision for "giving priority to the things that matter more to us," such a person will in fact be buffeted by one desire or impulse or another without any way of prioritizing them, and "that way . . . madness lies" (166). The democratic person is basically the oligarchic person without the pretense of a governing principle, one who in Socrates's words intentionally "puts his pleasures on an equal footing . . . always surrendering rule over himself to whichever desire comes along, as if it were chosen by lot" (168), and that way too no effective agency is possible: it is sheer accident whether such a person can even satisfy one desire before he is distracted by the next, so "he may be almost completely *incapable of effective action*" (169). Finally, the tyrannical person is one who is dominated by some single desire, "leaving the person an absolute slave to a single dominating obsession," and this is only "a horrifying imitation of the unity and simplicity that characterize justice" in the soul (169–70): Korsgaard does not spell this out, but presumably what she means is that while such a person might seem to have a unified will, since his desire is an obsession it is not clear that it should be considered a product of choice or will at all, and in any case the dominant desire might always change without any act of will on the part of the subject, once again rendering him a mere heap of contradictory impulses rather than a unified will. So the only candidate for an effective agent with a unified will that is left is the one who rules himself by "reason's own principle," which "unifies the soul and unifies it in a way that makes it capable of effective action" (175).

Korsgaard does not tell us anything more about the content of the prin- ciple that has thus been reached, and one could object that her characteriza- tion of "reason's own principle" thus far is tautologous: the principle that renders the will unified is whatever renders it more than a heap of impulses, that is, whatever unifies it. Be that as it may, Korsgaard moves on immediately to attempt to show that the principle "that really unifies us, and renders us autonomous, is also the principle of the morally good person," that "integrity in the metaphysical sense—the unity of agency—and in the moral sense— goodness—are one and the same" (Korsgaard 2009: 176). That is, she now wants to argue that the principle for the intrasubjective unity of the will is one that requires the intersubjective validity of reasons for actions, or the universal- izability of maxims—the moral law (although in chapter 9 Korsgaard refers to this as the categorical imperative, effacing the distinction she had earlier made). Here is where Korsgaard turns from Plato back to Kant; here her argument also becomes very indirect. First she mentions Kant's argument in *Towards Perpetual Peace* that states that are internally just, that is, republics (Korsgaard calls them "constitutional democracies," although Kant shares the traditional worry that democracies are not actually constitutional but are a form of mob tyranny), are also most likely to enter into externally just relations, that is, to remain at peace with one another (183). One might object that Kant's argument there runs in the wrong direction for Korsgaard's purposes: Kant's point is that international justice can be brought about only by states that are internally just, whereas what Korsgaard wants to argue is that justice in the individual soul or a unified will can be brought about only through moral interpersonal relations. So Korsgaard then turns to interpersonal relations directly, both long-term interpersonal relations such as marriage and friendship and "everyday interac- tion itself" such as making a promise (189). Here she claims that "When we interact with each other what we do is deliberate *together*, to arrive at a shared decision" (190), and her argument is then that shared deliberation is possible only if we "reason together," only if "I must treat your reasons, as I will put it, *as reasons*, that is, as considerations that have normative force for *me* as well as you, and therefore as public reasons." "And to the extent that I must do that," she continues, "I must also treat you as what Kant called an end in yourself— that is, as a source of reasons, as someone whose will is legislative for me" (183). The only way to deliberate successfully together is for all parties involved to seek reasons that are reasons for all, not just reasons for one, so the only way for "reason's own rule" to govern interaction is for it to act only on interperson- ally valid reasons—*quod erat demonstrandum*.

Surely there can be no objection to Korsgaard's claim that successful joint deliberation requires commitment to acting only on intersubjectively accept- able reasons—the only alternative to that is the forcible imposition of one party's will upon another, which is not joint deliberation at all, whatever inter- nal deliberation might seem to precede on the side of one party or the other. However, it is less clear that she has actually argued that the unification of the individual will entails the commitment to mutual deliberation in situa- tions of interaction, which is what needs to be proved. At least she needs to make a lemma for this inference explicit, either a negative one that not to be committed to mutual deliberation in such situations would really just be to allow oneself to be dominated by an impulse toward domination of others, or a positive one that to be committed to "reason's own rule" is to be committed to the rule of reason everywhere and always, thus in others as well as in oneself, thus to ensuring that others and not only oneself can reason in situations of interaction.

But let us suppose that the missing argumentation can be supplied, thus that Korsgaard can successfully show that the necessary conditions for intrasubjective unity of the will are also sufficient conditions for the intersubjectively validity of reasons or maxims. Even this concession will not forestall a general question about Korsgaard's overall argument, namely whether she has really shown that it is in any sense imperative for an actual person to strive to have a unified will. Kant himself, it will be recalled, did not want to settle for an analytic judgment that any rational being must act in accordance with the moral law, but wanted to establish it as a synthetic proposition that we actual human beings cannot but recognize the binding validity of the moral law. Can Korsgaard establish not just that to have a unified will one must act in accordance with the principle of the intersubjective validity of reasons but also that each and every human being must actually strive to have a unified will?

In my view, Korsgaard begs this question: she argues that one cannot *choose* any principle other than that of reason's own rule, that one cannot choose any of the defective constitutions of the soul, because souls so constituted are not unified wills, therefore cannot make genuine choices at all. Of course, one can choose to be a unified will and then fail in the execution of that choice, ending up as one of the defective sorts of soul, "in the same way that you can be a just person who fails on the rack," that is, who cannot maintain his commitment under extreme duress. "But you cannot decide in advance that this is what you will be" (Korsgaard 2009: 183), because in that case there is really no single *you* to do the deciding. Here is where I find Korsgaard's argument unconvincing. She appeals to Kant's analysis of moral choice in *Religion within the Boundaries of Mere Reason* as the choice between two competing fundamental maxims, the maxim of acting in accordance with self-love only when that is compatible with fulfilling all the demands of morality and the maxim of acting in accordance with morality only when that is compatible with self-love, in support of her view that failing to act out of morality is defective agency, something that cannot be considered a genuine choice but only an unsuccessful attempt to be moral (Korsgaard 2009: 162). But this is surely not the lesson that Kant draws from his analysis. In Kant's view, the selection of the maxim of self-love is a genuine choice, a product of the agent's freedom and fully imputable to the agent, although inscrutable because it is supposed to take place at the noumenal level of our reality where our causal explanations do not reach and where indeed because the choice is in some sense irrational justification by reasons also will not reach. Perhaps the choice of the principle of self-love will in some way shatter the future integrity of one's will, reducing one to a heap of impulses, but that does not make it any the less a genuine choice—just as the choice of suicide might be a genuinely free choice even though it will of course destroy one's possibility of making any further free choices, along with destroying oneself altogether. For Kant, the fact that the choice of the principle of self-love is the genuine choice of a real agent is also reflected in his view that it is always in the power of one who has made self-love his supreme maxim and thus chosen evil to reverse that choice, to undertake (not undergo) moral conversion and to make the moral law his supreme maxim after all. This could not be possible unless the choice of evil were the choice of a genuine will, and one that retains a certain kind of unity or continuity in spite of that choice, namely the continuity that would allow the very same will that has once chosen evil to reform and now choose good. Given that Kant's model of choice in the *Religion* is not obviously implausible (apart from its invocation of transcendental idealism, of course), it seems to me that we need much more argument than Korsgaard provides to show that self-rule by intersubjectively valid reasons is not merely a noble ideal but actually a necessary condition for imputable choice at all.

Korsgaard has attempted her transcendental deduction of the moral law without ever mentioning Kant's transcendental idealism. I have argued that Kant's transcendental idealism was never well grounded, and would hardly want to revive transcendental idealism in order to defend the proposition that the choice of evil is a genuine choice, not merely the defective execution of the one and only possible genuine choice of a real will, namely the choice of moral goodness. But even without the prop of transcendental idealism, Kant's depiction of the nature of moral choice in the *Religion* certainly captures much of our ordinary thought about responsibility. To be sure, we recognize extreme conditions, such as psychosis or schizophrenia, which excuse people from responsibility precisely because they render them such a mere heap of impulses that they cannot be considered to have a real will and to make genuine choices at all—we do think of such people as passive subjects buffeted by forces entirely beyond their own control, and even when we need to confine them for their safety or our own we do not think in moral terms of guilt and punishment but solely in terms of safety. But that is not how we think of ordinary evil-doers. Their behavior might fit the pattern of one or another of Plato's and Korsgaard's "defective constitutions" of the soul quite well, but we still think of them as responsible for their conduct because of choices they have made. We might agree that such persons do not have ideally unified wills in the sense that Korsgaard describes, and are defective for that reason, but we do not think that they do not actually have wills at all and have not actually willed their conduct. We are prepared to hold them responsible for their actions and think it fair to punish them for those actions.[19]

The most natural way to accommodate these ordinary assumptions about responsibility, it seems to me, is to say that Korsgaard's conception of a will that can be genuinely unified only if it makes the moral law its own law is certainly an or the ideal for human conduct, but not the necessary condition of the possibility of genuine choice at all. This is what Kant himself did in section III of the *Groundwork*, where no sooner had he attempted to prove that the moral law is actually the causal law of the noumenal self—and thus perforce the necessary condition of all action, since the noumenal self is the ground of the phenomenal self and thus the source of all its action—than he switched modality and for the remainder of the section referred to the moral law only as the ideal for our authentic self. And this is to say that the project of a transcendental deduction of the fundamental normative principle from the metaphysical necessities of the possibility of action fails—which is why Kant himself switched to the project of a transcendental deduction of the metaphysical necessity of freedom *from* the validity of the moral law in the *Critique of Practical Reason*. Here Kant conceded that the moral law will somehow have to stand on its own normative feet—the "ought" of the moral law cannot be derived from the "is" of the very nature of action itself—and I do not think that Korsgaard has proven otherwise. The ideal of the unified will as she has described it, following Plato as well as Kant, has a profound appeal, but it cannot be shown that action undertaken in the name of some other principle is not really action at all.

Where does this leave us? Korsgaard's attempt to take constructivism a step beyond Rawls by arguing that commitment to the moral law is a condition of the very possibility of genuine action fails because the unified will that she represents as a condition of the possibility of action is not in fact such a condition, but only an ideal, although a profound one, for action. Her transcendental deduction of the moral law is certainly not the same as Kant's in *Groundwork* III, but it ultimately fails for a similar reason, namely that it does not jibe with our ordinary assumptions about responsibility, assumptions that may not be unimpeachable but that would need to be impeached on grounds more plausible than either Korsgaard's assumption that only a fully unified will can genuinely act or Kant's transcendental idealist account of the noumenal will before we would have good reason to ignore them. So that seems to leave something like Rawls's strategy after all, namely we can construct the principles of justice that follow from a fundamental commitment to morality but cannot construct the fundamental commitment to morality itself. That we can certainly analyze, and we can also put it in as favorable

---

[19] Naturally the subject of whether what Peter Strawson originally dubbed our "reactive attitudes" to such people actually justify our moral and juridical treatment of them is the subject of another huge debate. For entry into that, see Wallace (1994).

light as possible, as Socrates himself was portrayed as doing in the extended argument of the *Republic*, but we cannot show that it is a condition of the possibility of acting at all.

Bibliography

Allison, H. E. (1983) *Kant's Transcendental Idealism: An Interpretation and Defense*. New Haven: Yale University Press.

Allison, H. E. (1993) "Kant on Freedom: A Reply to my Critics," *Inquiry* 36(4): 443–64. Reprinted in Allison (1996).

Allison, H. E. (1996) *Idealism and Freedom: Essays on Kant's Theoretical and Practical Philosophy*. Cambridge: Cambridge University Press.

Ameriks, K. (1981) "Kant's Deduction of Freedom and Morality," *Journal of the History of Philosophy* 19(1): 53–79. Revised in Ameriks (1982, chapter 6).

Ameriks, K. (1982) *Kant's Theory of Mind: An Analysis of the Paralogisms of Pure Reason*. Oxford: Clarendon Press. Rev. ed. 2000.

Beck, L. W. (1960) *A Commentary on Kant's "Critique of Practical Reason"*. Chicago: University of Chicago Press.

Bennett, J. (1966) *Kant's Analytic*. Cambridge: Cambridge University Press.

Bittner, R., and Cramer, K. (eds.) (1975) *Materialen zu Kants "Kritik der praktischen Vernunft"*. Frankfurt am Main: Suhrkamp.

Guyer, P. (1992) "Review of Kant's Theory of Freedom," *Journal of Philosophy* 89(2): 99–110.

Guyer, P. (1995) "The Possibility of the Categorical Imperative," *Philosophical Review* 104: 353–85. Reprinted in Guyer (2000b).

Guyer, P. (1998) "Life, Liberty, and Property: Rawls and the Reconstruction of Kant's Political Philosophy," in D. Hüning and B. Tuschling (eds.), *Recht, Staat und Völkerrecht bei Immanuel Kant. Schriften zur Rechtstheorie*, 273–91. Berlin: Duncker & Humblot. Reprinted in Guyer (2000).

Guyer, P. (2000a) "The Strategy of Kant's *Groundwork*," in *Kant on Freedom, Law, and Happiness*, 207–31. Cambridge: Cambridge University Press.

Guyer, P. (2000b) *Kant on Freedom, Law, and Happiness*. Cambridge: Cambridge University Press.

Guyer, P. (2002) "Kant's Deduction of the Principles of Right," in M. Timmons (ed.), *Kant's "Metaphysics of Morals": Interpretative Essays*, 23–64. Oxford: Oxford University Press. Reprinted in Guyer (2005).

Guyer, P. (2003) "Kant on Common Sense and Skepticism," in *Kantian Review* 7(1): 1–37. Reprinted as "Common Sense and the Varieties of Skepticism" in Guyer (2008), 23–70.

Guyer, P. (2005) *Kant's System of Nature and Freedom*. Oxford: Clarendon Press.

Guyer, P. (2007a) *Kant's "Groundwork for the Metaphysics of Morals": A Reader's Guide*. London: Continuum.

Guyer, P. (2007b) "Naturalistic and Transcendental Moments in Kant's Moral Philosophy," *Inquiry* 50(5): 444–64.

Guyer, P. (2007c) "Response to Critics," *Inquiry* 50(5): 497–510.

Guyer, P. (2008) *Knowledge, Reason, and Taste: Kant's Response to Hume*. Princeton, NJ: Princeton University Press.

Kant, I. (1996a) *Groundwork of The Metaphysics of Morals*, in *Practical Philosophy*, 41–108. Tr. and ed. M. J. Gregor. Cambridge: Cambridge University Press.

Kant, I. (1996b) *Critique of Practical Reason*, in *Practical Philosophy*, 137–271. Tr. and ed. M. J. Gregor. Cambridge: Cambridge University Press.

Korsgaard, C. M. (1999) "Self-constitution in Plato and Kant," *Journal of Ethics* 3(1): 1–29. Reprinted in *The Constitution of Agency: Essays on Practical Reason and Moral Psychology*. Oxford: Oxford University Press (2008).

Korsgaard, C. M. (2009) *Self-Constitution: Agency, Identity, and Integrity*. Oxford: Oxford University Press.

Quarfood, M. (2006) "The Circle and the Two Standpoints," in C. Horn and D. Schönecker (eds.), *Groundwork for the Metaphysics of Morals*, 285–300. Berlin: Walter de Gruyter.

Rawls, J. (1975) "A Kantian Conception of Equality," *Cambridge Review* 96: 94–9, reprinted in Rawls (1999).

Rawls, J. (1980) "Kantian Constructivism in Moral Theory," *Journal of Philosophy*. 77(9): 515–72.

Rawls, J. (1993) *Political Liberalism*. New York: Columbia University Press.

Rawls, J. (1999) *Collected Papers*. Ed. S. Freeman. Cambridge, MA: Harvard University Press.

Rawls, J. (2000) *Lectures on the History of Moral Philosophy*. Ed. B. Herman. Cambridge, MA: Harvard University Press.

Schönecker, D. (1999) *Kant:* Grundlegung III*: Die Deduktion des kategorischen Imperativs*. Freiburg and Munich: Verlag Karl Alber.

Stern, R. (ed.) (1999) *Transcendental Arguments: Problems and Prospects*. Oxford: Clarendon Press.

Strawson, P. F. (1966) *The Bounds of Sense*. London: Methuen.

Timmons, M. (ed.) (2002) *Kant's Metaphysics of Morals: Interpretative Essays*. Oxford: Oxford University Press.

Walker, R. C. S. (2006) "Kant and Transcendental Arguments," in P. Guyer (ed.), *The Cambridge Companion to Kant and Modern Philosophy*, 238–68. Cambridge: Cambridge University Press.

Wallace, R. J. (1994) *Responsibility and the Moral Sentiments*. Cambridge, MA: Harvard University Press.

Wood, A. W. (2006) "The Supreme Principle of Morality," in P. Guyer (ed.), *The Cambridge Companion to Kant and Modern Philosophy*, 342–80. Cambridge: Cambridge University Press.

9

Formal Approaches to Kant's
Formula of Humanity

Andrews Reath

My aim in this chapter is to explore different ways of understanding Kant's Formula of Humanity (FH) as a formal principle. I believe that a formal principle for Kant is a principle that is constitutive of some domain of cognition or rational activity. It is a principle that both constitutively guides that activity and serves as its internal regulative norm. In the first section of this chapter, I explain why it is desirable to find a way to understand the Formula of Humanity as a formal principle in this sense. In sections II and III I discuss two interpretive approaches to Kant's idea that rational nature or humanity is an end in itself, both of which may be construed as treating the Formula of Humanity as a formal principle. By focusing on the notion of formal principle, I hope to raise a set of issues about how to understand the idea of rational nature or humanity as an end in itself, and about the relation of the Formula of Humanity to the Formula of Universal Law (FUL). I do not resolve the issues in this chapter, though I briefly sketch some resolution at the end.

I. Two Poles to the Formula of Humanity

In the first section, I describe what we might think of as two poles of thought about FH, and then lay out a partial list of desiderata for an interpretation of FH.

1. RATIONAL NATURE AS THE SUBSTANTIVE
VALUE OF MORAL THOUGHT

The idea of rational nature or humanity as an end in itself introduces, or perhaps just makes explicit, the end that serves as the substantive value that animates moral thought and concern. Kant argues that the existence of an end in itself—an end of absolute and incomparable worth—is both a sufficient and a necessary condition of an authoritative categorical imperative and that persons are such ends: "rational beings are called *persons* because their nature already marks them out as an end in itself, that is as something that may not be used merely as a means, and hence so far limits all choice (and is an object of respect)"[1] (*GMS* 4: 428). The "absolute worth" of rational nature (and the ensuing principle of humanity as an end) is the "ground of determinate laws" that specify the proper attitude toward and treatment of persons and serves as the "supreme limiting condition" of all free action and choice of subjective ends (*GMS* 4: 429, 431). Arguably the idea of rational nature as an end in itself would provide Kant's answer to questions about the "subject matter of morality."[2] Morality is about persons—more specifically, it is about acting from principles that show proper respect for persons as rational agents with autonomy.

As ordinarily understood, the principle of respecting persons as ends in themselves is a requirement to acknowledge the moral standing that gives persons claims to certain kinds of consideration and treatment. It directs our attention as reasoners and agents to our attitudes toward persons (as rational agents) and to the ways in which our choices affect the rational capacities and interests of persons—as we might say, to persons, including ourselves, on the receiving end of our attitudes and actions. Let's call this the requirement of "respect for persons (as rational agents) in the standard intuitive sense." To many people, it is a way of framing what is at issue in moral concern that is both accurate and deeply appealing and that seems able to support the deliberative priority of moral considerations. One common philosophical rendition of respect for persons that aligns it with Kant's FUL is that it is the requirement to act from principles that can justify one's actions to those affected by them (as rational agents with autonomy), where the standard of justification is what can be willed as universal law for rational agents with autonomy. This understanding of Kant's principle is supported by his remark in the deceptive promise example that to value rational beings as ends in themselves is to value them as "beings who must be able to contain in themselves the end of the very same action" (*GMS* 4: 429–30). One treats others as ends when they can rationally endorse one's underlying maxim of action, where what is rationally endorsable is what all agents can jointly will as universal law (for agents with autonomy).[3]

---

[1] I use the translations of Kant's *Groundwork*, *Critique of Practical Reason*, and *The Metaphysics of Morals* from Kant (1996).

[2] To use T. M. Scanlon's phrase—see Scanlon (1998: 1–5).

[3] Here I follow Rawls (2000), "Kant III," especially pp. 190–92. Rawls interprets Kant's language that the recipient (here the promisee) be able to "contain in himself the end" [*den Zweck in sich enthalte*] of the action in terms of the recipient rationally endorsing the agent's maxim by seeing that it can be willed as universal law. Maxims that can be willed as universal law are mutually endorsable, thus serve as principles through which we can justify our actions to each other. For other treatments of FH that align it with FUL, see Hill (1992: 45) and O'Neill (1989: 137–43).

The introduction of FH follows a question: "is it a necessary law *for all rational beings* always to appraise their actions in accordance with such maxims as they themselves could will to serve as universal laws?" (*GMS* 4: 426) The FUL is already in hand at this point in the *Groundwork* (both as the principle presupposed by the ordinary notion of duty and as the principle that expresses the form of a practical law or unconditional practical requirement, which would appear to be part of the very idea of practical reason). But its authority remains an open question that FH helps to address in (I suggest) two ways. First, FUL is an abstract practical principle whose authority it is natural to question. FH tells us that acting from FUL is about respecting persons and relations of mutual respect between persons. These are values with strong intuitive appeal that it makes sense to care about and that can command our allegiance. Seeing that respect for persons is at issue in FUL helps to deflect questions about its authority and to motivate acceptance. In this respect FH (along with the Formula of Autonomy and the idea of the realm of ends) brings the moral law ("an idea of reason") "closer to intuition...and thereby to feeling" and "provide[s] access for the moral law" (*GMS* 4: 436, 437).[4]

Second, the sequence of the formulas of the Categorical Imperative (CI) through *Groundwork* II is part of a technical philosophical argument for the authority of the moral law. One component of this argument is the analytic claim that "a free will and a will under moral laws are one and the same," which I understand as the claim the moral law is the formal (or internal) principle of free volition (*GMS* 4: 447). The sequence of reformulations of the CI sets up this claim by showing that the FUL can be understood as a principle of autonomy—as the principle through which the will is a law to itself—and accordingly is the formal principle of free volition. The introduction of FH must advance this argument in some way—presumably by contributing to the transition from subjection to duty to autonomy.[5]

To summarize this pole: rational nature as an end in itself is the substantive value that underlies moral thought and concern and it leads to a requirement of respect for persons. Its introduction advances the argument for the authority of the moral law in different ways. It "provides access" for the moral law since it is a value that it makes sense to care about, and it is a reformulation of the basic principle that contributes to the technical argument of the *Groundwork* as a whole.

---

[4] Even if the introduction of FH "provides access" for the moral law, it cannot close the question of its authority at this point. The question how categorical imperatives are possible arises initially because of the unconditional character of duty: how can there be requirements that are independent of and take priority over desire-based reasons? (Do we have the motivational capacities to act from such principles and does it make sense to accept their authority?) Since FH purports to be an unconditional requirement, it cannot by itself resolve that issue.

[5] For discussion of this transition, see Reath (2006: 99–108, 137–49) and Engstrom (2009: 135–6, 149–51).

2. FH AS A FORMAL PRINCIPLE

A different pole comes to the fore when we consider Kant's view that the various formulas of the CI are equivalent. Kant holds that the FUL is a formal principle. Among other things, he refers to it as the "formal principle of volition" (*GMS* 4: 400) and as the "formal practical principle of pure reason" (*KpV* 5: 41).[6] Indeed the FUL is both the formal principle of morality and, given the arguments of the opening of *Groundwork* III (*GMS* 4: 446–7), the formal principle of free rational agency. If FUL and FH are "at bottom only so many formulas of the very same law," (*GMS* 4: 436) then FH is likewise a formal principle that functions in these capacities—both as the formal principle of morality and as the formal principle of free rational agency. Obviously if one rejects Kant's claims about the equivalence of the formulas, there is no need to consider whether FH can be understood in this way. But the assumption that FH is *not* a formal principle is one barrier to accepting Kant's claim about equivalence. Since showing that FH can be understood as a formal principle would accordingly remove some skepticism about this claim, it is worth giving this approach to FH a hearing.

To see what this approach to FH involves, let me explain what I think formal principles are for Kant.[7] Kant tends to regard the fundamental principles in some domain of cognition or rational activity as formal principles. This is quite clear in his moral philosophy, where he is explicit that the fundamental principle of morality must be a formal principle and that only a formal principle—a principle that determines the will through its form rather than its matter and that prescribes the formal condition of universal law—has the necessity of a practical law.[8] The connection between form and normative necessity is explained if we understand a formal principle as the internal constitutive principle of a domain of cognition or rational activity. It is the principle that defines or describes and makes it possible to engage in that activity, thus the principle that any subject engaged in that activity must follow. So understood, the formal principle of a domain of cognitive activity is uniquely suited to govern it with normative necessity because it is not coherently rejected by anyone engaged in that activity.

The contemporary conception of formal principles focuses on abstraction from content, as do many of Kant's own discussions of the basic principle of morality. As we know, the normative force of a categorical imperative or practical law does not depend on any purpose or an interest in the matter of the principle, but only on its form, and to that extent such a principle "abstracts

---

[6] Cf. *GMS* 4: 400: that in action done from duty the will "is determined by the formal principle of volition as such"; and *GMS* 4: 444: a good will, "whose principle must be a categorical imperative...contains merely the form of volition as such and indeed as autonomy...," indicating that the CI captures the form of volition as such.

[7] This and the next paragraph draw on section III of Reath (2010).

[8] Cf. *KpV* 5: 27, 34, 39, 41, 64.

from all objects."⁹ But the fact that the normative force of a practical law is independent of its matter provides no insight as to why only a formal principle can serve as a practical law, and does not explain what it means for its authority to depend on its form. Understanding formal principles as internal constitutive principles provides a positive explanation of their normative authority and foundational role.

A formal principle of a domain of cognition grows out of and expresses the self-understanding of that activity. It would appear that any kind of rational activity understands itself as having certain features that make it what it is—indeed that it is a formal feature of rational activities that they understand themselves to have a certain form—and that all genuine instances of the activity are normatively guided by this self-understanding. (Rational activity is self-conscious and is guided by its awareness of what it is.) The spontaneity of cognition or rational activity, in part, is that it is normatively guided by this self-understanding (of its own form).

In order to make this idea a bit less abstract, let me illustrate with an example taken from Stephen Engstrom (much simplified).¹⁰ Engstrom suggests that it is the mark of judgment that it is "self-consciously self-sustaining." The self-sustaining component is that a judgment understands itself to make an objectively valid claim that excludes incompatible claims and that agrees with all other judgments and is confirmed by this agreement. Judgment is *self-consciously* self-sustaining because it sustains itself through its understanding that it is making an objectively valid claim. Among other things that means that judgment self-consciously seeks agreement with all other judgments as its formal aim, both what Engstrom calls "subjective agreement" and "objective agreement." "Subjective agreement" is that all judging subjects are to agree with or hold a valid judgment, and "objective agreement" is that judgments with different content are to agree with and support each other. Thus the formal feature of judgment is that it understands itself, and so constitutively aims, to fit together with all other judgments in a single (mutually supporting) body of knowledge that holds for all judging subjects, and moreover that it sustains itself through its consciousness that it does fit together with all other judgments in this way. In the case of theoretical judgments of the understanding, since the categories and principles of the understanding are conditions of agreement or unity in one objective self-consciousness, they serve as the internal norms of judgment.

---

⁹ See *GMS* 4: 441: A categorical imperative "must abstract from all objects to this extent [*von allem Gegenstande sofern abstrahieren*]: that they have no influence on the will, so that practical reason (the will) may not merely administer an interest not belonging to it, but may simply show its own commanding authority as supreme lawgiving." In other words, a categorical imperative "abstracts from all objects" in the sense that its normative force does not depend on an empirically given interest in some object. A categorical imperative must carry its authority in itself, because it has the very form of volition.

¹⁰ Here I summarize Engstrom (2009: 98–118).

The structure here is that a judgment—in this case a theoretical judgment—understands itself to be making an objectively valid claim that stands with all other judgments in one body of knowledge. This is a necessary feature of judgment, in that a mental state that does not understand itself in this way is not a judgment. Further, this self-understanding leads to a set of internal principles that govern exercises of judgment in two respects. First, the internal principles describe and constitutively guide the operation of theoretical judgment and, because they are part of its self-understanding, tacitly guide all instances, even false judgments. One judges about items given in intuition (brings them to the objective unity of self-consciousness [*KrV* B141]) by bringing them under the categories and principles of the understanding. Second, these internal principles function as regulative norms that, again because they are based in the self-understanding of judgment, set authoritative standards of success and failure. A judgment that does not meet the condition of agreement with all other judgments must be withdrawn.[11]

What goes into construing FUL as a formal principle? For present purposes, I'd like to assume with Kant that FUL is the formal principle (the internal constitutive norm) of rational volition. FUL is then the principle that expresses the self-understanding that both (1) constitutively guides or describes rational volition, and (2) serves as its regulative norm. In its second capacity as regulative norm, it is familiar to us in imperatival form as the principle of a good will. In its first, constitutive capacity it is the internal principle that describes the operation of free rational volition. Since this notion is harder to come to terms with, let me say a bit about it, though without taking on the many large issues that it raises. Rational volition (I hold) understands itself to specify action by deriving actions from universal principles that provide sufficient rational support.[12] That is, rational choice understands itself as part of its form to aim at actions and ends supported by good and sufficient reasons, and it is guided by that self-understanding. This self-understanding is expressed by FUL—or so I interpret Kant's view. In that case FUL describes the operation of the will: volition involves deriving or specifying action through what are taken to be universally valid principles, or judgments of good reasons; and it tacitly guides all exercises of the will, including bad choice that does not conform to this principle in its regulative-normative capacity.

---

[11] Christine Korsgaard has also developed the idea that constitutive principles are both descriptive of an activity and normative. See, among other places, Korsgaard (2008: 7–10).

[12] In fact, following Engstrom, the self-understanding of rational volition is more complex. First, it understands itself both to be a form of practical thinking, that is a form of thought that can bring its object about, simply through its self-understanding as efficacious. This aspect of its self-understanding leads to norms of instrumental rationality (here see Engstrom 2009: 28–44). Second, it understands itself to aim at actions and ends judged to be good. I focus on the second aspect here.

One way to represent this conception of volition philosophically has been suggested by Barbara Herman. Kant tells us that the will is a capacity to derive actions from a representation of certain laws or principles (cf. *GMS* 4: 412). Herman adds that "among the laws that we can and do represent to ourselves is the law that is constitutive of the will's own causal power" (Herman 2007: 171). In all rational volition "an agent is moved by a perceived connection of the action to her representation of herself willing an end, which is to say, according to a representation of the will's constitutive principle...the principle constitutive of the will's own activity...[is] what we (always and necessarily) represent to ourselves in and as a condition of rational choice" (Herman 2007: 246). So here is a way to unpack the idea that rational volition is governed by its own self-understanding as aimed at good and sufficient reasons: all rational volition proceeds from a representation of the formal principle of volition and understands itself to specify action through the application of this principle—that is by deriving action from principles taken to be universally valid or to provide sufficient rational support. A bit more work will tell us that rational volition, so conceived, is free activity. It is robustly self-determining because it is governed by its self-understanding of its form as expressed in its internal norm, independently of certain kinds of outside influence.[13] Thus FUL is the formal principle of *free* agency.

Now the point I wish to make is that what we just said about FUL must also hold for and map onto FH in some way. FH must be the formal principle of morality, the principle of a good will. (So much is obvious. The issue here is whether it is actually the same norm as FUL.) At the same time it is the formal principle of free rational volition—the principle that describes the operation of rational volition and tacitly guides all instances, even those that fail to satisfy the moral norm. So, for example, if a representation of FUL in some way figures in all rational volition, so must a representation of rational nature as an end in itself.

---

[13] The idea is that this conception of rational volition satisfies Kant's conception of transcendental freedom. It is negatively free in various senses: it is governed normatively rather than causally, and since it is not bound to take its desires to indicate reasons, it is motivationally independent. Positively, it is guided by its own self-understanding as expressed in its formal principle—where that is a principle that it gives to itself a priori through its own self-understanding.Taking FUL to be the formal principle of free agency provides a nice account of how bad action is free: it is free because guided by a representation of the formal principle of the will, bad because that principle is *mis*represented (see Herman 2007; 171–2, 246). (On Engstrom's view the formal feature of all free action is that it contains the presupposition of universality; in morally good choice, the content of the maxim agrees with its form, while in morally bad choice it does not; see e.g., Engstrom 2009: 131–4.) If the thesis that FUL constitutively guides free volition is to succeed, it has to provide some substantive guidance— e.g., by setting out obligatory ends that can initiate practical reasoning. For recent accounts, see "The Scope of Moral Requirement," section III, and "Obligatory Ends" in Herman (2007), and Engstrom (2009: 188–223).

3. SOME DESIDERATA FOR A READING OF FH

With these remarks in mind, let me suggest a partial list of desiderata for a reading of FH.

1. If one takes seriously Kant's claim that FUL and FH are equivalent, a reading of FH should show that it is both the formal principle of morality and the formal principle of free rational volition—and moreover a formulation of this principle that is recognizably equivalent to FUL.

2. It should preserve the idea that rational nature as an end in itself (and respect for persons in the "standard intuitive sense") is the substantive value that underwrites moral thought and concern. I think that this is clearly Kant's intent and it is an important feature of his moral conception. Since, the equivalence of FUL and FH also presupposes that this substantive value is implicit in FUL, this point suggests a desideratum for our understanding of FUL. (Formal practical principles, in Kant's sense, need not be devoid of substantive value commitments.)

3. It should show how FH restates the moral law (as previously expressed by FUL) in a way that advances the argument for its authority, both (a) bringing the moral law closer to intuition and to feeling, and (b) advancing the overall philosophical project of the *Groundwork*. A reading of FH that satisfies desideratum 2 will satisfy 3a, since respect for persons is a value that it makes sense to care about (thus "provides access for the moral law"). Aside from that, we want an understanding of the role of FH in the sequence of formulas that shows how it advances the overall argument of the *Groundwork*.

4. Of various passages that a reading of FH should fit and make sense of, I'll mention three. First, prior to introducing FH Kant writes that "in [an end in itself], *and in it alone*, would lie the ground of a possible categorical, imperative, that is, of a practical law"[14] (*GMS* 4: 428; my italics). After claiming that persons are ends in themselves, he then says that without an end in itself "nothing of absolute worth would be found anywhere; but if all worth were conditional and therefore contingent, then no supreme practical principle for reason could be found anywhere" (*GMS* 4: 428). It is clear that the existence of an end in itself is a *sufficient* ground of practical laws: if there are such ends, than there are laws governing proper responses to them. But the claim that an end in itself provides a ground that is *necessary* for a categorical

---

[14] In a closely related passage Kant writes that while "the ground of all practical law-giving lies *objectively in the rule* and the form of universality . . . *subjectively*, however, it lies in the *end*" (*GMS* 4: 431)—raising the question in what sense an end in itself ("the subject of all ends") is the "*subjective* ground of law-giving." The three that I mention (in addition to the argument at *GMS* 4: 429) are obviously not the only relevant passages.

imperative should puzzle us. Kant's arguments for the authority of the CI—either the argument of *Groundwork* III or the Fact of Reason in the second *Critique*—do not directly refer to an end of absolute value. The FUL is a principle that appears able to stand on its own, and it specifies objective ends. In what sense is an end of absolute value a *necessary* ground of a categorical imperative?

5. Second, we want an explanation of the promissory note at *GMS* 4: 429n to the effect that the thesis that humanity is an end in itself will be made good in *Groundwork*, III. The claim that "every other rational being also represents his existence in this way [as an end in itself] consequent on just the same rational ground that holds also for me" is advanced as a "postulate" whose grounds are supplied in the third section (*GMS* 4: 429). Presumably the warrant for this claim has to do with the necessity of acting under the idea of freedom—that beings who necessarily act under the idea of freedom on that basis necessarily represent their existence as ends in themselves. That would show that rational agents necessarily represent themselves as ends in themselves, since the necessity of acting under the idea of freedom is a necessary feature of rational agency (and not just human agency). If so, the question to address is why the necessity of acting under the idea of freedom is a basis for representing one's existence as an end in itself.

6. A third important passage is the remark at *GMS* 4: 437: "Rational nature is distinguished from the rest of nature by this, that it sets itself an end [*dass sie ihr selbst einen Zweck setzt*]." In the balance of this paragraph, Kant says that the end that rational nature sets for itself is "the matter of every good will," is "an independently existing [*selbstän-diger*] end" that must always be valued as an end, and is the "subject of all ends" (which is the subject of a good will). Given what follows, it is clear that the opening sentence is claiming that rational nature sets itself a *single* end, namely *itself* as end in itself. Arguably every organized creature has itself as its own end—that is, has the end of maintaining itself in its form. What would distinguish rational nature, then, is that it *sets* itself as an end for itself—viz., that it freely and spontaneously makes itself its own end. This may mean that it self-consciously understands itself to be its own end and that this self-understanding in some sense guides its choices or activity.[15]

---

[15] Compare *GMS* 4: 412, where Kant claims that what sets rational beings apart from the rest of nature is that their activity is guided by principles that they self-consciously represent to themselves. Because they are aware of representing these laws to themselves, such laws can guide their activity normatively. Likewise, at *GMS* 4: 437, Kant may mean that every organized creature has itself (its form) as an end, but that only rational nature self-consciously sets itself as its end (and thus is normatively guided by that end).

Now these are "desiderata": it would be desirable to have a reading that satisfies these criteria, which is not to say that it is possible. But one might think that readings of FH can be assessed by how well they do against this, or a more complete list of desiderata. In the interpretative approaches to FH considered in the next two sections, I focus mainly on 1, 2, 4, and 6 (sadly, I don't yet have much to say about 5[16]).

II: One Formal Reading: The End for the Sake of which Other Things Have Value

I shall now outline two different ways of understanding FH as a formal principle, (focusing on its role as the formal principle of free rational agency), and then consider how well each does by the above desiderata. The first interprets FH along the following lines: That rational nature is an end in itself means that rational nature, that is, persons, are the ends for the sake of which other things have value and the end for the sake of which rational action is undertaken. FH would then be the formal principle of rational agency because valuing rational nature is a condition of rational choice—roughly, one exercises one's will by making rational nature one's end and by valuing it as an end in itself. I find this general approach in the work of Christine Korsgaard and David Velleman. They do not claim that FH is a formal principle in any sense; my contribution is to suggest their approach lends itself to this understanding.

Velleman interprets the idea of persons as ends in themselves as follows:

> when Kant referred to persons as ends he was saying merely that they are things for the sake of which other things can have value, as your happiness is valuable for your sake...In his view, persons shed value on other things by making them valuable for the person's sake...(Velleman 2006: 42, 43)[17]
>
> The statement that a person is an end, I interpret as expressing the fact that we ought to care about some things for the person's sake, by caring about them out of concern for the person. A person is an end in the sense that he is that for the sake of which—out of concern for which—some things are worth caring about. (Velleman 2008: 191)

---

[16] But see Herman (2011).

[17] Velleman stresses that that for the sake of which one acts need not be an aim to be produced. In action undertaken for the sake of a person, the person is the object of some attitude or form of concern that motivates the agent to undertake the action. He bases moral constraints of respect for persons on the idea of persons as ends for the sake of which other things have value as follows. That for the sake of which other things have value itself has a value that limits permissible choice, because there is a kind of practical irrationality in subordinating its value (using it, sacrificing it, exchanging its value, etc.) to goals that ultimately only have value for its sake. See Velleman (2006: 43, 88–92; 2008: 192–193).

Korsgaard does not explicitly characterize ends in themselves as ends for the sake of which other things have value, but I believe that she understands the idea of humanity or rational nature as an end in itself in the same basic way. For example:

> Kant saw that we take things to be important because they are important to us—and he concluded that we must therefore take ourselves to be important. In this way the value of humanity is implicit in every human choice.[18]

Korsgaard's view is that valuing humanity (one's human identity) confers normative force on one's particular practical identities. Valuing one's human identity is thus the ultimate source of the value of conforming to one's particular practical identities, a condition of having reasons for action, and accordingly a condition of (rational) action.

I trust that the idea that persons are ends for the sake of which other things have value is familiar, but let me begin to fill it out through two examples. Consider first a helping action motivated by the judgment that a person's needs are reasons that make a claim on you. Since the reasons for helping trace back to the value or standing of the other person, you take on the end of helping for the sake of the person and are moved by "respect for the person as an end in himself." Respect here acknowledges the value or standing of the person as a ground for taking on other concerns (here a concern for the person's good) and for taking certain facts about the person's condition as sufficient reasons for action. That is to say that "respect" is a recognition that the value or standing of the person is the basis of compelling reasons to treat that person in certain ways, to give consideration to the person's interests and good, and so on.[19]

For another kind of example: say I find that a certain area of scholarship interests me in a sustained way, and I take that fact as a sufficient reason (within the obvious moral parameters) to enter the field. For present purposes, I assume that this is a humanly good or worthwhile activity independently of my interest in it and that there are objective standards for how this end is to be pursued. Against this background, my interest is reason enough to devote myself to that field. Having done so, it now matters to me that I master the field and develop a sense of what is important in it, that I immerse myself in significant problems, that I make some original contribution, and so on. It matters to me both that I reach certain levels of achievement and that I live up to certain ideals of scholarship, and I regard my doing so to be objectively worthwhile. What goes into

---

[18] Korsgaard (1996b: 122).

[19] Here see Velleman, "Love as a Moral Emotion," in Velleman (2006: 88–93). This case needs to be distinguished from other cases of helping—for example, when one helps to impress another or to incur a debt (for one's own sake), rather than for the sake of the beneficiary; or when one helps for the sake of the beneficiary, but out of sympathy rather than respect (one is not guided by the idea that the person has a claim on one's action).

these things mattering to me? Obviously I have reasons to pursue these scholarly ends and to take the values of scholarship seriously. (That these things matter to me may also be reason to hold others to these standards.) Further, how well I do is a reason for certain kinds of affective responses—for example, there are grounds for pride if I make an original contribution, grounds for self-satisfaction if I live up to the ideals of scholarship and for disappointment or self-reproach if I do not, and so on. I am inclined to say that several features of this example (though not all) reflect a value that I place on myself—my initially taking my interest in the field to be a good reason for taking on this end, the way in which these things subsequently matter to me, and my thought that *my* reaching a certain level of achievement is objectively worthwhile. Furthermore, I am inclined to say that if my level of accomplishment matters through a value that I place on myself, then in taking on these ends and acting on the reasons and values of scholarship, I act for the sake of myself as an end.

What interests me in these examples is the implied view about the structure of value and reasons. The familiar thought is that rational action is undertaken for the sake of some person in the sense that the value of some end, or there being reasons for certain actions, are ultimately grounded in the value of some person. The value of rational nature is the terminus of rational support and the formal condition of there being sufficient reason for action. Absent this form of value, there would not be sufficient reasons for action. If the value of persons confers value on specific ends or actions, then in responding to those specific values and reasons, one is acting for the sake of that person, in effect making the person one's end.

Thoughts in this vein permit us to understand FH as the formal principle of rational volition. Rational volition understands itself to specify action through principles that provide sufficient rational support. If the value of rational nature or persons is a formal condition of there being good and sufficient reasons and the terminus of rational support—the end for the sake of which rational action is undertaken—then rational volition understands itself to be for the sake of persons. This self-understanding of rational volition would be expressed by FH. Roughly, you exercise the will by making rational nature or persons your end (in the "end in itself" sense): you find action to have sufficient rational support by reasoning from the value of persons or by framing practical reasoning in terms of that value. A representation of the value of rational nature as an end in itself then figures in all rational volition, and FH tacitly guides all rational choice, though often in defective form. The value of rational nature can be misrepresented (the value of persons can be tied to the wrong capacity or part of the self), it can be represented incompletely (one can value oneself without extending that value to others), agents can reason badly from that value to action, and so on.

The two examples I just gave are intended to fill out a generic version of the idea that persons are the ends of rational action and are not driven by a specific conception of agency and value. Both Korsgaard and Velleman have conceptions of rational agency that work this idea out in some detail. Let me first sketch some of Korsgaard's views, and then turn to Velleman, who develops a conception quite similar to Korsgaard's. Both offer neo-Kantian conceptions (rather than interpretations of Kant) that suggest renditions of FH as the formal principle of rational volition.

In *The Sources of Normativity*, Korsgaard argues that it is by valuing oneself as a human being that one comes to have reasons for action. That would make valuing one's humanity, or valuing oneself as a human being, a formal condition of rational choice that is implicit in all rational choice.

Korsgaard arrives at this conception of volition through a complex conception of the "reflective structure of human consciousness" that has much built into it (Korsgaard 1996b: 92–3, 103). First, it includes a conception of *negative freedom*: a reflective subject has the ability to step back from any impulse and ask whether it provides a reason (for belief, for action) and it can only move forward (to belief or action) by actually endorsing the impulse (93). This conception of negative freedom leads to a form of *voluntarism*—that a consideration or practical principle provides a reason for a subject only through an act of endorsement. This is not just the weak claim that a consideration or principle can motivate only by, for example, being endorsed or regarded as reason-giving, but rather the more controversial thesis that it gets its normative force, or validity as a reason, from the volitional activity of the agent (e.g., actual endorsement or identification) (121–3, 125, 254).[20] It also leads to a *"positive" conception of volition* according to which the characteristic activity of the will is endorsement and identification with a law or principle (understood as the exercise of the reflective self's authority over the acting self) (104). Volition involves "giving oneself a law," where the only constraint is that what one wills, or the "law" that one gives oneself, is a general principle.[21] Since to identify with a principle is to regard it as expressive of yourself, the laws that one gives oneself will

---

[20] In her well-known earlier article "Kant's Formula of Humanity," Korsgaard ascribes to Kant the view that in choosing rationally we suppose that "rational choice itself makes its object good" and thus is "value-conferring" (1996a: 122). Read in light of some of her later work, her view here, I take it, is that there are features of objects that interest us in them independently of our choices, though they may be features that objects have in relation to our interests, needs, patterns of response, and so on. Choice is an act of endorsement that is necessary for these features to be reason-giving. Further, an individual's choice (assuming that it is consistent with constraints set by the general value of humanity as an end in itself spelled out through application of the Categorical Imperative) makes it, say, a good thing in the judgment of anyone that the individual succeeds in pursuing the end or activity, thus gives others reasons to support her activity.

[21] As she says, "all that it has to be is a law." See Korsgaard (1996b: 98), and "Morality as Freedom," in Korsgaard (1996a: 162–7). FUL is the formal principle of volition, conceived as giving oneself a law, because it is the higher order principle of choosing a law, subject only to the constraint that the principle one elects have the form of law. As I understand her view, this constraint is simply that one choose a general principle (and not, for example, the richer constraint that it be a principle that all rational agents can accept as authoritative).

be the basis of a practical identity (or set of practical identities) that give rise to reasons for action and obligations in particular circumstances (101). Given Korsgaard's voluntarism, the normative force of these identities depends on their being endorsed by the agent.[22] "Autonomy is the source of obligation" in that substantive obligations are based on the laws that we (actually) give to ourselves through our willing (104).

Finally, these features of the reflective structure of self-consciousness point to a *conception of human identity*: it is a necessary feature of human agency that we are reflective animals "who need reasons to act and to live" (Korsgaard 1996b: 121), and since reasons depend upon practical identities, we "need to have practical conceptions of our identity in order to act and to live" (121, 129). One's human identity is "a reason" to conform to some of one's practical identifications in the sense that it is a fact about human agency that one must maintain and conform to some practical identity in order to have reasons for action and to exercise one's rational powers. But "it is a reason you have only if you treat your humanity as a practical, normative form of identity, that is if you value yourself as a human being" (121). That is, given her voluntarism, the normative force of this need of human agency depends upon a subject actually treating it as reason-giving. Thus, the normative force of one's particular practical identities, and presumably all reasons for action, depend on actually valuing (identifying with) one's humanity.[23]

If valuing oneself as a human being involves some volitional activity on one's part, it is something that one can fail to do—though at the considerable cost of complete normative skepticism, since then one would not have any reasons for action or see any value in the world. Presumably the default is that agents do value their humanity whenever they act for reasons, even if only implicitly. If ground level reasons depend on giving oneself some law, or

---

[22] Initially what I am identifying as a conception of negative freedom includes the claim that the reflective subject needs a reason, that is, some general consideration, to go forward. Elsewhere Korsgaard fills this claim out with her argument against "particularistic willing." Negative freedom requires minimally that a subject can move to belief or action only by endorsing some impulse. But a condition of there being a distinction between the acting self who endorses and the impulses within the self is that endorsement or identification be of some general principle that applies to a range of similar cases. For if willing were "particularistic"—if it could consist of endorsing a consideration or an action here and now, with no implications beyond the case at hand—the subject would wholly identify with and in effect be absorbed into the present motive or impulse. But then there would be no distinction between the self and the various desires and impulses in the self, and thus no active self (see Korsgaard 1996b: 225–33; 2009: 72–6.) Thus, the idea that a reflective subject can go forward only through an act of endorsement, when supplemented by the argument against particularistic willing, leads to the need for reasons (general considerations) in order to go on and the idea that volition involves giving oneself a law or general principle.

[23] See for instance Korsgaard (1996b: 125): "Our other practical identities depend for their normativity on the normativity of our human identity—on our own endorsement of our human need to be governed by such identities—and cannot withstand reflective scrutiny without it. We must value ourselves as human."

on some practical identifications, and the normative force of these particular identifications presuppose that one identifies with one's humanity and endorses the general need for reasons, then valuing oneself as a human being is implicit in all rational volition.

A brief digression: what does Korsgaard mean when she talks about valuing oneself as a human being or under one's human identity, and is it true that what appears to be a valuing *of oneself* underlies all volition? A practical identity is a "description under which you value yourself, a description under which you find your life to be worth living and your actions worth undertaking" (Korsgaard 1996b: 101). It is a self-conception that contains a set of interrelated norms, and (I take it) by providing some definition to the self, it makes possible concrete expression of the basic or primitive value that any subject places on him or herself. Valuing oneself involves caring about one's good and thinking that it matters how one's life goes. But in order to have this kind of concern for oneself, one's life needs some shape in terms of which it can go well or badly. Among other things, a practical identity specifies a notion of good and thus provides a substantive way in which to value oneself, giving content to basic self-concern. Valuing oneself as a human being then involves valuing oneself under the description of a reflective animal who needs reasons and stable normative conceptions of her identity. The normative element involves taking oneself to have reason to act and to exercise one's rational powers and thinking that it matters whether one is able to exercise these powers and how one does so. (Roughly it treats exercising one's rational powers as a form of good.) Since it is only an abstract mode of valuing oneself, it leads one to endorse the need for substantive reasons and more particular practical conceptions of one's identity. As one might say, valuing oneself as a human being is the form of taking oneself to have reasons for action and being concerned and thinking that it matters how one's actions and life go.

The thesis that valuing oneself under one's human identity is the ultimate source of value and reasons appears to commit Korsgaard to the view that all rational volition is guided by a basic form of self-concern (that needs specification and concrete expression through particular practical identifications). One might worry that this is false (clearly rational choice can be guided by concern other than for oneself) or that this conception of volition is unduly self-absorbed (should I always be valuing myself or my capacities when I act?). In response, it is important that Korsgaard holds that all reasons are public and are the basis of shared judgments about what is good that hold for anyone (see Korsgaard 1996b: 132–43). Thus, in valuing oneself as a human being one takes it to be good in anyone's judgment that one act and exercise one's rational powers, that one maintain and conform to a stable set of practical identities, and so on. And of course if my endorsement of my human identity is the basis of shared reasons, others' endorsements of their human identity are as well. Proper reflection on one's human identity (aided by some Kantian theorizing) should lead one to think of oneself as a Citizen in the Kingdom of Ends (1996b: 100).[24] Even so, given Korsgaard's voluntarism, that expression of human identity becomes normative through an agent's endorsement of it, in which case it is still a description under which one *values oneself* as a human being.

The second prong of this worry can be addressed by noting that valuing oneself as a human being remains empty until specified through some particular practical identity and that the identities through which this value can be expressed are entirely open. Valuing oneself under one's human identity seems to include a concern that one live and act well, that one achieve good, or that one act from good reasons, but at a level of abstraction that does not yet determine what counts as good reasons and achieving good. Here it is important that one *can* value oneself as a human being through the identity of a Citizen in the Kingdom of Ends. In that case, one will recognize binding moral obligations as ordinarily understood (by Kantians, at least). One will be committed to having a good will and acting from universally valid principles, one will have the ends of virtue (which include a requirement to have the attitude of respect toward the rational autonomy of others and oneself), and so on. Moreover, one will think that it matters that one act from these principles and values: they determine the good that one thinks it is important to achieve. Thus, the thesis that this formal notion of basic self-concern is a component of rational volition does not imply exclusive or undue influence on oneself.[25]

What then is the functional role of valuing oneself under one's human identity? As we have seen, "autonomy is the source of obligation" for Korsgaard in the sense that what ultimately confers normative force on any set of considerations is endorsement of one's human identity. Furthermore, identification with a set of values and principles gives them a motivational foothold in the subject by making it one's end to act from these values and principles.

There are two general points that I want to draw from Korsgaard. First, her conception of agency makes valuing oneself under one's human identity, or valuing one's humanity, a formal condition of having a reason for action, and thus of the possibility of rational choice. That is because valuing oneself as a human being confers normative force on one's particular practical identities, in relation to which certain ways of living and acting come to have value. In this way the value that one (tacitly) places on one's humanity is the ultimate source of the value and normativity that one finds in the world and the terminus of rational guidance for individual choices. If in valuing oneself as a human being

---

[24] Cf. also the arguments in "Kant's Formula of Humanity," in Korsgaard (1996a: 119–128).

[25] Concern for animals or for nature presents another obvious problem for the idea that persons or rational nature are the ends for the sake of which rational action is undertaken. The line of thought sketched in this paragraph may provide a way to address this objection, though I won't consider that issue here. (Perhaps Kant was not so far off the mark in classifying duties to animals and to nature under duties to oneself [*MS* 6: 442–3].)

one values humanity generally, then FH is the formal principle of rational volition: it is by (tacitly) valuing humanity as an end in itself that one comes to have reasons and exercises one's will.

Second, if complying with and sustaining some of one's practical identities is a condition of exercising one's rational capacities and of giving concrete expression to the value that one places on one's humanity, or on oneself, then we may say that the particular identities that are fundamental to one's self-conception are adopted for the sake of one's humanity (cf. Korsgaard 1996b: 102–3). In acting from these identities, one acts for the sake of one's humanity. Further, since these identities get their normative force from the value one places on one's humanity (from one's endorsement of one's human identity), the identities adopted for the sake of one's humanity inherit the value that one places on human identity. That suggests that the ends and projects that are central to one's fundamental practical identities have special normative standing, both for oneself and for others. They are sources of unconditional obligations, in Korsgaard's sense—reasons for action that an agent cannot ignore without loss of identity; and they create reasons for others, for example, to respect and to support one's pursuit of such ends.

In recent papers, Velleman develops the view that persons, in virtue of their capacity for autonomy, introduce value into the world—as he says, "persons shed value on other things by making them valuable for the person's sake" (Velleman 2006: 43). Moreover, he regards this fact as a necessary condition of things having value or being worth caring about; "Kant thought that a world without persons would be pitch dark with respect to value" (Velleman 2006: 43).[26] In "Beyond Price" (Velleman 2008), Velleman draws on certain ideas of Harry Frankfurt about caring to lay out the route by which the value of persons introduces value and reasons into the world. Caring is a specific motivational attachment that involves a disposition "to support and sustain [a] desire." Further, caring about certain ends is important for its own sake, independently of the intrinsic worth of what we care about, because "it is the indispensably foundational activity through which we provide continuity and coherence to our volitional lives."[27] Given the needs of human agency, then, we have reason to find ends that we can care about and love.

We need a few assumptions to get persons introducing value: (1) what is distinctive of persons is the capacity for autonomy, where that includes the capacity for self-governance through authoritative reasons, moral constraint, setting goals for oneself, and so on. (2) Persons have value (in virtue of their capacity for autonomy), and the value of persons confers value on their good (where a person's good is "what it makes sense to care about out of an appreciation for"

---

[26] See also Velleman (2008: 211): "what ultimately makes things worth caring about in the way that entrenches them in a person's good...is one's value as a person."

[27] Frankfurt (1999: 160, 162–3); cited in Velleman (2008: 208–9).

the value of the person).[28] (3) A person's good is the realization of his or her autonomy. Now, having continuity and coherence in one's volitional life is a condition of realizing one's autonomy, and having ends that one cares about in sustained fashion is what gives continuity and coherence to one's volitional life. So the value of persons and the good of realizing one's autonomy confer value on any ends that one can care about in a sustained manner and give individuals reasons to find and take on some such ends. At this point in the story, the value of persons introduces reasons or normative considerations: the value of persons makes any ends or activities that *would* unify and give coherence to an individual's volitional life candidates for inclusion in the individual's good and ends in which an individual has reason to take an interest. If the only way for value to enter the scene is through an activity playing this role in individuals' volitional lives, then the value of persons (persons' autonomy) is a necessary condition of value and reasons. (I expect that Velleman would accept some such claim, though I do not know for sure.) Note that specific volitional acts (of endorsement and identification, of choice) have not yet figured in this story, since the ends and activities that have value are those that *could* play a certain role in an individual's volitional life, not those the individuals have endorsed or chosen. In this respect, Velleman's view differs from Korsgaard's, since in her conception reasons and normativity depend on what individuals endorse. But choice comes next in Velleman's story. Once an individual settles on, or even stumbles into, some set of ends that provide continuity and coherence to his volitional life, these ends take on a special status. Those of an individual's ends that play this role in his volitional life are elements of his good.[29] Because they play this role, we may say that such ends and activities are chosen for the sake of the person's autonomy, thus for the person's sake. The value of autonomy now makes the pursuit of these ends objectively worth caring about and gives the person reasons to sustain interest in and take them seriously (cf. Velleman 2008: 211). Presumably this value gives other agents reasons to enable individuals to find and settle on ends that can figure in the realization of autonomy, and

---

[28] Following Anderson (1993), Velleman holds that something is "valuable if it is worthy of being valued in some way" (Velleman 2008: 200), or if it is the proper object of some evaluative attitude. I take it that he would support the assumption that persons have value through the idea that persons are the proper objects of attitudes such as love and respect, which are responses to persons that lead us to care about other things for the sake of the person.For Velleman the capacity for autonomy that is central to personhood has value in two respects. It is to be valued or respected in oneself, where respect for one's autonomy motivates one to realize that capacity by acting under the guidance of reasons. And it is to be respected and loved in others. The connection is that if there are reasons to respect the autonomy of others, respect for one's own rational autonomy that generates the aspiration to act for reasons motivates one to act on these reasons. See Velleman (2008: 202; 2006: 43–4).

[29] See Velleman (2008: 210): "Not all of [a person's] ends are of significant importance to his good—only those which he cares about in the way that sustains his desire for them. Things are worth caring about in that way because desires so sustained give structure and unity to his life, thereby providing scope for the fullest realization of his autonomy."

once an individual has chosen some such ends, reasons to support his pursuit of these ends. Agents who act on such reasons act for the sake of the person.

We now have the following points from Velleman's view. First, value flows from persons, through their capacity for autonomy and various needs of human rational agency, to ends and activities that can provide continuity and coherence in individuals' volitional lives. These ends and activities are candidates for inclusion in one's good, in which one has reason to take an interest. Second, we may say that ends and activities that do in fact play these unifying roles, through which the individual realizes his good of autonomy, are chosen for the sake of the person's autonomy or rational nature, thus for the person's own sake. These ends are objectively worth caring about because of one's value as a person, and others have reasons to support the pursuit of such ends once chosen.

Finally, as in Korsgaard's view, the value of persons is the formal condition of other values and reasons for action, and the terminus of rational support. For example, it is the formal condition of certain ends and activities comprising an individual's good and for these ends to be worth caring about. The capacity for rational choice is exercised by valuing rational nature or making it one's end (again, in the "end in itself" sense)—by reasoning from the value of rational nature or autonomy to specific ends and actions chosen for the sake of one's rational nature. On this conception of value and agency, FH is the formal principle of rational volition.

How does this general approach to FH fare by the desiderata listed in I.3 above? It satisfies 2. My focus has been on how to understand FH as the formal principle of rational volition, that is, as the principle that constitutively guides or describes rational volition. But the considerations that support this idea establish that rational nature is an end in itself and the substantive value that underwrites moral thought. (If FH is the constitutive norm, it is the regulative norm as well.) Desideratum 2 secures 3a—that FH advances the argument by bringing the moral law closer to feeling and intuition. This approach also fits 4 and 6: if the value of persons is the formal condition of other values and the terminus of rational support, that value would be a necessary ground of there being practical laws. And the end that rational nature sets itself is the "subject of all ends"—that being both the subject that sets ends (ends are set by rational agents) and the subject for whose sake ends are set (ends are set for the sake of persons, rational agents). This end is an "independently existing end," not an end to be produced, since it is the end for the sake of which other ends and activities have value and are chosen; and rational nature *sets itself* this end in the sense that rational volition self-consciously understands the rational nature of persons to be the end for the sake of which other things have value and the end for the sake of which it acts.

The question I have concerns desideratum 1: is FH the *same* formal principle as FUL? Among other things, this worry is fuelled by the way in which desideratum 4 is satisfied. If the value of rational nature or persons is a necessary condition of practical laws, FH appears to articulate a further condition not contained in FUL on there being principles that provide full rational support or sufficient reasons presupposed by FUL. Here is a way to articulate the worry. Kant argues that a statement of FUL (though not its authority for us) can be derived from the idea of a practical law as a principle that is the basis of fully sufficient reasons for action.[30] I interpret FUL to be the formal principle of free volition in the sense that rational volition understands itself to derive actions from principles that provide sufficient rational support, and that this self-understanding is expressed by FUL. If so, a representation of FUL figures in and tacitly guides all rational volition (e.g., as part of the self-understanding of what volition is, or as a premise in the reconstructed practical reasoning that underlies choice). We have just considered a conception of rational agency in which the value of the rational nature of persons is a formal condition of there being sufficient reasons for action, and rational volition understands itself to be for the sake of rational nature or persons. In this conception of rational agency, a representation of the value of humanity likewise tacitly guides all volition (again, as part of the self-understanding of volition or as a premise in the reconstructed practical reasoning). Are the formal principles of these conceptions of volition the same, or at least different expressions of a single idea? (This is just to raise the standard question of the equivalence of the formulas, but in the context of taking them to be the formal principle of rational volition, according to some conception of rational agency.) The worry is that they are not: that these assumptions about the value of persons do not follow from the idea of practical law from which Kant derives a statement of FUL, and that they add an element to the conception of practical reason and a further condition on the existence of sufficient reasons for action that is not contained in FUL.[31] To dispel this worry one would have to show that the above conception of rational nature as an end in itself (construed as the end for the sake of which other things have value) is implicit in the notion of practical law and sufficient reason, and that I have not done.[32]

---

[30] See *GMS* 4: 402 and 4: 420–21; and *KpV* 5: 19–30.

[31] This question should not worry Korsgaard or Velleman since they do not think that FUL and FH are equivalent. See Korsgaard (1996a: 143–4, 151–4) and Velleman (2006: 40).

[32] Kant thought both that a statement of FUL can be derived from the very idea of a practical law and that this principle has substantive implications for choice and action. To address this issue about equivalence, it is not enough to show that the existence of practical laws and sufficient reasons presupposes that rational nature is an end in itself: one needs to show that this conception of rational nature as an end in itself (construed as the end for the sake of which other things have value) is derivable from the very idea of a practical law or sufficient reason. It may be that there would not be sufficient reasons for choice unless rational nature were an end in itself, but that the absolute value of rational nature is not derivable from or contained in the idea of sufficient reason; that an independent argument is needed to show that rational nature is an end in itself. (And in fact it is natural to read the *Groundwork* as introducing new material at *GMS* 4: 428ff. that goes beyond what has been introduced so far, that is a condition of there being practical laws

III: A Second Formal Reading: The Formal End of Practical Reasoning

According to the second approach, that rational nature is an end in itself means that the formal end of practical reason is its own proper exercise, as defined by FUL. FH is then a formal principle because it is strictly equivalent to FUL. This reading is proposed by Stephen Engstrom in his recent book *The Form of Practical Knowledge*.[33] (It has also been suggested in passing by Barbara Herman.[34]) To explain Engstrom's approach, I need to give some background on his interpretation of the Categorical Imperative.

Engstrom connects the Categorical Imperative with reason by showing how it can be unfolded out of the idea of "practical knowledge" of what is intrinsically good, where the idea of knowledge introduces the conditions of universal validity expressed in FUL. He understands practical reason or the will as the capacity for practical knowledge of the good—roughly, knowledge of what ought to be that has the capacity to make its object real. For Engstrom, all rational volition is based on a judgment about what is good, where the formal feature of judgment (theoretical or practical) is that it understands itself to be making a universally valid claim, a claim to knowledge. Engstrom distinguishes two notions of universal validity. First, a judgment understands itself to be "subjectively universally valid"—to hold *for* all judging subjects. Second, it understands itself to be "objectively universally valid," or to hold *of* all objects that fall under the concept employed in the judgment. The Categorical Imperative is based on the formal features of specifically practical knowledge. In practical judgment, the subject and object of the judgment are identical: "practical knowledge is always knowledge cognizing subjects have of what *they themselves* are to do" (Engstrom 2009: 121). Thus in practical judgment subjective and objective universal validity coincide: they are judgments about what any subject in the relevant conditions is to do that are valid for all subjects with the capacity for practical knowledge. This "double universal validity" is the "form of practical knowledge"—the condition that practical judgments must satisfy to count as genuine knowledge of what is good (122–4). Accordingly

---

and sufficient reasons, etc.) Elsewhere I've argued that the condition on choice imposed by FUL is that a principle can be willed as universal law for agents with autonomy, where a conception of autonomous agency is a source of moral content. FUL may be understood in this way because some notion of autonomous agency is implicit in the idea of a practical law. Specifically it is part of the idea of a practical law that the agents subject to such principles must be regarded as their legislators (*GMS* 4: 431)—that is, they must have the practical and legislative capacities that go into Kant's conception of autonomy. If practical laws govern the conduct of agents with autonomy, then they must be universal laws for agents with autonomy (see "Agency and Universal Law" in Reath [2006, especially 204–8 and 211–20]). Perhaps one can use this argument to derive the value of rational nature as an end in itself from the idea of practical law or sufficient reason, say, as part of the self-conception of any agent with the capacity to act from a practical law. But space does not permit pursuing that line here.

[33] Engstrom (2009).

[34] Herman (2007: 250–53).

Engstrom interprets FUL as the imperative: to act from maxims such that all practical subjects can agree that any subject in the same conditions is to act from the principle (124–5, 221).

Two more preliminary points: First, Engstrom argues that, since the formulas of the CI are equivalent, this "double universality" is implicit in all of them. The different formulas all express the form of practical knowledge, though they highlight different aspects. FUL, which Kant connects with the concept of a practical requirement and subjection to duty, stresses the objective universal validity of a practical law—that a practical law is to govern the conduct of all agents who fall under it. The focus on humanity or rational nature articulates the idea that moral agents are "cognizing subjects" with the ability to make and act on the basis of judgments about good; thus it highlights subjective universality, that all judging subjects must be able to agree with and hold a valid practical judgment. The Formula of Autonomy (FA) highlights the coincidence of these two forms of universal validity—that "the subjects to whom law is given are necessarily the subjects in and through whom it is given by the practical reason... that they share in common" (Engstrom 2009: 136; cf. 150),[35] Second, Engstrom accepts a strong guise of the good thesis: all practical judgment, that is, all rational volition, understands itself to satisfy this double universality and carries what he calls the "presupposition of universality." It understands itself to be directed at objects taken to be good in this strong sense. That makes FUL the constitutive guiding principle of rational volition in the sense I have discussed.

Turning now to Engstrom's interpretation of FH, he takes "rational nature" or "humanity" to be the capacity for practical knowledge (i.e., practical reason), which is exercised through FUL (2009: 167–8). To treat rational nature as an end is to represent that capacity as an end in all practical judgment (170–71). Two points are involved here, that all practical judgments contain a *representation* of rational nature and that it is represented as an *end*. First, it is part of the form of practical knowledge that a practical judgment is about what some practical knower (i.e., an agent with rational capacity) is to do. For example, in judging that an action is choiceworthy or good, I make a judgment about what I, as a rational agent, am to do. The practical judgment contains a representation of rational nature because it represents oneself (or the agent about whom one makes the judgment) as having the capacity for practical knowledge—the capacity to determine oneself to act from a judgment about good that satisfies

---

[35] For Engstrom, the idea that practical laws are "self-legislated" appears to involve two elements. First, the agents subject to practical laws have the shared capacity for practical knowledge, the capacity to make judgments about objective good, through whose exercise the content of moral law is determined. Second (and perhaps more importantly), since these judgments are *practical*—that is, they have the capacity to bring their objects about—it is through the judgments of such subjects that practical laws are efficacious in determining conduct, and are thus real laws. As Engstrom says: "For a law whose efficacy, and so whose very being as a law, depends on its being known by those whose existence it can determine is precisely a self-legislated law" (2009: 136).

the presuppositions of universality. Here Engstrom says: "Humanity is thus represented in the subject position in all practical knowledge, prior to all acts of practical predication through which particular ends are adopted" (2009: 171).

Second, the capacity for practical knowledge is represented as its own end—again as part of the form of practical knowledge. A practical judgment understands itself to be making a universally valid claim and it sustains itself through self-consciousness of its own validity. It aims at and takes itself to be in agreement with all other practical judgments (including those of other judging subjects), it draws support from other practical judgments, and it withdraws its claim if these conditions are not met. Engstrom writes:

> humanity is always represented in such cognition as already actual and self-sustaining in and through such cognition itself. As Kant says, it is conceived as "self-standing" [*GMS* 4: 437]. Hence in practical cognition humanity is represented, not as to be produced, but as to be sustained, both in a negative sense (as not to be hindered) and also positively (as to be furthered) so far as practical cognition... is capable of developing and perfecting itself. (2009: 172)

His point, I take it, is that practical judgment is guided by its formal or constitutive aim of satisfying the presupposition of universality, and moreover it understands itself to be always on the way to satisfying this condition. Practical knowledge is not some distant aim of judgment: a practical judgment takes itself to be an instance of practical knowledge. In that sense, humanity or rational nature is not an end to be produced, but a capacity to be "sustained." Engstrom's larger claim, if I understand it, is that rational nature (practical reason) is represented as an end in practical judgment and knowledge in the sense that such cognition understands itself to have, thus is self-consciously guided by, the formal end of satisfying its own internal norm (the conditions of universality). That is, the claim that rational nature is an end in itself is—at least initially—the claim that rational nature has the formal end of its own proper exercise, and thus is its own end. Since all exercises of rational nature are tacitly guided by its own formal principle, this is an end that it is always on the way to actualizing; in that sense this end is "self-standing."[36]

---

[36] Engstrom relies on a particular understanding of what ends are: an end is "represented in practical knowledge as being for its own sake,...[F]or something to be deemed good as an end, or for its own sake, is for it to be represented in a practical judgment as furthering itself...[A]n end always sustains itself" (2009: 74–5). As I understand his view, ends sustain themselves through rational agents' representations of them (through rational agency). An end has features that, when represented by a rational subject, lead the subject to maintain the thought of the end. That is to say that the subject takes pleasure in the thought of the end, and the representation of the end leads to active interest in its actuality. What matters for our purposes is that practical judgment takes itself to satisfy the presupposition of universality and sustains itself through its awareness of satisfying these presuppositions. Since it is represented in practical knowledge as sustaining or furthering itself, it satisfies the concept of an end, and indeed is its own end.

The capacity for practical knowledge is properly exercised when a judgment in fact has the double universality that is the form of practical knowledge. The judgment will then "agree with humanity" because it fully conforms to the principle that defines humanity, or the capacity for practical knowledge. That means that one conforms to FH by conforming to FUL (Engstrom 2009: 173).

One virtue of Engstrom's interpretation is that it makes FUL and FH strictly equivalent. FH adds no fundamentally new ideas, since it is just another expression of the form of practical knowledge. It simply articulates a notion implicit in FUL: that the agents subject to moral requirements are "practical knowers" with the capacity to make judgments about good, and that it is a condition on any valid practical judgment that all such subjects can agree with or hold that judgment.

An additional virtue is that this interpretation aligns the idea of rational nature as an end in itself with the absolute value of the good will in an interesting way.[37] Bearing in mind that practical reasoning is the basis of volition, the formal end of satisfying the conditions of universality would appear to be that of having a good will. So the idea that rational nature is its own end, as understood by Engstrom, amounts to the idea that it has the formal end of good willing. Further, the formal aim of good willing has unconditional authority over all exercises of the will since having that aim is a condition of willing. If you don't aim to satisfy the internal norm of volition (the conditions of universality), you are not exercising the will. As we might say, no other aim can be put in the place of this formal end, and it is never to be abandoned for any other end. Thus, taking the formal end of rational volition to be good willing seems close to building recognition of the absolute value of the good will into the self-understanding of rational volition. Here consider the "practical" reading of the absolute value of the good will suggested by Thomas E. Hill, Jr.[38] To hold that the good will is good unconditionally and without qualification is to say that it is always worth choosing or maintaining in all circumstances, and never to be abandoned for any other kind of good. And one chooses or maintains a good will by recognizing the priority of moral reasons and conformity to universal law. The point that I want to make here is that assigning rational volition the formal end of good willing gives that end authority over all exercises of the will, and that amounts to building a thin version of the recognition of the absolute value of the good will into the form of volition.

A third strength is that this approach leads to a satisfying reading of Kant's claims that an end of absolute value is a necessary condition of a categorical imperative (desideratum 4). Given the fact that Kant treats FUL as a principle that can stand on its own, why is an end of absolute value a *necessary* ground of a categorical imperative? But what if rational nature were not an end in itself in the sense we are considering—that is, what if rational volition did not have

---

[37] Engstrom does not make this point, and I go beyond his account here.
[38] See "Is a Good Will Overrated?" in Hill (2002: 37–60, especially 42–3, 52).

the formal end of good willing, or that this formal end did not have authority over all exercises of the will and that some other aim could be put in its place (that is, it did not have "absolute worth")? Then there would be no authoritative reason to conform to the conditions of universality and they would not be the basis of true practical laws. (Rational volition would be free, as it were, to aim at something other than conforming to the conditions of universality, in which case it would have no authoritative standard and all practical principles would be conditional.) The "absolute worth" of rational nature is the ground of practical laws because it amounts to the recognition of the authority of the internal principle or formal end of rational volition.

But Engstrom's interpretation does have one feature worth noting. The requirement to treat rational nature as an end amounts to the injunction to agree with its formal end by reasoning in ways that do in fact satisfy the presupposition of universality. This is reflected in a passage cited earlier, where Engstrom writes that humanity (the capacity for practical reason) is "to be sustained, both in a negative sense (as not to be hindered) and also as positively (as to be furthered)" (2009: 172). What is to be sustained, I take it, is the proper use of practical reason. Since rational agents are already on the way to reasoning properly, (negatively) one should avoid influences that impede its proper use and lead to judgments that conflict with those of others; and one should perfect one's rational capacities, so that one's reasoning displays "positive agreement with humanity as an end in itself" and agrees with the practical judgments of others. (*GMS* 4: 430; II. 54).[39]

As Engstrom interprets it, the value of rational nature as an end in itself is not on its face the rich notion of respect for persons in the standard intuitive sense that underlies much ordinary moral thought. The rich notion requires giving certain forms of consideration to persons (including ourselves) on the receiving end of our actions and treating them in certain ways. But here treating rational nature as an end in itself requires a certain attitude toward that capacity: one is to recognize the authority of its formal end (exercising the capacity according to its own internal norm).[40] Note that the negative and positive

---

[39] I gather that "sustaining humanity" involves judging in ways that are consistent with the aim of shared practical judgments. Negatively one is to avoid practical judgments that lead to contradictions in conception; positively one's judgments should agree with judgments about the goodness of self-perfection and own happiness to which all agents are committed, thus avoiding contradictions in will. I'm grateful to Steve Engstrom for comments here.

[40] What has absolute worth or is to be "respected" as an end in itself is a capacity that one possesses—the capacity for practical reason, understood through its formal principle. There is, of course, precedent for this reading in the texts. At *GMS* 4: 428 and in the four examples (*GMS* 4: 429–31), it is clear that persons and their rational capacities are ends in themselves. But in a key discussion of "respect," Kant notes that "the object of respect is therefore simply the law" and that honorific respect for a person's accomplishments is "respect for the law...of which he gives us an example" (*GMS* 4: 401n). For an interesting discussion that understands respect for the moral law as respect for the idealized rational will that is the essence of the person and a law for the empirical self, see Velleman (2006: 77–81).

aspects of respecting the formal end of practical reason to which Engstrom points are a step removed from the negative and positive duties that Kant uses to illustrate the FH. The focus of these examples—negative duties proscribing suicide, deception, interference with the rights of others, and the positive duties of virtue (self-perfection and mutual aid)—is the proper attitude toward and treatment of persons and their rational capacities.

Is this a problem? Perhaps it is not, because the proper use of practical reason leads to choice that respects persons in the standard intuitive sense through the condition of subjective universal validity—that all rational agents be able to agree with or hold a valid practical judgment. (My judgment that I may deceive for self-interest cannot be generally shared, in particular by the person I deceive.) That subjective universal validity is a formal feature of rational volition that limits its proper exercise translates into the idea that persons as rational agents are "supreme limiting conditions of the freedom of action of very human being" and of "all subjective ends" (*GMS* 4: 431).

Regarding the six desiderata, Engstrom's approach does well by 6. The end that rational nature sets itself is its own proper exercise. It "sets itself" this end in that it is constitutively guided by its self-understanding of its formal end, and this is a "self-standing" end that it is always on the way to actualizing. As just discussed, it provides a satisfying, if spare, treatment of 4. It does very well on 1, since it treats FUL and FH as strictly equivalent. In particular, FH is as much a statement of the formal principle of morality and the formal principle of rational volition as is FUL. My question concerns desiderata 2 and 3a: is the link between Engstrom's interpretation of rational nature as an end in itself and the substantive value of persons sufficiently direct? Connecting the moral law with the formal end of good willing does not exactly bring it closer to intuition and feeling.

IV. Conclusion

I hope to have made the case that FH can be construed as a formal principle. The question then is how best to do this. If the approach drawn from Korsgaard and Velleman is to preserve the equivalence of FUL and FH, one needs to show that the key ideas of FH, for instance that persons are sources of value and that rational choice is for the sake of persons, are implicit in FUL. Whether that can be done is a matter for another occasion.

Since Engstrom's interpretation of rational nature as an end in itself is not on its face the rich notion of respect for persons, the question is whether it preserves the substantive value that underwrites moral thought in the right way (desiderata 2 and 3a). Now this may seem like a quibble, since the formal end of rational nature, once fleshed out, certainly gets us to the value of persons. The conclusion that I think we should draw is that this approach does satisfy 2 and 3a, and in a way that proves instructive. The value of rational nature as an end in itself (the value of the formal end of conforming to its internal norm) is as abstract as the requirement of conformity to universal law—unsurprisingly, since it is the same idea slightly redescribed. But one aspect of this end is the condition of subjective universal validity—that all subjects be able to hold a valid practical judgment. This idea gives some precision to the idea of respect for persons that underlies ordinary moral thought—for example, setting out an ideal of justifiability as what is owed to persons specifically as rational agents with autonomy. Furthermore, FUL leads to a set of duties and principles whose content is to respect the rational nature of persons. This indicates that FUL, at different levels of generality, contains the substantive value that is clearly worthy of our allegiance. Furthermore, since the value of respect for persons that drives much ordinary moral thought turns out to be implicit in FUL, Kant's foundational project would show that value to have a genuine basis in reason. In sum, what we might call "the formal formal approach" does surprisingly well on all of the desiderata.

Bibliography

Anderson, E. (1993) *Value in Ethics and Economics*. Cambridge, MA: Harvard University Press.

Engstrom, S. (2009) *The Form of Practical Knowledge: A Study of the Categorical Imperative*. Cambridge, MA: Harvard University Press.

Frankfurt, H. (1999) *Necessity, Volition, and Love*. Cambridge: Cambridge University Press.

Herman, B. (2007) *Moral Literacy*. Cambridge, MA: Harvard University Press.

Herman, B. (2011) "The Difference that Ends Make," in J. Wuerth (ed.), *Perfecting Virtue: New Essays on Kantian Ethics and Virtue Ethics*. Cambridge: Cambridge University Press.

Hill, T. E., Jr. (1992) *Dignity and Practical Reason in Kant's Moral Theory*. Ithaca, NY: Cornell University Press.

Hill, T. E., Jr. (2002) *Human Welfare and Moral Worth: Kantian Perspectives*. Oxford: Oxford University Press.

Kant, I. (1996) *Practical Philosophy*. Tr. and ed. M. J. Gregor. Cambridge: Cambridge University Press.

Korsgaard, C. M. (1996a) *Creating the Kingdom of Ends*. Cambridge: Cambridge University Press.

Korsgaard, C. M. (1996b) *The Sources of Normativity*. Cambridge: Cambridge University Press.

Korsgaard, C. M. (2008) *The Constitution of Agency: Essays on Practical Reason and Moral Psychology*. Oxford: Oxford University Press.

Korsgaard, C. M. (2009) *Self-Constitution: Agency, Identity, and Integrity*. Oxford: Oxford University Press.

O'Neill, O. (1989) *Constructions of Reason: Explorations of Kant's Practical Philosophy*. Cambridge: Cambridge University Press.

Rawls, J. (2000) *Lectures on the History of Moral Philosophy*. Ed. B. Herman. Cambridge, MA: Harvard University Press.

Reath, A. (2006) *Agency and Autonomy in Kant's Moral Theory*. Oxford: Oxford University Press.

Reath, A. (2010) "Formal Principles and the Form of a Law," in A. Reath and J. Timmermann (eds.), *A Critical Guide to Kant's "Critique of Practical Reason"*, 31–54. Cambridge: Cambridge University Press.

Scanlon, T. M. (1998) *What We Owe to Each Other*. Cambridge, MA: Harvard University Press.

Velleman, J. D. (2006) *Self to Self*. Cambridge: Cambridge University Press.

Velleman, J. D. (2008) "Beyond Price," *Ethics* 118(2): 191–212.

10

Kant's Grounding Project in *The Doctrine of Virtue*

Houston Smit and Mark Timmons[1]

Kant's project in *The Metaphysics of Morals* is to set forth and defend a wide-ranging system of general duties by deriving them from a single moral principle, the categorical imperative. In the introduction to this work, Kant claims that the moral law expressed by the categorical imperative "affirms what obligation is" and then he remarks that "the simplicity of this law in comparison with the great and various consequences that can be drawn from it must seem astonishing at first..." (*MS* 6: 225).[2] The great and various consequences in question compose the system of duties that Kant divides into juridical duties and ethical duties according to the type of lawgiving associated with the duty, and which are treated respectively in Parts 1 and 2 of the *The Metaphysics of Morals*: the *Rechtslehre*, or *Doctrine of Right*, and the *Tugendlehre*, or *Doctrine of Virtue*.

Our focus in this chapter is on the relationship between the categorical imperative and the "great and various consequences" featured in the *Doctrine of Virtue* (*DV* henceforth) that Kant attempts to derive from this imperative. (Call them "Kant's derivations.") These derivations feature the Formula of Humanity (FH) of the categorical imperative, which commands individuals to treat humanity as an end in itself, never merely as a means.[3] We construe

---

[1] This article is thoroughly collaborative. Order of authorship is alphabetical. We would like to thank Sorin Baiasu, Cole Mitchell, and especially Oliver Sensen and Robert Audi for helpful comments.

[2] Passages from Kant's writings in English are from the various translations in the Cambridge edition of the works of Kant listed among the references (Gregor 1997; Heath and Schneewind 1997; and Zöller and Louden 2007). In this particular passage, Kant is discussing the universal law formulation of the categorical imperative. Given the alleged equivalence of the various formulations and the fact that in the *Doctrine of Virtue* Kant almost exclusively employs the humanity formulation in his various derivations, his claim about the simplicity of the formula and the many consequences that can be drawn from it presumably applies also to the humanity formulation.

[3] The lone notable exception is Kant's argument for the duty of beneficence in which he employs the universal law formulation. We have more to say about this matter below in section IV. For a nuanced treatment of the notion of treating someone merely as a means, see Audi (n.d.).

the relationship between this formula and the particular duties featured in the
DV as intended by Kant to be *explanatory*—as expressing what contemporary
philosophers call a criterion of right and wrong action (or obligation). That is,
within the overall economy of Kant's ethics, we understand FH as purporting
to set forth, in very general terms, that in virtue of which actions have this or
that particular deontic status. Thus, on this construal, what *makes* an act of,
say, suicide morally wrong, a violation of duty to oneself, is that in performing
this kind of action an individual fails to treat her or his own humanity as an
end in itself. This way of interpreting the FH is perhaps about as uncontroversial as Kant interpretation gets.[4] And given this interpretation, one should view
Kant's efforts in *DV* as primarily an *explanatory grounding project*—the project
of using FH not only to derive (and thus justify) a set of duties, but also to
explain and thus provide insight into the deontic status of a range of actions.
Again, this understanding of Kant's work in the *Metaphysics of Morals* is perhaps uncontroversial.

What interests us are the details of Kant's derivations and how well they
succeed in providing plausible explanations of the deontic status of the various actions that are discussed in *DV*. As for the details, Kant employs a variety
of distinct explanatory considerations in his derivations, and one aim of the
present chapter is to sort them out and explain how they are connected to the
content of the humanity formulation of the categorical imperative. Getting
clear on the details will enable us to evaluate the success of those derivations.
One persistent worry about abstract moral principles is that they lack sufficient
content to enable genuine derivations of a full range of moral conclusions that
those principles are supposed to ground, so that attempts to ground relatively
specific deontic verdicts by deriving them in this way cannot succeed. And, of
course, the concepts featured in FH—the concepts of treating persons as ends
in themselves and refraining from treating persons merely as means—have been
subject to the sorts of indeterminacy worries that would undermine Kant's
grounding project. So one issue we will address as we examine Kant's derivations is the issue of determinacy.[5]

Here, then, is our plan. In section I we set up what is to follow by clarifying
what we understand to be Kant's explanatory grounding project in *DV*. As we
explain in this first section, addressing questions about Kant's project obviously requires, as a first step, clarifying as far as possible the content of FH

---

[4] What is controversial is the claim that the more formal formulations of the categorical
imperative are not best interpreted as criteria of right action. Timmons (1997; 2005; 2006) argues
that while Kant's humanity formulation purports to express an explanatory criterion of right
conduct, the universal law formula represents a kind of decision procedure or test of moral rightness and so its role is not explanatory in the way that FH is. One need not agree with Timmons's
claim about the universal law formula to agree that the FH does play the role of an explanatory
criterion in the overall economy of Kant's ethics.

[5] On this issue see, for example, Hill (1992; 1993; 1996) and Wood (1999: 2007).

and, in particular, clarifying the related a priori concepts of humanity, dignity, and respect, as they figure in Kant's thought. We take up this task in section II. Then in sections III and IV, we turn to Kant's *DV* derivations and proceed to examine them with an eye on the purported explanatory connection between FH and the duties being derived as well as the plausibility of those derivations. In section V we sum up and conclude.

I. Clarifying Kant's Project

There are important points of clarification that concern the limits, targets, and criteria of success that characterize how we understand Kant's *DV* grounding project. Let us take these up in order.

Limits. Our primary focus is on what we call Kant's *internal* grounding project—"internal" because it takes for granted that the categorical imperative has been established as the fundamental principle of morality. This project works within a moral system characterized by this principle in order both to establish and to explain the deontic status of various actions. In particular, the internal project takes for granted various claims that Kant makes about the concepts of humanity, dignity, and respect that we examine in the next section. By contrast, Kant's *external* grounding project involves the "establishment of the supreme principle of morality" (*GMS* 4: 392), which Kant addresses in the third section of the *Groundwork* and again in the *Critique of Practical Reason*. One might say, then, that Kant's grounding project in *DV* is limited in the sense that it does not purport to ground the various duties "all the way down." Rather, it addresses the question: Given that the FH is itself properly grounded, how can it be used to ground more particular duties?

Targets. Here we refer to the duties that Kant attempts to ground, and in particular to the fact that in *DV*, the project is to ground a set of mid-level moral generalizations about the deontic status of act types. More precisely, the explananda of Kant's derivations are act types as being duties *of a certain sort*, most fundamentally either to oneself or to others. Regarding Kant's explanatory project and its targets, there are two points worth stressing. First, in addition to purporting to explain the deontic status of act types, we also find Kant providing explanations of the following: (1) the comparative viciousness of certain actions and associated vices (e.g., gluttony being a greater violation of duty to oneself than drunkenness, *MS* 6: 427); (2) the relative priority of various duties (e.g., avoiding suicide as the "first" duty to oneself from among the duties to oneself qua animal, *MS* 6: 421; and moral self-knowledge as the "first command" of all duties to oneself, *MS* 6: 441); (3) the relative "width" of a duty (e.g., the duty of moral beneficence is relatively wide, allowing for more latitude in its being fulfilled compared to other, narrower duties, *MS* 6: 393); (4) the special status of certain duties (e.g., gratitude as a "sacred" duty, *MS* 6: 455); and (5) the psychological sources of various vices (e.g., misunderstanding of the basis of moral self-esteem in connection with vices that violate one's duties to others, *MS* 6: 459). Except for the last of these, which will figure in our discussion later on, we will have either little or nothing to say about Kant's explanations of these aspects of duties of virtue.

The second point is this. As Kant makes clear, a *metaphysic* of morals is restricted to the setting forth of duties at a certain high level of generality that can be derived from the a priori categorical imperative, perhaps together with fundamental and thus universal empirical facts about human beings (see especially, *MS* 6: 217 and 6: 468–9). Because of the generality of the targets, and the mostly a priori nature of the project, Kant's derivations can aspire to a high degree of rigor. Indeed, the apriority of these derivations consists in their laying out how the supreme principle of morality, given certain universal facts about human beings, is the ground of certain considerations constituting moral reasons and how it thereby grounds the duties in question. These derivations, then, do not merely establish *that* certain types of actions are required of us; they serve to explain *why* they are, by showing how the supreme principle of morality makes them moral requirements.[6] And, insofar as these derivations provide such explanations, they are to be contrasted with claims about duties that appeal to intuitive moral judgment.[7] The important point that we want to stress is that Kant's derivations are meant to do some genuine explanatory work, and that this work consists in explaining how the categorical imperative functions as a principle to generate the duty in question. And this point brings us to questions about the criteria of success associated with Kant's derivations.

Criteria of success. It is well worth dwelling on exactly what one is to expect from a successful explanatory derivation project of the sort we find in Kant. The general model here is clearly a "top-down" argument, going from general principle plus at least one additional premise about the nature of the action or

---

[6] Here we are suggesting that Kant works with the original notion of the a priori, on which to know (conceive, infer) something a priori is to know (conceive, infer) it from the grounds that make it true. For a development and defense of this reading of Kant's notion of the a priori see Smit (2009). Notice that, on this reading, when Kant describes his derivations of duties in the *Metaphysics of Morals* as a priori, he is claiming that these derivations provide the fundamental explanation of the deontic status of certain actions and attitudes. In "Indispensible Principles of Application in Kant's *Metaphysics of Morals*" (work in progress), we develop this model of Kant's derivations by attending carefully to the parallel Kant draws between his project in the *Metaphysics of Morals* and his project in the *Metaphysical Foundations of Natural Science*.

[7] Certainly moral judgment, understood as a fundamental capacity to apply general moral rules in particular cases to reach correct moral verdicts about those cases, plays an important role in Kant's views about moral deliberation. Kant's casuistical remarks appended to his derivations in *DV*, his remark at *MS* 6: 224 about competing grounds of obligation (and thus the implied need for adjudication that at least in some cases requires moral judgment), and his remark about the latitude associated with imperfect duties that "unavoidably leads to questions that call upon judgment to decide how a maxim is to be applied in particular cases" (*MS* 6: 411)—all make clear that there are cases of moral thinking and deliberation in which duties are not derived from moral principles. But the mid-level moral duties Kant catalogues in *DV* are not themselves supposed to be the products of intuitive judgment.

maxim being evaluated, to a conclusion about the deontic status of that maxim or action. There are three related criteria, satisfaction of which is central to Kant's project.

Most obviously, insofar as Kant's project is explanatory, FH purports to pick out the most fundamental features of an action that *explain* its deontic status.[8] Call this the *criterion of explanatory power*. Satisfaction of this criterion requires more than the principle's success in arguments that are sufficient to show true or "prove" various claims about the deontic status of actions. Judging how well FH satisfies this criterion involves the large task of evaluating Kant's normative moral theory as a whole, comparing it to competing theories. We don't take on that large task here. Rather, we propose to examine how well Kant's derivations satisfy the following two additional criteria. According to the *criterion of determinacy*, a moral principle features concepts whose application conditions are fairly determinate. Satisfaction of this criterion means that Kant's derivations featuring FH generate most, if not all, of the "great and various consequences" that Kant advertises in connection with the categorical imperative. Finally, according to the *criterion of independence* a successful derivation cannot simply pack the alleged duty into the FH as part of its very content. So a violation of this criterion occurs when, for instance, it is claimed of some action that it violates respect for persons (and is thus wrong) but this claim is, without motivation, simply being loaded into the very concept of respect for persons. Such are cases of "mere interpretation"—what is really going on is that the concept of respecting persons is being partly interpreted so that the action in question simply counts as part of the very concept of violating respect for persons.

Before moving forward, we wish to add, by way of further clarification, three related points about the formula of humanity and the related issues of determinacy and independence. First, the success of Kant's explanatory grounding project depends crucially on the content of this formula—content roughly equivalent to a principle requiring equal respect for all persons. But how determinate is the concept of equal respect? Not very, according to many philosophers, among them, James Griffin:

> Every moral theory has the notion of equal respect at its heart: regarding each person as, in some sense, on an equal footing with every other one. Different moral theories parlay this vague notion into different conceptions. Ideas such as the Ideal Observer or the Ideal Contractor specify the notion a little further, but then they too are very vague and

---

[8] See Guyer (2005) for an illuminating discussion of Kant's notion of system as it relates to *The Metaphysics of Morals*. Among the requirements of a system of duties that Guyer discusses is that the duties be derivable from a single principle where that principle is taken to be "the source of truth of what is derived from it" (246). Talk of a principle being the source of truth is, we take it, equivalent to our talk of the principle serving to explain the duties derived from it.

allow quite different moral theories to be got out of them. And the moral theories are not simply derivations from these vague notions, because the notions are too vague to allow anything as tight as derivation. (Griffin 1986: 208, see also 231 and 239)

Now we agree with Griffin that the *bare* notion of equal respect is too vague to figure in a moral principle that could be expected to yield determinate verdicts about the deontic status of a significant range of actions. And simply to take an abstract principle like FH (without drawing out in a principled way the content of the concepts it features) and proceed to offer "derivations" of a range of deontic verdicts would invite the complaint of theft over honest toil. But, as we are about to explain in the next section, Kant's FH is quite rich in content. Without having the various mid-level duties featured in *DV* simply loaded into its content, it is rich enough in content to provide illuminating explanations of the deontic status of many actions. In short, by and large, Kant's FH has the sort of determinate content needed to satisfy both the criterion of determinacy and the criterion of independence.

Second, it will be particularly important for our purposes to attend to the distinction between a *specification* of the content of FH and *derivations* involving FH. Specification involves spelling out at a fairly high level of generality the various principles and theses that serve to make more precise how Kant's notions of dignity and respect figure in the content of FH. A derivation (as we mentioned at the outset of this subsection) is an argument that draws from a general moral principle and at least one additional premise—typically one that indicates something about the nature of the action or maxim being evaluated—a conclusion about the deontic status of the item in question. As we shall see, some of Kant's derivations simply invoke conceptual claims about the nature of an action, which, together with the relevant principle, entail a conclusion about the deontic status of that action. But others appeal to nonconceptual, synthetic claims about an action in going from principle to deontic conclusion. These distinctions—both that between specification and derivation and that between two sorts of derivations—will become clearer as we proceed.

So, as we mentioned earlier, with respect to Kant's internal grounding project, we are interested in examining this question: Given the content of Kant's FH, how successful are his derivations in satisfying the criteria of determinacy and independence? To anticipate, we will argue Kant's derivations are generally, but not always, successful, and in some cases where they seem to fail, we think there are alternative derivations in the offing that are successful. We will also be arguing that with respect to certain duties (viz., to cultivate one's moral self-esteem and to strive toward moral self-perfection) Kant should not be understood as offering derivations. And indeed, one does not find arguments in the passages where these duties are discussed. Rather, these duties are part of the content of FH—which, of course, explains the lack of argument.

One final point. In his derivations, Kant often claims that such and so action constitutes treating humanity merely as means or that the action degrades humanity. Now granted, there are certain actions involving for example the manipulation of another person, whether through coercion or deception, which count as paradigm instances of treating another person merely as a means. And certain actions (think of the humiliating treatment of prisoners at Abu Ghraib who were made to wear dog collars and were treated as nonhuman animals) are paradigm instances of degrading treatment.[9] Regarding such clear paradigm instances of treatment merely as means and of degradation, one simply points to them as clear instances of the concepts in question. But in many other cases an explanation is in order. This is particularly true in the case of violations of duty to oneself. How is it that in willingly committing suicide or masturbating or overeating one is treating oneself merely as means? An explanation is in order. In general we think that Kant's appeals in *DV* to what constitutes treatment merely as means or what constitutes degrading behavior are subject to explanation or at least illumination in terms of various elements that figure in what we are calling a specification of FH. So let us now turn to the task of specification.

II. Humanity, Dignity, and Respect

For Kant, the concepts of humanity, dignity, and respect are a priori concepts. They provide grounds for insight into how moral principles permit or forbid actions and, to the extent that they provide grounds for such cognition of practical possibility and necessity, they are independent of experience both for their genesis and their justification.[10] Furthermore, the a priori concepts of humanity and dignity, as Kant understands them, have a certain normative significance—a significance that is more fully specified when certain empirical information about humans and their condition is brought to bear on questions of rational choice and action. In this section, we propose to articulate some of the main theses of normative significance (including some moral principles) that we think follow directly from the FH, simply given the very concepts of humanity and dignity as Kant understands them.

In what immediately follows, we proceed, in three stages, to explain how the concepts of humanity and dignity figure in the FH, in particular, how humanity, as an end in itself, grounds the special normative status that moral considerations have in Kant's moral theory. First, we bring out an important implication of Kant's claim that humanity is an end in itself: on his theory,

---

[9] We are not assuming that all cases of degrading treatment of persons are cases of treating them merely as a means. Degrading treatment can directly violate the requirement to treat persons as ends in themselves.

[10] See note 6, above.

ends ground reasons for action, and an end in itself is, as a nondiscretionary end, one that grounds unconditional and universal reasons. Second, we point out that, on Kant's view, autonomy is the constitutive element of humanity in virtue of which humanity is an end in itself and a nondiscretionary end. And third, we explain how the idea of humanity as inherently possessing dignity serves to illuminate the special normative significance that nondiscretionary ends and reasons possess within Kant's theory of practical rationality. All of this will allow us to articulate a series of normatively significant theses and related principles that constitute what we have referred to as a partial specification of FH and that will figure in various of Kant's derivations that we turn to in later sections.

Humanity, Kant claims, is an end in itself, distinct from other types of ends. Kant characterizes an end of action as "an object of the choice (of a rational being), through the representation of which choice is determined to an action to bring this object about" (*MS* 6: 381),[11] and he claims that "no free action is possible unless the agent also intends an end (which is the matter of choice)" (*MS* 6: 389). Kant distinguishes two sorts of ends: discretionary and nondiscretionary or, to use his *Groundwork* terminology, subjective and objective. Discretionary ends (in so far as one embraces them at a time) refer to the objects of one's sensible desires and aversions, and for Kant they possess merely relative, conditional value in the sense that their status as values depends importantly on being the objects of desire or aversion. By contrast, Kant claims that nondiscretionary ends are "given by reason alone, and must hold equally for all rational beings" (*GMS* 4: 427). He claims that there is one such end, namely rational nature itself (*GMS* 4: 428–9), which, in relation to the humanity formulation, serves "as the ground of this principle" (*GMS* 4: 428).[12] Humanity, understood as an agent having a rational nature, stands as a nondiscretionary end or, in Kant-speak, humanity is an end-in-itself—something having nonrelative (in the sense of nondependent) worth.[13] Since ends of action, in so far as they have normative significance for choice and action, provide reasons for action, one can say that discretionary ends provide (or can provide) desire-based reasons for action, while nondiscretionary ends provide

---

[11] Of course, humanity as a complex set of capacities is not an end to be brought about (see *GMS* 4: 437), and this particular passage is referring to what a human being can bring about *through her actions*. But this remark does apply to the ends of perfection and happiness that are grounded in humanity.

[12] In light of the previous note, the claim that humanity is an end is to be understood as the claim that considerations having to do with humanity provide or constitute reasons for freely adopting ends, and these in turn provide or constitute what we go on to call "humanity-based reasons" for action.

[13] In various places, Kant refers to the nondependent end of humanity as having "absolute worth," see especially *GMS* 4: 428. He also uses the terms "inner worth" and "absolute inner worth" in connection with dignity at *GMS* 4: 435–6 and *MS* 6: 435 respectively. For an illuminating discussion of Kant's concept of inner worth and of value generally, see Sensen (2009a).

what we will refer to as humanity-based reasons for action. That there are two types of reason for action grounded in distinct sorts of ends tells us nothing about the contents of those ends and, in particular, tells us nothing about the content of so-called nondiscretionary ends. And strictly speaking, this distinction between ends with conditional, dependent value and ends having unconditional (in the sense of nondependent) value does not tell us whether ends of either sort have relative normative supremacy in relation to each other. It is the dignity of humanity, as we shall see below, that is the basis for what we call the *normative superiority thesis,* namely, the thesis that humanity-based reasons have greater normative weight than competing desire-based reasons.[14] But before getting to this, more must be said about the contents of the concepts of humanity and dignity.

Regarding the concept of humanity, Kant writes that "The capacity to set oneself an end—any end whatsoever—is what characterizes humanity (as distinguished from animality)" (*MS* 6: 392). This end-setting capacity distinguishes rational agents in a sharp way from nonrational animals, because unlike so-called animal choice, human choice "is a choice that can indeed be *affected* but not *determined* by impulses... *Freedom* of choice is this independence from being determined by sensible impulses" (*MS* 6: 213–4). This aspect of human freedom—its independence—is what Kant calls negative freedom. And for Kant, having this sort of negative freedom implies positive freedom, "the ability of pure reason to be of itself practical," or what Kant calls autonomy. Autonomy is understood as a kind of noumenal causal power whose most fundamental law expressed most formally commands one to "act as if your maxims were to serve at the same time as a universal law (for all rational beings)" (*GMS* 4: 438). Presumably, which maxims can and which cannot serve as universal law, and thus which maxims and associated actions are and are not consistent with the law of autonomy (or morality) is something that can be explained by reference to nondiscretionary ends of action and thus ultimately on the basis of humanity-based considerations bearing on choice and action. This ability or power identified as autonomy includes various cognitive powers of understanding, imagination, and judgment that are necessary for exercising one's autonomy in being able, for example, to recognize which considerations constitute reasons for action and how best to achieve or realize the ends one

---

[14] This superiority can take different forms. Audi (2001: 162–3) distinguishes three. The first two concern moral reasons insofar as they constitute moral requirements. What he calls the *supremacy thesis* says that moral requirements have normative precedence over all other competing reasons, both individually and collectively. His *priority thesis* maintains that a specific moral requirement always takes normative precedence over any particular competing nonmoral reason. Priority does not entail supremacy: it may be that any moral reason taken alone will outweigh any single competing nonmoral reason, but might be overridden by multiple coalescing nonmoral reasons. The third form of superiority is expressed by what he calls the *paramountcy thesis*: moral reasons are the best kind of reason to act on when the same action is favored by a moral reason and one or more nonmoral reasons.

sets for oneself.[15] Humanity-based reasons for action, then, ultimately have to do with the fact that human beings possess autonomy, understood as a complex of powers that enable rational beings to set ends and act for reasons. So, the content of the concept of humanity for Kant, as we understand his view, includes these elements: (1) it is a power or capacity of rational agents to set ends that ground reasons for action; (2) this power involves a kind of causality that, when exercised, operates independently of the causal forces of nature;[16] (3) and in addition to the fact that it makes rational agents members of an "intelligible world," it involves rational powers of cognition, including understanding, imagination, and judgment. These elements are the *constitutive elements* of humanity. And from what was said in the previous paragraph, humanity has normative significance since it is of value, being the ground of nondiscretionary ends that in turn ground unconditional and universal reasons for action.

What is missing from the characterization of humanity so far is the kind of value and normative status it possesses, particularly in relation to nondiscretionary ends. Although in various places Kant seems to identify being an end in oneself with what he calls dignity,[17] the latter notion (even if basically equivalent to the former) highlights an important aspect of Kant's moral thought—the idea of humanity or autonomy as giving rational agents an elevated status. Oliver Sensen (2009b; 2010) has done much to illuminate this theme in Kant's ethics.[18] On Sensen's interpretation, Kant's concept of dignity is a relational concept having to do with something having an elevated status compared to something else. The

---

[15] See, for example, *V-Mo/Collins* 27: 357 where, in distinguishing moral self-esteem from moral self-love, we find, "We esteem what has inner worth...; understanding, for example, has an inner worth, regardless of what it is applied to"; and at *V-Mo/Collins* 27: 364, "So far as the perfections of our mental powers are bound up with the essential ends of humanity, it is one of our self-regarding duties to promote them. All our states of mind and mental powers have a bearing on morality. The autocracy of the human mind, and all of the powers of the soul, so far as they relate to morality, is the *principium* of the self-regarding duties, and thereby of all other duties." Also relevant is *V-MS/Vigil* 27: 544 where, in describing the duty of self-perfection, the notes say "for the more a man gathers knowledge, and cultivates his understanding and imagination, and the more he is in a position to direct the lower faculties of the soul, the fitter he becomes to attain ends."

[16] As Kant's so-called incorporation thesis (*RGV* 6: 23–4) makes clear, this is true not only in cases where one fully exercises one's autonomy by acting on the basis of reasons grounded in non-discretionary ends, but holds true for cases in which one acts on the basis of reasons grounded in discretionary ends.

[17] See, for example, *MS* 6: 435; *V-MS/Vigil* 27: 601, 628.

[18] According to one prominent interpretation, dignity for Kant is apparently a kind of ontological nonrelational value property possessed by human beings (and all rational creatures) that Kant uses as a basis for grounding the categorical imperative and which thus serves as a kind of ultimate ontological ground for the various duties that compose Kant's system. Such an interpretation would make Kant's ethical theory value-based, with the value of dignity at its foundation; see for example Wood (1997). This view is forcefully criticized by Sensen, who argues that (1) Kant's conception of dignity is essentially the Stoic *relational* notion involving the idea of being elevated; (2) this status does not require treating dignity as some ontological value property; and (3) more generally, no nondeontic value concept plays a foundational role in Kant's theory. As we have said, we are interested in how the concepts of humanity, dignity, and respect connect with the various

elevation in question has, as it were, two related dimensions that are reflected in Kant's remark that "morality, and humanity insofar as it is capable of morality, is that alone which has dignity" (*G* 4: 435). One dimension (already noted in the previous paragraph) concerns a capacity that all rational beings share (humanity as capable of morality), which Kant explains in terms of a rational agent's freedom of the will. First, in relation to nonrational animals, the fact that human beings have freedom of the will elevates them above such creatures.[19] Call this kind of elevation in status of rational beings, *elevation qua autonomous being.*

The other dimension of dignity as elevation is morality itself, which is understood as a person coming to fully realize the capacity for morality by making the moral law effective as one's fundamental principle of action; that is, by coming to have a virtuous disposition. Having such a "cast of mind" has a worth that elevates virtue above the worth of such mental traits as skill, diligence, wit, imagination, and humor, and above all other items that have what Kant calls mere price. Regarding the attitude of respect that reflection on a virtuous disposition prompts, Kant writes that "This estimation...lets the worth of such a cast of mind be cognized as dignity and puts it infinitely above all price, with which it cannot be brought into comparison or competition at all without, as it were, assaulting its holiness" (*GMS* 4: 435). Call this second sense of elevation in status of rational beings, *elevation qua morally realized rational being.* Full moral realization, what Kant apparently refers to as "holiness," represents an ideal having what Kant considers to be the highest degree of moral worth or value.[20] From the idea of humanity as having this dual elevated status, Kant is in a position to draw out a number of implications regarding its normative significance, implications that spell out the respect that humanity commands. These implications can be usefully sorted into three groups: (1) the first pair having to do with the concept of dignity itself and the reasons it grounds; (2) the second pair having to do primarily with relations

---

duties featured in the *Doctrine of Virtue* and, in particular, how those concepts figure in explaining why various actions and attitudes have the deontic status they do. That Kant appeals to the FH (and the concepts this formulation involves) in attempting to explain why certain actions and attitudes are either impermissible or required is clear. Metaphysical questions about the ontological purport of Kant's notion of dignity, and whether dignity is at the basis of Kant's entire ethical system (and thus whether the concept of dignity justifies the categorical imperative) are matters about which we can remain neutral. However, Sensen's claim that Kant's concept of dignity is a relational notion involving elevation will play an important role in the account we provide of Kant's derivation of duties.

[19] The sort of elevation conferred upon human beings in virtue of having freedom is something in addition to the higher value humans have compared to nonrational animals that Kant discusses at 6: 434–5: "Although a human being has, in his understanding, something more than [other nonrational animals] and can set himself ends, even this gives him only an *extrinsic* value for his usefulness...that is to say, it gives one man a higher value than another, that is, a *price* as of a commodity in exchange with these animals as things..."

[20] See also *MS* 6: 405 and *V-MS/Vigil* 27: 626 for references to humanity in its perfection as an ideal.

among persons; and (3) the final two having primarily to do with matters of intrapersonal significance. In what immediately follows we simply state these implications with brief commentary. Their normative significance is more fully revealed as they figure in Kant's derivations that we take up in the next two sections.

Respect as an appropriate response. First, because dignity represents a particular kind of value, something having an elevated status, having a value that is beyond anything having mere price, it demands, as it were, a certain *kind* of response on the part of rational agents. Kant claims that "*respect* alone provides a becoming expression for the estimate of [dignity] that a rational being must give" (*GMS* 4: 436). We shall say a bit more about respect later in this section.

Normative superiority of humanity-based reasons. Second, ends set by reason—nondiscretionary ends—because they concern respecting the dignity of humanity, ground normative reasons that are superior to[21] reasons for action that are grounded in discretionary ends. Kant claims that discretionary ends can only ground hypothetical imperatives while nondiscretionary ends can ground categorical imperatives (*GMS* 4: 428). Imperatives of the latter sort thus enjoy normative supremacy over imperatives of the former sort.

Moral equality. Third, and most obviously, because the elevated status of dignity is something all rational agents possess, and possess equally, as far as dignity qua autonomous agents goes, all such beings enjoy equal moral status. This equal status is the basis of a *principle of moral equality* which, stated most generally, would require at least that one refrain from actions that would show contempt for the moral status of other persons. As we shall see later in section IV, this principle concerns preservation of a person's moral self-esteem.

Impartiality. Fourth, given the moral-equality thesis, humanity-based reasons for action provide reasons for action for all relevantly situated agents. Certain facts about my humanity provide not only *me* with normative reason to adopt general ends and more specific maxims of action, but those same facts about my humanity provide *anyone* who is relevantly situated with such reasons to adopt ends and more specific maxims, and vice versa. That is, such considerations provide reasons to acknowledge in maxims and action the claims that the morally legitimate ends of others (particularly their needs) have on us. This thesis provides a basis for both a positive and a negative principle of impartiality. According to the *positive principle of impartiality*, one is to adopt maxims and perform corresponding actions that manifest a positive concern for the

---

[21] Talk of "superior to" is meant to include not only cases in which certain humanity-based reasons serve to categorically *require* some action or attitude (thus trumping, as it were, reasons grounded in discretionary ends), which pertain in particular to perfect duties, but also includes cases in which humanity-based reasons provide one with sufficient normative reason for engaging in some action or taking up some attitude in cases where one is not required to do so. Cases of the latter sort pertain to the fulfillment of imperfect duties.

ends (especially the needs) of others. And according to the *negative principle of impartiality* one is to avoid adopting maxims or performing actions that manifest a negative concern for the ends (especially the needs) of others. These principles concern the welfare of persons.

Finally, the dimension of dignity as full realization of one's rational nature provides individuals with an ideal that grounds humanity-based reasons that concern basic requirements of moral virtue.

Perfection of the will. This follows straightforwardly from the idea of dignity as an ideal, and provides a fundamental moral orientation when it comes to the morality of character. Such perfection is an individual's sole moral "vocation."[22] And the requirement to perfect one's will (or at least to strive to do so), involves self-governance. That is, as nonholy rational beings, human beings with a sensible nature are beings for whom the impulse to one's happiness "belongs to his essence" (*GMS* 4: 416).[23] Given that humanity-based reasons enjoy normative superiority over reasons grounded in one's happiness, and given that to act rationally on some occasion is to act for reasons that have the greatest normative weight, it follows as a requirement of rationality that nonholy beings ought to acquire a motivational structure such that in cases where reasons pertaining to one's happiness compete with humanity-based reasons, one can control one's impulses to act for reasons of the former sort and act entirely from reasons of the latter sort. In this connection, Kant mentions the duties of apathy and self-mastery. These duties correspond to so-called *structural virtues* and have to do with psychic strength or self-governance and thus with one's ability and willingness to govern one's choices and behavior by one's values and commitments.[24]

Apathy. This duty (mentioned at *MS* 6: 408) requires that one not let oneself be governed by feelings and inclinations, a necessary condition for achieving moral perfection; it represents a negative duty.

Self-mastery. By contrast, the duty of self-mastery is a "positive command to a human being, namely to bring all his capacities and inclinations under his (reason's) control, and so to rule over himself" (*MS* 6: 408). In the Vigilantius lecture notes on ethics we find this passage:

> The duty of self-mastery follows from the concept of duty; duty is the *ground* of the determination of free choice according to pure reason. This

---

[22] Kant's view about the actual attainment of one's moral vocation is that unlike nonrational animals that can individually fulfill "nature's purpose" in developing their "predispositions," "with human beings only the species reaches it" (*Anth* 7: 329).

[23] Strictly speaking, this claim about the essence of human beings is an anthropological claim, but one which, according to Kant, "can be presupposed surely and a priori" (*GMS* 4: 415), so in drawing out the normative significance of the concepts of humanity and dignity we are still dealing with necessary truths involving the concepts in question.

[24] Adams (2006: ch. 2), following Roberts (1984), usefully distinguishes motivational virtues such as beneficence that are defined by motives from structural virtues that have to do with will power.

ground is unconditioned and necessary, and hence the formula of duty is always an imperative, whereby the nature of the mastery is indicated. (*V-MS/Vigil* 27: 625)

We have been expressing the idea of "unconditioned and necessary" grounds associated with duty in terms of the nondependence of the value of nondiscretionary ends and the related thesis of the supremacy of humanity-based reasons. Since the concept of duty, applying to nonholy, sensuously affected wills, involves the idea of being rationally constrained by laws, the most fundamental of which set forth ends to be pursued, rationality as a property of an agent's will involves a duty of self-mastery—of striving to make humanity-based reasons motivationally dominant in relation to the desire-based reasons grounded in discretionary ends. This duty *is* the duty of moral self-perfection. In the Collins notes, Kant contrasts prudential with moral (true) self-mastery and characterizes the latter in a manner that makes reasonably clear that the duty of self-mastery is equivalent to the duty of moral self-perfection:

> But the true self-mastery is moral in character. This is sovereign, and its laws hold a categorical sway over sensibility, and not as the pragmatic laws do, for there the understanding plays off one sensible factor against the rest. But in order for it to have a sovereign authority over us, we must give morality the supreme power over ourselves, so that it rules over our sensibility. (*V-Mo/Collins* 27: 361)

So, on the basis of the contents of Kant's concepts of humanity and dignity one is able to draw out a number of key theses and principles of normative significance: (1) respect as the proper response called for by humanity-based reasons; (2) the normative supremacy of humanity-based reasons for action and maxim; (3) the moral-equality thesis and its related principle; (4) the thesis of impartiality and the related (negative and positive) principles; (5) dignity as full realization and the highest moral good provides individuals with humanity-based reasons to strive to realize their rational natures by making the law of morality motivationally dominant; perfection is thus a moral ideal; and (6), given the fact that human beings are nonholy, there are the duties of apathy and self-mastery that constitute a general requirement of self-governance that is entailed by the very idea of agents subject to duty. The duty of self-mastery (we claim) is the duty of moral self-perfection—one's guiding moral vocation. The duty of apathy is a necessary component in achieving full self-mastery.

Collectively these theses and associated principles serve to specify (in the sense of make more specific) partially the a priori content of the humanity formula. These theses are of obvious relevance to Kant's derivations, which we turn to in the following sections. In particular, the principles of moral equality, impartiality, and self-perfection specify what respect is, and in this role, provide the starting points for the derivations. In closing this section, we wish to say a bit more about Kant's concept of respect.

In Kant's ethical writings, the concept of respect has both volitional and affective uses. In its affective sense, respect is a feeling that is distinctive in its *object* (it is a response to one's awareness of the moral law), its *source* (reason as opposed to one's sensible nature), and its *content* ("it is the representation of a worth that infringes on my self-love"; *GMS* 4: 410n).[25] Used in its volitional sense (which is the sense relevant for present purposes), respect refers to actions (including the adoption of maxims) that can be freely chosen and are thus subject to moral commands (see *MS* 6: 449). Although Kant's official formulation of the formula of humanity does not make use of the concept of respect, it is reasonably clear from his writings that this concept (in its volitional sense) is meant to cover all modes of action that figure in duties. So, according to FH, one is required to perform actions (adopt maxims) that (given conscientious adherence to them) help maintain or promote respect for humanity as possessed of dignity, which FH expresses in terms of treating humanity as an end in itself and never merely as means.

However, as Kant's derivations make clear, there are various "modes" of respect. Perhaps the most basic form is honor, taken very broadly to include responses in which one either does or does not "live up to" one's nature as a being with the dual elevated status in virtue of which one is possessed of dignity. The idea that Kant's theory represents a type of honor ethic is reflected in some of the language he uses for characterizing actions that fail to respect humanity, terms such as "degrading," "defiling," and of course, "failing to make oneself worthy."[26] And as we shall see when we examine certain of Kant's derivations regarding duties to oneself, the theme of honor, which connects with the ideas of perfection and self-governance, is one major strand of moral thought in Kant's writings that pertains to the ethics of character. With respect to one's dealings with other human beings, respect for their dignity will involve the ideas of impartiality and equality that represent distinct strands of moral thought in Kant's *Doctrine of Virtue.*

So the various principles we have just formulated constitute a *partial specification of the content of FH.* (In our discussion of duties to oneself, we shall further specify respect by adding two more principles.) Our next task is to turn to those derivations to examine how they figure in Kant's attempts to provide explanations of various duties to self and to others.

---

[25] In addition to this *Groundwork* note, which provides a concise description of the feeling of respect, see also chapter 3 of the *Critique of Practical Reason* where Kant claims that in addition to representing a worth that infringes on one's self-love, this feeling also represents a worth that "strikes down" self-conceit.

[26] See *V-Mo/Collins* 27: 346–7 where in one place Kant mentions all of these negative responses in relation to violations of the honor owed to one's humanity. Other interpreters have either developed (Anderson 2008; Skorupski 2005) or pointed out (Baron 2002) the honor ethical aspects of Kant's moral theory.

III. Ethical Duties to Oneself

We turn then to part I of the doctrine of elements in the *Doctrine of Virtue* in which Kant deals with duties of self-perfection. In section 4 ("On the principle on which the division of duties to oneself is based"), Kant characterizes negative duties of omission as pertaining to the preservation of one's humanity, while positive duties of commission concern imperfect, wide duties pertaining to the cultivation of one's humanity. This is what he calls an "objective" division within this category of duty. The so-called subjective division involves a distinction between two ways in which a human being (a subject) can view herself: as a purely natural being with animal powers and as a being with the kind of end-setting powers that elevate the human being and in light of which beings of this kind possess dignity. Thus, we have the distinction between duties to oneself qua animal being, and duties to oneself qua moral being. The former comprise negative duties of self-preservation, the latter comprise both negative duties pertaining to the preservation of one's honor as well as positive duties of cultivation.

1. DUTIES TO ONESELF QUA ANIMAL BEING

The derivation of these duties invokes certain anthropological considerations: in particular, the fact that as animal beings of a particular sort, human beings have certain impulses that concern self-preservation, preservation of the species, and preservation of the capacity to use his or her powers to enjoy life. Because they aim at preservation of one's self and thus preservation of one's humanity, these impulses (and the powers associated with them) are positively oriented toward what has nondependent value. Nevertheless one can fail to govern these impulses in ways that harm the powers that partly constitute one's end-setting capacity. Associated with self-preservation is the duty to refrain from suicide and various forms of self-mutilation, with the sexual impulses—impulses that aim at the preservation of the species—the duty to refrain from masturbation, and with the bodily powers of taking in food and drink at least partly for enjoyment, the duties to refrain from gluttony and drunkenness. As we are about to explain, Kant's derivations of the duties to refrain from suicide, gluttony, and drunkenness can all be usefully viewed as appealing to (1) the (very plausible) claim that one way in which one can fail to respect one's own humanity is to destroy or cause serious damage to those rational powers that constitute one's end-setting capacity; and (2) the fact that the impulses Kant identifies as part of one's animal nature can lead one to adopt discretionary ends whose pursuit destroys or causes serious damage to one's rational end-setting powers. In light of the animal impulses Kant identifies, and the two points just made, it is reasonably clear that the following principle expresses one important constraint on respecting humanity and thus can be viewed as a partial explication of FH.

Moral harm principle. One way in which one can fail to respect one's own humanity as an end in itself is to perform actions (or be subject to habits) involving one's animal nature that destroy or damage those end-setting powers that constitute one's humanity. Such actions are violations of duties to oneself qua moral being with an animal nature.

Kant clearly thinks there are other ways in which one can fail to respect one's own humanity as an end in itself. But he often singles out this way. It is worth stressing that what makes suicide, gluttony, and drunkenness wrong, on his view, is not that they destroy or harm one's rational capacities. What makes them wrong is, rather, that they are ways—and particularly clear ones at that—of failing to respect one's humanity as an end in itself.

Let us now proceed to consider Kant's illustrations of actions that violate the moral harm principle.

Suicide and self-mutilation. Consider now Kant's *DV* derivation of the duty to refrain from suicide:

> To annihilate the subject of morality in one's own person is to root out the existence of morality itself from the world, as far as one can, even though morality is an end in itself. Consequently, disposing of oneself [*über sich... zu disponieren*] merely as a means to some discretionary end is debasing humanity in one's person (*homo noumenon*), to which the human being (*homo phaenomenon*) was nevertheless entrusted.... (*TL* 6: 423)

With a bit of massaging—taking Kant's talk of annihilating the subject of morality and morality itself as a reference to one's humanity, including the capacity for morality—this argument can be interpreted as appealing to (1) the moral harm principle, together with (2) the obvious effects of committing suicide, as a basis for explaining why killing oneself for some discretionary end violates FH. And Kant's argument here seems unassailable, given the moral harm principle.[27] Kant's remarks about treating oneself merely as a means can be understood as the idea that in cases where suicide is performed for a *discretionary* end it violates the principle of the normative superiority of humanity-based reasons, in that in this case one's reason to preserve one's humanity overrides all competing reasons grounded in discretionary ends.[28] This is *why* such action constitutes a debasing of one's humanity: one

---

[27] It is noteworthy that the conclusion of this argument is that committing suicide for some discretionary end is a violation of a duty to oneself. This leaves open the possibility that suicide for some non-discretionary end might be permissible, a topic Kant takes up in the casuistical questions after presenting his main argument. For further discussion of this point see Timmons (forthcoming, 2013).

[28] Here, the superiority that humanity-based reasons have over desire-based reasons is the supremacy asserted in what Audi terms the supremacy thesis (see note 14).

acts contrary to the normatively superior reasons provided by one's humanity and thus fails to respect the dignity, or elevated status, enjoyed by one's
humanity.[29]

Under the heading of "material" deprivation having to do with bodily parts,
Kant mentions castration as a means of enhancing one's singing prowess and
giving away or selling a tooth for purposes of transplantation into the mouth
of someone else as types of "partial" murder and considers them to be wrong-
ful. With these two examples, it is questionable whether Kant is able to clearly
explain their alleged wrongness by appeal to the moral harm principle; neither
type of action, as such, seems to result in harm to one's humanity. Nor does it
seem that any of the other elements we have identified as part of the a priori
content of FH can provide the basis of an explanation here. In short, FH does
not yield a negative verdict about these action types. Of course, Kant may have
been personally repelled by such actions and took them to be degrading, but
merely being repelled by some action and its striking one as degrading does
not constitute an explanation. To insist on their being violations of one's dignity would seem to violate the independence constraint governing top-down
explanatory derivations.[30]

Intemperance in the use of food and drink. Consider now what Kant says
about using certain of one's powers that are associated with enjoying some of
life's animal pleasures—eating and drinking—in ways that result in gross overindulgence in food and drink:

> Brutish excess in the use of food and drink is misuse of the means
> of nourishment that restricts or exhausts our capacity to use them
> intelligently. Drunkenness and gluttony are the vices that come under this
> heading. A human being who is drunk is like a mere animal, not (at the
> time in question) to be treated as a human being. When stuffed with food
> he is in a condition in which he is incapacitated, for a time, for actions
> that would require him to use his powers with skill and deliberation. It
> is obvious that putting oneself in such a state violates a duty to oneself.
> (*TL* 6: 427)

As in the case of suicide for discretionary ends, here again Kant can plausibly explain the wrongness of drunkenness and gluttony in terms of the
moral harm principle, particularly if one stresses the "brutish" nature of
such overindulgences. Obviously, being an alcoholic and being a glutton can
harm one's powers over time, or at least cause bodily damage and disease that

---

[29] For an interpretation of treating oneself as a mere means that is much the same as this
proposal, see Kerstein (2008).

[30] However, insofar as submitting to castration and selling a tooth are outward expressions
of an attitude toward oneself as being a "thing"—which is incompatible with proper self-esteem
(see the discussion of servility below)—Kant does have a basis in his theory for condemning such
actions.

can be incapacitating. But as Kant's remark about being incapacitated "for a time" indicates, he meant to argue that even occasional—perhaps one-off—instances of intemperance in the consumption of food and drink violate a duty to oneself. Notice that the moral harm principle as formulated (which seems plausible to us) does not cover particular instances of incapacitating overindulgence in which the use of one's powers on some occasion is "hindered." One could, of course, just add to the moral harm principle so that harms include not just destruction of or damage to one's rational capacities, but also *hindrance to* their operations. However, it isn't clear that such occasional hindrances need constitute a violation of duty to oneself, in the way that acts that harm one's rational capacities do. Indeed, many morally innocuous activities—e.g., amusement park fun rides—temporarily deprive one of control over one's powers, and thus hinder the use of one's powers. Here, then, is another place where one might question whether Kant is building into the content of his formula of humanity (by way of an expanded version of the moral harm principle to cover hindrances) more than is strictly dictated by the concepts of humanity, dignity, and respect, and thus in violation of the independence constraint.

But apart from appealing to the consequences of intemperate actions and associated habits, Kant condemns such actions in terms of what they indicate about one's character. In the Collins lecture notes, for example, Kant says "A drunkard, for instance, does nobody any harm, and if he has a strong constitution, does no harm even to himself. But he is an object of contempt" (*V-Mol Collins* 27: 341). If we take this remark as claiming that a drunkard may not harm his or her rational capacities, and we ignore the fact that while in an excessive state of intoxication one may not be able to make normal use of one's rational capacities, it would seem that Kant's condemnation here must rest with what we have called the principle of apathy. The drunkard is someone who has come to be dominated by the impulse to get drunk. Such domination exemplifies a failure of apathy—a failure to control one's inclinations. So there are at least two lines of argument—harm-based and apathy-based—that Kant employs in explaining why certain forms of intemperance are morally wrong. And given the plausibility of these considerations as elements of FH, Kant's arguments are fairly persuasive.

Masturbation. In arguing that "defiling oneself by lust"—masturbation—is a violation of a duty to oneself, Kant admits that "it is not easy to produce a rational proof that unnatural, and merely unpurposive, use of one's sexual attribute is inadmissible as being a violation of duty to oneself," and thus appears not to base his derivation on an appeal to natural teleology.[31] He writes: "The *ground of proof* is, indeed, that by it [masturbation] the human

---

[31] For discussion of this point regarding this example, see Gregor (1963) and Denis (1999). See Guyer (2002) for a general discussion of the role of teleology in Kant's ethics.

being surrenders his personality (throwing it away), since he uses himself merely as a means to satisfy an animal impulse" (*TL* 6: 425). Talk of using oneself merely as a means is not helpful here. *That* masturbation involves use of oneself *merely as a means* is what needs to be explained. One does many enjoyable things for the sheer pleasure of it, giving in to the pleasure, without using oneself merely as a means. So, here is one derivation that fails to provide a genuine explanation of the wrongness of the action in question. But there are two additional points worth making about this case.

First, if one considers an individual who is a compulsive masturbator, then Kant can perhaps argue that, like a compulsive drunk, this individual suffers from a failure to comply with the duty of apathy, thus constituting a failure to live up to one's humanity. Second, in *On Education*, Kant claims (presumably, in accord with medical experts of his day) that "nothing weakens the mind as well as the body of the human being more than the kind of lust that is directed at oneself." He goes on to say that educators must instruct youth that by engaging in masturbation, "his bodily powers are ruined the most, that it brings on premature old age and that his mind will suffer a good deal in the process" and concludes the passage thus: "The physical effect is extremely harmful, but the consequences as regards morality are far worse. Here one transgresses the boundaries of nature, and inclination rages without arrest because no real satisfaction takes place" (*Päd* 9: 497). If one stresses the alleged negative effects on those powers that partly constitute one's humanity, then this passage could be read as an argument that appeals to the moral harm principle. Doing so would allow a wide range of Kant's derivations regarding the use of one's animal powers to be explained by the principle in question. To sum up: the wrongness of suicide, masturbation, gluttony, and drunkenness are all susceptible to explanatory derivations on the basis of the moral harm principle together with empirical claims about the effects of such actions on one's rational capacities. Because such capacities constitute one's dignity qua autonomous being (as we explained in the previous section), it is the idea of the elevation of human being qua autonomous that plays a prominent role in these derivations. Focusing, then, just on the harm principle as a basis for explaining why these types of actions represent violations of duties to oneself, we depict the structure of these derivations in Figure 10.1 below.

Of course, the success of the various derivations depends on the plausibility of the empirical claims involved. In addition, these violations reveal something about one's character that is not represented in the above diagram, namely, that in performing such actions one fails (perhaps due to a failure to comply with the duty of apathy) to give humanity-based reasons motivational authority and thus, in this way, fails to "live up to" one's dignity. Such failure is what makes sense of Kant's claims that the actions proscribed in this general category degrade (if not defile) the dignity of one's humanity.

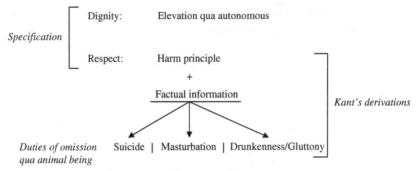

FIGURE 10.1 *Negative duties to oneself qua animal being.*

2. DUTIES TO ONESELF QUA MORAL BEING

Whereas the previous set of duties involves the control of basic animal impulses which, if not properly governed, can harm one's rational nature, duties to oneself qua moral being concern certain actions and maxims that promote or impede one's being able to strive successfully toward moral perfection and thus to realize one's humanity fully. Since the negative duties under consideration in one way or another concern interfering with one's fulfillment of the positive duty of self-mastery, let us first consider this duty.

Moral perfection (self-mastery). In section II, we claimed that the thesis of perfection of the will—a duty to perfect one's will—follows immediately from the idea of dignity as full realization of one's rational nature. So it should not be surprising that in the passages where Kant is discussing this duty, one does not find a derivation. Rather, Kant advances this duty as an immediate implication of the FH when he claims this "*idea* of moral perfection [is one that] reason frames a priori and connects inseparably with the concept of a free will" (*GMS* 4: 409). This connection is presumably analytic: the positive concept of free will just is the concept of the autonomous will, and the will realizes its autonomy in realizing its moral perfection. What the law of autonomy (free will), as the law of morality, demands is conformity to itself out of recognition of its authority, and this conformity *is* moral perfection. This aspect of one's humanity as dignity demands that one strive to fulfill one's moral obligations ("be perfect") while also striving to make moral considerations motivationally sufficient, at least when such considerations require that one perform or omit some action ("be holy"). So the duty of moral perfection (self-mastery) is really a partial specification of FH.

Although we do not find a derivation of the duty of self-perfection (self-mastery) in the *DV*'s treatments of this duty,[32] Kant does argue that this duty includes more specific positive duties whose fulfillment contributes to fulfilling the general duty of self-mastery. These more specific positive duties are, as we

---

[32] See *TL* 6: 387; 6: 392–3; and 6: 446–7.

are about to explain, what ground the negative duties of avarice, lying, and servility. In section II, we have already mentioned the duty of apathy—the duty to not allow oneself to be governed by inclination. In addition, Kant explains that one has a positive duty of moral self-knowledge:

> Moral cognition of oneself, which seeks to penetrate into the depths (the abyss) of one's heart which are quite difficult to fathom, is the beginning of all human wisdom. For in the case of a human being, the ultimate wisdom, which consists in the harmony of a human being's will with its final end, requires him to first remove the obstacle within (an evil will actually present in him) and then to develop the original disposition to a good will within him, which can never be lost. (*TL* 6: 441)

The sort of moral cognition in question involves accurate self-appraisal of one's character—one's motivation. Also Kant recognizes a positive duty of moral esteem that involves coming to understand the true basis of one's dignity. (We say more about this duty below when we discuss servility.) So, we find in Kant three positive duties—apathy, moral self-knowledge, and moral self-esteem— which, as we shall proceed to explain, provide a basis for explaining respectively the negative duties of avarice, lying, and servility.

In commenting on these vices and their general bearing on the dignity of humanity, Kant says that to fall prey to these vices is to "adopt principles that are directly contrary to his character as a moral being (in terms of its very form), that is, to inner freedom, the innate dignity of a human being, which is tantamount to saying that they make it one's basic principle to have no basic principle and thus no character..." (*TL* 6: 420). We read this as claiming that the vices in question, in one way or another, interfere with or hinder one's striving toward moral perfection or self-mastery as Kant understands this notion. This suggests the following principle whose explanatory function is analogous to the moral harm principle.

> *Lack of moral character principle.* One way in which one can fail to respect one's own humanity as an end in itself is to adopt maxims and/or perform actions that interfere with the positive duty of self-mastery, and so interfere with one's moral vocation of making humanity-based reasons motivationally dominant in one's overall motivational structure. Such maxims and actions manifest a lack of moral character and constitute violations of one's duty to oneself qua moral being.

Let us now consider the vices in question. We leave Kant's discussion of the positive duty of natural perfection for later in this section.

Miserly avarice. We find Kant's argument regarding the wrongness of miserly avarice in his casuistical remarks about this vice, where he argues that miserliness is not a mere matter of imprudence, and so

> ...miserliness is not just mistaken thrift but rather slavish subjection of oneself to the goods that contribute to happiness, which is a violation

of a duty to oneself since one ought to be their master. It is opposed to liberality of mind (*liberalitas moralis*) generally...that is...opposed to the principle of independence from everything except the law, and is a way in which the subject defrauds himself. (*TL* 6: 434)

What Kant is here calling the principle of independence, we referred to earlier as the duty of apathy (a partial specification of FH), and insofar as one suffers from a "slavish subjection" to discretionary ends, one is letting oneself be governed by a particular passion. And a failure of apathy means that one has failed to make nondiscretionary ends set by reason motivationally dominant. This failure may be due to a failure to understand or fully appreciate one's dignity and thus a failure to understand or fully appreciate the normative supremacy of humanity-based reasons. But, the kind of slavish subjection Kant is here referring to may be a mere failure of apathy, a failure to control one's passions despite having an intellectual understanding of one's dignity and the supremacy of humanity-based reasons. This seems to be how he is arguing in the above passage. And if so, then Kant's derivation involves the duty of apathy plus a characterization of avarice as involving slavish subjection which together yield the negative deontic verdict. And, in general, any slavish[33] pursuit of some discretionary end (whether acquisition of money or anything else) represents an obstacle to moral perfection, removal of which is instrumentally necessary for being in a position to cultivate virtue.

Lying. It is difficult to extract a clear argument for the claim that lying is a violation of a duty to oneself from the *DV* passages. Kant claims that, apart from any harm a lie may cause to another person, by lying one "throws away and, as it were, annihilates one's dignity as a human being" (*TL* 6: 429). Recall that dignity, on Kant's account, takes two forms: elevation qua autonomous being and elevation qua fully realized rational being. It is not so clear how or whether lying negatively impacts those powers (identified earlier in section II) that are constitutive of one's autonomy. But it is reasonably clear how lying can involve a use of one's rational capacities that is incompatible with their full realization, so that in lying one "throws away and, as it were annihilates"—or as he puts it later, "renounces"— one's status as a fully realized rational being. In this way, to lie is to fail to respect the value of one's humanity properly. But what needs to be explained (if possible) is why it is that in lying one renounces one's dignity. In any case, he follows this comment by what seems to be his main argument for this verdict.

A human being who does not believe what he tells another (even if the other is merely an ideal person) has even less worth than if he were a mere thing; for a thing, because it is something real and given, has the

---

[33] As Robert Audi pointed out to us, one might well worry that the qualification "slavish" weakens the point, making it virtually truistic. But the point of this qualification is to allow for the pursuit of a discretionary end in an exercise of autonomy which allots that end its proper normative weight, one that recognizes its subordination to nondiscretionary ends.

property of being serviceable so that another can put it to some use. But communication of one's thoughts to someone through words that yet (intentionally) contain the contrary of what the speaker thinks on the subject is ... directly opposed to the natural purposiveness of the speaker's capacity to communicate his thoughts, and is thus a renunciation by the speaker of his personality.... (*TL* 6: 429)

What is puzzling about this passage is that part of it (the first sentence) focuses on one's being of use to others and thus does not seem to be particularly relevant for explaining why lying is a violation of a duty to oneself. Granted, in various passages Kant does claim that an individual has a duty to make him- or herself useful to other individuals and to society generally, and lying arguably does violate this duty. But this more general duty is a duty to others, not to oneself. Kant's appeal, in this passage, to "the natural purposiveness of the speaker's capacity to communicate his thoughts" might address this concern: to lie is to violate the duty one has to oneself to fulfill the natural purposiveness of one's rational capacities, and so to fully realize these capacities. But such appeals to natural teleology are not obviously legitimate, and seem to pack in just the claim about the wrongness of lying that was to be derived. So, absent a satisfying defense of such appeals to natural teleology within his ethics, it is not clear how Kant can provide a direct derivation of the wrongness of lying as a violation of a duty to oneself, by appeal to FH plus additional nonmoral premises.

He can, however, provide an explanation of the wrongness of lying by appealing to: (1) the moral requirement to strive to know one's own motives with the aim of trying to discover "whether the source of your actions is pure or impure," the duty of moral self-knowledge (*TL* 6: 441); and (2) the lack of moral character principle. Kant distinguishes outer lies from inner lies (cases of self-deception), and it is reasonably clear that engaging in self-deception will likely hinder one's success in being able to attain "Impartiality in appraising oneself in comparison with the law, and sincerity in acknowledging to oneself one's inner moral worth or lack of worth [which] are duties to oneself that follow directly from this first command to cognize oneself" (*TL* 6: 441–2). So, it would appear that Kant can provide a derivation of a duty one has to oneself not to lie by appealing to the likely negative effects of lying together with the duty to acquire moral self-knowledge. Here, it is noteworthy that in the Vigilantius lecture notes Kant calls attention to the connection between self-deception and moral self-knowledge. "A man can tell himself lies about the good and bad in his actions and really imagine a situation that he is not in at all" (*V-MS/Vigil* 27: 609) and thereby represent his moral character as being "either better or worse by fabrication" (*V-MS/Vigil* 27: 608).

Servility (false humility). Under this rubric Kant discusses the duty to recognize and preserve proper moral self-esteem, understood as involving an attitude that one unavoidably takes toward oneself upon proper reflection on one's dignity, and correspondingly the duty to avoid actions that either outwardly express lack of moral self-esteem (and thus communicate a message to the effect that one does not hold oneself in proper esteem) or are expressions of a lack of self-esteem (regardless of what one's outward actions may officially communicate). That one has a duty of moral self-esteem—a duty to respect the dignity of one's own humanity—is directly entailed by FH. So that there is such a duty does not require a derivation. What Kant is doing in the passages under consideration is explaining in what this duty consists by connecting it to a proper understanding of one's dignity.

Consider first self-esteem as an attitude one is to have toward one's humanity. In the introduction to *DV*, we are told that persons who are subject to duty must come equipped with certain "moral endowments," which one does not have a duty to acquire, "because they lie at the basis of morality, as subjective conditions of receptiveness to the concept of duty" (*TL* 6: 399). Among them is the feeling of respect. Because one has no duty to acquire it, "Accordingly it is not correct to say that a human being has a *duty of self-esteem*; it must rather be said that the law within him unavoidably forces from him *respect* for his own being, and this feeling (which is of a special kind) is the basis of certain duties, that is, of certain actions that are consistent with his duty to himself" (*TL* 6: 402–3). Although acquiring the feeling of respect or (equivalently) a feeling of moral self-esteem is not a duty, Kant does refer to a duty of self-esteem in discussing servility, which concerns understanding what proper self-esteem is and cultivating the sort of attitude toward one's humanity that constitutes such esteem. What is particularly interesting about Kant's discussion is his characterization of the attitude in question as a fitting response to recognition of the dignity of one's humanity. Here what we find are remarks that purport to explain what proper self-esteem is by connecting this complex attitude to dignity understood as dual elevated status (see section II, above). Consciousness of one's dignity as an autonomous being whose fundamental constraint is the moral law and accurately comparing one's deeds and character to the demands of the moral law result in moral humility, and thus guard against moral arrogance. The Collins notes are helpful here. There we find this passage:

> Humility is thus the curbing of any high opinion of our moral worth, by the comparison of our actions with the moral law. Such a comparison makes us humble. Man has reason to have a low opinion of himself, since his actions are not only in contravention of the moral law, but also lacking in purity. Out of frailty he violates the law and acts against it, and out of weakness his good actions fall short of its purity. (*V-Mo/Collins* 27: 350)

But, as Kant later remarks: "This humility can, however, have injurious consequences, if it is wrongly understood." The dangers include timorousness (lack of moral courage) and self-abasement, that is, "belittling one's own moral worth" (*TL* 6: 435). But while proper moral humility comes from accurate moral self-appraisal, proper moral self-esteem includes not only such humility but also a kind of "exaltation" (*TL* 6: 436) or "elation of spirit" (*TL* 6: 437) that results from dwelling on one's capacity for internal lawgiving (dignity as autonomy) and on a "human being's feeling for his vocation" (*TL* 6: 437)—one's dignity qua fully realized rational being.

The duty of moral self-esteem considered in relation to how one is to view oneself, involves recognizing the ground of true self-esteem by dwelling on one's dignity, as a basis for the duty of preserving the corresponding self-directed attitude involving a combination of humility and exaltation, thereby avoiding the vices of moral arrogance (self-conceit) and self-abasement.

Let us turn now (briefly) to servility as expressed in action. Of such servility, Kant writes: "But belittling one's own moral worth merely as a means to acquiring the favor of another, whoever it may be (hypocrisy and flattery) is false (lying) humility, which is contrary to one's duty to oneself since it degrades one's personality" (*TL* 6: 436). It appears as if Kant is here appealing to the fact that certain actions are degrading to explain why belittling one's own moral worth is contrary to duty. But an appeal to what is degrading seems to call out for explanation, and the explanation would seem to be in terms of the fact that certain actions either express lack of proper moral self-esteem (given what such actions "say") or result from (and are thus expressions of) a lack of proper self-esteem. Kant's illustrations of such behavior at *TL* 6: 436–7 include failing to stand up for one's rights and being someone else's lackey. An important element of what makes such actions morally degrading is that they express or are expressions of a lack of moral self-esteem. So, we suggest that the true significance of this passage is not to provide an explanation of the wrongness of belittling one's moral worth. The passage rather is meant to call attention to the fact that apart from any attempt to manipulate another person by false humility or flattery, and thus apart from considerations of one's action being a violation of duty to others, servile actions by their very nature are contrary to one's duty of moral self-esteem: they violate the lack of moral character principle and are thus degrading for that reason. Kant's derivation of the duty to avoid servile attitudes and actions thus draws on the duty of moral self-esteem and a conceptual claim about the nature of servile attitudes and actions, together with the lack of moral character principle.

We summarize this battery of derivations in Figure 10.2 below.

Natural self-perfection. The duty of natural self-perfection requires one to develop or cultivate one's mental and bodily powers. With respect to mental powers, Kant distinguishes powers of spirit "possible through reason" and mentions the a priori disciplines of mathematics, logic, and metaphysics of nature as requiring the use of powers of reason, while powers of soul that are guided by experience and "at the disposal of understanding" include powers of "memory, imagination, and the like" (*TL* 6: 445). Arguably, powers of both sorts are part of what constitutes one's autonomy—and thus part of the constitutive

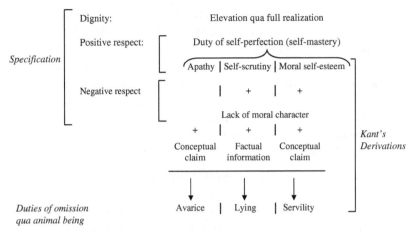

FIGURE 10.2 *Negative duties to oneself qua moral being.*

ground of one's dignity qua autonomous being. After making clear that the ground on the basis of which the duty of natural perfection is owed is not the "advantages their cultivation can provide" (*TL* 6: 445), and thus that this duty is not a matter of prudence, Kant writes:

> Instead, it is a command of morally practical reason and a *duty* of a human being to himself to cultivate his capacities (some among them more than others, insofar as people have different ends), and to be in a pragmatic respect a human being equal to the end of his existence. (*TL* 6: 445)

The key idea of "being equal" to the end of one's existence in a pragmatic respect concerns fully realizing the autonomy in virtue of which one has dignity. Developing these powers is part of fully realizing one's autonomy—one important aspect of an individual's moral vocation. So, one way of understanding Kant's argument regarding perfecting one's natural powers is that it invokes the idea that these powers are part of what constitutes one's autonomy, a dimension of one's dignity: since according to the principle of the perfection of the will one is to perfect that in virtue of which one possesses dignity, one has a duty (apart from any instrumental value such developed powers might have) to cultivate the powers in question. But what we take to be a more intuitively plausible way to read this passage is suggested by the following passage in the Collins notes, in which Kant comments on Baumgarten's perfectionist view about the ground of morality, according to which one is to "seek perfection as much as you can":

> The perfection of a thing and a man is different. The perfection of a thing is the sufficiency of all that is needed to constitute the thing, and so in general means completeness. But the perfection of a man does not yet signify morality. Perfection and moral goodness are different. Perfection here is the completeness of the man in regard to his powers, capacity

and readiness to carry out all the ends he may have. Perfection can be greater or less; one man can be more perfect than another. But goodness is the property of making good and proper use of all these perfections. So moral goodness consists in the perfection of the will, not the capacities. Yet a good will needs the completeness and capacity of all powers to carry out everything willed by the will. So we might say that perfection is indirectly necessary to morality, and to that extent belongs to it, and that the proposition [seek as much perfection as you can] is indirectly a moral one. (*V-Mo/Collins* 27: 265–6; see also 27: 363–4)

If this passage reflects Kant's mature view regarding the duty to develop one's natural powers, then as it indicates, the duty is indirect in the sense that the explanation being offered for the duty is that perfecting one's powers are instrumental to being able to satisfy the duty of moral self-perfection. Going back to the above quoted passage from *DV*, and approaching it in light of the Collins passage, the idea of being "in a pragmatic respect a human being equal to the end of his existence" is to be understood as being as able as possible, through the development of one's powers, to strive to realize the end of moral perfection or virtue. Doing so would make one "equal" to one's end or vocation in the sense of being as prepared as possible and thus "up to" the task of striving toward that end.[34]

What emerges from this examination of Kant's discussion of duties to oneself is a fairly clear explanatory picture of the various duties in question (we have noted a few exceptions). As one would expect, they all revolve around the duty of moral self-perfection, whose fulfillment requires moral knowledge and motivational self-governance, as well as maintenance of one's physical being. All of these negative duties are neatly explained by principles (moral harm, lack of moral character) that themselves represent partial specifications of the basic requirement of respect for the dignity of humanity. While the various negative duties to oneself involve avoiding actions that obstruct the fulfillment of (or progress toward) the duty of moral perfection, the positive duty of natural perfection is instrumental to fully realizing one's humanity.

IV. Ethical Duties to Others

Kant divides this batch of duties into duties of love and duties of respect, where the basis of the distinction has to do with whether performing an action

---

[34] Note also the remarks in Vigilantius where Kant is stressing the importance of occupying one's time in useful ways. "Now by cultivation of our abilities we become assured of our duties, and able to recognize and carry them out: it is a self-regarding duty for us, both to be busy and also to engage in that recreation that keeps us occupied." "Cultivation of our powers is a requirement for our vocation; a lazy man tramples both underfoot, and his punishment is therefore self-contempt" (*V-MS/Vigil* 27: 657–8).

called for by the duty puts another person under an obligation. Duties of love involve an agent conferring a benefit upon another party that is not strictly owed, thereby putting the beneficiary under an obligation of gratitude. By contrast, duties of respect, because they are owed, do not generate corresponding obligations of gratitude.

1. DUTIES OF LOVE

Under this category Kant discusses the positive duties of beneficence, gratitude, and sympathy as well as the corresponding vices of envy, ingratitude, and malice.

Beneficence. This duty involves adopting an unselfish maxim that disposes one to promote the well-being of others in need without, as Kant says, "hoping for anything in return" (*TL* 6: 453).[35] After characterizing the duty of beneficence, Kant proceeds to give the following argument:

> For everyone who finds himself in need wishes to be helped by others. But if he lets his maxim of being unwilling to assist others in turn when they are in need become public, that is, makes this a universal permissive law, then everyone would likewise deny him assistance when he himself is in need, or at least would be authorized to deny it. Hence the maxim of self-interest would conflict with itself if it were made a universal law, that is, it is contrary to duty. (*TL* 6: 453)

This argument is reminiscent of Kant's *Groundwork* argument at 4: 423 where he is illustrating the universal law formulation of the categorical imperative.[36] What this form of argument reveals is that a maxim of never helping others in need unless it serves one's own interest (the maxim of calculated self-interest) would involve a violation of duty. But an explanation of why adopting this maxim is a violation of duty, as well as an explanation of why one is morally required to adopt a maxim of practical beneficence, is provided by the sentence that continues the passage just quoted:

> Consequently the maxim of common interest, of beneficence toward those in need, is a universal duty of human beings, *just because* they are to be considered fellow men, that is, rational beings with needs, united by nature in one dwelling place so that they can help one another. (*TL* 6: 453, our emphasis)

---

[35] The content of this duty is open to various interpretations. Narrow interpretations stress the reference to "needs"; wide interpretations hold that the duty is not so restricted. See Baron and Fahmy (2009) for discussion. It is worth noting that in Collins at 27: 441, a distinction is drawn among acts of *charity* as a response to someone's distress, *kindness* as a response to "other needs," and acts of mere *courtesy*.

[36] Allen Wood (2009: 232) suggests that Kant's argument based on the universal-law formula rules out only a maxim of principled refusal to help others; it does not thereby support the duty to positively adopt a maxim of practical beneficence.

This passage can be read as providing an explanation—and, indeed, a derivation—by way of what we earlier labelled the positive principle of impartiality (implicit in FH), to the effect that humanity-based reasons for action provide reasons for action for all relevantly situated agents; that one is to adopt attitudes and perform corresponding actions that manifest a positive concern for the ends (especially the needs) of others. This principle presupposes that there are humanity-based reasons for individuals to set and strive to achieve ends (so long as those ends and the means chosen are morally permitted), and that achieving certain ends requires help and cooperation from others. The positive principle of impartiality makes explicit the claim that there are humanity-based reasons for those who are suitably situated to help those in need.[37] The crucial feature of this duty, which helps explain the duties of gratitude and sympathy (as we are about to see), is that it requires beneficence on principle, as against what Kant calls "well-doing from love" (i.e., love as a feeling).[38] When one is beneficent on principle, one responds to the fact that the humanity of the beneficiary involves the setting of ends the obtaining of which (by the beneficiary) partly constitutes a full realization of her humanity, that in virtue of which she has dignity. Such helping action, which is an expression of care for another, manifests recognition of the fact that another person's permissible ends (and in particular their needs) provides anyone with reason to help. In other words, in helping the person in need, the principled benefactor helps in recognition of the fact that the beneficiary is deserving of help apart from any desire the benefactor might happen to have for helping the beneficiary in question. In this way the duty of beneficence involves respecting the dignity of the humanity of others.

Kant's derivation, then, of the duty of beneficence involves the positive principle of impartiality plus the conceptual claim that beneficence on principle involves the kind of concern for the well-being of another that the positive principle of impartiality directs one to adopt.

We turn now to duties of sympathetic feeling. Beneficence involves a relation between benefactor and beneficiary. The duties of sympathetic feeling

---

[37] In presenting the thesis of the normative supremacy of humanity-based reasons (see above, section II), we expressed the key idea by saying that such reasons are "superior to" desire-based reasons having to do with discretionary ends. Here, we remind our readers that one way in which humanity-based reasons can be superior is by, in a context, categorically requiring that one perform or omit the action favored or opposed by the reason. Humanity-based reasons associated with perfect duties are presumably requiring reasons. But given the latitude characteristic of imperfect duties, the humanity-based reasons for action associated with beneficence, particularly with regard to cases of charity, are what we may call "justifying reasons"—instead of functioning to require that one perform some action on some occasion, they rather function to make rational the performance of an act of charity by providing a sufficient normative reason for doing it. For more on the distinction between requiring and justifying roles in relation to practical reasons, see Gert (2004).

[38] See *V-Mo/Collins* 27: 413.

and gratitude have to do respectively with the two positions constituting this relationship.

Sympathetic feeling. Kant mentions joy and sadness as feelings that are proper responses to the weal and woe of others. The capacity for these feelings is innate, "implanted in human beings" (*TL* 6: 456). Since having an occurrent feeling is presumably not something under one's direct voluntary control, one cannot be obligated to feel joy or sadness on some occasion. The fact that one's control over being a person who has the relevant feelings on the right occasions is indirect makes the duty of sympathetic feeling an "indirect" duty. And as a duty of cultivation, it is imperfect.

> But while it is not in itself a duty to share the sufferings (as well the joys) of others, it is a duty to sympathize actively in their fate; and to this end, it is therefore an indirect duty to cultivate the compassionate natural (aesthetic) feelings in us, and to make use of them as so many means to sympathy based on moral principles and the feeling appropriate to them. (*TL* 6: 457)

After illustrating a few derivative duties involving relatively specific types of action through which one could cultivate the feelings in question (e.g., visiting sickrooms and debtor's prisons), Kant concludes the just-quoted paragraph with this: "For this [capacity for sympathetic feeling] is still one of the impulses that nature has implanted in us to do what the representation of duty alone might not accomplish" (*TL* 6: 457). So the explanatory derivation Kant is here offering in defense of the duty of sympathetic feeling is instrumentalist: the successful cultivation of such feelings enables one to fulfill the duty of active sympathy (i.e., beneficence) both by making one more sensitive to the plight of others and by motivating one to act accordingly. But there is something additional to be said here that helps explain the particular significance of what Kant has in mind by sympathetic feeling and, we think, provides the basis for a noninstrumentalist explanatory derivation of this duty.

Sympathetic concern is not just an appropriate response to another's need: such concern registers the fact that the need of another is something that provides anyone relevantly situated with a reason for helping. Stephen Darwall expresses this idea well:

> On the one hand, sympathy presents itself as warranted by threats to *a person's good*. Welfare is normative for sympathy.... On the other hand, sympathetic concern presents itself as of, not just some harm or disvalue *to* another person, but also the *neutral disvalue* of this personal harm owing to the value of the person himself. In feeling sympathy for the child, we perceive the impending disaster as not just terrible for him, but as neutrally bad in a way that gives anyone a reason to prevent it. We experience the child's plight as mattering categorically because we experience the child as mattering. (Darwall 1998: 275)

In the first of the two above-quoted passages from Kant, the duty to cultivate sympathetic feeling is the duty to make use of such feelings of care for the plight of others in need "based on moral principles and the feeling appropriate to them." The kind of sympathetic concern in question is grounded in the principle of impartiality which, as Darwall puts it, involves a recognition of the value of the person in need—her dignity. Viewed in this manner, Kant's positive principle of impartiality—which requires one to adopt *attitudes* (as well as perform actions) that manifest concern for the well-being of others, together with a conceptual claim about the very nature of sympathetic feeling (as a kind of concern), yields a noninstrumentalist derivation of the indirect duty in question.

Gratitude. While sympathetic feeling concerns the proper moral attitudes of benefactors, gratitude concerns the proper moral attitudes of beneficiaries. Kant characterizes gratitude as "*honoring* a person because of a benefit he has rendered us" (*MS* 6: 454). He distinguishes affective from actional gratitude: the former is an attitude of appreciativeness directed toward a benefactor, the latter an outward act conveying to the benefactor an acknowledgment (and appreciation) of the benefit. He also distinguishes mere reciprocation (where the beneficiary is moved by the desire to receive further benefits) from genuine gratitude.[39] Focusing just on the duty concerning actional gratitude, nowhere in his writings or in the student lecture notes on ethics do we find a derivation of this duty. Gratitude is recognition of the benefactor's recognition of oneself and one's concerns as a source of reasons to act. This is why Kant characterizes gratitude as an honoring—something quite different from treating someone merely as a causal source contributing to one's welfare.[40] This suggests that the failure to be grateful constitutes a violation of a positive duty one has to honor the moral merit of our benefactor's act of beneficence.

Does this amount to a *derivation* of the duty of gratitude? Or is this better viewed merely as a way of specifying our positive duty to treat others as ends in themselves that is more expansive than Kant's own? The duty does not seem to follow from the positive principle of impartiality, at least as we have formulated it, because in expressing one's gratitude toward one's benefactor one need not be promoting the benefactor's ends or addressing that person's needs. Here it seems as if gratitude as a response to beneficence is a basic form of positive respect: genuine beneficence calls for a certain kind of recognition of the benefactor by the beneficiary. Of course, Kant's *DV* taxonomy does not include duties of positive

---

[39] In Collins, gratitude from duty is distinguished from gratitude from inclination. "We are grateful from inclination, insofar as we feel love in return" (*V-Mo/Collins* 27: 441).

[40] This point is made by Berger (1975), whose account of gratitude is Kantian. It is worth noting that Kant does indicate that there is a good moral reason—a reason pertaining to self-perfection—for having a grateful disposition and acting accordingly (see *TL* 6: 456). Being grateful allows one to cultivate one's love of human beings in that one is being sensitive to what one takes to be (and hopefully is) a benevolent disposition on the part of the beneficiary. This sort of reason for gratitude does not explain why it is a perfect duty to others.

respect. However, Kant does claim that beneficiaries should "take the occasion for gratitude as a moral kindness, that is, an opportunity to unite the virtue of gratitude with love of man, to combine the *cordiality* of a benevolent disposition with *sensitivity* to benevolence...and so to cultivate one's love of human beings" (*TL* 6: 456). This suggests, perhaps, another way of specifying Kant's FH—namely, to include a positive duty to promote the love of human beings, which could then be a basis for deriving the duty of gratitude. Unfortunately, this matter requires more attention than we can give it here. In Smit and Timmons (2011), we have said more about the issue of justifying the duty of gratitude in the context of examining the role of gratitude in Kant's moral theory.

2. VICES OF HATE

These correspond respectively to the virtues of beneficence, gratitude, and sympathetic feeling. The primary focus of Kant's remarks is on the traits of character associated with these vices, though he does have things to say about actions that are expressions of such traits. In the passages from *DV* in which these vices are discussed, Kant does not explicitly offer derivations of their wrongness. Rather he simply points to the fact that they involve attitudes that are directly opposed to the attitudes constitutive of the corresponding virtues. However, for each of these vices, Kant can provide an indirect derivation of their wrongness, a derivation that appeals to another duty: given that beneficence, involving a certain active positive concern for the welfare of others, is a duty, and given that envy (as a character trait) involves an attitude of harm directly opposed to positive concern, it follows that the attitudes and associated actions characteristic of envy involve a violation of duty.[41] Exactly parallel arguments can be given for the vices of malice and ingratitude. But, of course, even if beneficence and sympathy were not duties, Kant can explain the wrongness of the vices of envy and malice in terms of their inappropriateness as reactions to the well-being of others on the basis of the negative principle of impartiality.

Envy is described as "a propensity to view the well-being of others with distress, even though it does not detract from one's own" (*TL* 6: 458). We are told that when this propensity results in action aimed at diminishing the well-being of others, it is "envy proper," but if it results merely in ill-will toward others, it is called jealousy. Regarding envy, Kant says that it is "only an indirectly malevolent disposition" (*TL* 6: 458), because it results not from taking an immediate

---

[41] Kant here doesn't seem to worry about how we could have a (direct) duty not to have an attitude, such as the feeling of envy, which it would seem, is not under our direct voluntary control. But whether or not we have a duty not to have such affects, Kant it seems can say that we have the duty not to engage in acts of envy "aimed at diminishing the well-being of others" and that we also have a duty to strive to rid ourselves of envious feelings.

interest in decreasing the well-being of others out of hatred for them (such an attitude is constitutive of malice), but rather results either from a perceived inequality in comparative levels of well-being or from an ambition to exceed others in one's level of worth. This remark about envy's indirectness is an observation about its genesis, not about how its moral status is to be explained. As just noted, its status as a vice can be explained not only by appeal to the duty of beneficence, but also according to the negative principle of impartiality: there are obviously humanity-based reasons to refrain from positively harming others and for avoiding associated dispositions. So, Kant can easily provide a nonderivative explanation of this vice and the actions that result from it, an explanation that is independent of an appeal to the positive duty of beneficence.

Malice. As a character trait, malice involves being disposed to take an *immediate* joy (or pleasure or even satisfaction) in the ill-fortune of others and sadness at the good fortune of others; malice proper refers to actions resulting from this trait. The immediacy here is supposed to signal one difference between envy and malice. Whereas envy expresses a concern for one's own comparative level of well-being, malice (as least in the form of malevolent joy) expresses resentment of the good fortunes of others. Like the vice of envy, its psychological basis has to do with feelings of comparative inequality owing in particular to the "*haughtiness* of others when their welfare is uninterrupted, and their *self-conceit,*" the latter owing to good moral luck rather than to genuine moral strength of character (*TL* 6: 460). In discussing this vice, Kant gestures toward the kind of derivative explanation mentioned above: "to rejoice immediately [in the misfortunes of others,]...and so to wish for them to happen, is secretly to hate human beings; and this is the direct opposite of love of our neighbor, which is incumbent on us as a duty" (*TL* 6: 460). But again, apart from an appeal to the duties of beneficence and sympathetic feeling, Kant can argue directly for the claim that malice is a violation of duty by appealing to the negative principle of impartiality.

Ingratitude. For Kant this vice includes mere unappreciativeness (either not responding to a known benefactor in affect or action, or being displeased by the obligation that beneficence imposes upon one) and what Kant calls "ingratitude proper" which involves taking up a negative, hateful attitude which, in turn, results in a desire to harm one's beneficiary.[42] Psychologically this vice, like those of envy and malice, results from a perceived threat to one's self-esteem (and thus to one's sense of moral equality) as one judges this on the basis of comparing oneself to others with regard to, e.g., welfare.

In the passages under consideration, Kant offers two remarks about the significance of ingratitude.[43]

---

[42] See *V-MS/Vigil* 27: 694–5 for some of these details about ingratitude.

[43] Given how Kant begins the passage just quoted, it is plausible to read what follows as a psychological explanation of why ingratitude is so shocking. But as we are about to explain, the passage we think provides insight into the particular significance of gratitude in relation to the principles of impartiality and moral equality.

But ingratitude is a vice that shocks humanity, not merely because of the *harm* that such an example must bring on people in general by deterring them from further beneficence (for with a genuine moral disposition they can, just by scorning any such return for their beneficence, put all the more inner worth on it),[44] but because ingratitude stands love of human beings on its head, as it were, and degrades absence of love into an authorization to hate the one who loves. (*TL* 6: 459)

The harm-based argument alluded to here—to the effect that repaying beneficence with ingratitude may discourage a benefactor from future acts of beneficence[45]—is not the main consideration Kant is offering in explaining the moral significance of ingratitude. Rather, Kant's central claim is that ingratitude stands love on its head because an ungrateful individual who is not inclined to be grateful thereby lacks "love" for her benefactor, and because of feeling inferior in status in relation to her benefactor (which Kant cites as the main contributing psychological factor resulting in this vice) she feels justified (authorized) in taking up a hostile attitude toward that person. The inversion then is a matter of returning hate for love as if such a response were appropriate. And so, with respect to ingratitude proper, involving a hostile or even hateful attitude toward one's benefactor, such attitudes and actions are ruled out as violations of duty by the negative principle of impartiality, which forbids the taking up of attitudes and performing actions that manifest a negative concern for the well-being of others.

Let us sum up this discussion of duties of love to others. The positive principle of impartiality is the basis for a derivation of the duty of beneficence. We have also explained both how the duty of sympathetic feeling can be derived from this principle and how (as Kant's text suggests) it can be derived instrumentally from the duty of beneficence. Kant does not seem to offer a derivation of the duty of gratitude—where gratitude is understood as a natural response to another's beneficence—and we have speculated a bit about how a Kantian derivation might go. The vices of envy, ingratitude, and malice all stem from a false conception of one's dignity and thus of one's self-esteem—a conception that involves comparison of oneself to others on the basis of, e.g., well-being. These vices thus make clear the importance of the duty of moral self-esteem discussed in connection with the vice of servility. The wrongness of such vices and corresponding actions is explained by the negative principle of impartiality,

---

[44] This suggests a possible indirect derivation of the duty of gratitude: cultivating, in oneself and others, the disposition required to fulfill the duty of beneficence requires us to cultivate affective gratitude and to exhibit actional gratitude. But what Kant is offering in this passage is simply an explanation of the moral significance of gratitude, and not a derivation, direct or indirect, of the duty of gratitude.

[45] In Collins, Kant is reported as saying, "Ingratitude we hate amazingly, and even if not directed to ourselves, it still so rouses our wrath that we feel driven to intervene. This is because generosity is thereby decreased" (*V-Mo/Collins* 27: 443).

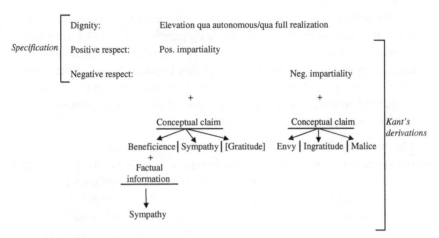

FIGURE 10.3 *Duties of love toward others.*

as depicted in Figure 10.3. We bracket the duty of gratitude, having for the present set aside the questions as to whether it is subject to a derivation (rather than simply representing a basic form of respect) and, if subject to a derivation, how the derivation proceeds.

3. DUTIES OF RESPECT

After repeating the claim that humanity itself has a dignity "by which he raises himself above other beings in the world that are not human beings and yet can be used, and so over all *things*," Kant writes:

> But just as he cannot give himself away for any price (this would conflict with his duty of self-esteem), so neither can he act contrary to the equally necessary self-esteem of others, as human beings, that is, he is under an obligation to acknowledge, in a practical way, the dignity of humanity in every other human being. Hence there rests on him a duty regarding the respect that must be shown to every other human being. (*TL* 6: 462)

The sort of respect under consideration in these passages concerns the preservation of the moral status of persons. Although in the "Remark" at *TL* 6: 463–4, Kant mentions positive duties of assistance in connection with respecting human beings "in the logical use of [a person's] reason," the only duties featured in his *DV* discussion of duties of respect concern the vices of arrogance, defamation, and ridicule.[46] Presumably, at the level of abstraction characteristic

---

[46] Here it is useful to distinguish the performance of actions expressing high esteem for someone, and actions that would help another person preserve or perhaps cultivate her or his self-esteem. At *TL* 6: 467–8, Kant denies that one's duties of respect for others include actions of the former types, but he does allow, as indicated in the "Remark," that respect for others can be

of mid-level duties, there aren't any commonly recognized types of action (again, abstracting from the varying circumstances of individuals) that constitute positive duties whose rationale is to cultivate the self-esteem of others. In contrast to the central duty of love—beneficence—that potential recipients have no right to demand, all human beings do have a right to demand respectful treatment from all others which, given human psychology, is most likely to be violated by actions that express arrogance, are defamatory, or involve ridiculing others.

Arrogance, defamation, ridicule. Kant characterizes all three vices partly in terms of a person's inclination or propensity (and thus aim) to treat others as worthy of contempt. Arrogance is explained as "...the inclination to be always *on top*...a kind of *ambition* (*ambitio*) in which we demand that others think little of themselves in comparison with us" (*TL* 6: 465). Defamation is "the immediate inclination, with no particular aim in view, to bring into the open something prejudicial to respect for others" (*TL* 6: 466). Ridicule in the forms of wanton faultfinding and mockery is "the propensity to expose others to laughter, to make their faults the immediate object of one's amusement" and is thereby "a kind of malice" (*TL* 6: 467). In explaining the wrongness of these attitudes and associated actions, we again find Kant appealing to the likely negative consequences of expressing contempt for others and thus giving what Kant calls scandal. "An offense against respectability is called *scandal*, an example of disregarding respectability that might lead others to follow it. To *give* scandal is quite contrary to duty" (*TL* 6: 464). Kant repeats this argument in his discussion of defamation (*TL* 6: 466) and the same argument might be used for explaining the wrongness of outward expressions of the other two vices. But the likely negative consequence of such outward expressions of contempt for others is not the fundamental consideration Kant uses to explain the wrongness of both the attitudes and actions associated with these vices. Rather, given that Kant's characterizations of arrogance, defamation, and ridicule include as a central aspect of these traits the aim of bringing about the lowering of another's self-esteem and thus prompting contempt for the targets of one's disposition, their wrongness is explained by appeal to the nature of these traits plus the principle of moral equality. As explained in section II, this principle requires that we preserve the self-esteem of others, and the character traits under consideration are defined partly by a motive that is directly contrary to the preservation of another's self-esteem. Thus, the derivations of these negative duties proceed from the principle of equality plus a characterization of the

---

expressed through actions of the latter type. In the Vigilantius discussion of friendship, there is passing mention of positive efforts to promote a friend's self-respect: "The mutual respect for humanity in the person of the other must at least be exercised negatively, albeit that the positive endeavor to increase and fortify respect is not thereby ruled out" (*V-MS/Vigil* 27: 682). So, even between friends, the emphasis is on refraining from doing anything that would lower a friend's self-esteem, though Kant allows room for positive action aimed at promoting another's self-esteem.

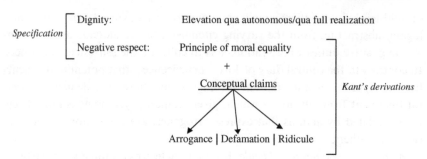

FIGURE 10.4 *Negative duties of respect toward others.*

nature of the action type (a conceptual claim), which together yield a deontic verdict about arrogance, defamation, and ridicule, as depicted in Figure 10.4.

V. Conclusion

We have covered much territory for a single chapter: the nature of Kant's explanatory grounding project in the *Doctrine of Virtue*, the content of the formula of humanity, and Kant's derivations of the central duties of virtue to oneself and to others. Our aim has been to determine the success of Kant's top-down derivations with an eye on both the "great and various consequences" that allegedly can be derived from the formula of humanity (the determinacy of these derivations) and the requirement that the duties being derived are plausibly explained by this formula and do not just represent unmotivated interpretations of the general idea of respecting the dignity of humanity (the requirement of independence). A central part of our project has been to sort out the various strands of argumentation one finds in the *DV* and relate them to the formula of humanity. As Griffin (1986: 208) rightly observes, there is no going from the bare, unspecified notion of equal respect to a rich set of reasonably determinate moral requirements. But, on our interpretation, the content of FH is quite rich, invoking Kant's conception of dignity as elevation both qua autonomous being (capable of morality) and qua fully realized rational being (virtuous). On the basis of this general conception of human dignity, principles of self-perfection, moral equality, and impartiality are implicated in the requirement to respect the dignity of humanity, as well as the principles concerning moral harm and lack of moral character. And on the basis of these principles, which constitute a partial specification of FH, one can (so we argue) provide top-down derivations of most if not all of the duties to oneself and to others that represent mid-level duties of virtue. Many of the derivations involve an appeal to one of the specification principles plus a conceptual claim about the action and attitude under consideration. We claim that such arguments count as derivations because they involve an illuminating explanation of the duties in question—explanations that compete with, say, the sort of explanation forthcoming from a utilitarian moral perspective. We also noted that with regard to a few of the mid-level duties (e.g., moral self-perfection) no derivation is offered, which is explained by the fact that they represent partial specifications of FH. So what we find in Kant is a largely successful project of working from a particular conception of dignity and the respect it demands which, together with various conceptual and factual premises, yields a fairly determinate set of mid-level duties to oneself and to others while generally respecting the requirement of independence.

Bibliography

Adams, R. M. (2006) *A Theory of Virtue: Excellence in Being for the Good*. Oxford: Oxford University Press.

Anderson, E. (2008) "Emotions in Kant's Later Moral Philosophy: Honour and the Phenomenology of Moral Value," in M. Betzler (ed.), *Kant's Virtue Ethics*, 123–45. Berlin: Walter de Gruyter.

Audi, R. (2001) *The Architecture of Reason: The Structure and Substance of Rationality*. Oxford: Oxford University Press.

Audi, R. (n.d.) "Two Anchors of Moral Judgment: Merely Instrumental and End-Regarding Treatment of Persons." Unpublished MS.

Baron, M. (2002) "Love and Respect in the *Doctrine of Virtue*," in M. Timmons (ed.), *Kant's "Metaphysics of Morals": Interpretative Essays*, 391–402. Oxford: Oxford University Press.

Baron, M., and Fahmy, M. S. (2009) "Beneficence and Other Duties of Love in the *Metaphysics of Morals*," in Hill (2009): 211–28.

Berger, F. (1975) "Gratitude," *Ethics* 85(4): 298–309.

Darwall, S. (1998) "Empathy, Sympathy, Care," *Philosophical Studies* 89(2–3): 261–82.

Denis, L. (1999) "Kant on the Wrongness of 'Unnatural' Sex," *History of Philosophy Quarterly* 16(2): 225–47.

Gert, J. (2004) *Brute Rationality*. Cambridge: Cambridge University Press.

Gregor, M. J. (1963) *Laws of Freedom*. Oxford: Basil Blackwell.

Griffin, J. (1986) *Well-Being*. Oxford: Oxford University Press.

Guyer, P. (2002) "Ends of Reason and Ends of Nature: The Place of Teleology in Kant's Ethics," *Journal of Value Inquiry* 26(2–3): 161–86. Reprinted in Guyer (2005).

Guyer, P. (2005) "Kant's System of Duties," in Guyer, *Kant's System of Nature and Freedom*. Oxford: Clarendon Press: 243–74.

Hill, T. E., Jr. (1992) "A Kantian Perspective on Moral Rules," in J. Tomberlin (ed.) *Philosophical Perspectives* 6: 285–304. Reprinted in Hill (2000).

Hill, T. E., Jr. (1993) "Donagan's Kant," *Ethics* 104(1): 22–52, Reprinted in Hill (2000).

Hill, T. E., Jr. (1996) "Moral Dilemmas, Gaps, and Residues," in H. E. Mason (ed.), *Moral Dilemmas and Moral Theory*, 167–98. Oxford: Oxford University Press Reprinted in Hill (2002).

Hill, T. E., Jr. (2000) *Respect, Pluralism, and Justice*. Oxford: Oxford University Press.

Hill, T. E., Jr. (2002) *Human Welfare and Moral Worth: Kantian Perspectives*. Oxford: Oxford University Press.

Hill, T. E., Jr. (ed.) (2009) *The Blackwell Guide to Kant's Ethics*. Oxford: Wiley-Blackwell.

Kant, I. (1996) *Practical Philosophy*. Tr. and ed. M. J. Gregor. Cambridge: Cambridge University Press.

Kant, I. (1997) *Lectures on Ethics*. Ed. P. Heath and J. B. Schneewind. Tr. P. Heath. Cambridge: Cambridge University Press.

Kant, I. (2007) *Anthropology, History, and Education*. Ed. G. Zöller and R. Louden. Tr. M. J. Gregor et al. Cambridge: Cambridge University Press.

Kerstein, S. J. (2008) "Treating Oneself Merely as a Means," in M. Betzler (ed.), *Kant's Virtue Ethics*, 201–18. Berlin: Walter de Gruyter.

Roberts, R. (1984) "Will Power and the Virtues," *Philosophical Review* 93(2): 227–47.

Sensen, O. (2009a) "Kant's Conception of Inner Value," *European Journal of Philosophy* 19(2): 262–80.

Sensen, O. (2009b) "Dignity and the Formula of Humanity," in J. Timmermann (ed.), *Kant's Groundwork: A Critical Guide,* 102–18. Cambridge: Cambridge University Press.

Sensen, O. (2010) "Kant's Conception of Human Dignity," *Kant-Studien* 100(3): 309–331.

Skorupski, J. (2005) "Blame, Respect and Recognition: A Reply to Theo van Willigenburg," *Utilitas* 17: 333–47.

Smit, H. (2009) "Kant on Apriority and the Spontaneity of Cognition," in Newlands, S.. and Jorgensen, L. (eds.), *Metaphysics and the Good: Themes from the Philosophy of Robert Adams,* 188–251. Oxford: Oxford University Press.

Smit, H., and Timmons, M. (2011) "The Moral Significance of Gratitude in Kant's Ethics," *Southern Journal of Philosophy* 49 (4): 295–320.

Timmons, M. (1997) "Decision Procedures, Moral Criteria, and the Problem of Relevant Descriptions in Kant's Ethics," *Jahrbuch für Recht und Ethik* 5: 389–417.

Timmons, M. (2005) "The Philosophical and Practical Significance of Kant's Universality Formulations of the Categorical Imperative," *Jarbuch fur Recht und Ethik* 13: 313–33.

Timmons, M. (2006) "The Categorical Imperative and Universalizablity," in Horn, C., and Schoenecker, D. (eds.), *Kant's "Groundwork of the Metaphysics of Morals": New Interpretations,* 158–99. Berlin: de Gruyter.

Timmons, M. (2013) "Perfect Duties to Oneself Qua Animal Being," in A. Trampota, O. Sensen and J. Timmermann (eds.), *Kant's "Tugendlehre": A Comprehensive Commentary*. Berlin: De Gruyter.

Wood, A. W. (1999) *Kant's Ethical Thought* Cambridge: Cambridge University Press.

Wood, A. W. (2008) *Kantian Ethics*. Cambridge: Cambridge University Press.

Wood, A. W. (2009) "Duties to Oneself, Duties to Respect Others," in Hill (2009): 229–51.

11

Kant and Libertarianism
Howard Williams

Libertarians place the individual at the centre of their political outlook. They stress the need to allow individual freedom to flourish and argue that all social institutions that hamper this flourishing should be restrained and minimized. Like anarchists, libertarians are thoroughly antistatist but are more prepared than anarchists to accept the necessity for a minimum form of state organization. Libertarianism is a *modern* outlook, presupposing the emergence of modern individuality and the institution of private property with the breakdown of feudalism. Each contemporary libertarian thinker will have as their model a particular favorite classical thinker, but John Locke's political philosophy is often a significant starting point—particularly the sections on property ownership in *Two Treatises of Government*—as is John Stuart Mill's essay *On Liberty*. Two well-known twentieth-century political philosophers who have often been connected with libertarianism are Friedrich Hayek and Robert Nozick. Indeed Robert Nozick is perhaps the most significant champion of the doctrine whose conclusion neatly sums up where many libertarians stand now:

> a minimal state, limited to the narrow functions of protection against force, theft, fraud, enforcement of contracts, and so on, is justified; . . . any more extensive state will violate persons' rights not to be forced to do certain things, and is unjustified; and . . . the minimal state is inspiring as well as right. (Nozick 1974: xi)

A variety of libertarian writers have warmed to Kant's moral and political philosophy, seeing in it classical inspiration for their own standpoint. He retains this enthusiastic following amongst libertarian thinkers today (see Otteson 2009). They are particularly drawn to his account of autonomy in his pure moral philosophy, and the view of freedom presented in the philosophy of right. They see the depiction of legal freedom that Kant gives as being independent from the arbitrary interference of others as very close to their own understanding of an unhindered freedom. They concur with Kant's view expressed in the *Metaphysics of Morals* that "freedom (independence from being constrained by another's choice)" is "the only original right belonging to every man by virtue of his humanity" and hold also that "this principle of innate freedom already involves" "innate equality, that is, independence from being bound by others to more than one can in turn bind them" (*RL* 6: 337–8). Libertarians are strongly of the view as well that a human being possesses the "quality of being his own master" and he is "authorized to do to others anything that does not in itself diminish what is theirs" (*RL* 6: 238). From an external, legal standpoint Kant permits and indeed encourages each individual to determine spontaneously for himself the grounds upon which he acts.

The object of this chapter is to demonstrate that, although there are these close affinities between Kant's views and those of contemporary libertarians, Kant's political philosophy as a whole is not libertarian in spirit, and that it indeed possesses overtones of the political standpoint that libertarians often most dislike: socialism. The focus will be on Kant's justification of social provisions for those who are unable to meet their basic needs, as an implication of Kant's claim that the idea of general will is presupposed by the specific way in which legal norms are applied in particular cases in societies.

Individual freedom is at the core of libertarian political philosophy. According to the libertarian, initiatives should derive from individuals and any necessary social organizations that are created should reflect and facilitate this. From the libertarian's perspective ceding freedom represents a loss of independence, personality, and scope for action. As social and political organizations grow in their power and influence libertarians see individuals as diminished in their freedom. Libertarians are not in favor of reciprocity between public institutions and individual freedom but instead favor a subordination of institutions to individuals. As Katrin Flikschuh puts it, "they generally regard legitimate government functions as restricted to upholding the rule of law internally and defending the state's sovereignty externally"; moreover "most libertarians are suspicious of state-enforced social welfare policies that involve the redistribution of resources from the better-off to the worse-off: they prefer to let the mechanism of the market determine allocation of resources" (Flikschuh 2007: 63).

Kant can be seen as sharing some of the libertarians' concern about the significance of liberty and the dangers of the subjugation of individuality to public power. However, he does not wholly share their antipathy to the state, nor does he share the sense of absolute priority that should be given to individual liberty over other considerations, such as equality and community, that they do. As I see it, there are some libertarian strands to Kant's political philosophy but they are counterbalanced by other more significant strands, such as the extraordinary mix he tries to bring about between patriotism and cosmopolitanism (neither of which outlooks looms very large in libertarian thinking) in his mature political philosophy. Kant is rightly identified with cosmopolitan politics with his goal of a federation of free states which show hospitality to all visitors, but he expects of the citizens of these free states that they show loyalty and respect towards their homelands, since a state is a society of human individuals "which no one other than itself can command or dispose of," like a tree "it has its own roots" (*ZeF* 8: 344).

Where the libertarian strand is apparent in Kant's thinking is in his strong dislike of paternalism in politics. One of the prime functions of the social order in Kant's vision is for it to facilitate human liberty which consists in individuals being free to pursue their happiness in their own way. This comes across clearly in the essay "On the Common Saying: That may be correct in theory, but it is of no use in practice," published in the wake of the French Revolution in 1793: "Each may seek his happiness in the way that seems good to him, provided he does not infringe upon that freedom of others to strive for a like end" (*TP* 8: 290). Kant goes on to say, in a manner that would gladden the heart of any libertarian, that "a government established on the principle of benevolence toward the people like that of a father toward his children" is "the greatest despotism thinkable" (*TP* 8: 290). The freedom and equality of individuals should be matched by their independence as citizens. Independence is the cornerstone of a thriving civil society. Thus there is always a tension between the authority of the state and the autonomy of individuals that requires constant vigilance on the part of subjects. But Kant's answer to this problem is not to keep government wholly at bay in the manner of the libertarian, but to seek to help bring into being a "patriotic" government. Kant sees a powerful reciprocity between individual freedom and state authority. He is not a libertarian because he sees our right to freedom belonging to us as a "member of a commonwealth" from which we have arisen and "which we must leave behind as a cherished pledge" (*TP* 8: 291).

Kant's position is arguably compatible with Robert Nozick's strikingly Lockean view that "individuals have rights, and there are things no person or group may do to them (without violating their rights)" (1974: ix). However Kant's position leads to a different interpretation being put on the role the possessive verb "have" plays in this sentence. For Kant the claim that individuals naturally *have* rights is primarily a moral claim around which political institutions have to be erected rather than an existentialist or ontological claim that denotes an already established state of affairs. Kant's view can be taken to be more along the lines that all human individuals as intelligible beings *potentially* or provisionally possess rights, such as the right of ownership or the right of free speech; however the historical conditions for their realization represent an arbitrary factor which the theory itself cannot control. Thus the ideal theory has to be confronted with the historically inherited situation where we have to see how "our" rights as rational beings should be realized. Whereas the libertarian Nozick homes in on the individual, and deploys John

Locke's political philosophy, especially its view of the state of nature (Nozick 1974: 10),[1] to see how the individual's rights can be made compatible with those of others, Kant deploys a different conception of the state of nature (as a wholly imagined condition of humans as rational animals[2]) and also pays strong regard to the inherited social conditions. Where a civil society is already in existence (however rudimentary) we have to seek to reform it to bring the ideal arrangements into being. So, in Kant's political philosophy, the individual and the society are the joint central actors in seeking to realize the ideal arrangements. The individual who has acquired rights with Kant is already the *socialized* individual, and the individual who has innate rights is one who anticipates the realization of those provisional rights as a socialized individual in a civil society.

I. The Libertarian Challenge: A Negative Concept of Liberty

Looking at Kant's thinking in the light of libertarian philosophy in this way is also motivated by several readings of my *Kant's Political Philosophy* (1983) which suggest that in some key passages I present a picture of Kant as a libertarian political thinker. Partly in this chapter I try to show that an alternative reading of *Kant's Political Philosophy* is possible which is closer to my original intention in writing the book and presents him more as a mutualist thinker. Partly also in here I shall try to present an understanding of Kant as a mutualist thinker more fully by looking closely at the idea of reciprocity under law. This is an important theme in Kant's writings which has been somewhat overlooked and can lead to a limited picture of the social-welfare provision Kant is prepared to countenance (LeBar 1999: 199). In the doctrine of right at the beginning of the *Metaphysics of Morals* Kant accords the state a significant role in the alleviation of poverty and suggests several lines of economic intervention which aim at radically altering inherited forms of the distribution of property. This is sharply in contrast to contemporary libertarian views. I want to explore closely Kant's justification for this interventionist standpoint and demonstrate how it distances him from the libertarian model of political thought, exemplified by Robert Nozick and Hillel Steiner, whilst at the same time demonstrating his commitment to a powerful conception of individual freedom.

Nozick draws two important implications from his support for the minimal state which is to be limited to a small number of distinctive functions. They are

---

[1] For Locke and Nozick the state of nature is very much a condition that is to be found here and now amongst human beings. As Locke strikingly puts it: "men living together according to reason without a common Superior on Earth, with authority to judge between them, *is properly the state of nature*" (1967: 280).

[2] For a fuller account of how Kant sees the state of nature in the manner of Hume as "a philosophical fiction" which may legitimately be deployed by reason see Williams (1983: 168–9).

that "the state may not use its coercive apparatus for the purpose of getting some citizens to aid others, or in order to prohibit activities to people for their *own* good or protection" (Nozick 1974: ix). There are notable echoes in Kant's writings of such an approach. For Kant it is equally a prime concern for the state to afford protection to the individual against criminal wrongdoing, but for Kant this implies a good deal more than Nozick's "minimal state," since achieving the rule of law requires broader powers than those of merely punishing infractions. Potentially free individuals who respect the rule of law are not just found or existentially present in Kant's political theory, Kant is acutely aware that the modern independent individual has to be created by a process of civilization and development. It seems unlikely that Kant would be inspired by Nozick's skeletal state since as a matter of historical fact (related to this process) Kant thinks it important that there should be an emotional identification between the individual and the state, sufficiently at least for the individual to identify with his or her state both as "the maternal womb" and as the "paternal land, from which and on which he has arisen and which he must also leave behind as a cherished pledge" (*TP* 8: 291). Thus although Kant is highly opposed to the state using its power in a paternalistic way to make individual citizens do what it deems good for them, he does favor the state using its coercive powers to make citizens help each other when in need.

As Hillel Steiner (a left libertarian) notes, it is Kant's concept of legal freedom that is attractive to the libertarian mind.[3] Kant distinguishes between the duties of right and duties of virtue. Duties of right are duties for which external lawgiving is possible and duties of virtue are ones for which external lawgiving is unworkable (*RL* 6: 239). Thus it is possible from the standpoint of strict justice to act in accordance with public law without embracing this as a duty. The standpoint of strict justice leaves the individual entirely free to decide on the grounds for acting. "That is to say, just as right generally has as its object only what is external in actions, so strict right, namely that which is not mingled with anything ethical, requires only external grounds for determining choice; for only then is it pure and not mixed with the precepts of virtue" (*RL* 6: 232). In terms of the distinction which Isaiah Berlin makes between the concepts of negative and positive liberty (1969: 118–32), it is clear that our freedom from the standpoint of right or law within the Kantian perspective conforms with this negative concept. Within the sphere of right we have the space to be ourselves: freedom appears as the absence of restraint. This is an undoubtedly libertarian "moment" within Kant's practical philosophy which represents a fascinating aspect of his doctrine of right. Libertarians sees their own values reflected in

---

[3] "The virtue of an action depends, for Kant, on the intention with which it is done: that is, on whether it's done pursuant to your primary rules (and their prioritization). Whereas its justness has to do with whether and how far it restricts someone else's freedom. Any action can be appraised from both these standpoints" (Steiner 1994: 211). Steiner adds later you can "act justly without acting virtuously" (1994: 212).

Kant's apparent rejection (from the juridical standpoint) of the views, interests, and well-being of other individuals and the institutions of which they are
part in determining our motives in conforming to public law. Kant has great
respect for the private sphere where we must be free to determine our own ends
independently of the authority of the state. This is not because he recommends
that we take irresponsible attitudes to our action but because he wants us to be
wholly unhindered in determining the grounds for our action in so far as they
concern our own happiness.

Kant's negative take on the concept of liberty as regarded from the political and legal standpoint also comes out, as we have seen, in his treatment
of freedom in "On the Common Saying: That may be correct in theory, but
it is of no use in practice," where there is a clear restriction placed on what
Nozick calls "paternalistic aggression" or "using or threatening force for the
benefit of the person against whom it is wielded" (1974: 34). Kant sees the
interests of each individual as distinct. Each person has their own life to lead;
they must pursue their projects from the standpoint of their own preferences.
Clearly Kant endorses the view that everyone has the right to make their
own mistakes, and conversely the right to be the originator of their own success. Emancipation involves thinking for yourself and above all acting for
yourself.

II. Offending Passages

There are self-evidently libertarian strands in Kant's moral and political
thought. But this does not make him into a fully-fledged libertarian. The
dangers of conceding too much to this libertarian strand in Kant's thinking
are made apparent by the critical readings of my *Kant's Political Philosophy*
dealing with welfare. Two authors who concern themselves with the issue as
it arises in Kant's doctrine of right, Susan Holtman Williams and Alexander
Kaufman, have suggested that in *Kant's Political Philosophy* I overemphasize
the libertarian aspect of Kant's social thinking at the expense of its humanitarian dimension (Kaufman 1999: 4, 26; Holtman 2004). The passages that
have received the most attention occur where I am discussing Kant's notion
of the "well-being of the state" (*Heil des Staates*). There I argue that "Kant's
notion of the 'well-being of the State' is based on the premiss that the principal agent in the pursuit of welfare is the rational individual. The State must
not, and cannot, pursue his welfare on his behalf" (1983: 194). I note that for
Kant the well-being of a state arises not from the happiness of its subjects
but from the harmony in the relationship between the three independent powers of the state: the legislature, executive, and judiciary. I suggest that this
inevitably leads to a limited role for government in relation to the flourishing
of a country's citizens: initiative for this has primarily to come from citizens

themselves. I impute to Kant "laissez-faire and antipaternalist sentiments" that leave "little for the government to do other than to deal with disasters and emergencies" (1983: 196). However, I do not conclude from this that Kant is a fully-fledged libertarian but seek rather to imply that Kant is a liberal in the style of John Stuart Mill and Kant's own former student Wilhelm von Humboldt.

Susan Williams Holtman includes me among those writers on Kant who attribute to him a minimalist view of the state. "According to the minimalist, social welfare programs that supply basic necessities are legitimate only as a tool to insure against crises (political upheaval, famine, severe economic depression) that threaten the state's very existence" (2004: 86–7). Although Holtman does not mention libertarianism in her article it appears that her object is to refute strictly libertarian interpretations of Kant. For her,

> the minimalist interpretation was common among Kant scholars for a time during the second half of the 20th century. Though many recent interpreters have abandoned it, it remains a popular understanding of Kant particularly among non-specialists. (Holtman 2004: 87)

Arguably Holtman tends too much in the direction of overlooking the "libertarian moment" in Kant's political philosophy, however the general drift of her argument quite correctly highlights the humanitarian, socially interventionist side of Kant's political outlook. There is a need to balance Kant's general attitude of noninterference at the individual level with his commitment at a societal level to creating a genuine civil society where all subjects have the opportunity to flourish. This need for balance is not, I now recognize in retrospect, properly brought out in *Kant's Political Philosophy*.

The libertarian moment in Kant has to be accommodated within both his wider moral philosophy which emphasizes a strong regard for others as ends in themselves and his empirically sensitive political philosophy which recognizes the nonideal nature of current social relationships where many are not capable of functioning independently. Political intervention is necessary both in the first instance to establish independent citizenship and subsequently to preserve it. Thus both the libertarian and the mutualist (or, put more bluntly, the socialist) moment in Kant's thinking have to be kept in focus. In the final section of this chapter I explore how this can be done.

III. Why Kant is not a Libertarian

However one tries Kant cannot be pushed wholly into the libertarian camp because there are two fundamental ways in which he marks off his political philosophy from that school. The most striking difference is, first, that in his moral philosophy as a whole the theory of virtue and the theory of right although distinct are also complementary.[4] The highest political good (perpetual peace) and the highest ethical good are indeed different but they are also strongly related.[5] Libertarians see right as justice as detachable from ethics or the theory of virtue. Steiner for instance describes his liberalism as "an exploration of justice alone" that is "not derived from any particular conception of what constitutes 'a good life' " (Steiner 1994: 282). The idea of the unencumbered individual that determines wholly from a self-referential point of view what he or she should do is not one Kant shares—even if it is a standpoint permitted within his system from the perspective of strict right. The standpoint preeminently recommended from the perspective of Kant's system as a whole is voluntary obedience to the moral law. It is far from clear what ultimate view of the moral aspirations of the human individual that libertarians hold, since they think that as far as is possible this is something for individuals themselves to determine, but Kant has many specific ideas on what morally we—of course acting on our own volition—ought properly to aspire to. It is difficult (although admittedly not impossible) to see the libertarian subscribing to Kant's ideals of virtue as "our own perfection" and "the happiness of others" (TL 6: 385).

We have noted that Kant and libertarians converge on the point that legal freedom entails an absence of internal constraint on our motives in acting. Juridical law ought not to seek to interfere with freedom to set our own goals. But with Kant this legal space created for independent action is to be deployed not to exercise an arbitrary autonomy but rather for us to pursue virtue which is attained through self-restraint and guidance by the moral law. From the standpoint of public law we may of course do otherwise, but from the standpoint of Kant's moral philosophy as a whole—which encompasses ethics and right—we should exercise our freedom in a presumed realm of ends with others. Public law provides legitimate external restraints on our action but does not extend to our choice of ends because the free person should choose and will choose ends which are compatible with the external freedom of others. Where the libertarian sees a loophole—or, more charitably, a sphere—for the unfettered deployment of individual discretion the Kantian will see an opportunity for the pursuit of duties that are also ends such as "cultivating our faculties" (TL 6: 387).

Libertarian interpretations of Kant's notion of legal freedom also overlook the fundamentally reciprocal nature of Kant's concept of political and legal freedom. Kant is a republican and the libertarian aspect of his thinking has to fit within this mold. As legal freedom is enjoyed only with others it cannot simply focus on the minimization of interference and restraint. What Kantians are looking for

---

[4] This is a point which Isaiah Berlin strongly sensed. Although in some respects he interprets Kant wrongly as an advocate of positive freedom in his political philosophy, Berlin does register correctly Kant's moral antipathy to regarding "all ends of equal value" (Berlin 1969: 153n).

[5] On the nonindividualistic aspect of Kant's ethics, see Wood (2008: 78–9).

are the conditions where the freedom of one person under the restrain of coercive public law is compatible with the freedom of all others. Unlike the libertarian, the Kantian political philosopher has to absorb the standpoint of the limiting others within the vision of one's own freedom. As Kant puts it in *Perpetual Peace*:

> rightful (hence external) freedom cannot be defined, as it usually is, by the warrant to do whatever one wants provided one does no wrong to anyone. For what does warrant mean? The possibility of an action insofar as one thereby does no wrong to anyone. So the definition would go as follows: freedom is the possibility of actions whereby one does no wrong to anyone. One does no wrong to anyone (one may do what one wants) provided one does no wrong to anyone, hence it is an empty tautology. My (rightful) freedom is, instead, to be defined as follows: it is the warrant to obey no other external laws than those to which I could have given my consent. (*ZeF* 8: 350)

As the mutuality with others is a condition of exercising liberty so others have to be subsumed as compliant with the exercise of our liberty. Clearly this cannot be an open-ended compliance. We may have an infinite choice in terms of the grounds of our actions but we cannot expect complete tolerance with regard to their external impact. Potential collisions in terms of their external impact have to be carefully monitored and an agreement reached on mutual limits. When deliberating about public law we have to take into account both our ethical and juridical selves.

In deducing rights Kant is just as much a social-contract theorist as a state-of-nature thinker. The a priori model that Kant deploys to deduce the rights that individuals should enjoy in a properly organized civil society emphasizes, in other words, not only the starting point of an imagined state of nature but also the point of synthesis in a social contract. This is an important consideration in evaluating Kant's political theory from the perspective of libertarianism. The libertarian has always in view the original supposed condition of the complete lack of limitation on the scope of action of the individual and any social contract that precedes an actual civil society has always to work around it. But Kant is as conscious of the need for an agreement amongst individuals (symbolized by the social contract) as he is of the original condition of complete liberty, so his view of the ideal social order embodies a dimension of solidarity *in* the realization of outward freedom.[6] Thus there are responsibilities

---

[6] These issues are discussed in Varden (2008). She argues that for Kant "civil society is not primarily a prudential requirement for justice; it is not merely a necessary evil or a moral response to combat our corrupting nature or our tendency to act viciously, thoughtlessly or in a biased manner. Rather civil society is constitutive of rightful relations among persons because only in civil society can we interact in ways reconcilable with each other's innate right to freedom," and she concludes that "Kant's account, therefore, provides ideal reasons to support the claim that voluntarism cannot be the liberal idea of political obligations" (1).

that Kant is happy for the state to take on that the libertarian finds at best strange and at worst unacceptable.

Two such responsibilities stand out. The first is the responsibility that the supreme authority in the state has to maintain those individuals, such as orphans, the elderly, and the sick, who are unable to help themselves (*RL* 6: 326), and the second is the responsibility that the public authority has to guide the national economy, administer the public finances, and manage the police (*RL* 6: 325). The state is able to take on these responsibilities with Kant's model because it relies so strongly on the social contract for its authority. This comes out most clearly in the justification of the taxation of the better off to help the needy. This can occur because "the general will of the people has united itself into a society which is to maintain itself perpetually; and for this end it has submitted itself to the internal authority of the state in order to maintain those members of the society who are unable to maintain themselves" (*RL* 6: 326). In this context what the libertarian interpretation of Kant most overlooks is the transition that occurs from the first development of Kant's model in the imagined sphere of the state of nature to its actual realization in a current civil society. What occurs in this transition is that the authority of the state over the individual grows. Kant believes that one cannot rely on the sketch of rights in the state of nature to bring them into being empirically, for that to occur actual civil societies have to come into existence. This can occur only through coercion—an irresistible public force has to be brought into being (*RL* 6: 307). This need is so urgent that the manner of achieving it is almost a matter of indifference to the citizen of the subsequently existing civil society. In demanding that historically existing societies should embody the rights to which we are entitled as human beings, the a priori analysis has to be supplemented by a more concrete reasoning taking into account the institutions of a specific society. Here Kant begins from the premise that "the presently existing legislative authority ought to be obeyed, whatever its origin" (*RL* 6: 319).

The model of the origins of civil society which includes the ideas of the state of nature and the social contract does not for Kant parallel the actual development of modern states but is rather a measure of their conformity to reason. In his philosophy of history it is clear that he sees progress coming about as much through violent conflict amongst individuals and states as by agreement. The model has therefore always to be juxtaposed with the actual conditions of the societies being evaluated in such a way that the analyst always respects what has already been achieved by public authority. This weighs Kant's model in favor of the social-contract consideration as a context within which the state of nature conditions are observed. The united general will is the lynchpin of the model. Individual rights, such as the key one of property ownership, rest just as much on the approbation of the right by the general will as they do on our inborn rights. Kant rejects the Lockean deduction of property rights within the state of nature on the grounds that it supports only empirical possession whereas he is also concerned to establish a simultaneous intelligible possession. There is an irreducible social dimension to property ownership. Property must be conceived of as being held through the consent of others. This can be seen as coming about only through the supposition of "an innate possession in common of the surface of the earth and on a general will corresponding a priori to it" (*RL* 6: 250).

IV. Kant and William Godwin

It is difficult to characterize the libertarian position in a way that fully permits us to contrast Kant's political philosophy accurately with it. Libertarianism as a political philosophy largely has, as we have noted, developed since Kant's day and its main proponents are twentieth-century figures. However there is one contemporary of Kant, the English political theorist William Godwin, whose ideas prefigure those of the libertarians and is a well-known source for the ideas of their occasional bedfellows the anarchists. As Godwin is one of the most liberal of the early anarchist thinkers arguably he might best be characterized as a protolibertarian thinker rather than a full-blooded anarchist.[7] Godwin published his major work *Enquiry Concerning Political Justice* in 1793. We can see the libertarian overtones of his thinking in his contention that "the injustice and violence of men in a state of society produced the demand for government" but, although government was "intended to suppress injustice," "it offers new occasions and temptations for the commission of it" (Godwin 1976: 75–6). Godwin treats the centralization of political power with the utmost suspicion, contrasting the proper independence that should be enjoyed by the individual with the overweening majesty of the sovereign state. Government, in his view, "by concentrating the force of the community" "gives occasion to the wild projects of calamity, to oppression, despotism, war and conquest" (76). Godwin does not reject the role of government outright but, as with today's libertarian, he believes its further growth beyond the minimum to preserve peace has immeasurably harmful effects.

Equality is of considerable importance to Godwin in the realization of his just society. According to him "we are partakers of a common nature, and the same causes that contribute to the benefit of one will contribute to the benefit of another" (Godwin 1976: 183). We do not need to look to others, least of all to government, to tell us what is right. We are all endowed with reason which we are all capable of employing to judge what is true. We ought not then under any circumstances seek to hand over this capacity to judge to another individual or body. The use of our reason will tell us that "there are certain opportunities

---

[7] Cf. Sowell (2007: 127). Sowell argues here that Godwin can legitimately be presented as a contributor to libertarianism, indeed as much so as Ayn Rand or Friedrich Hayek.

and certain situations most advantageous to every human being, and it is just that these should be communicated to all, as well as the general economy will permit" (183). It is unnecessary to impose authority to bring this about from the outside, for each individual's private judgment will tell him what to do with respect to his neighbor and fellow citizen. Godwin envisages the path to progress lies through the severe curtailment of national authority. In keeping with his deep distrust of any form of government Godwin is extremely suspicious of the power of national assemblies. He does not believe that there can be such a thing as a *corporate* person. As he sees it, a multitude of persons remains a multitude even if they are artificially constrained by a sovereign. The will of a sovereign can never be more than the will of one person since "the acts of the society can never rise above the suggestions of this or that individual" (550). Thus national assemblies serve only to bring about a false unanimity, which is justified only by an appeal to necessity. Gradually, Godwin thinks, national assemblies should release their hold over local communities so that true justice might be served. Great optimism attends Godwin's vision of political progress. He believes that our essential goodness will be brought out by the relaxing of centralized political constraints. For him national political authority is justified only as a temporary expedient. He concludes in a highly libertarian mode that

> government is, abstractly taken, an evil, an usurpation of the private judgement and individual conscience of mankind; and that, however we may be obliged to admit it as a necessary evil for the present, it behoves us, as the friends of reason and the human species, to admit as little of it as possible, and carefully to observe, whether, in consequence of the gradual illumination of the human mind, that little may not hereafter be diminished. (Godwin 1976: 408)

There is no doubting that Godwin's political theory as a whole, with its reliance on an immutable reason to which we can all look to frame our conduct (Godwin 1976: 236),[8] differs a good deal from the thinking of today's libertarians; however, there are strong common foundations that his thinking shares with libertarianism which allow us to draw out important differences from Kant's political reasoning. I mention some of them here. The suspicion of national authority is not one that Kant shares. Even in advocating a federation of free states as the way forward for the world Kant relies upon the achievements of progressive nations that have adopted republican governments to press it along. Kant also has powerful objections to relying solely on the private judgments of individuals to direct government. He is, unlike the libertarian, as prone to stress the duties

---

[8] Godwin asks "who is it that has authority to make laws?" "The answer to this question is exceedingly simple: Legislation, as it has been usually understood, is not an affair of human competence. Immutable reason is the true legislator, and its decrees it behoves us to investigate" (Godwin 1976: 183).

that subjects possess as their rights. In many respects Kant shares the distinction that Rousseau makes between the particular will of the individual and the general will and Kant clearly believes that a society ought to be directed by a united general will rather than succumbing to the appeals of an outright individualism. Unlike Godwin, Kant thinks effective government essential to individual flourishing, and does not portray it necessarily as representing a diminution of individual freedom. Indeed that sphere of personal discretion that libertarians find most attractive in Kant, the sphere of autonomy sketched out so clearly in the *Groundwork to the Metaphysics of Morals*, becomes possible for Kant only through the creation of state authority in a civil society. Thus although there is a clash that exists between paternalist government and individual freedom Kant sees no clash between a patriotic government and free citizenship.

The libertarian interpretation of Kant emphasizes the independence of individuals as highlighted in the essay "What is Enlightenment?" in the invocation to "argue as much as you will and about whatever you will" at the expense of the second clause of the epigram which sternly notes *"but obey!"* (*VA* 8: 37) In his political philosophy Kant is as much concerned with the proper conditions for the exercising, as he is with the flourishing, of our innate right to freedom. Unlike the libertarian Kant acknowledges that "everywhere there are restrictions on freedom"; what concerns him, however is "what sort of restrictions hinder enlightenment, and what sort does not hinder but instead promotes it" (*VA* 8: 37). Thus Kant does not enter into political philosophy with the aim simply of limiting the hold of state authority on the individual but rather to seek out those forms of state authority which enable us to arise from our self-incurred immaturity properly to think and act for ourselves.

V. Conclusion

Society and self are intensely intertwined in Kant's understanding of external freedom. So the libertarian strand in his thought has to be accommodated within a view of society that demands strong elements of mutuality. In order to pursue happiness in the way we individually see fit we have to accommodate an authoritative state with powers of intervention most libertarians deplore. The state that commands us we must envisage as structuring its power in ways we ourselves shape through our representatives in the legislature and the executive. Although we cannot resist, much less rebel against, the state we have the right to have our complaints against it heard. The state enables our freedom, but to do so we have to obey its authority, even where we may consider it to be acting wrongly.

Moreover, one marked feature of much libertarian thinking is its insistence on the principle of self-ownership. Again this principle derives from the political philosophy of John Locke. The assumption of self-ownership is a key step in his deduction of property rights in the state of nature. I get to own what I acquire in the natural condition because it is shaped from nature by my limbs. As my limbs are mine so also the things I shape with them can be regarded as mine. Libertarians like Robert Nozick recognize that Locke's arguments for the derivation of property from "body rights" does not work as well as Locke had thought but none the less the adhere to the principle of self-ownership (cf. Flikschuh 2007: 81). Libertarians may embrace this principle with such enthusiasm because they see it as providing a powerful foundation for the independence of the individual both from others and nature. However, it is not a view that Kant shares. In his *Lectures on Ethics* he explicitly argues against the idea of self-ownership and that in a context where it is often deemed essential by libertarians: sexual relations. In a discussion of prostitution Kant states:

> Man cannot dispose over himself because he is not a thing; he is not his own property; to say that he is would be self-contradictory; for in so far as he is a person he is a Subject in whom the ownership for things can be rested, and if he were his own property, he would be a thing over which he could have ownership... Accordingly, a man is not at his own disposal. He is not entitled to sell a limb, not even one of his teeth. But to allow one's person for profit to be used by another for the satisfaction of sexual desire, to make oneself an Object of demand, is to dispose of oneself as over a thing and to make of one a thing on which another satisfies his appetite, just as he satisfies his hunger upon a steak.[9]

One final concept that Kant deploys which must throw considerable doubt on his libertarian credentials is that of the "supreme proprietor." The concept underlies Kant's understanding of individual property ownership, a cornerstone of freedom both for libertarians and Kant. "This supreme proprietorship" is an idea "of the civil union that serves to represent in accordance with concepts of right the necessary union of the private property of everyone within the people under a general public possessor" (*RL* 6: 323). Kant notes that this general public possession does not involve the direct ownership of the land by the sovereign but rather indicates the power the sovereign enjoys over the ascription of property holdings. For Kant one can say of this supreme proprietor that he "possesses nothing of his own except himself," "but one can also say that he possesses everything since he has the right of command over the people, to whom external things belong" (*RL* 6: 324) Final authority for the division of property amongst the people within a state lies with the sovereign. Thus in strong contrast to the usual libertarian view, for Kant property rights emanate from the state outwards (albeit in the form of the united general will) and not upwards or inwards towards the state from individuals.

---

[9] Quoted in Morelli (1999). Moreover, this "passage clearly shows Kant's rejection of what is sometimes called the 'self-ownership' view of the body" (320). The passage can be found in the original at *V-Mol Collins* 27: 386.

It is very much to Kant's credit—and this demonstrates the fecundity of his political philosophy—that a variety of doctrines can claim inspiration from his work. However, just as with liberalism and democratic socialism—which can also claim affinity with Kant's political writings—so also the libertarian can learn a great deal from the cautious remarks which Kant makes about the relationship between the individual and the state that can give pause to think more carefully about the larger conclusions concerning political affiliation that are being drawn.

Bibliography

Berlin, I. (1969) "Two Concepts of Liberty," in *Four Essays on Liberty*. Oxford: Oxford University Press.

Byrd, S., and Hruschka, J. (eds.) (2006) *Kant and Law*. Farnham: Ashgate.

Flikschuh, K. (2007) *Freedom*. Cambridge: Polity.

Godwin, W. (1976 [1793]) *Enquiry Concerning Political Justice*. Harmondsworth: Penguin.

Holtman, S. W. (2004) "Kantian Justice and Poverty Relief," *Kant-Studien* 95(1): 86–106.

Kant, I. (1996) *Practical Philosophy*. Tr. and ed. M. J. Gregor. Cambridge: Cambridge University Press.

Kaufman, A. (1999) *Welfare in the Kantian State*. Oxford: Oxford University Press.

LeBar, M. (1999) "Kant on Welfare," *Canadian Journal of Philosophy* 29 (2): 225–50. Reprinted in Byrd and Hruschka (2006: 245–72).

Locke, J. (1967 [1690]) *Two Treatises of Government*. Cambridge: Cambridge University Press.

Morelli, M. (1999) "Commerce in Organs: A Kantian Critique," *Journal of Social Philosophy* 30(2): 315–24.

Nozick, R. (1974) *Anarchy, State and Utopia*. Oxford: Blackwell.

Otteson, R. J. (2009) "Kantian Individualism and Political Libertarianism," *Independent Review* 13(3): 489–509.

Sowell, T. (2007) *A Conflict of Visions: Ideological Origins of Political Struggles*. New York: Basic Books.

Steiner, H. (1994) *An Essay on Rights*. Oxford: Blackwell.

Varden, H. (2008) "Kant's Non-voluntarist Conception of Political Obligations: Why Justice is Impossible in the State of Nature," *Kantian Review* 13(2): 1–45.

Williams, H. (1983) *Kant's Political Philosophy*. Oxford: Blackwell.

Wood, A. W. (2008) *Kantian Ethics*. Cambridge: Cambridge University Press.

12

Kant's Practical Justification of Freedom

Henry E. Allison

Practical justification in Kant comes in two distinct forms, which reflect the different sorts of proposition that require justification.[1] One concerns the justification of practical propositions and it encompasses both the categorical imperative, as the fundamental principle of morality, and particular categorical imperatives or duties such as "Never lie." Practical justification in this sense might also be termed "justification of the practical" and is a task that is generally viewed as encumbent on any moral theory. Kant attempted a justification of the categorical imperative as the fundamental principle of morality in both the third section of *Groundwork*, where he presented it as a deduction of the categorical imperative, which is at least loosely modeled on the transcendental deduction of the categories in the first *Critique*, and in the second *Critique*, where it took the form of an appeal to the consciousness of the moral law as a "fact of reason." By contrast, *MS*, Kant's last systematic work in moral theory, is devoted largely to the justification of particular duties.

The second type of practical justification concerns certain *theoretical* propositions. For Kant these are propositions regarding God, immortality, and freedom, which in *KpV* he refers to as "postulates of pure practical reason," because morality requires that they be presupposed, even though they are not susceptible of a theoretical justification. It is with this type of practical justification, which to distinguish it from the first might be termed "practical justification proper," with which I shall be concerned here. Or, more precisely, I shall be concerned with one aspect of such justification.

The situation is complicated, however, in two ways. The first is by a distinction that Kant draws between the kind of practical justification that he finds available for God and immortality, on the one hand, and freedom, on the other. Although in the second *Critique* Kant includes freedom along with God and

---

[1] This chapter, originally wirtten for this volume, was first published in Allison (2012: 110–23), and is here reproduced by permission of Oxford University Press.

immortality among the postulates of pure practical reason in the Dialectic of pure practical reason (*KpV* 5: 132–3), he does not treat it *merely* as a postulate, since in the Analytic he offers a deduction of freedom from the moral law as a fact of reason (*KpV* 5: 47–50). Thus, while God and immortality are postulated as necessary conditions of the highest good on the dual grounds that we have a duty to promote the highest good and the familiar "ought implies can" principle, Kant holds that freedom "in the strictest, that is, the transcendental sense," is (again by the "ought implies can" principle) a necessary condition of morality in general (*KpV* 5: 29).[2]

The second complication concerns the difference in the way in which Kant endeavors to provide a practical justification of freedom in various texts, particularly in *GMS* and *KpV*. In the former work, Kant links the justification of freedom with a reflection on the consciousness of being a rational agent, that is, having the capacity to act in accordance with one's representation of laws or on principles, without any special reference to *moral* laws or principles. In some of his later writings, however, most notably *KpV* and *RGV*, Kant maintains that it is only our consciousness of standing under the categorical imperative (as "the fact of reason") that assures us, from the practical point of view, of our freedom. In the first two parts of this paper I shall deal briefly with each of these attempts at a practical justification of freedom, while in the third I shall offer some reflections on the ontological issues posed by both of these modes of practical justification.

I.

Early in *GMS* III, Kant remarks that "to every rational being possessed of a will we must also lend the idea of freedom as the only one on which he can act" (*GMS* 4: 448).[3] In his lectures on metaphysics from about that time, he makes essentially the same point, claiming that, "Freedom is a mere idea and to act according to this idea is what it means to be free in the practical sense," to which he adds: "Freedom is practically necessary—man must therefore act according to an idea of freedom,

---

[2] In the second *Critique* Kant defines freedom in the transcendental sense as "independence from everything empirical and so from nature generally" (*KpV* 5: 97). Kant generally contrasts it with "comparative concept of freedom," by which he understands the Leibnizian conception. It is the latter that he contemptuously dismisses as "nothing better than the freedom of a turnspit" (*KpV* 5: 97). In the Dialectic of the first *Critique* Kant defines transcendental freedom as "the power [*Vermögen*] of beginning a state spontaneously [*von Selbst*]" (*KrV* A533/B561). There, and in his lectures on metaphysics, Kant generally contrasts transcendental with practical freedom, which he defines in a number of different ways. For my analysis of this issue, see Allison (1990: 54–70).

[3] Translations from *GMS* are my own. Quotations from other works of Kant use the translations from the Cambridge Edition of the Works of Immanuel Kant.

and he cannot act otherwise" (*V-Mol/Mron* 29: 898). Our initial task is to uncover and evaluate the line of argument underlying this sweeping claim.[4]

I begin with a brief look at Kant's first published statement of this line of argument in a review of a deterministic moral theory by Johann Heinrich Schulz, which appeared in 1783 (two years before *GMS*).[5] In response to Schulz's speculative determinism, which Kant characterizes as fatalism and compares to the doctrines of Joseph Priestley, Kant makes two main points. The first turns on a sharp contrast between the speculative and practical points of view. According to this line of thought, when confronted with the question of what ought to be done, even the speculative fatalist, for whom the future is presumably already decided, will unavoidably proceed as if the decision were up to him, that is, he will "always act *as if he were free*" (*RS* 8: 13). The second is a parallel between the freedom to *think*, that is, the idea that one's judgment is based on objective grounds, which the cognizer takes as reasons to believe, rather than being the product of "subjectively determining causes" and the freedom to *choose*, which is presumably likewise based on objective grounds (*RS* 8: 14).

The restatement of this line of argument in *GMS* III is contained in a paragraph with the heading: "*Freedom must be presupposed as a property of the will of all rational beings*" (*GMS* 4: 447–8), which Kant evidently regarded as a preparation for his central argument rather than as a constituent of it.[6] The overall task of *GMS* III is to establish the validity of the moral law or categorical imperative, which has already been shown to be a synthetic *a priori* practical proposition. Building on the previously established connection between the *concepts* of the categorical imperative and the autonomy of the will, Kant begins the section by arguing for what I have termed the "reciprocity thesis," that is, the proposition that "a free will and a will under moral laws are one and the same" (*GMS* 4: 447).[7] Given this thesis, the natural strategy for Kant to pursue would be to argue that we are free, from which the claim that we really are subject to the categorical imperative would follow immediately. But since Kant was precluded from adopting such a strategy by the teaching of the first *Critique* that theoretical reason is incapable of proving (or disproving) the reality of freedom in the requisite transcendental sense, he was led to adopt

---

[4] In Allison (1997) I dealt with this thesis from a more thematic, less historical point of view, arguing against thinkers such as Dennett and McDowell, who endeavor, albeit in quite different ways, to give a naturalistic reading to this claim. The present account will be more sharply focused on the Kantian texts.

[5] Schulz's work, the first part of which likewise appeared in 1783 and was the only part that Kant reviewed, was entitled: *Versuch einer Anleitung zur Sittenlehre für alle Menschen, ohne Untersschied der Religion, nebst einem Anhange von den Todesstrafen* [Attempt at an introduction to a doctrine of morals for all human beings, regardless of religion, together with an appendix on capital punishment].

[6] See *GMS* 4: 447.

[7] I analyze the reciprocity thesis, which also appears in slightly different form in *KpV* in Allison (1986; 1990, 201–213).

the fallback strategy of arguing for the necessity of presupposing freedom and contending that for practical purposes this is equivalent to proving that we really are free, that is, that we really are subject to the categorical imperative.

Kant prefaces his account by emphasizing the necessity of establishing the strict universality of the attribution of freedom. In order to serve the purpose of Kant's argument, freedom must be attributed to the will of all rational beings or, as he also puts it, to every rational being with a will. This follows from the combination of the underlying methodological assumption of *GMS* and the reciprocity thesis. The assumption is that inasmuch as morality expresses a law for every rational being as such, its principle "must be bound up (fully *a priori*) with the concept of the will of a rational being as such" (*GMS* 4: 426). And since the reciprocity thesis maintains that freedom is the property of the will from which subjection to moral requirements is derived, it follows that the legitimization of morality, which for Kant means the categorical imperative, depends crucially on the premise that freedom is a property of the will of every rational being. Although the restriction of the attribution of freedom to rational beings with a will may seem trivial, since in order to have a free will it is necessary to have a will, we shall see that it is crucial to Kant's argument.

Our immediate concern, however, is with Kant's actual argument, which contains two steps, each of which is presented by Kant in the form of a bald assertion:

> 1) Now I say: Every being that cannot act other than *under the idea of freedom*, is for that very reason actually free in a practical respect, that is, all laws that are inseparably bound up with freedom are valid for it, just as if its will had been shown to be free in itself and in theoretical philosophy. (*GMS* 4: 448)
>
> 2) Now I assert that to every rational being that has a will we must necessarily lend also the idea of freedom, under which he acts. (*GMS* 4: 448).

As Kant makes clear in a footnote, the point of the first step is "to free ourselves from the burden that pressures theory" (*GMS* 4: 448), which is to say that even if the theoretical question regarding the reality of freedom remains unsettled, the necessity of appealing to the *idea* of it suffices to establish the validity of the categorical imperative. In evaluating this assertion, it is crucial to determine what is meant by acting under the idea of freedom and the grounds for the alleged necessity of so acting. To begin with, it seems clear that if we take acting under the idea of freedom to mean something like believing that one is free, the argument lacks plausibility; for it appears to be open to the determinist simply to deny that he really believes that he is free, even if he might grant that he sets aside his determinist convictions when engaged in practical deliberations.

But if acting under the idea of freedom does not mean acting with the belief that one is free, what does it mean? The answer lies in the nature of an idea for

Kant, which, simply put, is a normative principle that is a product of reason. Otherwise expressed, it is a *thought* that one necessarily brings with oneself, when one takes oneself to be deliberating or acting, not a *fact* that we might discover about ourselves through introspection or in some other manner. In Kantian terms, it is a regulative idea that governs our conception of ourselves as agents. Moreover, as such, it has normative force. In Sellarsian language, to act under this idea is to place oneself in the logical space of [practical] reasons and, therefore, to take oneself as subject to rational norms of both a moral and prudential sort.

This explanation of Kant's first claim puts us in a position to understand the second, which was already articulated in the review of Schulz and which turns on what he there termed "freedom to think." Kant does not mean what is usually understood by that expression, namely, the freedom (independence from external constraint) to hold whatever beliefs seem warranted. Indeed, "freedom" is not the appropriate term, since what Kant has in mind is really the spontaneity that for him is an ineliminable ingredient in discursive cognition. The basic idea is that the human understanding is spontaneous in the sense that it is not a mere receptacle of sensory data (this is how Kant regards sensibility); rather, it is an active faculty that takes what is sensibly given and brings it under concepts.[8] Schematically expressed, the understanding takes (judges) x as F, where the "taking" is an act of spontaneity, something that the subject does, rather than, like association, a causal process that occurs in the subject's mind/brain. As Kant puts it in yet another bald assertion:

> Now I assert that one cannot possibly think a reason that in its own consciousness is directed from outside with regard to its own judgments; for in that case the subject would attribute the determination of his power of judgment to an impulse rather than to reason. (*GMS* 4: 448)

This thesis, which Kant expressly limits to the first-person point of view ("in its own consciousness"), sets the stage for completing his argument for the necessity of lending the idea freedom to the will of every rational being that acts, by extending, as he had already done in the Schulz review, the conclusion from reason in its cognitive to its practical capacity. Thus Kant writes:

> It [reason] must regard itself as the author of its principles independently of alien influences; consequently, as practical reason or as the will of a rational being, it must be regarded by itself as free, that is, the will of a rational being can be a will of its own only under the idea of freedom and must therefore in a practical respect be attributed to all rational beings. (*GMS* 4: 448)

---

[8] Elsewhere I characterize this as "epistemic spontaneity" to contrast it with the "practical spontaneity" that Kant attributes to the will. See Allison (1990: 36–8 and passim; 1996: esp. 129–42).

Kant is here affirming a symmetry between theoretical and practical reason or, more precisely, between epistemic and practical spontaneity, both of which are expressly linked to a first-person point of view and speak to how a (thinking or acting) subject is rationally constrained to regard itself, qua cognizer or agent. Just as one cannot regard oneself as a cognizer without conceiving of oneself as a subject who judges something to be the case by bringing sensory data under concepts on the basis of normative principles (principles of the understanding), so one cannot regard oneself as a rational agent without taking oneself as incorporating the data of volition (incentives) into one's maxims (subjective principles of action) under the direction of normative rules (hypothetical and categorical imperatives).[9]

Even assuming the general framework of Kant's account of cognition, which cannot be dealt with here, there are three problematic features of this line of argument, which may have been recognized by Kant and help to explain his relegation of this relatively straightforward approach to a merely preparatory status and to embark on an extremely complex deduction, which makes extensive use of the concept of an intelligible world and his "two-standpoint" doctrine. The first we may term the "bindingness problem." By raising the specter of a "hidden circle" (*GMS* 4: 453), Kant seems to be suggesting that the argument from the necessity of presupposing freedom is insufficient to account for the claim that the categorical imperative is really binding on all rational agents, even when strengthened with the thesis that whatever laws are valid for a being whose freedom can be established theoretically are also valid for one who can act only under the idea of freedom.[10] Although Kant is notoriously unclear at this point, his worry seems to be that the most that the above argument can prove is that if we must presuppose that we are free, then (by the reciprocity thesis) we must likewise presuppose that we are subject to the categorical imperative; but this falls short of showing that we really are bound by it, as a deduction requires.

A second source of possible concern is the assumption of a strict symmetry or isomorphism between cognition and volition with respect to their spontaneity. In fact, we have evidence from both the first *Critique* and the *Reflexionen* that Kant was agnostic or at least somewhat ambivalent regarding the move from theoretical to practical spontaneity, with the latter denoting a causality

---

[9] I am here referring to what I term the "incorporation thesis," which I take to lie at the heart of Kant's conception of rational agency. In its canonical formulation it states that "freedom of the power of choice [*Willkür*] has the characteristic, entirely peculiar to it, that it cannot be determined to action through any incentive *except so far as the human being has incorporated it into his maxim* (has made it into a universal rule for himself, according to which he conducts himself); only in this way can an incentive, whatever it may be, coexist with the absolute spontaneity of the power of choice" (*RGV* 6: 24). For my discussions of this thesis, see Allison (1990: 5–6, 40, 47–8 151, 189–90; 1996: 118–23, 130–35, 139–42).

[10] For my analysis of the circularity problem, see Allison (1990: 218–21).

through reason.[11] Moreover, I believe that Kant can be taken as acknowledging the problematic nature of this move in *GMS* III, through the restriction of the scope of his arguments to rational beings with wills. This reflects Kant's recognition of the conceptual possibility of rational beings *without wills*, that is, cognizers who are not agents, or, what amounts to the same thing, beings with reason but not *practical* reason.[12] Although one might think that Kant could dismiss such a worry as idle, on the grounds that we are conscious of our agency and it can have no effect from the practical point of view, the fact is that he did not.

Finally, an additional problematic feature of Kant's move from epistemic to practical spontaneity involves the relationship between two different senses of freedom recognized by Kant: spontaneity and autonomy or, as he also describes them, a negative and a positive conception of freedom (*GMS* 4: 446). By the former Kant understands the opposite of natural necessity, that is, a causality that is effective "independently of alien causes determining it" (*GMS* 4: 446). By the latter he understands "the property of the will of being a law to itself" (*GMS* 4: 447). Although Kant says at one point that the concept of the latter "flows" (*fleisst*) from that of the former (*GMS* 4: 446), this is not obviously the case.[13] In other words, it seems perfectly possible that a will might be free in the contracausal sense of not being causally necessitated by antecedent conditions and yet ineluctably heteronomous in the sense that its menu of incentives (or motives) all stem ultimately from its sensuous nature.[14] Moreover, since it is quite clear that the bindingness of the categorical imperative requires autonomy, it follows that, even if it were successful, the argument from epistemic to practical spontaneity would be inadequate to establish the goal of the deduction. But since analyzing that argument is not my concern here, I shall abandon *GMS* at this point and consider Kant's very different strategy for a practical justification of freedom in *KpV*.[15]

---

[11] These texts include *KrV* A547/B575, A548/B576, and A557/B582, where Kant expresses uncertainty about whether reason has causality, which I take to be equivalent to the question of whether reason is practical or whether rational beings have a will; and *Refl* 5442: 18: 183, where Kant distinguishes between logical and transcendental freedom and denies the possibility of inferring the latter from the former.

[12] Kant entertains such a possibility in the teleological reflections that he interjects in support of his claim that the good will is the only thing that is good without restriction. The idea is that if reason had been given us only for the purpose of better enabling us to attain happiness, which is a belief to which those who deny Kant's claim about the good will are supposedly committed, then it would not have chosen the best means, since that could be more easily attained through instinct. For our purposes, what is relevant about this is that Kant held open the possibility of beings who are cognitively rational, but whose choices are governed by instinct rather than practical reason (See *GMS* 4: 395–6).

[13] I discuss this issue in Allison (1996: 137–8). A similar point is made, albeit in different terms, by Hill (1992: 93–4, 106–10).

[14] For my discussions of this possibility, see Allison (1990: 59–70; 1996: 109–14).

[15] For my analysis of the deduction, see Allison (1990: 218–29).

II.

Kant's practical justification of freedom in *KpV* reverses the strategy adopted in *GMS*. In both cases the argument presupposes the reciprocity thesis, but whereas in *GMS* Kant began with an argument for presupposing freedom that is based on a general conception of rational agency, rather than on any specifically moral premises, and proceeds from this to a deduction of the categorical imperative, in *KpV* Kant begins by appealing to the notorious "fact of reason," that is, a presumably self-certifying consciousness of the moral law as supremely authoritative, and proceeds from this to a deduction of freedom. As Kant puts it, "the moral law, which itself has no need of justifying grounds, proves not only the possibility but the actuality [of the power of freedom] in beings who cognize this law as binding upon them" (*KpV* 5: 47).

The obvious problem with this strategy is the seemingly question-begging appeal to a fact of reason, which Kant characterizes differently in different places and in his more careful moments describes as a "fact as it were" (*gleichsam als ein Faktum*).[16] Unfortunately, both the reasons for what has been termed Kant's "great reversal" and the cogency of his appeal to the fact of reason are extraordinarily complex and contentious issues with which I cannot deal adequately with here.[17] Nevertheless, I shall say something about how I believe this "fact, as it were" is best understood and its relevance to the justification of freedom.

I shall begin with the distinction drawn by Lewis White Beck between a "fact for" and a "fact of pure reason."[18] By the former Beck understands a pre-given value that is cognized by pure reason. On this reading, pure reason is regarded as a theoretical capacity or, more precisely, a capacity for intellectual intuition, which is a capacity that Kant denies being possible, not only for humans, but for finite rational beings in general. Thus, in addition to its question-begging nature, which it shares with other forms of moral intuitionism, such a Platonic view stands in direct contradiction with a central tenet of Kantian epistemology, which seems more than sufficient to preclude taking it as a serious interpretative option.

Beck suggests, however, and I believe him to be correct, that things look considerably different if we take Kant to be referring to *the fact of* pure reason.[19] Beck characterizes the latter as the "fact" that pure reason is practical, that is, that it can of itself determine the will; not, to be sure, in the causal sense, but in the normative sense that it provides the will with a principle that is objectively

---

[16] In Allison (1990: 321–32), I cite Kant's eight characterizations of this "fact" in *KpV*.

[17] I offer my analysis of the fact of reason in Allison (1990: 230–49). The expression "great reversal" was used by Karl Ameriks to characterize Kant's change of approach to the issues of the justification of the categorical imperative and freedom (see Ameriks 1982: 226).

[18] See Beck (1960: 168–70; 1965: 200–214).

[19] I say "the fact of" because Kant refers to it as "the sole fact of pure reason" (*KpV* 5: 31).

necessary and, as such, binds or obligates finite rational agents.[20] Faced, for example, with the Humean thesis that "Reason is, and ought only to be the slave of the passions, and can never pretend to any other office than to serve and obey them,"[21] and its many modern variants, one may be tempted to dismiss this Kantian claim as likewise question-begging. Moreover, it could be argued that, since the purported goal of *KpV* is to show that pure reason is practical, by simply appealing to it as a fact of "fact as it were" Kant is making things rather too easy for himself.

Tempting as it may appear, however, this dismissal of Kant's procedure is itself too easy. To begin with, the appeal to the fact of reason, so understood, reflects Kant's realization, presumably brought about by the recognition of the failure of the deduction in *GMS* III, of the impossibility of proving that pure reason is practical by an argument that relies on extramoral premises. And if this is the case, then arguably the only viable strategic alternative left is to establish that pure reason *shows* itself to be actually practical, which is just what Kant claims to have accomplished by the appeal to the fact of reason.[22] In other words, much like the affirmation of the necessity of acting under the idea of freedom in *GMS* III, the turn to the fact of reason may be seen as a fallback position to which Kant was led by the recognition of the restricted options left open to him by his underlying critical commitments.

Kant's procedure is perhaps best described as phenomenological, where the phenomenon in question is the ordinary moral consciousness. As such, it occupies some common ground with *GMS* I, where Kant was likewise concerned with the ordinary moral consciousness or, as he there characterizes it, "common rational moral cognition." The difference is that whereas there this cognition was used as a point of departure for a Socratic-like analysis of what is implicit in it, Kant's concern here is with the express commitments of this consciousness, which amount essentially to the recognition of the supremely authoritative status of a moral principle that fits the general description of the categorical imperative. In this respect, there is also a certain overlap with the contents of *GMS* II and the opening portions of the Analytic of *KpV*; though in these texts Kant's avowed method is conceptual analysis rather than phenomenological description. Perhaps the most phenomenological moment in *GMS* is Kant's account of what we find if we attend to ourselves in the transgression of duty. As he describes the situation, rather than actually willing that our (impermissible) maxim become a universal law, since that is impossible, we

---

[20] In *GMS* Kant repeatedly emphasizes that what is objectively necessary as a prescription of reason is subjectively contingent for finite beings like ourselves with a sensuous as well as a rational nature. Accordingly, to claim that we are bound by the categorical imperative is not to say that we necessarily obey it.

[21] Hume (2000 [1739]: 266).

[22] See *KpV* 5: 42. Kant here characterizes the "fact" through which pure reason shows (*beweiset*) itself to be practical as "autonomy in the principle of morality."

will rather that its opposite (the morally permissible maxim) should remain the law; "yet we take the liberty of making an exception of ourselves, or (even only for this once) for the advantage of our inclinations" (*GMS* 4: 424). Otherwise expressed, we recognize the authority of the moral law even in violating it and, therefore, recognize a need to justify this violation to ourselves (and perhaps to others). Save for the complete sociopath, whom I do not believe Kant would regard as a responsible moral agent, I do not think that this is a bad bit of moral phenomenology and I also think that it sheds a good deal of light on how Kant understood the fact of reason, that is, as the consciousness of an authoritative demand that stems from one's own will rather than from an external source such as the will of God.

The major question, of course, is whether we are to regard this putative fact of reason as a genuine fact of *reason*, rather than, say, of the Nietzschean will to power or the Freudian superego. Although I am not sure how Kant would address this challenge, which strikes me as something like the "What about quantum mechanics?" objection to the second analogy, I believe that his best line of response would be a variant of his critique of the project of grounding morality in human nature, which is in fact what Nietzsche and Freud did, albeit on the basis of very different conceptions of human nature than Kant had envisaged. Simply put, the point would be that approaches of this type cannot account for the *kind* of necessity, with which moral requirements address us. In Kantian terms, the latter is an *objective* necessity, which bespeaks an origin in reason, as contrasted with a subjective necessity that is to be understood in psychological or anthropological terms, which, expressed in Kantian terms, is what Nietzsche and Freud (among others) have to offer.

Be that as it may, the central question for us is the move from this fact of reason to freedom, which Kant himself describes as "the deduction of freedom as a causality of pure reason" (*KpV* 5: 48). Although it is clear that the principle underlying this deduction is the ubiquitous "ought implies can"; the issue is made more complex by the nature of the ought. The crucial point is that the categorical imperative requires not merely a capacity to do what reason (or duty) requires, independently of, and even contrary to, one's needs and interests as a sensuous being, but also (and primarily) a capacity to do what reason requires *precisely because it requires it*. In the terminology of *GMS*, it requires not merely that one's action *accord with* duty, but that it be *from duty*; otherwise, the accordance with duty would be a contingent matter and one's maxims would lack moral content or worth. And this requires not merely negative freedom or independence from causal determination in accordance with laws of nature, but also positive freedom or autonomy, which involves a capacity to determine oneself to action on the basis of principles of reason that make no reference to our needs as sensuous beings. Moreover, what the fact of reason supposedly shows is not simply the necessity of presupposing autonomy, but its actuality as a capacity to be motivated by purely by moral considerations, a capacity of which we are conscious even if it is never exercised.[23]

Finally, this difference in the conceptions of freedom makes it possible to avoid an apparent contradiction between Kant's accounts in *GMS* and earlier writings and in *KpV* and later works. As we have seen, in *GMS* and *RS* Kant treated freedom as an idea that is presupposed by the conception of oneself as a rational agent, quite independently of any specifically moral considerations. Accordingly, the claim that we can act only under the idea of freedom is not to be understood as maintaining that we can act morally only under this idea, but rather that it is only under this idea that we can exercise rational agency in all of its dimensions. By contrast, in the second *Critique* Kant tells us that,

> [W]hereas freedom is indeed the *ratio essendi* of the moral law; the moral law is the *ratio cognoscendi* of freedom. For, had not the moral law *already* been distinctly thought in our reason, we should never consider ourselves justified in assuming such a thing as freedom (even though it is not self-contradictory). (*KpV* 5: 4n)

If Kant meant the same thing by freedom in this and similar texts as he did in *GMS*, when he insisted that we can act only under the idea of freedom, he would not only have directly contradicted his earlier view, but have affirmed a seemingly implausible thesis; for no matter where one may stand on the free will question, it does not appear to make much sense to claim that, apart from the recognition of being morally obligated, we would have no basis for assuming anything like freedom. After all, if I am or take myself to be a free agent in something like the manner that Kant affirms in *GMS* and other earlier texts, am I not as free in matters of prudence as in matters of morality?[24] But if, as I believe to be the case, Kant is referring in *KpV* and other later texts, where our awareness of freedom is specifically linked to our consciousness of being

---

[23] Kant's clearest illustration of this point is his oft-cited contrast between someone who asserts that when inclination and opportunity are present he finds the desire irresistible and someone of whom a prince demands on pain of immediate execution that he testify falsely against an honorable man. Of the first, Kant asks rhetorically whether if a gallows were erected in front of the house where he finds the opportunity to satisfy his lust and he were certain of immediate execution upon satisfying it, he would be able to resist his inclination. Of the second, Kant remarks, far more circumspectively, that, "He [the one put to the test] would perhaps not venture to assert whether he would do it [sacrifice his life by refusing to testify falsely] or not, but he must admit without hesitation that it would be possible for him. He judges, therefore, that he can do something because he is aware that he ought to do it and cognizes freedom within him, which without the moral law would have remained unknown to him" (*KpV* 5: 30).

[24] For example, in *KrV* Kant remarks with reference to the causality of reason, which he equates with freedom: "Now that this reason has causality, or that we can at least represent something of the sort in it, is clear from the **imperatives** that we propose as rules to our power of execution in everything practical" (A547/B575). I take it that the imperatives to which Kant refers here include the hypothetical as well as the categorical variety. Similarly the "rules" are both moral and prudential and "everything practical" is not limited to moral matters.

bound by the moral law, to freedom as autonomy, then there is no contradiction. Indeed apart from this consciousness, it is difficult to conceive how an agent could have an awareness of a capacity to govern itself by pure reason, independently of any empirical interests or desires that the agent might have.

III.

One of the questions that inevitably arise regarding so-called practical justifications of ostensibly theoretical claims concerns their metaphysical implications. This is especially true for Kant, since much of what he says on the topic suggests that he is offering solutions from the resources of practical reason to questions that are necessarily posed by, yet unanswerable for, theoretical reason. In the case of freedom, Kant insists at several points in *KpV* that the moral law, through the fact of reason, establishes not merely the (logical) possibility but the *actuality* of freedom, which certainly gives the impression that he regarded his claims as having metaphysical import.[25] Nevertheless, both my overall interpretation of transcendental idealism as methodological or epistemological rather than ontological in nature and my understanding of Kant's use of this idealism to resolve the antinomies make me highly suspicious of a metaphysical reading.[26]

Before turning to this issue, however, I wish to emphasize that Kant usually qualifies his claims regarding the moral grounding of freedom (as well as the postulates of God and immortality) with the caveat that they hold only for practical purposes. Although Kant expresses this caveat in a number of ways, I believe that they all come down to the same thing, namely, that the claims are valid merely from the standpoint of the agent who is concerned with the question: "What ought I do?" With regard to freedom, the fact of reason purportedly shows that we are really bound by the moral law and, as such, are beings whose actions are imputable. For Kant, on my view, this is neither a theoretical truth about the nature of our noumenal agency of which we somehow become aware through our consciousness of standing under the moral law, nor a heuristic fiction that we adopt when we view ourselves as subject to moral requirements.[27] It is rather a standpoint that we are compelled (by reason) to adopt in virtue of our consciousness of ourselves as bound by the moral law.[28]

---

[25] See, for example, *KpV* 5: 6, 42, 105, 134, 143.

[26] For my views on these matters, see Allison (2004; 2006).

[27] The classical formulation of the fictionalist view is by Vaihinger (1935: esp. 271–301). In addition to misconstruing the function of Kantian ideas by regarding them merely as heuristic fictions rather than principles of reason with a certain necessity and normative force, Vaihinger's reading denies any real normative force to the categorical imperative.

[28] Kant states that, "The concept of a world of the understanding [*Verstandeswelt*] is only a *standpoint* [*Standpunkt*], which reason is compelled to take outside of appearances *in order to think itself as practical*" (*GMS* 4: 458). In my view, Kant argues for essentially the same thesis in

My interpretation of transcendental idealism has been criticized from a variety of directions, but with respect to the question at issue the most germane is that of Karl Ameriks. According to Ameriks, the problem with non-metaphysical versions of transcendental idealism, such as my own, is that they "give no reason to think that the non-ideal has greater ontological status than the ideal" (Ameriks 1992: 334). Although Ameriks is correct in pointing out that on my reading (and perhaps others) the nonideal has no greater ontological import than the ideal, I question his further claim that this is incompatible with Kant's deepest philosophical commitments. On the contrary, I think that the denial of greater ontological import to the nonideal is in accord with these commitments and that this is nicely illustrated by Kant's treatment of freedom.

To begin with, let us note the well-known difficulties in which one finds oneself enmeshed in the endeavor to place Kant's account of freedom in the ideal-real metaphysical framework. Setting aside the variety of two-object (or -world) and two-aspects readings, at the end of the day, one who considers Kant's account of freedom as a metaphysical thesis is forced to choose between two alternatives: (1) to take Kant's view to be that we *really are* free and only *seem to be* causally determined; or (2) to read him as maintaining that the noumenal self is free and the phenomenal one causally determined. Unfortunately, neither view seems particularly attractive. The former undermines Kant's empirical realism and the latter commits him to a seemingly incoherent doctrine of two selves and to a highly counterintuitive view of moral responsibility. As Beck once put the latter point, "We assume the freedom of the noumenal man, but hang the phenomenal man" (1972: 42–3).

This suggests that the fundamental problem confronting any attempt to attribute a metaphysical status to Kant's conception of freedom is that it tacitly assumes that there must be some "fact of the matter" regarding freedom. Moreover, this applies equally to critics of this conception, who affirm a hard determinism, or the favored contemporary view of a "soft determinism" or compatibilism, as well as to Kantian naturalizers such as Guyer, who regards Kantian freedom as something one experiences, that is, a sort of psychological or anthropological fact, which is where one is unavoidably led if one wishes to preserve a factual status for freedom, while rejecting any attempt to locate it in the "noumenal world."[29]

KpV, except that reason is not required merely to conceive itself as practical, but also (in view of the fact of reason) as bound by the moral law.

[29] See Guyer (1993). In fairness to Guyer, it must be admitted that on occasion, particularly, but not exclusively, in pre-Critical texts, Kant does speak of a sense of freedom that is empirical. And, of course, in his political writings he is concerned with "outer freedom" or freedom of action. Nevertheless, as a matter of interpretation, I find it difficult to see how one can deny that Kant's deepest view about the problem of freedom is to be found in remarks such as: "The transcendental idea of freedom is far from constituting the whole content of the psychological concept of that name, which is for the most part empirical, but constitutes only that of the absolute spontaneity of an action as the

Admittedly, as with all the transcendental questions posed by Kant in the Dialectic, but particularly the antinomies, it does *seem* as if there must be a fact of the matter. After all, is it not the case that the will or, if one wishes to avoid "faculty talk," the human being, is either free or not free in whatever sense of "freedom" one wishes to affirm or deny. Indeed, must not this be the case even if, as Kant seems to suggest, we are incapable of determining by theoretical means which party is correct?

As I have argued elsewhere, however, though perfectly natural, this way of viewing the situation reflects a virulent combination of transcendental illusion and transcendental realism.[30] Although the illusion is both natural and unavoidable, indeed, it is the inevitable outcome of reason's engagement in its inherent project of attempting to grasp the whole (the totality of conditions for any conditioned); transcendental realism, which is the counterpart of transcendental idealism, is both avoidable and the source of the metaphysical errors that Kant methodically diagnosed in the Transcendental Dialectic.[31] Transcendental idealism does not remove transcendental illusion, that being impossible (for example, it still seems natural to assume that there must be some matter of fact regarding freedom); but by discrediting transcendental realism, it makes it possible to avoid being taken in by this illusion. In this respect at least, the function of transcendental idealism is largely therapeutic.[32] Consider the problem of the age and size of the world, which is the concern of the first antinomy. It certainly seems as if the spatiotemporal world must either have a first beginning in time and an outer limit in space or be infinite in both respects, which is to say that there appears to be a fact of the matter regarding the age and size of the world, independently of the question of how we are to determine it.

According to Kant's analysis of the antinomy, however, this is an illusion, albeit a highly persistent one that takes a transcendental critique to uncover; for if one assumes that the world (the totality of appearances) exists in itself, independently of the conditions of its cognition, which is the view to which transcendental realism is committed, then it follows that this whole must be regarded as being either finite or infinite in the relevant respects. Moreover, even though Kant characterizes the third antinomy as dynamical rather than mathematical and claims that this entails that both sides could be correct, I believe that the same principle is at work, namely,

---

real ground of its imputability; but this idea is nevertheless the real stumbling block for philosophy, which finds insuperable difficulties in admitting this kind of unconditioned causality. Hence that in the question of the freedom of the will which has always put speculative reason into such embarrassment is really only *transcendental* and it concerns only whether a faculty of beginning a series of successive things or states *from itself* is to be assumed" (*KrV* A448/B476).

[30] See Allison (2004: esp. 307–448).

[31] The definitive account of this issue is by Grier (2001).

[32] I am not claiming that the function of transcendental idealism is *entirely* therapeutic, but simply that this is its major role in the Dialectic. Obviously, it also plays a constructive role in the Aesthetic and Analytic.

that the source of the seeming conflict is the assumption that there must be some fact of the matter regarding freedom. Notice, if one continues to make this assumption in the face of Kant's official resolution of the antinomy, which appeals to transcendental idealism, one is led either to endorse an outright contradiction (we are both free and not free at the same time) or, more plausibly, we find ourselves back in the situation where we must affirm either that we really (noumenally) are free and only appear (phenomenally) to be causally determined or, equally unattractive, that there is one self that is really free and another that is causally determined. Notice also, however, that none of these consequences arise if we take the point of the resolution to be that there is no fact of the matter regarding freedom, but merely two regulative principles, each with its own sphere of validity.

Where, then, does this leave us with regard to Kant's practical justification of freedom? In my judgment, it is not with any ontological thesis regarding freedom; nor, I might add, does it push us in the direction of the fictionalist view associated with Vaihinger, according to which acting under the idea of freedom means acting *as if* we were free, even though we know that we are not. As the label suggests, the basic problem with this view, which has many contemporary variants, is that it too assumes there to be a fact of the matter, albeit a negative one. Rather, adopting the language of Dummett, Putnam, and others, we end up with what I call a doctrine of "warranted assertability from a point of view," where the point of view is practical.[33] In other words, qua rational agent engaged in a process of deliberation regarding what I ought to do (in either a moral or prudential sense), I must consider myself as free in the negative sense of being independent of determination by natural causes; while qua bound by the moral law I must regard myself as free in the positive sense of possessing autonomy. The former is the thesis of *GMS* and the latter of *KpV*. Together they constitute Kant's practical justification of freedom, which, once one is liberated by transcendental idealism from the illusion that there must be some fact of the matter regarding freedom, I believe to be sufficient for "practical purposes."

Bibliography

Allison, H. E. (1986) "Morality and Freedom: Kant's Reciprocity Thesis," *Philosophical Review* 95(3): 393–425.

Allison, H. E. (1990) *Kant's Theory of Freedom*. Cambridge: Cambridge University Press.

Allison, H. E. (1996) *Idealism and Freedom, Essays on Kant's Theoretical and Practical Philosophy*. Cambridge: Cambridge University Press.

Allison, H. E. (1997) "We Can Act only under the Idea of Freedom," *Proceedings and Addresses of the American Philosophical Association* 71: 39–50.

---

[33] See Allison (2004: 48; 2006: 18).

Allison, H. E. (2004) *Kant's Transcendental Idealism*. Rev. and enl. ed. New Haven: Yale University Press.

Allison, H. E. (2006) "Transcendental Realism, Empirical Realism and Transcendental Idealism," *Kantian Review* 11(1): 1–28.

Allison, H. E. (2012) *Essays on Kant*. Oxford: Oxford University Press.

Ameriks, K. (1982) *Kant's Theory of Mind: An Analysis of the Paralogisms of Pure Reason*. Oxford: Clarendon Press.

Ameriks, K. (1992) "Kantian Idealism Today," *History of Philosophy Quarterly* 9(4): 329–42.

Beck, L. W. (1960) *A Commentary on Kant's Critique of Practical Reason*. Chicago: University of Chicago Press.

Beck, L. W. (1965) "The Fact of Reason: An Essay on Justification in Ethics," in *Studies in the Philosophy of Kant*. Indianapolis: Bobbs-Merrill.

Beck, L. W. (1972) "Five Concepts of Freedom in Kant," in J. T. J. Srzednick (ed.), *Philosophical Analysis and Reconstruction, Festschrift to Stephan Körner*, 35–51. Dordrecht: Reidel.

Grier, M. (2001) *Kant's Doctrine of Transcendental Illusion*. Cambridge: Cambridge University Press.

Guyer, P. (1993) *Kant and the Experience of Freedom: Essays on Aesthetics and Morality*. Cambridge: Cambridge University Press.

Hill, T. E., Jr. (1992) *Dignity and Practical Reason in Kant's Moral Theory*. Ithaca, NY: Cornell University Press.

Hume, D. (2000 [1739]) *A Treatise of Human Nature*. Ed. D. F. Norton and M. J. Norton. Oxford: Oxford University Press.

Kant, I. (1996) *Practical Philosophy*. Tr. and ed. M. J. Gregor. Cambridge: Cambridge University Press.

Kant, I. (1996) *Religion and Rational Theology*. Tr. and ed. A. W. Wood and George di Giovanni. Cambridge: Cambridge University Press.

Kant, I. (1999) *Critique of Pure Reason*. Tr. P. Guyer and A. W. Wood. Cambridge: Cambridge University Press.

Vaihinger, H. (1935) *The Philosophy of "As If"*. Tr. C. K. Ogden. London: Kegan Paul. 2nd ed. London: Trench, Trubner.

13

The Place of Kant's Theism in His Moral Philosophy

John Hare

One stimulus that occasioned the writing of this chapter is that I gave a set of lectures in Glasgow on the topic "Loving the Neighbour as the Self," together with a Jewish philosopher, a Muslim philosopher, and a Secular Humanist. I said that Kant holds that the attempt to carry out practical love for the neighbor without believing in God is "rationally unstable." The reference to instability is from Volckmann's notes to Kant's lectures on the Philosophy of Religion (*V-Th/Volckmann* 28: 1151).[1] The Secular Humanist (A. C. Grayling) objected that this could not be Kant's view because of the opening of *Religion within the Boundaries of Mere Reason*, and he proceeded to quote at length, emphasizing the clause "Hence on its own behalf morality in no way needs religion." The same passage is emphasized by Merold Westphal (1998). Westphal calls *Religion* "Kant's Fourth Critique" and he says, "The first thing Kant says about the relation of religion to morality in his 'Fourth Critique' is that 'morality does not need religion at all'." My project is first to correct what I see as a misapprehension of Kant's project as Kant describes it in this passage. This will take some time, because the first two paragraphs of this work are very easy to misconstrue. I then pass to another famous passage from *Religion*, the beginning of the General Remark at the end of book one, which also seems to be at odds with the connection between morality and religion that I am trying to attribute to Kant, and which also limits "morality" (or in this case moral worth) to a particular kind of connection with freedom. The third and final part of the chapter will be an attempt to relate these two passages to what Kant says is wrong about the moral systems of the Stoics and the Epicureans, and I will

---

[1] I owe the reference to Patrick Kain.

attempt to draw these threads together into an account of what Kant means by moral depravity.

I. The First Sentence of *Religion*

Kant begins the preface to the first edition of *Religion* with the following sentence, in the Cambridge translation, "So far as morality is based on the conception of the human being as one who is free but who also, just because of that, binds himself through his reason to unconditional laws, it is in need neither of the idea of another being above him in order that he recognize his duty, nor, that he observe it, of an incentive other than the law itself." Kant is interested here in how we *recognize* our duties and in how we *observe* them; and he claims that we do not need to bring in God in either case, so far as we think of human beings as free and as binding themselves to the moral law. The mistake it is easy to make here is to detach the consequent. It is to think that since humans are free, on Kant's view, and do bind themselves to the moral law, it follows that we do not need to bring in God for our recognition or our observance of the law. But this cannot be Kant's view, because he moves during the first two paragraphs to the following statement that begins the third paragraph: "Morality thus inevitably leads to religion, and through religion it extends itself to the idea of a mighty moral lawgiver outside the human being, in whose will the ultimate end (of the creation of the world) is what can be and at the same time ought to be the ultimate human end." So we need to understand the first paragraph, and in particular its first sentence, in such as way as to be consistent with the third paragraph. Fortunately there is no difficulty in providing such an understanding. We emphasize the first three words, *so far as* morality is based on the conception of the human being as free. Kant's point, as I understand it, is that we are not merely free beings; we are also what he calls "creatures of need." If we *were* merely free, then we would not need the idea of a being over us, because we would be like God, who has no idea of a superior being.

In the *Groundwork*, Kant distinguishes between the ordinary members of the kingdom of ends and the head of the kingdom, who is also a member, but who (unlike the other members) is not subject to the will of any other (*GMS* 4: 433). Moral law is the law of this kingdom of ends, but the relation of the king of this kingdom to this law is different from the relation of the other members. The sovereign is not *under* the law, since the sovereign has a holy will and therefore needs no constraint. We, however, have inclinations toward our own happiness that need to be controlled. This is not to say that there is anything wrong with wanting to be happy, but it makes our relation to morality different.

To contrast this reading, then, with Westphal's, Kant does *not* on my view say, as Westphal *quotes* him as saying, that "morality does not need religion at all." What he does say is that morality does not *on its own behalf* need religion.

This phrase "on its own behalf" (or in the Greene and Hudson edition "for its own sake") makes an important difference. When we add this phrase, we see that the sentence is quite consistent with saying that *our* morality does need religion, because of the sorts of beings we are, and this is in fact just what Kant goes on to say. Westphal takes it that Kant is arguing that morality presupposes the idea of man as a free agent, and that since free beings do not need the idea of a superior to keep them in line, morality does not need religion at all. But Kant agrees that morality presupposes that we are free, but does *not* agree that freedom exhausts the features of our agency by which *our* morality is structured. We are also, in his view, creatures of need who do in fact have the end of our own happiness, and will always do so.

It is instructive to compare Kant's formulation here with Luther's point in his treatise on Christian Liberty, one of the central texts of the Reformation. Luther replies to people who say, "We will take our ease and do no works and be content with faith," by making a distinction: "That would indeed be proper if we were wholly inner and perfectly spiritual men. But such we shall be only at the last day, the day of the resurrection of the dead. As long as we live in the flesh we only begin to make some progress in that which shall be perfected in the future life" (1970: 294). A Christian, says Luther, is both "a perfectly free lord of all, subject to none" and "a perfectly dutiful servant of all, subject to all" (1970: 277). Luther says about the Christian, "Insofar as he is free he does no works, but insofar as he is a servant he does all kinds of works." Because we are not merely free, but also we remain in this mortal life on earth, we have to control or discipline our own bodies, and "here the works begin." Luther, like Kant, is insisting on our composition. We are not merely free, not merely inner men, but we live in the flesh, remaining "in this mortal life on earth"; and therefore we have to hold the body and its inclinations in check.

Kant makes the point in terms of *ends*, and this is a term that needs discussion. *So far as* we are merely free, our morality needs no end, that is, no material determining ground of the free power of choice. I think one key here is the distinction between matter and form, which recurs several times in these two paragraphs. The lawfulness of an action or maxim is the *formal* determining ground (*RGV* 6: 4) or the *formal* condition of the use of freedom in general (*RGV* 6: 5). But there are four possible *material* determining grounds, of which this passage mentions only three. They are my own happiness, the happiness of others, my own perfection, and the perfection of others (*MS* 6: 398). Kant does not need to mention the fourth of these, as he shows in the *Metaphysics of Morals*, because we do not have responsibility for the perfection of others; they do. But the other three possibilities for ends Kant does discuss in our passage. (1) To say that I should make my own happiness the determining ground would leave me outside morality. I will return to this possibility in my remarks about the Epicureans. (2) To say that I should make my own perfection the determining ground is ambiguous. I might be aiming at my *moral* perfection, but then that is the same as making the lawfulness of an action or maxim the ground, and so is the same as the formal determining ground. Or I might be aiming at my *natural* perfection, for example skill in the arts and sciences, taste, physical agility, and so on. But these are only conditionally good; they are only good in the service of a morally good will. (3) To make the happiness of others the determining ground is also only conditionally good. Here Kant departs from certain forms of utilitarianism. We should, he says in the *Groundwork*, share the ends of those affected by our actions to the extent possible, and he explains in the *Metaphysics of Morals* that the extent possible is the extent to which those ends are consistent with the moral law.

It is important to note here that Kant says that these three or four ends are the *only* possible ends, or determining grounds. Thus, after eliminating the first, namely my own happiness, he says: "But then there are only two determining grounds left," and goes on to name them as my own perfection and the happiness of others. This means that we can free Kant of one problematic kind of interpretation. He might be taken to be arguing that morality does not need the representation of any end in a *different* sense, namely anything to be achieved in the action or any content in the maxim proposed to the will. This will be clearer with an example, and we can take Kant's own example of truthfulness in testimony before a court of law. He says, "There is no need to demand an end which I might perhaps propose to realize by my declaration, for what sort of end this would be does not matter at all; rather, one who still finds it necessary to look around for some end when his testimony is rightfully demanded of him is in this respect already contemptible." What kind of end is Kant ruling out here? I think it must be one of the four I have just mentioned. Kant is *not* saying that I should not be intending to bring about any result at all, for example, my telling of the truth in court. For it would not make sense to entertain a maxim for action, and not thereby intend to bring about the result that would be constituted just by one's doing that thing, namely telling the truth in court. Kant is not a utilitarian, to be sure. But he is not denying, either, that we are to be judged morally on the basis of what we are intending to bring about. He is not saying that we should be indifferent to the intended consequences of our actions; and this is because if we were indifferent in this way, we would not be acting on a maxim at all. So what Kant intends to rule out, is that morality on its own behalf requires one of these four material determining grounds: my own happiness, my own perfection, and the happiness and perfection of others.

If this is right, we can make good sense of what Kant means in the second paragraph by saying that morality *does* have "a necessary reference to such an end, not as the ground of its maxims but as a necessary consequence accepted in conformity to them." Kant proceeds to propose an end which is the collecting together of the four material determining grounds, namely the happiness of all of us proportionate to the perfection of all of us. *This* end, which he also calls an ultimate end that reason can justify, *is* necessary for us, but necessary not as a ground but as an intended consequence. It is the *result* of our right conduct that our reason proposes to us, the world that our reason would create if this were in its power.

But we cannot adopt this end as an intended consequence without believing it possible; and we cannot believe it possible without assuming "a higher, moral, most holy, and omnipotent being who alone can unite the two elements of this good." Here we have in very brief compass the argument, given at greater length in the second *Critique*, for God as a postulate of practical reason. This is how Kant is led to say at the beginning of the third paragraph that morality inevitably leads to religion.

II. The First Sentence of the First General Remark

I want next to consider a second passage in which Kant limits the connection between our morality and God's work on our behalf. I will first need to set up some background for the passage. At the beginning of *Religion*, on my reading of it, Kant has made the point that our morality is a morality of creatures of need, and has a material as well as a formal aspect, where the matter can be collected together under the heading of the pursuit of the highest good. The fact that our morality is mixed or composite in this way does not yet give us depravity. Kant is not saying that there is anything wrong with desiring our happiness. This is not the place for a historical excursus, but I have tried to show elsewhere that he is in the tradition of Crusius and behind the Reformers, in the tradition of the Franciscans in this respect (2007: 91–7, 125–32, 162–71). The key distinction that Kant takes from this tradition is that motivation is not finally single, directed at one's own happiness or perfection, but double, directed both by what Scotus calls the affection for advantage and by the affection for justice (which is moved by what is good in itself, without any attachment to oneself). There is nothing in itself wrong with the affection for advantage, but wrong comes in the ranking of the affection for advantage over the affection for justice. The place of God so far in the discussion is that believing in God makes it possible for us to believe in the real possibility of the highest good. But when we add Kant's view of our propensity to evil, this gives God another role with respect to our morality. Believing in God makes it possible for us to believe in the possibility of the revolution of the will. Otherwise we would have the problem that Kant attributes to "the valiant Spener" about how creatures born under the Evil Maxim, so that their fundamental maxim is corrupt, can accomplish a reversal of the order of incentives, so that they will pursue their happiness only to the extent that it is consistent with their duty. (*SF* 7: 54) The solution Kant adopts to this problem is to invoke divine assistance, or what he calls an "effect of grace." The problematic passage I want to consider next is the first sentence of the general remark at the end of book one of *Religion*, where Kant says, "The human being must make or have made himself into whatever he is or should become in a moral sense, good or evil" (*RGV* 6: 44).

My conversation partner for this discussion is Nicholas Wolterstorff, who calls the doctrine of this sentence "the Stoic maxim," and abbreviates it as the doctrine that a person's moral worth is determined entirely by that person himself (1991: esp. 48f.). Wolterstorff continues: "Yet it is essential to Kant's particular project of a rational religion that God be able to alter our moral status for the better. Here then we have not just implausibility or tension, but internal contradiction." Wolterstorff supports his reading of the Stoic maxim by appealing to the general observation at the end of the fourth book of *Religion*, where Kant says, "what is to be accredited to us as morally good conduct must take place not through foreign influence but through the use of our own powers" (*RGV* 6: 191). Wolterstorff thinks that Kant tries to solve the difficulty here by appealing to the incomprehensibility of how the "supernatural factor" and our freedom might work together. But Wolterstorff continues: "It seems clear, however, that such an appeal is illegitimate here. To affirm the Stoic principle is to affirm something which *contradicts* the claim that God wipes out guilt. Our situation, given the Stoic principle, is that we know God does not." Then he ends:

> What Kant affirms is that only the worthy are saved—and that God, so as to bring it about that some are saved in spite of the wrongdoing of all, makes those of worthy character worthy in action as well. Kant affirms this without ever surrendering the affirmation that each can make only himself or herself worthy.

I want to ask whether Kant is in fact caught in a contradiction here. I am going to claim he is not. But this does not mean that I think his account of the removal of guilt is unproblematic. Kant rules out any substitutionary account of the atonement on the grounds that guilt is not a transmissible liability (*RGV* 6: 72).[2] I think he is wrong about this, but that is a matter for a different discussion. I am going to confine my defense to the point that it is consistent, noncontradictory, to say both that we are morally accountable only for what we do, and that we are made better by God's assistance. There is a relatively easy way to show this is consistent, but I am not denying that there are deep difficulties in Kant's account that remain.

The relatively easy point is that Kant is here restricting the word "moral" so that it covers not the whole of our being pleasing to God but only the part for which we are responsible, and so accountable. To make the parallel explicit with the first section of this paper, Kant could have made his point this way: Moral improvement *on its own behalf* has no need for religion or for the idea of a being over us. Kant goes on to make the limitation to the concept of morality explicit in the second sentence of the general remark. Let me quote them together:

---

[2] I have responded to this attack by Kant in Hare (1996: chapter 10).

The human being must make or have made himself into whatever he is or should become *in a moral sense*, good or evil. These two characters must be an effect of his free power of choice, for otherwise they could not be imputed to him and, consequently, he could be neither *morally* good nor evil.

I say that this is a "relatively" easy point, because there remains something counterintuitive about Kant's restriction here, that we can count as moral improvement only what we contribute. But this is nonetheless what he is saying.

What is important to see here is that Kant is not saying that our *goodness and badness* are entirely a consequence of our own efforts. Indeed he is going to go on to deny exactly this in what follows, as I shall describe. But he is saying that the part of our becoming good or bad that is *moral* is imputable to us, and this is because the term "moral" carries this implication within its sense. Then he goes on to grant that some supernatural cooperation is also needed to our becoming good or better, whether this cooperation only consists in the diminution of obstacles or also a positive assistance. These two possibilities are a staple of pietist reflection, as for example in Francke's account of his own conversion.[3] So it is not a contradiction to say that we must make ourselves into whatever (good or bad) we become *in a moral sense*, and then to say that God's assistance is necessary to make us good or better. And it is not illegitimate to appeal to lack of comprehension about how the resulting cooperation might work. God does something and we do something, and there is a reason in principle to think that we cannot understand how these fit together. Kant's defensive point is merely that we cannot show that such cooperation is impossible.

This is the relatively easy point, but it does not eliminate all the difficulties. For if we are born under the Evil Maxim, how can we do anything good to cooperate with God's assistance? Kant says that "the human being must make himself antecedently worthy of receiving" the supernatural cooperation, and it is not at all clear how, given the propensity to evil, we could do that. If our fundamental maxim is the Evil Maxim which subordinates duty to happiness, does not that corrupt every choice we make, so that nothing we do could make us morally worthy to receive God's help?

I have an initial suggestion to help with this difficulty, but it is not going to solve all the problems here. The suggestion is that what we can do to make ourselves worthy is simply the activity of what Kant calls the "germ of goodness left in its entire purity, a germ that cannot be extirpated or corrupted" (*RGV* 6: 45). The seed of goodness is, alternately described, the predisposition to good. ("Predisposition" is Kant's term for what controls the development of a thing, for example an organism.[4]) This language of a germ or seed is something Kant takes from his theological background, which he is constantly engaged in

---

[3] For Francke's mention of the two kinds of assistance, see Erb (1983: 140–41).
[4] See Wood (1999: 211).

translating within the Boundaries of Mere Reason. Even the Reformers who had a strong doctrine of total depravity still talked of a seed of religion that is planted in all human beings, even those who in other aspects of life seem least to differ from brutes. Total depravity is not, for Calvin for example, the view that every part of us (every faculty) is totally depraved, but that no part of us is without corruption, and this is consistent with the survival in us of a seed of goodness. Kant takes this language of a seed further by saying that because of our propensity to evil which lies over the top of our predisposition to good, the seed does not produce what it would otherwise produce, namely the fruit of a good life. "Over the top of" the predisposition is one way to express the relation between the propensity and the predisposition, relating to the parable of the sower in the Gospels (e.g., Matthew 13), where the seed can be prevented from producing grain by thorns and thistles growing over the top. But the seed can also be prevented by poor soil or being trampled by animals or humans. Kant also uses various metaphors, for example the language of weight, where the propensity "preponderates" (*RGV* 6: 42), the language of pollution, where the propensity produces "stain" (*RGV* 6: 38), and the language of dynamics, where the propensity provides "resistance" (*RGV* 6: 23). In all these different expressions, he wants to insist on the point that the seed is essential to us, unlike the propensity that we can lose without losing our humanity. The predisposition is given along with the concept of our humanity, and the propensity is not.

So there is the activity of a seed in us that is fighting against the propensity to evil. Later on in the general remark in book one, Kant says:

> We cannot start out in the ethical training of our connatural moral predisposition to the good with an innocence which is natural to us but must rather begin from the presupposition of a depravity of our power of choice in adopting maxims contrary to the original ethical predisposition; and, since the propensity to this [depravity] is inextirpable, with unremitting counteraction against it. (*RGV* 6: 51)

This picture is of an internal war in which the maxims adopted are in tension with the countervailing activity of the surviving predisposition that is continually being overruled but also continually fighting against this defeat. Someone might object that this cannot be Kant's view since he denies that a human being can be "morally good in some parts, and at the same time evil in others" (*RGV* 6: 24). But Kant has something particular in mind by "parts" in this passage. This is shown by his explanation in the attached footnote about the ancient philosophers who debated whether a human being can be virtuous in some parts and vicious in others. Kant approves of those (like Aristotle) who denied this possibility. But Aristotle and Kant are united here in a rigorism that denies that a *life* can be virtuous in some parts and vicious in others (for example brave and stingy). This is consistent with holding that a person can be divided in such a way as to have internal conflict. And while Aristotle does not, on my view, have a doctrine of the will, he does share with Kant the project of giving an account of this kind of conflict.

If my interpretation of the internal war is correct, we have to qualify the common picture of Kant's rigorism as requiring a totally unified agency. It is true that Kant thinks we are under one fundamental maxim, either the Good Maxim that subordinates happiness to duty or the Evil Maxim that subordinates duty to happiness. But this is consistent with his also saying that we have nonintegrated origins of movement (though not "parts" in his sense) that are in tension with the fundamental maxim. I have been talking about a nonintegrated good origin. I want to say a word also about a nonintegrated bad origin, and this takes us to the obscure notions of frailty and impurity. Frailty is not the same as being creatures of need, where this means that we have desires or inclinations whose satisfaction constitutes our happiness. Here being creatures of need corresponds on the affective side of our lives to being creatures of sense on the cognitive side, and is associated with our finitude in both cases. Being creatures of need is necessary for frailty, but not sufficient. Frailty is not merely the possibility of moral failure but the actuality of it, and this means that frailty is not (unlike being creatures of need) built into the concept of being human. Frailty is where the inclination is not only present (because we are finite) but subjectively *stronger* than the good will when we ought to be following a good maxim. Incidentally the Cambridge edition translates "*whenever* the maxim is to be followed," but this is not required by the German and creates the misleading suggestion that frailty is continuous and uninterrupted defeat. The possibility of frailty is necessary for the possibility of depravity, but again not sufficient, because depravity requires in addition that the higher status of inclination is adopted into the maxim.

In explaining frailty, Kant quotes the example of the Apostle Paul in Romans 7, and he interprets the passage as referring to Paul's state after conversion, though this is not certain in the original Pauline text. Kant is thus giving a reading within the Boundaries of Mere Reason of Luther's *simul justus et peccator*, at the same time justified (and so, in Kant's terms, after the revolution of the will) and a sinner. The person Kant is thinking of has already adopted the Good Maxim as her fundamental maxim, (Kant says, "I have adopted the good into the maxim of my power of choice"; *RGV* 6: 29), but she still sometimes fails to follow this maxim. This does not mean that she in fact has two fundamental maxims, for she has to be understood from God's point of view as already under the Good Maxim. But, in Luther's terms, "In myself outside of Christ, I am a sinner; in Christ, outside of myself, I am not a sinner" (Luther WA 38: 205).[5] Here is Luther in his commentary on Romans 7:23 (where Paul says "I see in my members another law at war with the law of my mind"):

---

[5] See Spitz (1963: 246), who talks of the kingdom of grace and the kingdom of nature (as in Leibniz), quoting from Luther's *Disputation Concerning Man* (WA 39, I).

From this it is obvious that he is speaking of himself as a pugilist between two contrary laws, but not as a defeated fighter for whom there is no longer a war between the law of the members and the law of the mind, because the mind has given in, as is the case with the carnal man. Rather, he shows that he is serving the one law, that he is dedicated to it and that he is standing up to the other law which attacks him and is not serving it, rather, that he is struggling against it. We all know that this kind of resistance or reports of resistance are never heard of in the case of the carnal man. (WA 56: 346)

Frailty is in Kant's terms "the general weakness of the human heart," whether the revolution of the will has been accomplished or not.

Frailty, in turn, needs to be distinguished from impurity. This notion is very difficult to understand.[6] Impurity, Kant says, "is that although the maxim is good with respect to its object and perhaps even powerful enough in practice, it is not purely moral, i.e. it has not adopted the law *alone* as its *sufficient* incentive." But what would purity be here? A will unmoved by inclination would be a holy will, and this is in principle unavailable to us. But would a pure will have inclination so transformed that there was no longer the possibility of conflict with duty, or would it be (less ambitiously) one without actual conflict, though still possibly conflicting? Kant seems to prefer the latter.[7] But in any case impurity adds to frailty that the moral law is not adopted as sufficient all by itself for doing actions that conform to the law. If we grant that inclination is always going to be present for human motivation, it cannot simply be the simultaneous presence of inclination that Kant is objecting to, or even sometimes the victory of inclination, since this is merely frailty. Rather, with impurity, even if the choice to do what conforms with the law prevails, it needs inclination to come alongside it.[8] This is different from depravity, because there is no decision in principle to make duty subordinate to happiness. But impurity is a worse state than frailty because the commitment to the good is weaker, needing a supplement from inclination that is more than just respect for the law.

There are all sorts of difficulties in understanding these mixed cases of motivation. But the fundamental difficulty for Kant, one felt by every defender of Kant, is how to relate freedom and temporality. Talk about a revolution of the will requires that there be noumenal change in a person from being under the Evil Maxim to being under the Good Maxim. When and where is this change supposed to take place? Kant is going to refuse the validity of both these questions, and he is justified within his framework in doing so. But the cost of this move is to add a large measure of unintelligibility. This is a difficulty that affects

---

[6] I have been helped by Lipscomb's discussion of it (2002).

[7] See especially *KpV* 5: 83–4.

[8] There is an example of one such inclination at *MS* 6: 457. I have tried to understand impurity by means of the notion of inadequate respect, see Hare (2011).

Kant at many places in his moral system. For example, he requires that the soul progresses infinitely toward holiness of the will, without ever reaching it, and presumably that is also noumenal change. To give another example, Kant requires noumenal change in the initial choice to put oneself under the Evil Maxim. To say that Kant's theory adds a large measure of unintelligibility in these sorts of cases is not yet a refutation, since we do not know in advance of some theory how much unintelligibility is acceptable. If I have been right to trace the problematic back to Luther, it may well be that these difficulties are deeply embedded in some versions of the Christian tradition, and Kant simply makes them acute by giving them an explicit philosophical formulation. But any satisfactory defense of Kant's moral theory has to concede the problem, and then show that no higher degree of intelligibility is likely to be available in a rival theory.

III. Moral Depravity

In the third and final part of this chapter I consider what Kant thinks is wrong about the moral systems of the Stoics and the Epicureans, and tie this together with the two passages I have already discussed into an account of what Kant means by moral depravity. I am not going to talk about whether he understood the ancient schools correctly (I think he did not), but about the use he makes of the reading he gives to them. This takes us onto the territory of the antinomy of practical reason laid out in the second *Critique*. Kant sets up the antinomy by proposing that the highest good contains these two elements, happiness and virtue, which are connected through action (since the highest good is a practical good) and which are connected synthetically and not analytically. We therefore require a causal connection between the two elements, and the two most plausible candidates here are that "either the desire for happiness must be the motive for virtue, or the maxim of virtue must be the efficient cause of happiness" (*KpV* 5: 113). Because we have a tendency to believe both of these things, finite practical reason seems to be stuck in a dialectical position, unable to propose for itself the object which at the same time it requires.

The two ancient schools both make too intimate the connection between the two elements of the highest good, but in opposite ways. Both tried to "search out the *sameness* of the practical principles of virtue and happiness" (*KpV* 5: 112). The Stoics maintained that virtue is the whole highest good, and happiness adds only the consciousness of possessing it. The Epicureans maintained that happiness is the whole highest good, and virtue only the form of the maxim for seeking to obtain it. We can associate the distinction between these two schools with the first two paragraphs of *Religion* as follows. The first paragraph emphasizes what our morality would be like if we were merely free. This is like the Stoics. The second paragraph emphasizes what our morality is like due to our status as creatures of need. This is like the Epicureans.

If, however, we separate virtue and happiness, and make the connection between them synthetic and causal, there are still two ways to see this connection that we might call a "Stoic extension" and an "Epicurean extension."[9] These two extensions go beyond the Stoics and the Epicureans themselves, as Kant sees these two schools, because the extensions acknowledge that the highest good requires a synthetic connection between two different items. But the extensions can be seen as the closest we can get to the two ancient positions while still making this acknowledgment. The two extensions are the two competing candidates for a synthetic connection between virtue and happiness proposed in the antinomy of practical reason. The Stoic extension thinks of virtue as producing happiness all by itself. This would be what Kant calls in the first *Critique* a conception of "self-rewarding" virtue, and would be plausible only if we conceived of humans as sufficiently virtuous collectively so that they could rely on each other's virtue to produce each other's happiness. The failure here is to take seriously what Kant calls our "radical evil" together with the limitations of our knowledge. The Epicurean extension thinks of happiness as the motivation for virtue, in the way that eudaimonists have always done, including Aristotle in the first sentence of the *Nicomachean Ethics*. Kant is in the tradition that denies we would have properly moral motivation at all if this were the case.

It is interesting to contemplate the survival power into contemporary moral philosophy of both the Stoic extension and the Epicurean extension. On the one hand some philosophers complain that Kant is polluting morality by bringing happiness into the highest good. I read a paper at the APA Pacific Division in 1995, defending Kant's notion of the highest good, and Fred Beiser replied that it "is a boil, a tumor, a cancer within the critical philosophy, which is necessary to remove surgically." One of the significant markers of the change in Kant scholarship over the last decade or so is that Beiser has changed his mind about this, and his view of the relation in Kant between morality and religion is now much more benign (Beiser 2006). On the other hand other philosophers (like Philippa Foot at one stage) propose that Kant was wrong to make morality a categorical imperative, and it should better be seen as a system of hypothetical imperatives, directed toward the best human life.[10] Kant's own position, by contrast, his own solution to the practical antinomy, is to insist that we have to believe in a causal connection between morality and happiness; but we cannot construct such a connection out of our own powers to run the world and understand it, and we need to bring in the idea of God who can bring about a world in which virtue and human flourishing go together.

---

[9] These are Matthew Caswell's terms, and I have been helped by his dissertation, *Kant's Conception of the Highest Good* (2005).

[10] Foot (1972). She changed her mind about this, though not her dislike of Kant.

I want to propose that we get an illuminating account of depravity by juxtaposing the two passages from the first book of *Religion* that I have been discussing. We can see that both the views of the ancient schools, as Kant construes them, and their extensions in the antinomy of practical reason, fail to understand the nature of human radical evil, as Kant imputes it to us, and so the need for God's help in overcoming it. The Stoics exaggerated the capacity of the sage to be "free from everything morally evil." They supposed this embodiment of Wisdom, like a god, to be immune from temptation, because his will was free from any need for that "special object of human desire," namely happiness (*KpV* 5: 126–27). This is like the thought experiment in the first sentence of the first paragraph of *Religion* about what our morality would be like if we were merely free. On the other hand the Epicureans do not even see subordination to the evil maxim as vice. They identify Wisdom with prudence, and hence capitulate to the maxim that subordinates everything else to the agent's own happiness.

In order to get the possibility of depravity we have to have a very complex mixture, a balance that could be disrupted in either direction. Kant identifies preconditions that have to obtain so that we are not, so to speak, too good for the possibility of depravity, and preconditions that have to obtain so that we are not, so to speak, too bad for it. This is a slightly odd way to put it, but I hope you will see what I mean. I have already discussed the preconditions so that we are not too good. These are our being creatures of need, our being frail, and our morality being impure. We could not be depraved if any of these did not obtain. But we would also not be depraved in Kant's sense if we were not able to choose to be under the Evil Maxim. Depravity is innate and *imputable*. As Kant says, in what Wolterstorff calls "the Stoic maxim," we have made ourselves into what we become morally and this includes *moral* depravity. There is a relevant thought experiment that Scotus took from Anselm (*Ordinatio* III, suppl. dist. 46). Suppose there were an angel who had only the affection for advantage and not the affection for justice. Such an angel would not be free, and so would not sin, even if the angel did what was contrary to God's command. Kant gives the same role to the predisposition to good that Scotus gives to the affection for justice, namely as necessary for freedom and so imputability (*RGV* 6: 41); but to have the predisposition is not yet to be *able* by our own devices to put ourselves under the Good Maxim. We have to be able to receive God's assistance, and this takes two different forms. There is first the assistance in accomplishing the revolution of the will, either a negative removal of hindrances or a positive increase in power. Second there is God's counting our progress toward holiness as sufficient for our being pleasing to God, so as to merit eternal reward without God's compromising God's own justice. Our contribution and so our *moral* improvement is the activity of the predisposition to good (even under our subordination to the Evil Maxim) and our resultant reception of these forms of divine assistance in reversing that subordination.

I want to conclude by locating Luther as a source for what I take to be one of Kant's key insights about human depravity in *Religion within the Boundaries of Mere Reason*. In *The Bondage of the Will*, Luther dissents from the view that the source of evil is the flesh, in the sense of the "lower and grosser affections," and locates it instead in "the highest and most excellent powers of man, in which righteousness, godliness, and knowledge and reverence of God, should reign—that is, in reason and will" (1957: 280). His point is that because the reason and will themselves are corrupt, they do not have the power in themselves to choose what is good. Erasmus had argued that if we are subject to this radical incapacity of our own resources, then it does not make sense to hold us accountable to the law. He says: "It would be ridiculous to say to a man standing where two roads met: 'You see two roads; go by which you will', when only one of them was open". Luther replies:

> Here is the very thing that I said of the arguments of human reason: reason thinks that man is mocked by an impossible commandment, whereas I maintain that by this means man is admonished and awakened to see his own impotence. It is true that we stand where two roads meet, and only one of then is open—indeed, neither is open; and the law shows us how impossible is the one, that leading to good, *unless God bestows His Spirit*. (Luther 1957: 158; emphasis added)

Luther means that the way leading to good *is* possible, but *not* by our own devices. Even the way to evil is only *open* because of God's permission.[11]

I do not want to exaggerate Kant's Lutheranism here. Kant's project in *Religion* is to translate within the Boundaries of Mere Reason the major elements of Christianity as he grew up with it. After the translation, what emerges is something that Luther would regard as mere Pelagianism. But I want to make two points nonetheless. The first is that in order to understand what Kant is up to in *Religion*, we need to understand *what* doctrine he is translating. The answer is that he is translating the theology he encountered in the Lutheran catechisms in his youth, and which he was not much interested in changing. The second point is that even after the translation, there is much of this doctrine that survives. Kant is not, in my view, reducing theology to ethics. He is not proposing to eliminate the outer of the two concentric circles of revelation he imagines in the second preface to *Religion* by reduction to the inner circle, to reduce historical revelation to the revelation to reason. In particular there are items in the outer circle, adjacent to the inner circle, which he calls *parerga*, and we can make room for them even though Reason cannot use them in either its theoretical or its practical employment.[12] To sum up what seems to me a recognizably Lutheran

---

[11] Earlier in the same work he accepts from "the Sophists" the view that we have the "dispositional quality" and "passive aptitude" to receive God's assistance, and plants and animals do not. He quotes the proverb "God did not make heaven for geese" (Luther 1957: 105). See Lohse (1999: 257): he thinks Luther had Bonaventure in mind: Sent. 2 dist. 29, art. 1 qu. 1.

[12] I have stated this baldly. For a longer discussion, see Hare (2007: chapter 5).

remainder: We are born under radical evil, which is both innate and imputable to us. This is not because we are creatures of need or creatures of sense, but it is because we have the disposition to prefer in the *will* our happiness to our duty. Because of this radical evil, the very ground of our maxims is corrupt, and therefore we do not have the capacity to raise ourselves out of the evil by a good choice. But this does not mean that we are not under the obligation to obey the moral law, on the excuse that we cannot and "ought implies can." For God provides the "divine supplement," by which the "seed of goodness," already present in us but unable, is enabled to produce the fruit of a life pleasing to God.

Bibliography

Beiser, F. C. (2006) "Moral Faith and the Highest Good," in P. Guyer (ed.), *The Cambridge Companion to Kant and Modern Philosophy*, 588–629. Cambridge: Cambridge University Press.

Caswell, M. (2005) *Kant's Conception of the Highest Good*. PhD. diss. Notre Dame.

Erb, P. (1983) *Pietists: Selected Writings*. New York: Paulist Press.

Foot, P. (1972) "Morality as a System of Hypothetical Imperatives," *Philosophical Review* 81(3): 305–16.

Hare, J. E. (1996) *The Moral Gap*. Oxford: Clarendon Press.

Hare, J. E. (2007) *God and Morality: A Philosophical History*. Oxford: Blackwell.

Hare, J. E. (2011) "Kant, the Passions, and the Structure of Moral Motivation," *Faith and Philosophy* 28(2): 54–70.

Lipscomb, B. (2002) *Binding Force: A Study of the Concept of Moral Law*. Dissertation Notre Dame.

Lohse, B. (1999) *Martin Luther's Theology*. Minneapolis, MN: Fortress Press.

Luther, M. (1883–2009 [WA: Weimarer Ausgabe]) *D. Martin Luthers Werke*. 120 vols. Weimar.

Luther, M. (1957) *The Bondage of the Will*. Tr. and ed. J. I. Packer and O. R. Johnston. Westwood, NJ: Fleming H. Revell.

Luther, M. (1970) *Three Treatises*. Intr. and tr. C. M. Jacobs, A. T. W. Steinhaeuser, and W. A. Lambert. Rev. ed. Philadelphia: Fortress Press.

Spitz, L. W. (1963) *The Religious Renaissance of the German Humanists*. Cambridge, MA: Harvard University Press.

Westphal, M. (1998) "Commanded Love and Moral Autonomy: The Kierkegaard–Habermas debate," *Kierkegaard Studies*: 1–22.

Wolterstorff, N. (1991) "Conundrums in Kant's Rational Religion," in P. J. Rossi and M. Wreen (eds.), *Kant's Philosophy of Religion Reconsidered*, 40–53. Bloomington: Indiana University Press.

Wood, A. (1999) *Kant's Ethical Thought*. Cambridge: Cambridge University Press.

14

Freedom, Temporality, and Belief

A REPLY TO HARE

A. W. Moore

Hare's initial concern in his extremely interesting chapter, indeed a concern that informs the whole of it, is an apparent contradiction in Kant's moral-cum-religious philosophy. On the one hand, Kant seems to hold that morality has no need of religion. On the other hand, he seems to hold that morality has a very particular need of religion.

The key to resolving this apparent contradiction, on Hare's account, is to distinguish between what morality needs "on its own behalf"—this is a phrase that Kant himself uses—and what morality needs, or, more strictly perhaps, what *we* who are subject to the demands of morality need, if we are to keep those demands properly in focus. "On its own behalf" morality does not need religion. That is to say, if we were purely rational, lacking any of the nonmoral inclinations of the animals that we are, then we would be able to recognize the demands of morality and we would be motivated to act on them without the assistance of any religious props. In fact, however, we are not purely rational. We are animals with nonmoral inclinations. And this means that we cannot recognize the demands of morality, nor are we motivated to act on them, except in so far as we cherish certain hopes about the consequences of our doing so. Since it is through religious convictions of various kinds that we succeed in cherishing these hopes, this furnishes a sense in which morality, by virtue of our animality, does need religion.

This exegesis strikes me as fundamentally correct. It means that what Kant's philosophy of religion is, at root, is an exploration of our bipartite nature. That is, it is an exploration of our nature as beings that exhibit both rationality and animality, both the infinitude of subjection to a self-imposed categorical imperative and the finitude of subjection to biologically imposed hypothetical imperatives. Much of Hare's own chapter is likewise concerned with that split-level picture of what we are like. Throughout his chapter, but especially towards the end of it, he helpfully locates this picture in a broader Christian tradition extending back to Luther. There is far more in the chapter than I can hope to cover in these comments. I shall fasten on a few points that I take to be of especial interest.

First, I want to say something about grace. Even if we accept the story sketched above about the sense in which, for Kant, morality needs religion, and even if we accept that this absolves Kant of the original apparent contradiction in his position, there still appears to be a more local contradiction between the orthodox Christian conception of grace and his own conception of morality. For, on the orthodox Christian conception, God can wipe away our sin—God can make us as if sinless, and God will do so provided that we repent of our sin (Psalms 103:12; Romans 5:15–21 and 8:1; and 1 John 1:9). On the Kantian conception, by contrast, we can never be *as if* sinless except by being sinless, and we can never be *made* sinless except by dint of our own efforts (this is the so-called "Stoic maxim"). In the second part of his chapter Hare addresses this difficulty.

His solution is to deny that Kant endorses an orthodox Christian conception of grace.[1] What Kant endorses, on Hare's account, is something considerably weaker, whereby, first, God improves our nature in *non*moral ways, thereby removing certain obstacles to our own moral efforts, and, second, God *treats* us as if sinless—provided that we, for our own part, not only repent of our sin but turn away from it and embark on an infinite journey of self-improvement. Once again, I find myself broadly in agreement with Hare in his exegesis. Nevertheless, I do wonder whether he makes Kant out to be a little more sure-footed on these matters than he in fact is. In the General Remark at the end of *Religion*, Kant struggles with the orthodox Christian conception, to which, it seems, he wishes he could give greater allegiance, and there are some decidedly odd results— including his refusal to rule out the possibility that something "supernatural" should act "as surrogate for the independent yet deficient determination of our freedom" (*RGV* 6: 191).

Now the reference above to our "turning away from" our sin and "embarking on" a journey of self-improvement signals what Hare describes as "the fundamental difficulty for Kant," (p. 309)[2] a difficulty which he thinks may be "deeply embedded in some versions of the Christian tradition," (p. 310) and which is certainly deeply embedded in Kant's overall system: namely, "how to relate freedom and temporality" (p. 309). In Kant's system, although we recognize exercise of freedom in its temporal manifestations, it is not in itself temporal— something which, by Kant's own admission, we cannot ultimately understand. In one respect I think that Hare understates the difficulty; in another, that he overstates it.

I think that he understates the difficulty in that he does not mention its apparent foreclosure of the very possibility of *real* self-improvement. Given that we have all acted sinfully, or immorally, in the past, it seems to follow that we are all, in our atemporal being, simply imperfect: there seems to be nothing

---

[1] Or so it seems to me. At the conference of which these are the proceedings it emerged that Hare and I differ somewhat in our conceptions of Christian orthodoxy.

[2] Page references are to Hare, chapter 13 in this volume.

that any of us can any longer do about that. However our lives may pan out, they will only ever provide further temporal manifestations of this irremediable atemporal fact. (It is partly in response to this problem, of course, that Kant has God treating an infinite life of temporal self-improvement as if there had never been anything morally wrong with it in the first place. Unless God showed us this indulgence, an infinite life of temporal self-improvement would be to no real avail.)

The respect in which I think that Hare overstates Kant's difficulty concerns the question of what, at the noumenal level, corresponds to change in how we manifest our exercise of freedom. Hare talks, as it seems Kant himself would ultimately be forced to talk, about "noumenal change," which is of course a contradiction in terms if "change" is interpreted in literally temporal terms. On Hare's account, this indicates the strain that Kant's system is under at this point, and it adds considerably to the professed unintelligibility of the system. To some extent, such a verdict is beyond dispute. But let us not exaggerate. "Change" can also be interpreted in metaphorical, nontemporal terms, as when we talk of the change of scenery along a particular route. On such a metaphorical interpretation, there is no obvious impediment to "noumenal change"—articulation at the level of things in themselves—nor, in particular, to noumenal change corresponding to change in how we manifest our exercise of freedom.

What Hare describes as "the fundamental difficulty for Kant" thus seems somewhat less severe to me than other difficulties that he confronts in this area. Consider, for example, Kant's conviction that we must believe in God. Kant holds this because he holds that we must believe in a being capable of securing the alignment of happiness with virtue which constitutes the highest good. This is an alignment which—contra Epicureans, for whom virtue consists in the procurement of happiness, and contra Stoics, for whom happiness consists in the exercise of virtue—is not conceptual, an alignment which does indeed therefore need to be "secured." There are some large and fascinating questions about the sense of "must" in which we "must" believe these things. Clearly, it is in part a practical sense, relating back to our bipartite nature; and one of the many merits of Hare's chapter is how well he draws this out. But what follows when we take a critical step back from these questions, as indeed we are doing now?

Are we not free to concede that what we "must" believe may yet be false? In a sense, obviously, we are: we are free to concede that our having no alternative but to believe something does not entail its truth (not, at any rate, where the belief in question concerns things in themselves). In another sense, equally obviously, we are not free to concede this: we are not free to convert that first concession into genuine agnosticism, for, if we really do have no alternative but to believe something, then we have no alternative but to *believe* it. That said, there must now be a question about how robust the "must" really is. Taking the critical step back is bound to put doubts in our minds, especially when, as in this case, the explanation for why we "must" believe what we "must" sounds more like a subversive explanation than a vindicatory one. There are important historical and exegetical questions about just how concerned Kant would have been to have unsettled our religious beliefs in this way. But to the extent that he would have been, which, if I read Hare correctly, he takes to be a considerable extent, then it may well be here that "the fundamental difficulty for Kant," in his philosophy of religion, really lies.

Bibliography

Kant, I. (1996) "Religion within the Boundaries of Mere Reason." in *Religion and Rational Theology*. Tr. and ed. A. W. Wood and G. di Giovanni. Cambridge: Cambridge University Press.

{ INDEX }